SIXTY-ODD
A Personal History

SIXTY-ODD

A Personal History

by

RUTH HUNTINGTON SESSIONS

STEPHEN DAYE PRESS : *Publishers*

BRATTLEBORO : VERMONT

COPYRIGHT, 1936, BY
Ruth Huntington Sessions

Designed by John Hooper
Director of Stephen Daye Press

Printed by Stephen Daye Press
Brattleboro, Vermont, U.S.A.

To My Grandchildren

Nigel Lyon Andrews, 1922-
William Shankland Andrews 2nd, 1925-
Jane Ann Byrne Sessions, 1929-
Sarah Fisher Sessions, 1931-

CONTENTS

Boston in the Sixties

CHAPTER | PAGE

I Rich Man, Poor Man 1
The Huntington House on Boylston Street—
Three Worlds—The Runaway Child.

II Forbears and Familiars 8
The Sargents and the Porters—A Heretic—Fred-
eric Huntington—Early Life in Cambridge—
The Huntington Children.

III Ninety-eight Boylston Street 16
"Jerusalem Crickets"—The Boston Bag—Foreign Visitors—Boston Speech—The Young Victorian—Family Prayers—Basques and Peplums
—Grandmother Sargent's House.

IV ABC'S and Dickens 27
Oliver Twist—The Household Book of Poetry—
The Children's Garland—Miss Gage's School.

V Child's View of the Civil War 31
Ominous Gray—Cannonading on the Common—John Brown's Body—"Richmond's Evacuated"—Worse than Murder.

VI Music in Boston 38
The Handel and Hayden Society—Italian Operas—Church Music—Te Deums in the Dark—
Music Lessons with Mlle. de la Motte—Harmonious Blacksmith.

VII Bishops and Broken Legs 46
Father Becomes a Bishop—Mitres and Robes—
Hoppetty, Kicketty—Departure for Syracuse.

Syracuse in the Seventies

I Old Syracuse 57
   "The Great West"—*The Vanderbilt*—The New
   House—Miss Mary Jackson's School—"Don't
   Wait for the Crutch."

II New People 63
    The Andrews and the Whites—The Pecks and
    the Sedgwicks—An Agriculturist of Parts—
    Child's Play.

III Grant and Colfax 66
     The Grapes of Wrath.

IV Music in Syracuse 69
    Music Lessons for an Indian Girl—Harriet
    Waits on a Savage—Ernst Held—The Music
    Club—Prisoners' Base—Organ-playing.

V Relief and Welfare 75
   The Bishop's Experiments—Arria Huntington's
   Work—The Shelter—Diamond Nell—Branches
   of the Knowledge Tree—The Hospital—Dr.
   Van Duyn.

VI Invitation to the Waltz 82
    Maggie the Mantua-maker—The Light Fantas-
    tic—Jovial Wall-flower.

VII Educational Facilities 88
     Research in Father's Study—Miss Jackson's
     Curriculum—"In Our Day We *Studied* Latin"
     —Father's Amanuensis—Mission Work in the
     German Neighborhood.

VIII Realities 94
      Marriage of George Huntington—James Hun-
      tington's Mission Work.

IX Congress of Women 98
    Louisa Alcott—Dr. Mary Walker—Mrs. Mary
    Livermore—Miss Maria Mitchell—Elizabeth
    Cady Stanton—Catherine Beecher—Mrs. Julia

Ward Howe—Mrs. Jennie Croly—"Chemistry
in the Kitchen"—"The Aesthetics of Dress"—
"Superfluous Women"—Spring in Syracuse.

Forty Acres

I   The Farm   109
Aunt Bethia's Supper—Rediscovery of the
House—The Prophet's Chamber—The Barn—
Old Max—"Who Sells the Bog Hay?"—The
Stoop.

II   Sun to Sun   116
A Prelate Becomes Farmer—A Boat on the Con-
necticut—George—Harnessing the Horses—The
Young Inventor—Books at the Farm—The
Chimney Swallows—A Visit from Harriet
Beecher Stowe.

III   New England Portrait Gallery   122
The Rye Is Ripe—Matty-the-conqueror—The
King of Builders—Henderson Tailer—*Mar-
chons!*—Billy Phelps.

IV   Behind a Horse   132
The Hadley Mill—Village Store—The Black-
smith—Riding for the Mail—Northampton—A
Formal Call.

V   Thunder and Lightning   137
The Voice of God—The Haymakers—"The
Wind Is in the Northwest"—The Ferry—Into
the Hills—Blueberry Pie—The Valley.

VI   An Altar in the Haymow   146
Childish Petitions—The Unerring Eye—Candy
for the Bishops.

VII   Victorian Sunday   150
The Amherst Church—Infant Baptism—The
Bishop Preaches in a Hill Village—*Antioch*—
Collation at the Parsonage—Seats of Culture—
God of the Gentians.

VIII Experiments in Education 155
  The Will of Sophia Smith—Robert Peabody—
  Child's View of Smith College—Summer School
  at Forty Acres—Letters to Turnip.

IX Year by Year 160
  Birds Fly South—Barmecide Feasts—October
  Holiday—The Dickinsons in Amherst—"Next
  Summer We Shall Come Back Again."

End of Childhood

I A Visit to Hingham 167
  Uncle Epes and Spiritualism—Advice to a Westerner—The Boarding-house—The Bryants—Return to the Farm.

II A Mark and a Meaning 174
  Mount Warner—New Conclusions—The Fourth
  Child Grows Older.

III The Young Victorian 177
  Chameleons—Disillusionment at Cornell—Victorian Courtship.

IV Enchanted Week 183
  Descendant of Moses Porter—Secret Signals—
  The Grammar of Assent—A Supernatural Seal.

V Decision To Go to Germany 190
  End of Church Work—A Visit in Roxbury—Dr.
  Zakrzewska—Prospects of Germany—"Good-
  bye."

Music in Germany

I Eastward 201
  The City of Brussels—Boat Journey—A Naval
  Knight.

II London 206
  The Yardleys—Celia Thaxter—Opera—Windsor.

III The Channel 214
     Royal Encounter.

IV Leipzig 216
     Fräulein Hernnsdorf—Plagwitz—Lessons in German—Music.

V Nihilists in Leipzig 224
     Royal Gossip—Fugitive Droschken—The Bomb.

VI Music in Leipzig 229
     The Choir — Belfry Family — Opera — *Hohe Messe.*

VII German Easter 233
     Bach Passion Music—Dresden Easter—Faust—Letters Abroad—Brass Bands.

VIII Reassurance 238
     Garfield—A Visit from Dr. Zakrzewska—Chaperon in Thuringia—Back To Work—James Becomes a Monk.

IX Six Together 243
     Cafés and Concerts—Winter Dancing—Rubinstein—Hans Von Bülow and the Late-comers—Clara Schumann.

X Gaiety 248
     We Give a Ball — Dresden Again — The Johannesgarten—Heidelberg—A Prince at Pontresina—Doubt and Dogma—Country of Saints—Organ—"Barnby in E."

XI Country of Saints 252
     Lessons—Return of a Book—Flowers and Green Garlands.

New York

I   Engagement 261
        Probation—Mrs. Piatt's Seminary—Contempo-
        rary Affairs.

II   Mrs. Sessions 270
        The Wedding—Forty Acres.

III Exciting Months 273
        Apartment — New York Hospitality — Diver-
        sions—The Blizzard of '88—Englewood.

IV Hannah 279
        Spring Visits—The Nurse.

V   The Butcher, the Baker 281
        Family Code—"Bill Rendered"—Mary Calligan.

VI Christianity and Anarchy 287
        Brooklyn Heights—Leonora O'Reilly—Note on
        Labor—Double Life—Influenza.

VII Loss and Hope 294
        Mary—Dr. Mosher—Mourning—The Phelps
        Farm—Life Again.

VIII The Eighteen Nineties 301
        Tammany—The Young Men's Democratic
        Club—Theodore Roosevelt—Knights of Labor—
        The *Cail*—Henry George—"Jacob Armitage."

IX A Part in Politics 308
        Frederick Hinrichs—Election Days—Apollyon
        Laid Low.

x   The Consumers' League 313
        The White List—Investigation of Working Con-
        ditions—Public Speech—Achievement.

xi   The Social Reform Club 321
        Discussion of Unions—Charles M. Spahr—Fa-
        bians.

xii   Counterpoint 326
        "The Bird House"—Proofs for the Printer—
        "That Child's Going To Be Musical"—Trial by
        Jury—Ainslee's and Munsey's Magazines.

xiii   Sorrowful Events 336
        Death of a Common Ancestor—*Noblesse Oblige*—
        The Death of Henry George—"Oh Lord! Van
        Wyck."

xiv   Weary Patriotism 339
        A Small Forum—The Old Rhythm of Capital-
        ism—The Singing Baby.

xv   Season's Mutations 344
        Editorial Work—John—Concert for Roger—
        Turn of the Century—The Bishop Interviews
        President Seelye—Departure from the "Bird
        House."

Northampton

i   New England Again 355
        Forty Acres—Northampton—"Quite, *Quite* An-
        other Thing"—Smith College—The First Group
        —Monday Club—Irving Wood and Plain Speak-
        ing—President Seelye.

ii   Henshaw House 363
        Alterations—Mary Brown—Solicitous Parents—
        Reading Aloud—Senda Berenson—The College
        Girl of 1904—A Memorable Mountain Day.

III   The Inevitable 373
        The Bishop—George—The Bells Toll—A Hand
        in Farming—Death of Mother—Milk Route.

IV   Departures 381
        President Seelye Retires—Nan in Europe—
        Roger at Harvard—Miniature Opera—Archie—
        Sabbath at Smith.

V   Inherent Pacificism 387
        The War—Roger at Smith—John—Madam
        Breshkowsky—Leonora O'Reilly Again.

VI   New Order 392
        President Neilson—Military Wedding—The
        Star Spangled—1918—Adelynrood—Arria—
        "Paul's Brigade Left Last Night."

VII   "Cook and Houseworker" 397
        Occasional Reflections—Influenza—Armistice—
        The Ninth Symphony—Interview with a Gov-
        ernment Official.

VIII   Woman Suffrage 406
        Pompadours — Plain Justice — Salesmanship —
        Max Eastman—Chocolate Cigarettes.

IX   Nineteen-Twenty 411
        Marriage of Roger—Forty Acres—O. Henry—
        Play-writing.

X   "They Tell Me You're Going Away" 415
        A Growing College—The Final Transaction.

ON THE STOOP AT FORTY ACRES, JULY, 1936 . . 419

Family Tree 422

Index 423

Boston in the Sixties

1

RICH MAN, POOR MAN

In the eighteen-sixties on Boylston Street, facing the Public Gardens in Boston, there was a row of prim brick dwellings, with granite steps and dark green doors on which brass numbers gleamed hospitably. Small iron balconies jutted out above the area-windows and the square-yard-allowances of grass. Frederic Huntington, the Rector of Emmanuel Church, lived in number ninety-eight, next door to Judge Putnam. Farther along came the Bowditches, Tildens, Reveres, Lincolns, Sumners, Gannetts: good neighbors who thought more or less alike, were interested in city and state, and friendly among themselves.

The houses were mostly of one design. Front entrances opened into narrow halls with staircases mounting rather steeply on the left. About three-quarters of the way up there were niches in the wall to hold busts; ours had a rather stark representation of my grandfather's head and shoulders in plaster. Opposite the foot of the stairs on the right was a long parlor with French windows opening on the balcony, and a fireplace with a small grate and chilly marble mantel. The room was carpeted with a sprawling Victorian pattern, and held plenty of good comfortable furniture; rockers were having their day, and sofas were short and bulgy. A square Chickering piano stood against the wall, good engravings decorated the space above, and the prevalent what-not stood in its corner. A center-table with a green cover completed the make-up of this living-room. It might have been commonplace if its atmosphere had depended on such furnishings. But while larger establishments boasted formal drawing-rooms, splendidly upholstered and scrupulously shaded, we of the rectory lived in our one parlor, and were

privileged to use our "best things" all the time, with respectful
handling of that which was frail or fadeable.

Behind the parlor was the Rector's study, full of books and
tributes. His large desk in the center of the room was always in
order, and never gave signs of hurried or disorganized work. He
wrote his sermons with a quill pen which squeaked as it travelled
over the square sheets. Sometimes he spoke in whispers the words he
wrote, hissing the s's, letting his eyebrows draw together and his
face twist into funny grimaces, at which he did not mind our
laughing. When he went out the desk bore evidence of a finished
task, his pen laid across the pedestal of a great brass inkstand, the
sermon-paper in a neat pile, the row of devotional books ranged
between two book-ends of ebony studded with mother-of-pearl discs
which were fascinating to the tips of childish fingers. We might not
often linger to count them, however, or do more than deliver a
message, unless the big horsehair arm-chair was pushed back and
the intruder lifted to a place of dignity upon the pastoral knee.

Dining-room and kitchen were in the basement. Above the
parlor our mother's room looked out on Boylston Street; we had a
nursery behind it, where Nurse Harriet presided, and there was
much sunshine on that east side of the house. Our view, however,
was limited by the high walls of the Providence Railroad station,
across a narrow alley where grocery carts and loads of freight passed
monotonously. There was a deep closet between the two rooms, for
bedding, our mother's piece-bag, and the family's best hats on high
shelves. Two more stories, above, furnished rooms for the older
children and maids, with an unused dormer-windowed room at the
front, which was to have served as a sort of study-retreat for the
Rector, but had finally come to be a repository for discarded furniture and the overflow of his library.

From our front windows we could look across at the Public
Gardens. Brilliant flower-beds and blossoming shrubs adorned
them the season through, winding paths led to secluded benches
or opened out on sunny malls. The pond was dotted with pleasure-
boats. Noble statues stood out against backgrounds of clustered
foliage. We spent most of our afternoons there among maids and

perambulators, trotting hand in hand, or now and then dodging the policeman, that bogy so often invoked by exasperated nurses, dashing across a bit of lawn to hide behind a bush, in defiance of KEEP OFF THE GRASS signs.

Behind these Elysian fields stretched Beacon Street, the highway of the aristocracy. We could see from our house its rows of curtained windows, with tall blue glass bulb-jars of daffodils and hyacinths in bloom. It was a world of which we children had little comprehension. Our parents sometimes stepped out of their sphere, and went across to dine at sumptuous tables, and our pretty grown-up sister, in evening clothes which made her look like one's image of fairyland, would be driven now and then to a dance given by some wealthy parishioner.

Our own particular joy consisted in watching, with round faces pressed between the iron palings of the Gardens, processions of carriages, admiring the finely dressed ladies and gentlemen, envying the coachmen, and coveting the long graceful whips with which they flicked the necks of their prancing steeds. It must be bliss, we felt, to guide those super-horses; no wonder the coachmen were distinguished by rich liveries and brass buttons. There was a rhythm in the trotting hoofs, bearing one's fancy along in dreamy delight as one watched the carriages move majestically past the Gardens, up the slope of Beacon Hill, with the Boston Common to the right and the State House crowning the Hill on the left. In the opposite direction they drove more briskly toward the Back Bay, which was then very near: a broad body of shallow water with tossing waves when breezes blew, crossed by the Mill-Dam, a causeway to the lovely suburb of Brookline.

Once or twice we were driven across the Mill-Dam, and found charming houses and gardens, close-clipped hedges and magnificent cultivated trees under which children played on their own grounds, not walking primly beside guardians over prescribed paths with menacing KEEP OFF signs. We were interested in having at last crossed the horizon-line, as it were, but it was not the realization of a dream nor the fabric of romance. It led only to comparison. We decided that there was more variety in city life: the risk and thrill of crossing Boylston Street by skilful dashes after waiting for the thinning of a line of vehicles; of eluding the policeman in the Gardens, and pulling down a lilac-branch to the level of one's nose; of throwing bread to the great swans in the pond, and watching them swim away with ragged pieces, their long necks twisting and their yellow bills opening now and then to emit harsh squawks that turned the magic birds into greedy animals. No, our own world was worth living in, and we were willing to remain in it.

But as a matter of fact there were three worlds in our universe, one of which we inhabited; from this we looked out at the other two. There was the World of the Rich, as we saw it through the iron palings of the Garden; the people who owned the fine horses and carriages, kept greenhouses, and had music-boxes and long mirrors in their parlors; wore costly clothes and furs, and dressed their children in white with Roman sashes and openwork stockings. Some of them had beautiful little dogs with bells on their collars. The nurses and babies perambulated on the sidewalks of Beacon Street more often than in the sunshine of the malls. The glimpses of their glory were like watching a pageant enacted for our benefit, very entertaining but not exactly real. Even their wonderful dolls— and the French dolls of the day were exquisite, with kid figures made in perfect proportion to imitate the human form, and Parisian faces with lifelike complexions—did not seem to us so friendly as our own battered companions in the nursery. And the visits of our family among the aristocracy—even the relatives who moved in its midst and came out to us from its background—did not bring us any nearer to that world. It was like another planet. The sphere in which we ourselves moved was made up of everyday folk who lived in plain houses, and did some work about them, and whose children wore sensible clothes, and perhaps attended public schools. The expression "old families" was quite incomprehensible to us. We had an idea too that our sort was especially privileged in having books and loving them, but I don't know just how it got into our heads; it is merely an association which comes to the fore in recalling our youthful outlook.

Beacon and Arlington and Charles Streets represented the

boundaries of these zones, even though we sometimes ventured into unclassified regions. It was about as much of a horizon, that quadrangle, as infant perceptions could grasp. And the third world, the World of the Poor, was a distant, strange country from which natives came now and then to the areas of Boylston Street to beg for "cold pieces," which the cooks meted out in the shape of dried crusts and even potato-parings. These creatures wore ragged shawls over their heads, and carried baskets on their arms, sometimes bringing wan babies. Of that world we knew little more, but we heard about its filthy houses, drunken husbands, and blind or lame old women to whom kind ladies carried food, and read the Bible, and preached submission and content. God took care of them, we learned; in fact was apparently responsible for the World of the Poor, and its status was considered as unchangeable as that of the Rich. We were reminded of it when a drunkard reeled across our path in front of the baby-carriage, steered out of his way by the competent Harriet; and there was some curiosity in our minds with regard to its denizens in the tenement regions, which we had been told were not far from Boylston Street.

As the fourth child of the family, I watched with some fascination a band of rubbish-gatherers who could be seen from Berkeley Street bridge (then on the outskirts of civilization) to which we were sometimes taken for a walk. An embankment above the railroad-yard was their gathering-place in the afternoon, as the Public Gardens were for us. God was supposed to have ordered it so. Dirty and tattered children accompanied their mothers, and now and then when some particular track was unused they descended upon it, and the little ones helped push out bits of coal from between the rails with sticks, or collected them in baskets. The misfortunes of the many and privileges of the few were taken for granted. There were some signs of an awakening, with charity doing its best, but the actual social conscience of Boston, in ignorance of any possible cure, remained dormant.

The child looked and wondered, gazing down over the railing of the bridge at what seemed to her a rather jolly company. She longed to join those children, and help with the rubbish-collecting and sorting, among the heaps of refuse on the embankment. Would they let her play too, she wondered, and could she take off her stockings, and cling with curving soles and toes to the warm rails, balancing as the children did, or jumping from one tie to another? It became so absorbing to watch them that she wanted to be taken over the new land to Berkeley bridge every afternoon. She turned impulsively back one day while following nurse Harriet and the perambulator as they headed for the Garden, and ran along Boylston Street with all the vigor of her short legs, reaching the goal quickly. She clambered down the narrow, unguarded stone steps, and strolled along at the foot of the embankment, between the moving engines. She was timid about sudden explosive sounds, but the rush of a locomotive did not alarm her, nor even the whistles, though they made her jump. The faces of the rag-pickers looked dark and wild, near to; they were Italians, and they did not notice her in their care for their own toddlers. She felt just a little afraid to go near them. It began to be a bit bewildering there with so much clanging and so many wheels revolving near one's eyes. A man with a shaggy beard and an oil-can in his hand came hurrying toward her; would he pick her up and carry her off? Then she heard her name, and turned to find her father's disturbed face looking down at her. He was panting; Harriet had rushed into his study with news of her flight, and they had thought at once of the bridge and the tracks. He swung her up to his broad shoulder, and strode away, past the foreign people, who waved and smiled at her now.

She still remembers the quick homeward stride, and how tightly she held to him. Then the going from the hot September sunshine into his cool study, and his explaining to her quite gently, so as not to quench her four-year-old valor, that little girls did not go alone to railroad tracks, and that one could have a much better time on such excursions if one took a companion. She quite agreed with him, and having accomplished her own private bit of research was entirely ready to promise anything; but he did not ask that, and concealed his perturbation. She was still buoyed up by the elation of high adventure. She little knew that all life, for her, was to be that; that nothing would really be commonplace, even the least eventful of days; that looking back after seventy years there would be a thrill which would be comparable only to the ardor of looking forward in childhood, to those same ever-new experiences; and that this was the first vivid chapter of a long, interesting story. At supper-time, between mouthfuls of bread and milk, her tongue ran on, describing the breathless scamper to Berkeley Street, the steep stone steps, the blaring whistles, the whirling, pounding wheels, the man in the blue jeans with dirty hands and face and the smell of oil.

The Rector and his wife did not at all want for their children that destiny which Gerald Stanley Lee describes as "a petrified life, imbedded in Grandma and Grandpa." But they found themselves confronted with an immediate problem. The Runaway Child had not yet been tabulated by psychologists. They could not turn to science for aid. So plain common sense came to the fore. If a certain child was likely to attempt further flights from the parental roof, she must be taught how to do it properly. They began to send her on little errands about the house and to near neighbors, stimulating a sense of responsibility which cultivated a cooperative obedience, not a tense adherence to laws. Whether it came from a recalcitrant ancestor in a northern borderland, or an English maid who had crossed the ocean in disguise a century before to marry the man she loved in defiance of paternal obduracy, there was a suggestion of resistance in the child's round, brown face, different in its contour from those of her brothers and sisters. It might be the Phelps great-grandfather after all. In the confidence born of subconscious freedom, however, she slept and waked, played and climbed, and ran and grew. But there were no more walks to Berkeley Bridge. The Natural History Museum, with its mastodon and monkeys, its stuffed birds and models, took the place of that. For five years, her glimpse at the World of the Poor lasted as a clouded memory.

2

FORBEARS AND FAMILIARS

We had only one grandmother, Grandmother Sargent, who lived in Roxbury. She had told us stories of her young days, and we knew that our Grandfather Sargent had been a sea-captain, who sailed his own merchant-ships, and had travelled in Russia and other countries. Grandmother herself was the daughter of Abner Lincoln, a son of General Lincoln, Washington's aide-de-camp. We heard about "Grandfather General" very often, of course. Abner Lincoln, our great-grandfather, had been a Harvard man and an outstanding educator of his time, and kept a school at Hingham in which his daughter Mary taught. Epes Sargent, the young captain, was a widower with five children, who left his boys and girls at the school while he went sailing. And they loved Mary so dearly that when Captain Sargent came back from his voyages and found them clinging to her, he came to love her too, so the story went, and married her, after which they had five more children. He gave up his seafaring life, and when our mother and father became engaged the Sargents were living in a big hospitable Boston house.

Our father's ancestors were Puritans, and had settled in the Connecticut Valley, at Hadley. There Captain Moses Porter built a fine house which later became our summer home. We children were interested in hearing about his little girl Betsey, who grew up to be our great-grandmother. She was only eight years old when her father went to the French and Indian War and was killed by the Indians at the Battle of the Morning Scout, near Lake George. The details were not made very clear to us, but we had seen our great-great grandfather's sword, and knew that Betsey and her mother were left all alone at Forty Acres when it happened; that as a result the mother was sad and lonely, while her child grew up to be a very bright, energetic young person, much interested in her village neighbors, and in the great farm to which she fell heir.

Her daughter, Elizabeth Phelps, (for there were five successive Elizabeths, mothers and daughters) had grown up in Hadley too. She, the third Elizabeth, married Dan Huntington, from Connecticut, and had eleven children, of whom our father was the youngest. We loved to hear him tell stories of his boyhood; of the stern regimen in the household, although his father, a genial retired clergyman of the orthodox church, was not as strict a disciplinarian as his mother. Her children loved her in spite of it, and one episode in her life made a deep impression upon them, especially on the little boy who had grown up to tell the story to his children.

My father's mother was a Calvinist. We had a curious impression of Calvinism and could not make out whether it was really a religion or not, with its references to hell-fire and devils, which we mentally illustrated by association with the Doré pictures. My father spoke of a far milder interpretation of the Bible by a preacher named Channing, whose books his mother read and who persuaded her to believe no longer in devils or eternal punishment. But the pastor of the village church had told Grandmother she must not believe such a doctrine as Channing's Unitarianism, and that she would be put out of the Calvinist society if she did not give it up. He sent the deacons of the church to ask her questions about it, and they went to Grandmother and spent whole afternoons arguing with her, which made her children frightened and unhappy.

From Father's vivid story we could picture the farmyard at Forty Acres, the shadow of great elms and the still summer afternoons. The men were away in the fields, and the blinds closed. There was the sinister portent of two high-springed, stiff buggies, with their horses tied to hooks in the wall of the shed.

They had brought a delegation from the orthodox society to labor with a heretic. The swishing of flies and the fretful pawing of hoofs kept up a steady accompaniment as hours wore away and the orthodox dignitaries prolonged their attempts to dislodge the demons of unbelief from our grandmother's soul. The boy Frederic would hang about, miserably, watching those grim scouts go in by the south door and seat themselves on high-back chairs in the darkness of the "long room." Elizabeth would come down the stairs, tall and dignified in her Sunday garb. Through the syringa-bushes which grew against the windows, the child could hear querulous voices of old men and crisp, laconic answers from their victim. The argument lasted long. Toward supper-time the visitors would emerge, blinking at the late sun-rays as they left the darkness of the shaded room behind them, and silently untie their impatient horses, back them round and drive away with vacant, sullen faces and reins lax over the dashboards. Our grandmother, white and manifestly wearied, but with victory after siege apparent in her shining eyes, would watch them climb into the high seats of their chariots, bidding them a grave "good-afternoon." Little whirls of dust followed the retreating wheels. Her husband, returning from the fields, would take the affair with easy, semi-amused temper of mind, his habitual attitude. He was as firm as she, but confident of her loyalty and poise, proud of the uncompromising front she was able to maintain in the face of antagonism. They came again and again, however, and finally cut both wife and husband off from communion with the Hadley congregation. It was a grief to be denied the sharing of that privilege with neighbors and relatives. Peace and serenity had nevertheless been gained through their change of faith, and they never relinquished it. There is no doubt that to their descendants they have bequeathed a measure of independent conviction and fearlessness of departure from time-honored or accustomed dogmas, as also a revolt against religious persecution which has shown itself more than once in the family history.

Of course these stories were not actually brought to the nursery for the entertainment of small children, but we listened when they were told to grown-ups, and they made a lasting impression. We loved the story of our father's courtship and marriage to Hannah Sargent. She was a very pretty Boston girl, only twenty when she became the wife of Frederic Huntington, who had graduated from Amherst in 1839, and was a popular young Unitarian minister.

After their wedding journey to Niagara Falls they went to Forty Acres, so that Frederic might show his wife the river and hills, and the old house. Perhaps at first Hannah found the Puritan household stern and reserved, but she grew to be very happy there, and made lifelong friendships in Northampton and Hadley.

I was born in Cambridge, on a November day in 1859. At that time Father was Plummer Professor of Christian Morals at Harvard College, and the family was settled in the old house afterward occupied by Professors Palmer and Peabody, on the corner of Quincy Street and Massachusetts Avenue, overlooking the Yard. The town was a country-like suburb then, connected with the city of Boston by a long bridge, and its inhabitants a rare company: a concentration of some of the best minds of the time.

This delightful community of intellectuals (would that I could find a less-worked term for them!) had opened its doors to the new professor and made an ideal place for the rearing of his children. Mr. Agassiz's school for girls, a progressive school with various original methods, was a matchless educational opportunity for our sister Arria. The Danas, the Nortons, the Lowells, the Longfellows, the Loverings, the Eliots, the Palfreys, the Agassizs and many others with their fine old houses and their gracious and ready hospitality and informal courtesy, made for a rare and delightful neighborhood life.

It was into this circle that the fourth child came, and for two years looked upon the faces of Cambridge friends and basked in their smiles as a new baby. The students, on excellent terms with their Professor, whose sympathy with their athletic pursuits was a work of supererogation so far as requirements of the Plummer Chair was concerned, ran in and out of the house at all times of day. It was owing to his efforts that the first Harvard Gymnasium was built, and boys came to him with their enthusiasms as well as problems. His wife welcomed them also, and made them at home in the family circle, even letting them rock the cradle on occasions, when it had to be brought down into the family sitting-room in winter weather. How many celebrated characters may have jogged those short wooden rockers we do not know. Jogged they were, however, sometimes with absent-minded jerks, and again quite slowly with concentrated attention.

But the child was too young when removed from the house of her birth to know that the pleasant life on Quincy Street was abandoned because her father had discovered a Trinitarian trend in his theology and had eventually felt his position at Harvard to be an equivocal one. It was then a trying time; a time of struggle for the nation, of doubt and questioning, of passion and political conflict. War was in the offing. When Frederic Huntington, counted upon by the men who stood for their idea of the one enlightened and rational theological position, announced his intention of embracing the Episcopal faith, it was received with active dismay. His many Unitarian friends felt hurt, puzzled, and some of them indignant. With many of his more intimate companions the relation was never quite the same. Deep underneath lay stores of affection and loyalty which survived the shock, but when he accepted the rectorship of Emmanuel Church, Boston, and was confirmed, as were his wife and oldest son, there was a severance of many ties. He always, however, acknowledged his deep respect and admiration for the high type of Christian manhood represented by those Unitarian men of the time, and their influence in the community. The rest of the family kept their Cambridge friendships and contacts. We children grew up to love those friends of our mother's, and never knew that there could be any difference in the matter of religious belief between ourselves and the many relatives and comrades about us.

There were five Huntington children. Our oldest brother, George, had graduated from Harvard and was spending his winters at a theological school in Minnesota for the sake of its climatic effect upon a chronic affection of the throat. He had spent many weeks at home, sometimes tutoring with our mother whose classical foundation enabled her to help him as she had her own brothers. This had given him a love of research, and the out-of-door life during succeeding summers at our old farm brought out his bent for natural history and botany. Added to this, an artistic sense and a love of music and poetry rounded out a resourceful personality, fascinating to his younger brother and sisters. I owe to him and to his contagious enthusiasm the most satisfying associations of my life. He was especially fond of Italian verse and a student of Dante, and his rhythmic intonation of the *Divina Commedia* caught our youthful ears like song. Recitations of Greek hexameter also stirred us, and fired the enthusiasm of all three juniors, who vied with one another in repeating the lines with him, sometimes moving to the swing of it as we listened. In his company we also came into companionship with nature; the sort of companionship, along with comradeship, which we try today to bring to our young children in nursery schools, recognizing it as a first step in education. And yet our brother never lectured. It was an almost casual unfolding, an opening of magic doors, to disclose wonders of which we might have been dumbly unaware. His own children, grown now to manhood, pay fervent tribute to that quiet, rich influence on their early lives.

Next came our one older sister, Arria, just growing up into young ladyhood. She had a profile like a cameo and a low brow around which her hair waved in delicate ringlets. Her eyes were like our mother's, deep blue with dark lashes; a face which expressed in every line the forceful character that made her a level-headed reasoner, a leader among her mates, and even in the days of her girlhood an altruist with constructive vision. After we had moved from Cambridge she studied at Miss Wilby's private school on Beacon Hill, an institution through which the higher education of women was made available, without any discussion as to its worth, to the privileged girls of Boston. Their mothers had been able to obtain the same advantages, and Arria Huntington probably took for granted, as her friends did, the belief of educators and social leaders in a literary and classical equipment for the well-born. My sister studied Latin, and supplemented her Greek lessons by taking a Testament to church on Sundays, to follow the Bible readings in that language. We still remember the little gray-brown volume with red edges to its leaves, tucked under her arm. She spoke French with ease and a good accent; Italian she read with our older brother; history had always a special interest for her.

The child next younger was a curly-headed schoolboy, very attractive, with a good development of the filial virtues and a natural amiability that brought him many friends. A Sunday child according to the calendar, James bore out the tradition connected with that distinction. Endowments seemed to have been showered upon him; if I say in the language of the past that they came "from the hands of the Graces," it is not, be sure, because that mythological beneficence was believed to have been really potent in the provision of talent. Versatility kept him too busy to be spoiled by adulation, and along with it went a spiritual quality of mind which foreshadowed the deeper claims to which he was eventually devoted. From our point of view he was an ordinary, active youngster, popular at school and at home, absorbed in making experiments of a mechanical or chemical sort with his particular friends on the upper floor of the house. Girls were barred from these processes. There were things burning in crucibles up there (I remember that in early days I got the word *crucible* mixed up with *crucifer* and was rather muddled as to the religious significance of both) and mysterious strings and wires, pinchers, saws and pulleys and otherwise dangerous implements, weirdly attractive to pryers, but too damaging to clothes for feminine participation.

The families, however, maintained a sympathetic point of view and looked for great achievement in the little hall bedroom. We lived for some time on the hope of owning a cart that could be wound up and would travel across the nursery floor. Such things could not then be bought at five-cent-stores. But beyond a few quite useful little contraptions which our parents enjoyed, these creative attempts came to naught, and as *Darius Green and His Flying Machine* had appeared about that time from Trowbridge's pen, the boys came in for much raillery in verse. But Jamie took his share with the equanimity of a person who can well afford to enjoy a joke on himself. His taste ran to legerdemain after that and the role of wizard compensated the disappointed mechanic. And his remarkable memory furnished the family with much entertainment. It was from him that we in the nursery learned to rattle off the Greek alphabet as a sort of voluntary exercise, and rivalled him in repeating

Horatius at the Bridge, getting credit for precocious achievement
which we did not deserve. We were merely small parrots, copying
his intonations and gestures automatically.

The fourth child found herself wedged in between her brilliant
elders, whose superiority was luckily taken for granted, and her
little sister, who, though too small to have developed any special
brand of precocity, was much loved and petted as the youngest of
the family. Molly was a good and dear child, but independent and
almost uncannily discerning. No amount of flattery could make her
vain, nor did she ever betray the boredom which attentions from
interested visitors brought upon her, but sat on their laps quite
patiently and waited for release. It was the price paid for many
pretty gifts; toys and beads and other adornments which did not
come the next older sister's way. I cannot remember any commendations of my behavior or appearance except an occasional
compliment bestowed upon my substantial and active legs,
clothed in the scarlet wool stockings that were then worn by small
girls. "Those red legs!" old ladies would exclaim sentimentally in
after years. "How they did fly up and down Boylston Street!" Meantime I would have vastly preferred my little sister's golden curls,
brushed around a polished stick each morning by the adoring Harriet. Yes, curls and a real locket, one that would open—these were
the fabric of my dreams and the burden of my nightly prayers.

3

NINETY-EIGHT BOYLSTON STREET

Our household was by no means a segregated one. Possibly the elders of the family cherished that elusive vision, which many devoted families do, of some day "having a nice time all by themselves," without realizing that it is about the most severe strain to which the nerves of any group of relatives can be subjected. At all events that was never achieved. There were all types of visitors at the rectory. Queer, tiresome people turned up with bags in hand and quondam introductions from strangers, and stayed till it taxed all the family resources to get them away. Forlorn people who had nowhere else to go drifted in and accepted, with a sort of blank alacrity, the slightest cordiality. There were "Jerusalem Crickets," so-called because they chirped perseveringly on the hearths of clergymen, all over Boston. Guests came who recommended improved parental methods for our upbringing. It amused us to see our mother's handling of them. We never caught her put about in any way; she was serene, executive and attentive. There was however a certain dry politeness in her manner which subdued the forthputting visitor marvelously. She had a less easy-going tendency than my father, who was apt to invite in haste and repent at leisure. The fine inclusive spirit of Forty Acres had clung to him but could not be worked successfully in pastoral hospitality. Yet he had a passion for helping people and his door was open to everyone who needed advice or a listening ear. His wife welcomed them warmly and fed them graciously.

They were rewarded, these two, by many delightful friendships. Thinkers, writers, and travelers gathered about them. We children were fascinated by discussions, often over our heads, which went on in such assemblages. Our mother's friends whom we adopted as relatives, brought in a cheery atmosphere. Many of them were Cambridge women who had begun their married life when our parents were at Harvard, and whom we adopted as aunts because of their close associations with the family. One, I recollect, was aunt Mary Cooke, the young wife of a brilliant scientist, Professor Josiah P. Cooke. She was a distant relative, as a matter of fact, and her visits were events.

All the "aunts" came at times to spend the day, and married ones brought their pretty lace caps, which matrons young and old wore then, neatly folded in bags. The Boston bag had a special place in the universe. Sometimes it was "worked," in cross-stitch with quite an intricate design, having handles of black patent leather and a bottom rather like a shoe sole. Or else it was made of beads or of silk with little bead mountings. But despite these exterior variations it was unique, and none but New England women carried it. Aunt Mary always breezed in with an especially capacious and interesting one: interesting because it was worth one's while to be lingering about when she opened it. One tried not to seem anxious for the ceremony to take place, and Mother forestalled any such eagerness if she could. Still, it was hard work to manage the proper detachment when you knew there might be a package of big white peppermints or maybe a string of beads. Once she brought two real silk parasols, brown-checked and blue-ruffled, with fold-up handles —wonderful acquisitions. She had a hearty laugh and a demonstrative grace of manner; she talked so fast and told so much exciting news that we listened breathlessly. We never minded the fact that she corrected us quite as frankly as Mother did and told us to stand up straight, all in the same easy, interesting sort of way which never stung us with mortification. Aunt Mary Cooke lived to be a most delightful old lady and was aunt to my children as she had been to me, sheltering, mothering and managing my daughter at Radcliffe with the innate psychological perception which made her leadership universally potent.

Other visitors came. Guests from abroad brought letters of introduction to the Rector and were taken quite simply into the family circle. Mrs. Wedgewood, wife of one of the famous pottery-makers of England, came to make a prolonged stay. She was a very attractive, albeit thoroughly Victorian, type, quite ample and rotund, with a pronounced manner and such a grand cap, upstanding in the front and accentuated by long lappets which she used to toss back over her shoulders as she sat talking. Her full skirts spread out into a train on the floor. She was entertained by a good many Boston people, and her comments on American life were greatly relished. Weeks after her departure, a truckload of barrels arrived at the door of Ninety-eight. The Rector and his wife were dazed, their family on tiptoe, as this stupendous cargo was landed and unpacked. The casks were from overseas and contained breakfast and dinner sets of real Wedgewood manufacture, provision for dozens of guests. The dinner set bore the familiar old trefoil, or rather strawberry leaf, a design still used. I saw it some years ago in a Swiss shop. The color of it can never be quite settled, as between blue and green. And the breakfast set was also of a design still in vogue, folksy little brown figures and tiny roses. Then there were some wonderful vases of the finer ware with the white cameo reliefs on a blue-violet background. It kept us reminded of Mrs. Wedgewood for many years and we have some of those delightful plates still in use.

There were other visitors from abroad whom I recollect less vividly, but I know we learned to understand the British accent in very early years and can remember saying over to myself, with a child's fascination for new expressions, "oh!"—that short-cut little "eoh" which puckers one's lips a bit, "how *virry* kind of you!" and "Fancy that!" The mellow, throaty voices of men and women alike made our Yankee intonation seem thin and nasal.

But after all, Bostonian speech had less of that than we were to experience later in districts farther west. A good many of the more travelled women of the time were fond of cultivating a foreign accent, and while it amounted sometimes to affectation, there were purely indigenous customs which made the society of Beacon Hill and its neighbors less distinctively Yankee than that of other places. Aristocratic old ladies dropped their final g's:—talked of *comin'*, *talkin'*, *feelin'*, chopped off their syllables with precision and called "pleasant" *plesunt*, with a slight hyphenization after the sibilant. If you accepted an invitation you said "I should *admire* to come." Going out to tea meant going out to supper; there were no afternoon teas as we have them. We talked of *going visiting* when we made visits longer than formal calls. We addressed our parents as Pa*pa* and Mam*ma*. *Dad* was an appellation supposed to be used only by the British working class, and we spoke very freely of classes then, but not of *masses*. Social limitations were taken quite as much for granted by the lower classes as the higher.

Some of the rules governing the behavior of children rested upon subtleties that have since disappeared. Comments on the possessions, customs, or appearance of other people were discouraged. One might neither disparage nor compliment the cut of a lady's gown, her china or her silver, her latest ornament, or anything in her house or on her person; such attentions came under the head of *personal remarks*; the very sound of which words I still remember with more or less perturbation. If one chose to exhibit one's treasures and invite appreciation, it was different, but *display*, we were told, might border on vulgarity. Great diplomacy must be used, in fact, in connection with such little matters.

Another great impropriety consisted in divulging the fact that one had had and refused an offer of marriage. Naturally small girls were not tempted to commit this indiscretion, but our older sister was the recipient of many proposals, far more than we little ones imagined. They were practically always made by letter, since a suitor rarely saw the object of his affections alone for a long enough time to make an avowal of love by word of mouth. There were endless little ways of insinuating it, subtleties quite unknown in the twentieth century, and very exciting. But the actual proposal arrived with a postage-stamp on it, or was left at the door by special messenger. A very slight stir followed one of these events. Intimate girl-friends, of course, heard about it in strictest confidence.

Arria was beautiful to look at, clever, and attractive to all kinds of swains, from the shy and dull to the fascinating and brilliant. A very curious little sister could glean something of such happenings, but the object of these multiplied affections seemed entirely unruffled, and apparently had not the slightest desire for matrimony. And one did not ask about those things. Curiosity was vulgar. Under no circumstances must one ever probe into the contents of a letter, a travelling-bag, or even the simplest of brown-paper parcels. Better wait till one could have a moment alone with a bundle and poke a hole in it with a sharp finger-nail. That was not really quite as offensive as the questioning.

Reproofs of these breaches of etiquette did not often come from either our mother or our father, neither of whom was a nagger. They really emanated from the surveillance of the watchful Harriet, or filtered down to us from admonitions and discussions of young people who visited us or from the occasional applications of a general code, and the directions issued to us when we went visiting by ourselves. The young Victorian was much more anxious to comport herself with due respect to form than are our children of today. That was the Boston of it. There were no comparisons with other places or customs. Country villages were naturally outside the pale; one took for granted that their inhabitants were untutored. But we had not the slightest doubt, we children, that we were living in the exact centre of the universe, or that the standards applied to our Boston life and manners were of primordial origin, fixed like the habits of the moon and the tide and the equinoxes.

The more ordinary details of our life as young Bostonians may have their interest for people of today. Before breakfast invariably came family prayers, one function at which attendance was compulsory. The whole family assembled, waited in silence and solemnity if anybody was late, so it was horribly embarrassing to appear before them. We gathered in the study, the two little ones sitting on low chairs with backs of Gothic design like those in the chancel at church. It was the desire of our lives to outgrow those chairs, with worsted-work seats into which we ground our elbows when kneeling. The pattern of mine, a variegated dog on a green background, not exactly ecclesiastical, was burned into my soul. Kneeling up straight did not become a custom till years later. But first we "read round," each person reading three verses at a time. Then we got to our knees, and the Rector made quite a long extemporaneous prayer, a little too departmental and subjective to be enjoyable. It brought one an uncomfortable feeling that our parents and the Almighty were taking our faults pretty seriously, and gave us uneasy consciences for the moment. Our minds wandered somewhat before the end came, and we joyously swung into the Lord's Prayer. Truth compels me to admit that the whole ceremony was, as we should have agreed, nicest when it was over. But we had a vague idea that somebody must have enjoyed it, God perhaps, or Father and Mother. And then after a rather tense silence, we scrambled to our feet and made for the dark stairway which led to breakfast.

There was no gleam of beauty about an area dining-room, with its bare walls adorned only by a few unattractive engravings. The windows let in but little light, and our upward glances through them revealed, from the table at least, a monotonous procession of legs, passing and re-passing on the sidewalk. Nevertheless, that room was a warm and happy meeting-place, and breakfast, even by the flare of a dim gaslight on gray mornings, was lavishly, indigestibly, adequate. It is amazing to think of the meat and fried potatoes, boiled eggs, hot biscuit (the maids got up at five o'clock to set those biscuit) and piles of buckwheat cakes with unlimited syrup. I remember when cereals came in, and were advertised by dietitians. Oatmeal was the first to appear, not predigested but quite solid and only soluble after hours of cooking. But it was Scotch, and the Scotch were proverbially healthy, so we ate it. Fruit was never considered as part of a matutinal menu.

After breakfast our mother went through the daily dishwashing task which was considered indispensable to an average New England family regime. It was understood that the lady of the house washed her breakfast glass and silver at least, and generally china also, with her own hands. The plates and dishes were gathered up, piled according to rule, in which process we daughters helped, and then the maid brought in on a tray a little wooden tub with brass hoops, filled with boiling hot suds, and laid thin spotless towels, smooth from the iron, beside it. The washing was done with a fluffy long-handled mop with which the tumblers and spoons could be deftly lifted out of the hot water and transferred to the edge of the tray. Our mother had no faith in the integrity of a household where this ceremony was not duly performed. If anything went wrong with the arrangements of a young married relative, in after years, she invariably asked anxiously, "Well, but *do* you wash your break-fast-dishes? I'm sure it would all go better if you did!"

Father always sat on with his paper in hand, and read aloud bits of news for his wife's comment; the mail came and family letters were opened. On some mornings, Arria told amusing experiences of the night before, and made everyone laugh over the latest *bon mot* of Boston's wit, Tom Appleton, or the delightful humor of Minnie Pratt and Helen Bell, daughters of the brilliant Rufus Choate, who were parishioners of my father.

Next came the departure to school after a search for caps and mufflers in the dark basement closet of Ninety-eight. The light went out in the dark dining-room after our goodby hugs, and we set sail from it as from a snug harbor—joyous crafts with varied destinations. There was much to be done by the mother of so active a family; marketing, planning, and sewing. Our clothes were at that time something of a problem. She herself always dressed well and suitably; her morning gowns quite simple, and handsome black silk for afternoon or colored ones, their full skirts trimmed with a large *Grecian key* pattern in black velvet for dinner-parties, and fine lace caps with little velvet bows. My sister wore plain school or street dresses, made often with straight loose jackets, but she had light silks with low necks, short sleeves and lovely sashes for parties. Our dressmaking was done by a Miss Balze. She used to be with us for quite long periods in the spring and fall; a tall, healthy person, whose knowledge of the fashions inspired us with unbounded confidence. We used to watch, fascinated, her mouthful of pins and the great shears from whose adventurous path the breadth of silk and cloth fell away in a shimmering swath as she balanced across her knees the cutting-board. It was a large affair with a semi-circular opening on one side that looked as if a giant had taken a bite out of it; this was designed to make it fit better against one's thighs and give a purchase to the cutter by supporting her elbows.

In wartime there were few garnishings to be bought for gowns, so they were adorned with varied arrangements of their own material. Here Miss Balze shone. She could "ketch down" a fold of silk with such cunning, and such invisible stitches, as to make it assume a corkscrew effect, very fetching indeed when four or five rows of it encircled a full skirt. Our mother had a mouse-colored alpaca street-dress trimmed with it one spring, which we thought marvelous. Then she could make, with remarkable speed, sharp pointed trimmings for the edges of basques and peplums, turning the fabric in and pinching it with her powerful thumb into the necessary outlines. We children did not expect anything so elaborate on our little plaided or checked frocks. As Scotch plaids were much in vogue then, every lady possessed a cloak of blue-and-green tartan to wear in rainy weather. Those Boston plaid cloaks were as characteristic as the Boston bags. Even younger people wore them; and men often hung plaid shawls over their coats in cold weather.

The rectory children heartily disliked dancing classes, but were more willing to attend the occasional children's parties to which we were invited, although society life brought its disappointments too. Most of the other little girls wore white frocks and lovely sashes, with openwork stockings, gloves, and slippers to match them, and blue lockets of enamel or turquoise on gold chains; lockets that opened. Our poplins, thought to be in better taste for ministers' children, seemed dark and thick, and we had light brown kid gloves instead of white ones, a real trial. We used to wish mother were not quite so sensible. But the fact that wherever we went we were graciously received and affectionate messages sent to our parents, made us come home in a more contented mood. After it was all over the home verdict was that clothes did not matter, so long as one was "neat," as it was put; I must say that seemed to us rather a meagre alternative.

After one birthday feast at the Gardiners', six-year-old Molly lapsed slightly from her accustomed politeness. She thanked our hostess prettily for giving us such a pleasant time and supper, added, however, with just a tinge of disappointment, "But I *could* have had cut-up oranges at home." Harriet, who came for us, was deeply mortified by this; her pride in the infallibility of the family breeding had received a blow.

One great source of happiness was our visits to Grandmother Sargent's house in Roxbury. They were the delight of our childhood, eagerly anticipated by older and younger ones alike. The house and grounds stood at the top of the hill above Cedar Square, a sloping, rocky little park whose paths wound about between clusters of the small, straight trees which gave it its name. You could get out of the horse-car, as we called it then, at the square and walk up a steep grade. But there was a far more interesting way of reaching the place. You took a Forest Hills car and rode out through the South End, along a continuation of Washington Street, and past the Roxbury Post Office and drug-store and Dr. Putnam's church with its quaint spire. That was like a real country village. Then pretty soon came a sort of cliff rising up out of the sidewalk, a ledge of rock on top of which the old Guild estate was built. An early chronicler says of it: "Up westward from the town it is something rocky; whence it hath the name of Roxberry."

Now you reached a place where a long, steep flight of steps had been cut into the rock, and the car conductor would obligingly let you out when requested at the stop known as Juniper Terrace. It was a deliciously private, special way of getting to Grandmother's, which we felt belonged to us exclusively. When we had climbed to the top of the steps, there stood a little house, built after a Swiss pattern, I think, different from the usual city architecture, so that it was like being in a foreign country. We called it going to Switzerland. Finally we reached the steps and terrace at the summit of which stood the large white house, a commanding mansion with spacious verandas on its east and west sides. It looked out over the then picturesque slopes of Roxbury and Jamaica Plain, rocky hillsides with patches of woods and scattered estates.

Grandmother was always at the door to welcome us, hearing our excited voices as we came along under the hedge. Mary Lincoln had never lost the fine presence of her girlhood. Tall, straight, with the bright serenity which carried her unruffled through years of family change and care; loving but not over-demonstrative, sympathetic and resourceful; dignity and repose in her bearing, few wrinkles on her calm brow: this was the woman whom her stepchildren had loved as an own mother, the revered mistress of the big house.

On entering, one noticed at once the handsome curving staircase, below which ticked a tall clock. At the right of the hall was the sunny library, and behind it a dining-room with heavy mahogany table and chairs and on a side-table the big samovar, a relic of Grandfather Sargent's Russian trips. But the portal through which we passed with greatest exhilaration led into the back hall, and there at one's right was the "Christmas closet," entrance into which was a privilege rarely accorded to children but a distinction of the highest order. The moment Grandmother turned the key in the door one perceived a fragrance, exotic and rare; a mixture of spices, fruits, syrups, nuts—words cannot describe the richness of that mixture, the product of age-old sweetness to which Europe and Asia had contributed and which seemed to cling to the very walls and shelves, immaculate though they were. There stood cases of figs, boxes of great juicy prunes, chests of tea from China, bottles of rare wine, tight little kegs of olives, blue-and-white ginger jars with basket handles, Guava jellies, tins of pilot-biscuit and hard crackers, red Edam cheeses, sewed-up bags of coffee beans, raisins, preserved strawberries and round cans with the thin, scalloped sugar cookies that only Grandmother's cooks could manufacture to perfection. And a cake-box with plum cake—what child could view these dainties without a watering mouth? Eating between meals was not allowed at ninety-eight Boylston Street, but there was always special indulgence at Cedar Square and if we really got into the Christmas closet at Grandma's heels, we did not leave it empty-handed.

When we spent the night at Grandmother's we were tucked into great softly pillowed beds, in rooms which, like the Christmas closet, were redolent of refreshing odors. Whether it was from the fragrant sheets—perhaps a suggestion of lavender—or the pungent, stimulating camphor in which the blankets had been laid away, or the fine Castile soap, or the delicate, faintly perceptible aroma of old polished mahogany, or possibly a little vase on the bureau with a sprig of rose geranium or lemon verbena offsetting a few flowers, I would not venture to say. Probably all those perfumes had mingled and stayed in the air for years, renewed from season to season. Sea air blew in at the windows, and an old chair with high back and flowered chintz hangings seemed to keep guard over the dreamers. That upper story was very like Dickens' description of Bleak House. The halls, reaching away back and overlooking the kitchen garden, had little steps up and down and the windows gave views of lovely country foregrounds, with the Boston dome and spires visible beyond.

The top floor, the sunniest of all, with slanting ceilings and dormer windows, was a unique and fascinating place. Here lived our Aunt Frances who was a little old lady with a face and figure which bore startling resemblance to Queen Victoria (it pleased her very much to be told that), and many talents and peculiarities which were inextricably mixed. She had the whole third story to herself and kept it bright with blooming plants and canary birds in every variety of cages, whole families of singing feathered creatures. An unsatisfied maternal instinct made her love children. We liked to help her make scrap-books for hospitals, dress dolls and collect toys for sick or neglected babies. She addressed us in extravagantly affectionate terms, and demanded more demonstration than we, ungrateful little creatures, were capable of giving in return. But we turned over her scraps of silk, and the beads and worsteds from which she made pretty trifles, ate her marvelous molasses candy, welcomed her visits when illness laid us low and she brought soft jelly, or when her cool currant shrub and lemonade refreshed us on hot afternoons. We always climbed to her attic in jovial mood.

By and by Jamie, or Father, would come to take us home and Aunt Frances and Grandmother would stow away something worthwhile in our coat pockets and send a package to Mother too. Cedar Square was the happiest of hospices. My Grandmother lived on to welcome us there until we had grown almost into young-ladyhood.

4

ABC'S AND DICKENS

I never remembered actually learning to read. I only recall three neat little blue volumes with stories in words of one syllable which were loose in the nursery for a long time, and *Mother Goose* in a gayer binding lying trampled among the blocks on the floor. One knew its rhymes by heart and didn't have to spell them out. But upstairs there was an unused room to which I went when Harriet was busy with my little sister. The books there represented an overflow from the study, where new library-acquisitions were always crowding out the old. Most of them consisted of theological works, which I rather suspect had been orthodox and Unitarian reading displaced by Episcopalian exegesis. Turning them untidily out on the floor to find pictures, I came upon three or four tall thin black volumes, between the covers of which grotesque illustrations and quite fine-printed text appeared alternately. They were an original English edition of Dickens' earliest works, with the Cruikshank engravings. I had never seen anything like them. I got hold of *Oliver Twist* first of all, and every one of those prints stands out vividly in my memory yet. Oliver trembling behind Mr. Brownlow at the book-stall, with Noah Claypole lurking near by; Fagin gnawing his fingernails in the prison cell; in another volume Mrs. Nickleby and Kate looking up at the leering old gentleman on the garden wall; Nell and her grandfather in still another volume, sitting on the hillside gazing down on London; Quilp's horrible dog—Heaven knows why that didn't give me bad dreams—frothing and straining at his chain. Those three or four books were the only ones we owned then, but they were utterly absorbing to me. How long I looked at those illustrations and wondered about them before I discovered that I could read the black printed words of the story, I do not know. There is a blank between those first discoveries and a winter day when I had brought *Oliver Twist* down from the chilly attic into the warm nursery and was lying face downward perusing it, and suddenly heard my sister's voice:

"Mother! What do you suppose this child is reading?"

There was an investigation and a subdued "Mercy! where did she find it?" Then Mother's decision, given with the bright, practical finality which settled all such problems:

"Well, she certainly can't get any harm from it at the age of six." So Oliver and the rest remained my special and beloved friends. I went back to them again and again, finding companionship and amusement as well, for my humor responded even to phrases I could not understand. The very exaggerations delighted me. I heard my brothers and sister observe now and then that people they met were *Dickensy*—indeed that was rather a family habit; and I instinctively knew what it meant and whence their amusement came. Those first bits of enjoyment took a definite place in my mental background, and little by little other joys followed. There were more books in the attic bookcase which appealed to me. Some volumes of a not very good edition of Shakespeare had been put there, and I had heard of remarkable little girls who read Shakespeare at a tender age. But the unfamiliar language repelled me. It was the same with Scott; Dickens had spoiled me for that too; the settings at the beginning of many of the novels were too hard to visualize, and the humans too long in coming forward dramatically. But poetry was different; into that I plunged with abandon, finding a copy of Dana's anthology, the *Household Book of Poetry* and carrying it up from downstairs to the dingy old armchair whither I fled on Harriet's sweeping days. My older brother discovered me there, finally, and it was a delight to him to find how much I could repeat of the verses he loved. He bought me my first own poetry-book, compiled by Coventry Patmore, *The Children's Garland*. A book has always had a personality for me, and this was so trim, so smooth in its soft red shiny covers, with leaves of a creamy fineness and delicate, clear print. The delight of cutting the leaves of a new book came to me thus early in life, and I gradually learned to do it with the reserve and suspended enthusiasm of the passionate reader. I have that beloved copy of *The Children's Garland* still; worn and faded but brave and intact.

But my parents began to feel that these energies would better be put under training; the educational advantages to be derived from promiscuous reading were not clear. A school was found for me, conducted by Miss Mary Gage, who lived in a little house at the corner of West Cedar and Mount Vernon streets; it had a sunny schoolroom jutting out over the sidewalk, looking down toward the Charles River and up toward Louisburg Square.

The principal was a fine woman, broad-minded, large and awe-inspiring, quite strict. The children read from First Readers; very easy and very dull after my more exciting home-reading. We did arithmetic from large pasteboard cards with columns of figures which could be made into addition, subtraction, multiplication or division-sums. I didn't like that either; I had not begun with the rest, and my card was always dog-eared. Geography was nicer, learned from little square books with maps and pictures. And the nicest thing of all was French, for which there was a good native teacher and small brown books, Chouquet's *First French Books*. And music, chiefly do-re-mi-sol-fa out of text-books by Lowell Mason—oblong-shaped.

Miss Gage was assisted by a pupil-teacher, a big girl with reddish hair who wore a dress of dull blue and was named Lily. She used to take the children into the back schoolroom to get drinks of water from a faucet and see that they did not play with it. She seemed to dislike her job, and moved and talked very slowly. But she was considered a mine of information, I discovered. There was a question that I did not want to ask of superior older sisters or brothers; to do that would be to admit their superiority, which, however, unquestioned, was not readily acknowledged by the inferior members of the family. Quite enough grist came to their mill as it was, and they had no patience, either, with foolish inquiries. It was best to try Lily and see what she could do. So one day after gazing at her intently over the top of a china water mug, I ventured to inquire;

"Can you think?"

"Why yes, of course I can," was the answer.

"I can't. I don't know how, and I want to. I've got to find out. Could you tell me how you do it?"

"No," said the big girl, "I can't tell you. It does itself."

"Yes, but how do you know when it is doing it?"

No answer. I concluded it wasn't of much use to go to school if you couldn't find out a thing like that. I did not pursue my inquiries further. Not long after, however, I started as I found myself saying to my nurse, "I don't think so." Of a sudden, realization burst upon me.

"Harriet," I cried. "Did you hear that? I've *thought*!"

"No, you said you *didn't* think," interrupted Molly.

"I said I didn't think that time, but it means I must have thought another time. Yes, it does do itself. How nice! I can think; I can think!"

The audience appeared mystified, not having appreciated the problem. But another step in the slow, involuntary process of self-realization had been taken. I had no more idea than before what thinking was. But *I could do it;* there was no more to worry about. It would happen, just as jumping and running, laughing and crying would happen. And it was the same power that my brothers and sisters, with their superior talents, possessed. I could take for granted that I was thinking whether I had learned how or not. And so that little conversation was fraught with a significance which sends the memory of it back to me after many years.

5

CHILD'S VIEW OF THE CIVIL WAR

But life at ninety-eight Boylston Street had its dark side. Over that warm protected circle lay the shadow of the Civil War. We were scarcely out of babyhood when it made itself felt in our experience. We learned that as little children learn all situations, from the words and looks of those about us; there was some struggle going on in the world which touched all life, brooded in faces, came out in phrases and exclamations and pitiful sights. South and North were incomprehensible distinctions, but we grew to realize that there were spaces on the earth, not bounded by gardens and brick blocks, where there was cruelty and darkness. There were people, we heard, who were trying to make things better and to stop the fighting, and men who were doing their best to put an end to them with musket and cannon. A picture of General McClellan hung in the dining-room; we were told that he was a brave soldier, and so were General Sherman and General Grant, of whom we also saw pictures. We did not think General Grant looked so brave as the others, but we knew he was, of course. We knew, by the time we were four years old, what blue coats and brass buttons stood for. The streets were full of boys in blue, marching over the pavements in squads. We heard that there were other soldiers in gray, and gray was an ominous color; those were the men that had to be "all killed up." Our soldiers would fire guns at them, and they would fall down dead. The boys played soldiers and made them do that. No one would care if the gray soldiers, the rebels, were killed; they were bad; an enemy.

We sang *Hang Jeff Davis to a sour apple tree* and hoped somebody would; he was a *terrible* person, Jeff Davis! There were many such songs, echoing on street corners, floating out of open windows, squeaking from melodeons, tinkling from piano-keys, whistled or hummed. We heard words like *tragic, ghastly, strategy* and *surrender,* and guessed what they meant by the tones in which they were spoken. Such expressions seemed to compete with one another for effect in common conversation. Our mother and aunts were away whole forenoons working at the rooms of the Sanitary Commission. Our sister and her friends scraped lint, knitted stockings, rolled bandages. People came to the house bringing all sorts of things to be sent to the soldiers. We heard of poor black people in the cotton-fields and men standing over them with whips. We had the kind, rugged face of President Lincoln imprinted on our memories, from pictures and descriptions.

All this meant to us a rather eventful, taken-for-granted activity which did not touch us very deeply nor frighten us. The sharpness of calamity reached us in other ways. As a baby I had experienced the extremity of terror. Once the little carriage in which I sat had been pushed into a crowd on Boston Common by a too-curious young nurse who wanted to see what was going on. A cannon was touched off and exploded with awful suddenness before the bystanders had fallen back to a safe distance. I had been brought home in a nervous convulsion which alarmed the family seriously and left its traces in twitching muscles and agonized sensitiveness to loud sounds. As I grew older the cannonading on the Common was an almost daily horror, and the military funerals an unbearable experience, long-drawn-out. Some forenoon or afternoon when the Garden was quiet and the hum of traffic monotonous, I would be conscious of a dull, persistent sound like the beating of a heavy pulse, no clang, no reverberation, merely a soft thud, the vibrations making their way through the thick rumble of vehicles and the clap of horses' hoofs over pavements. It did not seem to grow louder, but it kept up mercilessly, that horrible pulse-beat, and I knew what was coming. Then there would be another sound, even more mournful, the tolling of bells—sometimes one, sometimes many. And to the eye of a tense watcher, there would appear a procession coming up or down Boylston Street, a train of black carriages (with some of their curtains down) drawn by horses with plumes and trappings that made their eyes glare out of round holes. Then came biers, sometimes one, sometimes more, on catafalques, with sable hangings and coffins draped in flags. I knew that dead bodies of soldiers were inside; it was only necessary to hear the talk of the crowd on the sidewalk, in which we were caught if a funeral train surprised us in the Public Gardens.

Harriet and the other nurses told about wounds, and legs shot away and bullet-holes in foreheads, though they had never seen any. Sometimes a horse with an empty saddle was led along behind an officer's bier; then the old men sitting on the garden benches would cry and wipe their bleary eyes with bandana handkerchiefs. And all the time there was the muffled beating of the drums and the slow, slow clopping of hoofs.

Then came the band, playing a dirge. That was a musical experience, solemn, gripping. It was not cheap, inadequate music, but a fit accompaniment for a grand and dignified burial pageant. Out of the midst of the dark, moving masses came the strains of the Dead March in *Saul* or the tragic minor chords of Beethoven and Mendelssohn; not common things. We heard our mother say how beautiful and fitting those dirges were. I listened with a thumping heart, dreaded it, but I could not get away from it while the carriages and the biers and the soldiers crawled mournfully along Arlington Street, around to Beacon, and finally disappeared along Charles Street on their way to Mount Auburn.

More exciting and less mournful were the parades of victorious soldiers after a battle. First there was the cannonading from the Common. I would rush in an agony of fright to the dark closet and bury my head in the mattresses and pillows stored there till nurse Harriet or an older sister or brother opened the door, crying, "It's all over!" But there was still marching and shouting to be lived through and the blare of the bands and the repugnant strains of the *Star Spangled Banner*. And that began with "Oh, say"—a phrase which the well-bred child was forbidden to utter under any provocation! But I fervently chanted "My Country 'tis of Thee," feeling its dignified musical background instinctively. We sang Julia Ward

Howe's *Battle Hymn of the Republic* which gave us deep confidence. Our father loved to troll out its impressive lines. *John Brown's Body,* which had furnished the melody for it, was rather cheerful; one didn't like to think of bodies mouldering in graves, but souls getting out of them and marching on suggested something interesting.

The Rector, who did not believe in running away from scarey things, helped his little daughter to endure the clanging of the brass bands sometimes, by holding her close with his strong arm, her feet on the sill of the basement dining-room window where solid earth broke the vibrations somewhat. Feeling that bulwark I could face the music, which at the bottom of my heart I loved. When it was over I could experience with spent breath and pounding heart a sort of heroic exaltation. This was the nearest a child came to war and its atmosphere.

I remember vividly the story told to a little group in Mother's room about a young soldier who had been mortally wounded in the war. As he was about to die he kept repeating, "They killed us! We had a right to live." The listener, shocked at this, felt it to be an unpatriotic attitude for a dying soldier to take, a boy who had given his life to save his country. He must have been out of his mind, they felt. Father listened, but only said something about taking the sword and perishing by the sword. I was puzzled because I knew that the young soldier had been killed by a gun or a cannon. Mother said that perhaps a time would come when the world would feel as the boy had, but the others felt that no one could feel that way *now,* not while we were fighting for such a noble cause. So the debate ended in a wave of patriotism.

The long winter ended at last. Before the snow melted there was some sort of victory, perhaps the occupation of Charleston; then out of a blur of events flashes recollection of a moist, bright early spring forenoon when Jamie came rushing into the house and up the stairs with a cry of "Mother! Mother! Richmond's evacuated!"

"You don't say so!" we heard Mother answer. "Is it really true?"

"Yes," called the Rector, not far behind him. "The news is just in."

People were hurrying along the street; boys were carrying armfuls of papers. The windows were thrown up to let in the warm air; the sunshine lay across the garden-beds; there was an odor of damp earth. Bells rang, cannon boomed; one didn't mind that so very much, somehow, for there was gladness in the sound of them. Our jolly uncles stopped in, bringing bulletins, and ran up to my mother's room, where she sat smiling, at her table sewing. *Evacuated* was a new, puzzling word. "What had they done to Richmond," we inquired of Harriet.

"Oh, got out of it," she said. "Stopped fightin'. It means the end of the war, I guess." And she hurried downstairs to spread the news in the basement. Our sister Arria arrived with some friends; they had still more to tell; they had read the dispatches, posted in an apothecary's window. All that day fresh news kept coming in. Our father joined the gathering in Mother's room. I remember his solemn, rhythmic tones:

> "They shall beat their swords into ploughshares,
>   and their spears into pruning-hooks."

Other great days followed. We heard about Lee's surrender. The story seemed to take some of the temporary frivolity out of the public mind. We didn't know exactly what had happened, but we heard them talking about General Lee in a different way after that, almost as if they were sorry for him. Harriet said he was giving up fighting. It sounded as if he had turned out to be a nice man after all.

Then there were two weeks of hope and glory, and jubilant, weary regiments coming home. Then came Easter, the first we had understood very much about.

But we found the house strangely still when we came down to breakfast. Something had happened—had happened to the world. The faces of our elders were solemn; the family prayers breathed of sorrow. There was talking outdoors under the windows, but it was subdued, intense. Then we were told. President Lincoln, the good, the wise, the fatherly, the savior of the nation, was dead. The triumph of that last fortnight had ended in bitter bereavement.

I seem to have no recollection of what happened through the day except that people were reading things all day long out of newspapers. I caught some words about a theatre, and about a man coming forward on a stage and shouting out a thing that sounded like the hissing of a snake. I could repeat it long after, making an attempt to imitate that hissing.

"S-s-sic s-s-s-semper-r tyr-r-rannis-s!" So they said it, and the sound seemed worse than the shot. And that was assassination! I flew to Harriet; she could get tragedy down to our level.

"Harriet! Harriet! *What* is assassination? Is it shooting? Is it murder?"

"It's worse than murder," she answered shakily. "It's the dreadfullest kind of killing." And we could elicit nothing more from her. The calamity was beyond comprehension. Our only course was to accept it and wait; no one wanted to be asked questions. I have a recollection of going out with Father toward the end of the day and seeing black drapings nailed up somewhere and an old negro standing in front of a bulletin with tears streaming down his cheeks; of Father's long, absent-minded stride, and of the side-ache I got running to keep up with him.

Before going to bed that night we learned to our great relief that the funeral was not to be in Boston, so nothing dismal marred our vision of the loved President. Father and Mother were prudent enough to keep from us the accounts of the fugitive Booth and his final apprehension. We only knew that he, too, was gone beyond our ken and judgment, and it did not trouble childish dreams.

Thenceforth our daily life returned to a more peaceful course. We knew little of the nation's great upheaval and of the sad aftermath of the War. But bits of current news reached us; only bits, yet things not understood at once made sense as better comprehension came with growth. Father went as he had gone during the previous years to many meetings of an important kind in "Flannel" Hall, as we called Faneuil Hall: meetings where Garrison, Phillips, and others, spoke. We heard Father tell about them at breakfast, and he would read comments about them out of the newspapers to Mother. Then when a new *Atlantic Monthly* came or Littell's *Liv-*

ing Age our whole family shared them. Lowell was still bringing out his *Biglow Papers*—and I don't think anybody was tired of his genial pacifism clothed in irresistible humor. Jamie, whose phenomenal memory reproduced anything he had once heard read aloud, would reel off quotations on all occasions, and we little ones caught phrases also. I see myself hopping down the stairs at Ninety-eight, repeating

> "John P.
> Robinson he
> Sez he wunt vote fer Guvener B."

in a chant that lent itself to dancing-steps. And I recall a misty morning on Boston Common, waiting beside my father while he talked to a spare little gentleman whose face went into a hundred humorous wrinkles as they too quoted Lowell:

> "Ez fer war, I call it murder,—
> There you hev it, plain an' flat . . . ."

I lost the next lines but caught the last;—

> "An' you've got to git up airly
> Ef ye want to *take in* God."

6

MUSIC IN BOSTON

Through all the ravages of the Civil War Boston had continued a city of special cultural advantages. The Huntingtons, who had moved into a larger house not far from ninety-eight Boylston Street, enjoyed theatres, lyceums, and concert courses. My older brother and sister had heard the great Ristori, seen the charming Fanny Kemble act, heard Dickens' famous readings during his visits to this country, when people crowded the sidewalks sitting on camp-chairs for hours to make sure of their seats.

The Handel and Hayden Society, a large chorus, was singing the great oratorios. It was a special honor to sing in those choruses, which were given in Music Hall with the accompaniment of the great organ, and Boston's finest men and women attended. Italian operas were given in Boston during those years, and echoes from them sounded everywhere; even the war-songs were interspersed with bits of *Martha* and *Lucia di Lammermoor,* and *The Bohemian Girl.* New England was then overrun with organ-grinders; one heard them on street corners all day long. I heard the sextet from *Lucia* in a café on the esplanade at Lugano a few years ago. In a second the lovely lake and its setting of mountains disappeared. I saw instead a thin, tattered little old man standing on a Boylston Street curb grinding out the melody from his organ, its faded red silk front all worn out, its bellows squeaky, the pennies and two-cent coppers dropping sparsely into a tin cup. After hearing them ground out thus we knew the familiar arias by heart and hummed them or sang the translated words. Mother sang us *I Dreamt that I Dwelt in Marble Halls,* and *How So Fair Stood She There,* and even told us the story of *La Somnambula* as she had heard it produced.

On Sundays the great joy of the day was the music in church. It was the busiest day of the week at the rectory, and we ourselves were part of the activity, getting put into our best frocks, and at ten o'clock setting sail in the wake of our mother and sister. The neighbors marched to the joyful ringing of the bells in Dr. Gannett's church. The Rector went ahead, of course, his sombre black cape wrapped about him, his manuscript enclosed in a purple velvet sermon-case. As the door of Emmanuel Church was opened for our entrance a burst of triumphant organ music poured forth, and we went up the aisle in tune with a brisk march which bore us along "on wings of sound." The church, finished in dark wood, would look gloomy and severe today, but it was dignified, with Gothic arches and pillars. The clerestory of the chancel, however, was the most churchly feature; the chancel's ceiling was dark blue studded with gold stars like the real firmament. The thick carpeting of the aisles deadened all sound of footsteps; so there was nothing to divert the sonorous organ-tones which filled the church.

When we got into the Rector's pew, just under the pulpit, we all went down on our knees, and as we were very punctual but not ahead of time, that was usually the exact moment when the processional march wound up and the organ quieted down to slow soft chords, then came to a stop. An instant's silence followed. Then from far off, as if he were up among the stars, Father's voice rang out declaring, "The Lord is in His Holy Temple." That turned the place into a Holy of Holies. Afterward all the music seemed worshipful, although it must be conceded that most of the church music of the day was inferior. But we didn't know that. Only now and then could we get a fine English anthem or a solo from a really great oratorio. When we did have that happiness, it was imprinted indelibly on our memories. I can hear Annie Louise Cary, a famous contralto who began her career in Emmanuel choir, as she sang Mendelssohn's *O Rest in the Lord* to a rapt congregation. We listened for the words, "And wait"—that long, sustained, clear note that made one's own breath come deep and long as we, too, waited absorbed and confident until the tone sank, softly repeating the command; "Wait patiently,"—but it was more anticipation than mere patience—"for Him."

After the uplifting effect of music, one was rather let down by having to sit through the sermon. We felt the eloquence of our father, but we took in little of his discourse.

On Sunday afternoons we often went to meet our parents when they returned from the second service. Boylston Street was quiet except for a few strollers and a group of parishioners walking slowly homeward. Dr. Gannett, leaning on his two canes, would stop to talk to Father; Dr. Bowditch would salute us from his steps; the Putnams' long window next to our house would be open if it were warm spring weather, and the Judge would look down over his spectacles from a chair on the balcony, as we all came in at our own door to the shelter of Ninety-eight. Before we went to bed, Mother would play for us on the piano which was always piled with good music, mostly bound in portentous volumes with her name on them in gilt letters.

As a result of Mother's playing and the choir-inspiration, I longed to make music for myself during the week. The old closet where the pillows were kept and to which I had fled from the cannonading of wartime had ceased to be a refuge, and was now a dungeon for the impenitent. It was my mother's wise idea to shut me in there, knowing as she did that the solitude and darkness would quiet me down. Once alone, I forgot grievances and misdemeanors, and began improvising anthems and *Te Deums,* singing as I went. All manner of embellishments in bravura, variations, trills, now alto, now soprano, now falsetto, poured from the small cantatrice's throat as she sat on a rolled-up mattress playing choir to an imaginary congregation. The family, delighted to have me disposed of so satisfactorily, would nearly forget my existence.

There was another incident which connected the *Te Deum* more directly with family history. The Rector, writing one forenoon in his study, was interrupted by the sound of a shrill voice on a high key. It was his fourth child singing to the invisible church congregation from the nursery upstairs.

"When Thou hadst overcome the sharpness, the sharpness—of Death, Thou didst open the Kingdom of Heav'n, of Heav'n to all believers."

The music dropped from high heaven to wobbly tones below the staff, and stopped short. There was a dash of rapid steps along the hall and down the stairs. In at the door burst a tense little figure. "Papa! Papa! What *are* believers? Can nobody get into the Kingdom of Heaven, only just them? And where is it? Up in the sky? How do we know that they have only believers there?"

The Rector raised his eyes from a passage that had been hard to express with a pen. He saw the old doorway at Forty Acres, felt a breath of warm air blowing on the face of a worried little boy, squeezed between the syringa bush and the closed green blinds of the Long Room. He was there waiting in case of need to defend his mother, whose unfaltering tones, low and distinct, answered the strained interrogations of the believers from the Orthodox Society.

He bent down and put his arm around me, helping me to climb up over the arm of his chair.

"Listen," he said. "The Kingdom of Heaven is right here, right in this house and on Boylston Street all round us. All children are in it anyway; the Lord Himself said so. It is wherever His friends are. We get into it just by loving Him and doing the things He loves to have done. That's what friends do, isn't it? And friends believe in each other. You and I do that, don't we?"

The child bent down her head, and looked straight into his eyes. "That's a *good idea,* papa! I see; don't you? Friends first, then you believe in the friends. And in the Kingdom of Heaven all the while."

I was still for a moment—he told me this long afterward, when he was old and I had forgotten—and then climbed down and ran away. From the stairway echoed: "Cherubim and seraphim, cherubim and seraphim, cherubim and seraphim, continually do cry."

It was the only approach to a theological discussion the Rector ever had with his second daughter.

Meanwhile our parents, coming slowly to the conclusion that their fourth child might really be "musical," as they put it, began to think about a training for me. I could not spend my days in the airless and feathery closet. It would be as well to curtail the *Te Deums* for the time being, and as father suggested, try the effect of

tempo upon temper and temperament. There were no psychiatrists
at that period but common-sense was an excellent substitute. My
parents discovered that a first-rate music-school existed in Boston,
under the direction of Mademoiselle Gabrielle de la Motte, a
Frenchwoman whose methods were said to be European, and her
knowledge of great musicians and their works authoritative. The
Rector felt well satisfied with what he heard of her instruction. He
went to see her, and arranged that she should take his little daughter as a pupil, the younger the better, she had said. So it was announced to me that I was going to learn to play the piano.

It was a thrilling announcement. I laughed aloud in my delight;
a habit which was annoying to the more polite in the family circle.
Why so boisterous on all occasions? But the elders had a theory, or
rather a sort of general principle, that spontaneity should be at
least tolerated, since bottling it up might increase my self-consciousness. I needed training of all sorts, but especially manual training,
which was ignored in the contemporary methods of education. Both
sisters were "handy," the older one with a distinct talent for drawing
and water-color painting, small Molly for the household arts. I
did not know how to hold anything but a book; I dropped things,
let doors slam. But now, to learn piano-playing would be my
own accomplishment, not just like those of my family; and to play
as Mother did—to get beautiful sounds out of the big books and the
white keys—to be able to sit in Grandmother's shady parlor as Aunt
Kate could do, playing on and on with people listening—that was
the sum of my ambition and desire. I could not get to sleep for a
long, long time that night. It was not the hour for indulging in *Te
Deums,* but I sang them inside my head, as I would have described
it. Lessons, lessons—what would they be like?

I found out next day what a music-school was like. It was decided that as I was now eight-years-going-on-nine, and had already
been to day school without Harriet, I might be allowed to walk by
myself to the house of Mademoiselle. One can hardly imagine a
child of eight making that trip alone from Boylston Street to the
State House in this generation, but old Boston was safe and slow.

Once inside that house you were in America no longer; you

seemed, as the Rector said, to have been suddenly transported to France. The street might have been in one of the quiet corners of Paris. Even a child could appreciate the foreign air of the place, and my first reaction was a wave of homesickness. I would have failed at the very first lesson if it had not seemed such a wonderful thing to take music-courses, and if I had not known there were other children there. The very walls, the quaint old prints and portraits, the oval mirror in the hall with a prim little white-spread stand beneath it, seemed to go with the teacher and her French figure. She was about forty then; a wiry person with high forehead slightly receding, gray hair drawn tightly and smoothly back from her temples, gray eyes which looked you keenly but kindly through, a pointed chin above a close white collar; an invariably simple, perfectly fitted gray gown and small black silk apron. She was not unkindly, but a child could not feel drawn to her on first acquaintance. I resisted my first temptation to rush home in a panic, and reflected that after all I had good legs and knew the way to Boylston Street when the affair was over.

In the room which would have been a parlor stood four square pianos, back to back with two high stools at each. This was the classroom, with provision for eight at a time. The technical part of the lesson was performed by teamwork, two children at each piano. One other little girl and I were younger than the rest of our class. We were taught finger-exercises, without books or notes, but Mademoiselle read us portions of a book she was about to publish, and made us learn by heart simple instructions in theory. She stood in the middle of the room and beat time with a little baton. We had to keep very much alive when the eight played together, as a misstep stopped the whole class and frightened the stumbler.

After the lesson I was sent upstairs into a small hall where there was an upright piano, and given a practice lesson under a young woman named Miss Jones. She had a thin, red face and black corkscrew curls bunched at the back of her head. She traversed the ground that had been gone over by Mademoiselle, and then had me play exercises and scales again and again, rapping my fingers sharply with a wooden knitting-needle if I made mistakes. One other day in the week was devoted to private lessons, and learning simple little "recreations" as our leader called them. If I did well, I was presented with a bar of delicious French chocolate, said to be imported direct from Paris, and ate it on the way home, in defiance of a point of etiquette which forbade chewing on the street.

So the spring term passed, and after the summer vacation we went to work again. Mademoiselle had written to the Rector that his little girl had made very unusual progress thus far. She was to be trained for a performance in the annual *soirée* given by the pupils of the school in February, at which eight children, all but two of them about ten years of age, were to play an octette on four grand pianos. She felt sure that I, though younger, could take part in this, and offered to give me instruction one more day in the week without extra cost.

The performance in which we were drilled for the *soirée* was most cleverly arranged by Mademoiselle de la Motte. It was the theme from Handel's *Harmonious Blacksmith,* written in parts for eight children to play on four grand pianos. Each part was extremely simple, but represented a section of the harmony, and played together gave it complete. We went over and over it till we had memorized every note and accented every phrase, and could keep our eyes on Mademoiselle's baton. That was not all we were to play, however. Our teacher had set her heart on having us do the scales, major and minor, a heavy contract for a child who had had lessons for only about seven months. But the teamwork carried us along. Even the terrible double sharps in some of the scales were surmounted by dogged perseverance—Mademoiselle's, not ours— and by the appointed date we were at home with our task.

When the concert was played in Chickering Hall before a selected audience we all felt it was the beginning of a real career. We had no self-conciousness and no appreciation of the audience, for our eyes were glued to the figure of Mademoiselle, in a full-skirted black silk gown with a fine lace collar. We admired the costume because it was not "slinky" like her everyday one. We sat on our slippery piano-stools, arranged our fingers lightly on the keys, ready for action, and followed her baton with automatic precision. The blacksmith's hammer tapped responsively from one pair of pianos to the other, and there was no breakdown in the scales, for which crisp orders were given, though I suspect there were notes missed here and there without interruption of the rhythm. It was a tribute to the excellent method we had been taught, and which I believe is the best system for the acquisition of early technical *fertigkeit*. For me, at all events, that evening was a high-spot, and the best part of it was the great concession my parents made in letting me hear some of the performance of the more advanced pupils, who gave fine renderings of *classical* music, as it was then called.

My study of music was definitely beneficial to my development. It gave me a new world in which I could live alone, independent of my parents, my brothers, and sisters. In enjoying it, I had no obligation to anyone but myself.

7

BISHOPS AND BROKEN LEGS

It was not very long after the concerts that a new prospect, sudden and thrilling, appeared on the horizon of the rectory family. Something was happening. The Rector himself was silent and preoccupied. The lively meal-times had changed. Jamie was the only person who laughed and brought in tales of school affairs. He did not know, we felt. Our mother and sister talked together in low voices. Once they walked about the parlor looking at the furniture and suggesting what should be taken. Taken where? We began to grow unhappy over the mystery when one day our father waked up at the dinner-table and seemed to have reclaimed his old brightness of spirit. He said:

"Children, how would you like to go to Syracuse to live?"

"Why?" I inquired. "*Are* we going there?"

Yes, that was the plan. Father was going off to be a bishop, and take us all with him, in a railroad train. The furniture was going to be packed and stored for the summer, and in September we should move to a new home, have a new school and a new circle of friends. Harriet would go too. It was way, way off out West.

"And shall we have little bags of our own?" asked Molly, to whom the journey by rail appealed. No doubt we should. Father could not be certain of that; it was for mamma to say. And mamma, promptly interrogated, allowed that we might have to have bags, and even trunks. She did not look worried any more. "Arria will be the one to feel it most," we heard her say to someone later.

It was very, very exciting. We thought about bishops. We knew a little what they were like because a few had visited us. Bishop Clarke of Rhode Island always told such lovely funny stories. And

Bishop Coxe of Western New York was nice, only he used to get excited in talking sometimes, and say that some people were headed for Rome, whatever that meant. He liked a rich service but thought red altar-cloths were dreadful. We had never seen an altar-cloth, red or any other color. And Bishop Eastburn, who lived right in Boston, talked like that too, only more so. They had said so much about *Catholics* that we had asked Harriet why there was any harm in them when we said "the holy Catholic Church" in the creed on Sunday. Harriet had said: "Well, there's two kinds; there's the *holy* Catholic church and the *Roman* Catholic church; I guess that's the kind they don't like." But Jamie, overhearing us, had said, "No, Harriet, catholic means all-over-the-world, that's all."

"Oh." I was silenced for the time being. But bishops—bishops— what did they do? "Are bishops grand?" I asked my older sister.

"Not in America. In England they are, sometimes. But they have power." Of course. The power-and-the-glory-forever-and-ever- amen. Father would have power. He didn't look any different yet, however. Then we found there was to be a great service to consecrate him. A new word, *consecrate*. I had learned to go to the fat Webster's Dictionary which must be tumbled to the floor because it was too heavy to lift. I knocked it carefully down, got to all fours, and looked up *consciousness, conscription, consecrate*; "to exalt to the rank of a saint." I guessed at *exalt*, though that was a new word too. So they were going to make Father a saint, that was it. I wondered if he would look different that way. How would they do it? Harriet, summoned to help replace the Dictionary, suggested that they put robes on him and something on his head.

"What is it they put on bishops' heads?" I inquired of my eldest brother.

"Mitres, do you mean?"

"I guess so. Real bishops, not chess-bishops. Will father have a mitre on when they consecrate him?"

My brother was amused. "Hardly," he said. "That would be a rather startling departure for Boston. Fancy Bishop Eastburn's state of mind," he added to his sister Arria.

"Why?" I persisted. "Would he think it was worse than a red

altar-cloth?" At which the other laughed immoderately. I looked up
mitre, and found a picture of one in the dictionary. It was the mitre
of a Pope, whoever that might be: a heavy thing really like the top
of a chess-bishop. I was glad Father would not have the embarrassment of wearing one in church; it might get askew or tumble off
when he bowed his head. "Uneasy lies the head that wears a crown,"
I reflected. It might be the same with bishops.

Then came a box with some bishop's robes in it. A wealthy parishioner had sent them to her departing pastor. Beautiful thick
black satin and very full white sleeves with fine ruffles at the wrists.
Our mother was showing them to one of our aunts from Cambridge
next day.

"Yards and yards and yards," was her comment on the wrist
bands. "Isn't that rather discouraging? They have to be done up by
hand, and those tiny pleats crimped with a penknife; think of the
time it will take."

"Yes," was the answer, I imagine from Aunt Mary Cooke. "And
they're one of those things that only a lady can do perfectly—like
making a sponge cake. But you're just the person for a Bishop's
wife, Hannah; you'll carry it off grandly, I know."

Grandly, yes. Mamma would. She was so large, fine-looking,
dignified, and gracious in her ways, as everybody said. But we all
sympathized with her in the matter of the ruffles.

When the great day came, it seemed to fill Boston—the rectory
family's Boston, that is—with ministers in black coats. They
strolled across the Public Gardens, they hurried along Arlington
Street, they got out of horse-cars, they came down Boylston Street
in groups. The Bishop-to-be had moved out of his house, and we
younger children were staying with Aunt Kate, our mother's sister,
on the next block. I wanted to go to the service, feeling sure there
would be grand music, but Mother said that was too long for me to
have to sit still.

So I went off to school as usual, but in the afternoon when Aunt
Kate was lying down, I stole away with another child in the neigh-
borhood to play in a vacant lot where there was building going on.
There were many such lots near by full of shavings and bricks.

But we were not supposed to go there to play alone: I knew that. I can never forget that mild April afternoon nor the quiet of Newbury Street just opposite the church, where all the people had gone after the morning ceremonies. We two children balanced on boards, sat on a pile of bricks, then walked up to a great building-ladder which was lying full length against a wall. The other child said, "Let's pull this over," and took hold of the upper edge. It tumbled toward us. I was knocked over backwards, down a slight bank; the edge of the heavy ladder pinned me by one leg, which pained. I cried out, but the other child ran away. Then a man's strong arm pulled up the ladder and dragged me out, very quickly. He was a tall, fine-looking young man, as it turned out, the son of one of the bishops who was in town. He lifted me in his arms, carried me to the sidewalk, and stopped two old ladies who were driving by in a carriage. "Why, that's Dr. Huntington's little girl!" exclaimed one of them. The young man climbed in with me and held me on his lap till we got to Aunt Kate's house, then carried me upstairs where my tired parents were trying to rest.

The doctor who came was a soft looking person who evidently prided himself on his success with children. He approached the bed looking sentimental, pulling his moustache.

"My dear little girl, you've been real brave not to make any fuss. But I must tell you that your leg is broken, and you'll have to have it put in a splint, and lie still for awhile."

My eyes opened wide, fairly dilating with joy. Two seconds of imagination—visions of lame children, Jenny Wren with her crutch (Hoppetty, Kicketty, Peg-peg-peg), the Little Lame Prince, Tiny Tim, myself hopping about with two croquet-mallets under my arms as I had done last summer. And people pitying me. I laughed, boisterously, gleefully.

"Broken!" I cried. "Really *broken*? How *interesting*! I shall be a real cripple, shan't I?"

The doctor was amazed and frankly disgruntled. A most disconcerting child—dramatizing a serious situation like that, taking the thing so lightly, calling it interesting! He had expected to wipe my tears away and promise me some candy.

Now came some truly delightful weeks, weeks of being carried each morning to a couch across the bay-window, on which I spent the day, looking out at the Gardens in their spring verdure. People came every day to see me, out of love for the whole rectory family; brought books and puzzles and fruit. It really did make one a little bit important, apparently, to break one's leg.

One visitor, however, made a mistake. She told me she had once broken her own leg, "And I had to learn to walk all over again." That made a strong impression. Learning to walk somehow did not look attractive; it was being like a baby. And it wasn't like a real *bona fide* cripple either. Hopping on a crutch was something unusual, something really entertaining, not such a trivial thing as calculating which foot to put out first. I spent a good deal of time planning how to begin.

The weeks passed quickly, what with all the visitors and amusements, and the long letters which were coming from Syracuse. The new Bishop was being received there with open arms, and had been fêted and introduced everywhere. He had seen some real Indians. People were kind and warm-hearted; many asked after his little girl with the broken leg. This was balm to my soul, and I resolved to make a still greater impression when I reached there.

Life continued in smooth, protected fashion. There were last visits and invitations. Little Molly was staying at Cedar Square with Grandmother Sargent, our older sister. Aunt Kate took some of the care from my mother's shoulders, and was a most entertaining nurse, bringing out treasures from her mental storehouse in the way of jokes and verses, creative ventures and musical snatches. Sometimes she sat down in the parlor and played, making up things as she went along. Our older brother had been ordained to the ministry the day after our father's consecration, and was settling down to parish work; he could not be often with us.

One day the surgeon came to take the starch bandage off the broken leg, bringing a neat little saw which he operated, lengthwise, from the toes to the knee. It was thrilling. I was a bit afraid, naturally, that he would saw through to the bone, and he did make a few slight scratches on the flesh, but not "so's to hurt." Then he took hold of the two sides and bent them back with a mighty grip, and pulled off the whole shell, which by that time was yellow. And the unimportant fracture, lo and behold, had behaved beautifully. I could now, as he said, begin to walk.

There seemed to be no reason whatever for me to use crutches, which was terribly disappointing. I had set my heart on it and pictured myself using them for a long time to come. It was exhilarating to be told one could really walk off, however, and I gaily put out a foot, ambitious if not wholly satisfied. But there was something wrong after all; it wouldn't hold me up even long enough to get the other foot going. I tumbled and clung abjectly to my mother's hand. My sense of balance seemed to be gone. I tried again, without success. It was true, evidently, that I must learn to walk all over again. But not that way; one had to rest and begin again later. Travelling had lost its lure; the familiar couch was easier.

Things didn't go very fast. Even Mother, who could be Spartan when it came to bracing and encouraging her children, began to think she ought to give in on the crutch question. It was suggested that the bad backward tumble might have disturbed the nerves of my spine in some way. But it was straight and strong, and the doctor said it would do its duty all right. And meantime his young patient kept the pose of a cripple, acting the part with great detail and effect. I was quite happy in it, not appearing to mind being carried and helped. When the time came to travel to Forty Acres, the lameness was worse than ever. The Bishop had come back with glowing accounts of his new diocese, and of Syracuse. All of us would enjoy it; I must put forth all my efforts and be ready to run about and see things. He made me a little cane with a cross piece at the top on which I could rest both hands and help myself without the shortening of the leg and heightening of the shoulder which the doctor feared from a crutch. The day we journeyed to Hadley for the summer, I carried it in my hand, but did not use it much. When the train stopped at Palmer Junction we had an hour to wait for the New London train, and I got my father to lay me out on a baggage truck on the platform. I felt that people would notice me there and be sorry for me. But most of them hurried along, unnoticing. Finally a stout, curious lady stopped, and greeted me.

"What's the matter with you, little girl?" she inquired.

This was precisely what "the lame one" wanted. "I'm a cripple," I said pathetically, rolling up my eyes. "I've broken my leg."

" 'Tain't your hip, is it?" The woman set her bag down on the truck. "Hip-disease is kind o' bad."

"No, it's a-an unimportant fracture. A ladder fell on it. I can't walk on it. Maybe I never shall."

"Well, you look healthy. It ain't made you peaked. Is that stick all they could afford to give you?"

This was an unpleasant suggestion. "No," I answered truthfully, "The doctor wouldn't let me have a crutch."

"Oh, well, I guess there can't be much the matter. You'll be running around all right pretty soon." And she started for the lunch-room. Nobody else came along but a friendly brakeman who had lifted me out of the train, and he just whistled and laughed. It was a rather unsympathetic world, somehow.

All summer the cripple-obsession lasted, and was perseveringly carried out, but was far from disturbing my serenity. It was one of the jolliest summers I ever had. The other day I came across a letter which one of our Phelps cousins, when a young girl, wrote to her mother describing a visit at our house during that time. It says:

"We saw the little girls. Ruth is pale, but prettier, and her face has a more peaceful expression."

I could not but think how delighted I would have been to have known the impression I had made. Pale, pretty and peaceful—the equipment most desired for my role as a patient invalid. But alas! recognition is only too apt to come late in this uneven life.

The departure for Syracuse took place on a misty September morning at the old Boston and Albany station. We climbed into a Pullman car—one of the first used on the Boston and Albany road— and sank, or rather bounced, into its grand red plush upholstery, feeling that this was the adventure of our lives. A crowd of faithful women and courteous gentlemen finished their leave-taking on the platform of the cheerless *depot,* as it was called. Arria tore herself from the clinging arms of her mates. Harriet sniffed into a large cotton handkerchief as she disposed of bags and lunch-basket. Our eldest brother's strong embrace made one more sob rise in my throat, but that yielded to the excitement of getting started, to the tune of a vigorous "All aboard!" from the uniformed conductor. Bells clanged, engines whistled; we slid out under old Berkeley bridge, the second time in my life that I had looked up at it. Away, away from the ordered, protected existence, from the city blocks and the golden dome of the State House, from Miss Gage and Mademoiselle de la Motte, from Dr. Gannett's steps and the Public Garden. We little knew what a turning point it was in the road the rectory family was to travel.

Syracuse in the Seventies

1

OLD SYRACUSE

Central New York represented the great West to an average Bostonian in 1868. Not that the Valley of the Mississippi was unknown, nor that travelers had not already explored and settled in California, Texas and other distant lands. But somewhere between Syracuse and Utica, as my father put it, there was a psychological line which fenced off the West from home-abiding New Englanders. Furthermore, a good day's journey separated both those cities from Boston. Utica contained old families—the Devereux and Millers, Bacons and Beardsleys, Conklings and Coventrys, Seymours, Williamses, Kernans, Watsons—a society with traditions and formalities and social partitions, like Albany with its Dutch aristocracy. Syracuse, somewhat newer, still kept a spirit of pioneer enterprise, and her representatives of birth and pedigree were not in such close communication with Boston as with New York. Our family of Bostonians were emigrating to an altogether new world.

We soon forgot the sad little group of friends who had come to the Boston and Albany station in gray morning fog to bid us goodby. The twists of the railroad tracks and crossings of many streams between Springfield and Pittsfield gave us our first impression of romantic scenery, and kept us exclaiming. The Berkshire hills were brilliant in autumn colors. When we crossed the State line, rather disappointed that it was not drawn in visible shape, there came a contrast: flat and monotonous country. Albany had been prepared for by consultation with our green-covered geographies, which had told us that the Catskills would appear "like a purple cloud in the distance"; and in the September sunshine they actually did. The Hudson, with its crowds of small craft and the old

Daniel Boone at her pier, seemed far more important than the Connecticut.

Twilight found us still far from our destination. There were halts every now and then, when the passengers, silent and sleepy, wondered about sundry metallic bangs under the car. The brakeman apparently hit the wheels with iron instruments. A few men would climb out to watch the process, which was accompanied by smells of oil, and would trickle back, mentioning that a "hot box" was causing the delay. Then the last of the spectators would climb in hastily, the train would start up with a jerk, and proceed for a few miles, only to stop suddenly again and repeat the banging process. Darkness, and sleep fell upon us after we had consumed the remains of Grandmother Sargent's lunch. Toward midnight we were wakened by Father's announcement that we were reaching Syracuse. Lights grew more numerous, the engine slowed down; a short dash through a tunnel, and then a glimpse at a strange dark place where half-naked men, a weird glare on their figures, were moving about bright molten masses.

"The Glass Works," Father announced, and Jamie pressed his face against the window-pane to look back, as the train moved on more and more slowly. We were rolling through city streets, as travelers do to this day; only the streets were silent, and houses dark. An occasional informal welcome blazed from some illuminated saloon, but otherwise we received a blurred impression of many buildings; then there was a jarring stop, and we were hustled out into a crowd on a sidewalk, in front of the temporary shed which served just then as a station. Somebody held on to us, and we straggled across the street to a hotel on a near-by corner, The Vanderbilt.

All the rest of the night a clanging of engine-bells, screeching of whistles, and the bustle incident to trains, went on under the windows. The rooms were stuffy, the din unbearable to our elders; but we slept through it all, and awoke early, to find a string of freight-cars standing on the tracks below, a yellow fog surrounding the buildings opposite, and Harriet looking glum over the scanty furnishings of our apartment.

"Towels no bigger than a pocket-handkerchief," she muttered, "and no water in the pitcher. It's a queer place we've come to."

What matter about water? Anybody could draw it out of a faucet. But to be in a real hotel, with engines and cars so handy that one could watch them all the time one was dressing, and meals served in a long dining-room with a printed choice of food, was glorious enough to fill our souls with content. That first breakfast in the new country! The escape of savory vapors through a swing door, the black waiters, the clatter of cutlery, the piles of fried cakes and fishballs and corn bread, the ham and eggs, the clusters of little china-ware bathtubs round our plates! We studied the menu, and made plans for meals ahead.

From the windows of the hotel one could look along the business blocks which towered above the railroad tracks, and the street from which we started for our walk to the new house. Across it, far over our heads, floated a huge banner on which was inscribed GRANT AND COLFAX; it was an election year. Farther on was another banner: SEYMOUR AND BLAIR. We passed Hanover Square, an open space where market carts and hayloads stood ranked, and pigeons moved back and forth. Beyond, an arched iron bridge, toward which the street sloped upward, spanned the Canal—our first introduction to what was then the glory of Central New York. Just at that point came the meeting-place of the Erie and Oswego canals, with other bridges beyond.

We were in ecstasies as we passed on, over the bridges and up a broad residence street which rose smoothly and gradually to a considerable height beyond, with elm-shaded sidewalks on either side. We were obviously strangers—a middle-aged clergyman in a black cape, his pleasant-looking wife, a pretty daughter in the twenties, a tall lad of fifteen in a Scotch cap, two little girls in frocks of fine brown-plaided gingham with short sacques of brown cloth, and straw hats with brown streamers; and an elderly nurse, attired according to her "station" in a plain calico gown, black jacket and a severe bonnet with black strings. The "lame one" still limped, and carried a sort of crutch-stick, upon which she did not lean very heavily. We all looked eagerly about us.

We passed large houses with grounds and shrubbery, solid brick edifices built by families of distinction, and many smaller wooden ones, often constructed in the fashion of Greek temples with pillars in front and upper stories with small windows opening on the pillared porticoes, an architecture unfamiliar in New England.

All this made its impression on the eager and enthusiastic newcomers, as they passed along James Street: this was a *growing* community, not a finished one. They, too, were pioneers, and for them it was a fresh-discovered country.

The party came to a great house built on a terrace high above the sidewalk, with stone steps leading up to it. It had Greek columns like the other houses, only it was taller and grander. On either side of the steps were lions, crouching lions of iron, painted dark green. It looked like the house of a king, or a president, we thought. There were grounds beyond, with a group of tall oaks, bronzed by the Autumn sun.

Molly ran ahead. "Papa," she called. "Who lives here?"

"Our next-door neighbor, General Leavenworth," answered the Bishop. "And here is our own; look!"

We had reached a shady yard with elms on either side of a smooth walk, at the farther end of which stood a large square house of dark red brick. It had a porch in front, and windows with churchly pointed arches above them. Not a grand mansion like the one we had just seen, but a comfortable and dignified one. To our eyes it was far more beautiful than the houses on Boylston Street.

Molly flitted off to make her own explorations. After a while she could be seen with a little girl, walking about under the bronzing oaks, examining a playhouse which was built with pillars to match the great mansion. When it was time to go back to the hotel we had to call her, and she came breathless, flushed with excitement.

"I've been to see her!" she cried. "Her name is Mary, just like mine, only she's called Minnie; and she's exactly as old as I am, and her birthday is the fifteenth of November, too, and everything; and we're going to be friends and go through the hole in the fence. She's got dolls, and so have I, and we'll play in the dog-house 'cause the dog doesn't sleep in it, and she doesn't go to school just now, and she has a mother and father and a *great* uncle; a *great* uncle, you know; what kind is that? Oh, I like it here!"

So Molly's social future was assured. She was an independent little person in her likes and dislikes, usually rather shy about making friends, but this one seemed to have been made on purpose. Harriet showed signs of a little jealousy; she was to be a second-maid pure and simple now; she could not be spared for the higher rank of nurse any more, with all the work of the large house. Beside that, freedom from close supervision was open to us; not organized freedom, such as parents struggle to give their children today but freedom in its widest sense. It was in the Syracuse air.

School soon had to be considered. James, or Jim, as the family now called him, was to be sent to a Church school at Manlius, one of the Bishop's new undertakings. Miss Mary Jackson, a Syracuse woman with excellent ideas for the training of girls, kept a small private school in her own house, and it was decided that the girls should be sent there. Miss Jackson had as assistant an enthusiastic young woman who loved children, and knew how to hold their interest. After we came in from play there was always singing, out of a book called *The Silver Bell.* The songs we sang were of sentimental character, some hangovers from wartime, like *The Vacant Chair* and *Marching Through Georgia,* and some of the folksong order like *How Can I Leave Thee?* and *O Where and O Where Does My Highland Laddie Dwell?* Instead of a reading-lesson-book, we had Dickens' *Child's History of England,* which was far nicer.

That night, after my first day of school, there was something rather serious to think about. In the bay-window at Miss Jackson's a little girl of my own age, with a sweet happy face, had sat, in a wide chair with a cushion. When she got up to walk one saw her bend forward and twist painfully. One leg was paralysed, and hung like a dead weight, and on the foot below was a great laced boot with a sole three or four inches thick. She used no crutch, and the heavy leg had to be dragged at every step. But she was bright and full of fun; nobody was pitying her, and evidently she didn't want to be pitied. Somehow I perceived that my own lameness had been a mistake. It had been very tiresome lately. Queer, when it had seemed so interesting at first. . . . . .

In the morning there was a hurry in getting off to school. I was not quite ready when the other children came. "Come on!" they cried. "We'll take hold of your hands; don't wait for the crutch. Come!" And with jacket half on, and hat askew, I joined them. The Bishop was looking from his study window.

"Hannah!" he called. "Look here."

His wife was not far away. She caught a glimpse of the little flying figure between its two companions, running down the street.

"There she goes. She's forgotten herself."

Mother found the crutch-cane, lying crosswise on the back hall floor. She picked it up with a smile.

"Someone will break his neck over this, sooner or later," she observed, "if we don't look out. I think I'll put it away." It was never asked for, and never seen again.

2

NEW PEOPLE

School was but one phase of the new world into which we had moved. Learning the plan of the city was another interest.

On our own street we took great delight in the horses; most of our neighbors drove up and down the hill, but not in grandeur like that of Beacon Street. We soon learned the ownership of the many carriages. The solid, steady pair of bays, drawing a comfortable family coach in which sat a broad-faced, dignified gentleman, judicial in appearance, and a lovely gracious lady with gray hair who alighted often at our own door, were Judge Andrews' horses, and the whole equipment upheld the authority and precedence of its owners. The "fancy match," a black horse and a white one, with a high, smart vehicle in which a stylish lady and two pretty little girls accompanied him, was General Wood's turnout, and his fine house crowned the summit of the hill. Mr. Andrew D. White, later President of Cornell University, and afterward Ambassador to Germany, drove a couple of sorrel horses, finely paired, and his pleasant dwelling, with its valuable library built out from it, stood near us. Next door to him lived General Peck, who had been in the Mexican war and was a *real* General. The Peck horses were the most romantic, as we put it, of any on the street: a cream-colored pair, which looked as if they might have come straight out of the Arabian Nights. They drew a low victoria in which the General and his stately wife drove of an afternoon, with three pretty girls, who turned out—wonderful discovery—to be our schoolmates and instant friends. Never shall I forget the rapture of our first drive with them behind the marvelous steeds, and the opportunities we had to see the horses groomed and to admire their manes and tails and arched necks.

But processions, like constellations, were interrupted often by a comet: an open wagonette with two small horses, traveling at full speed, and driven by a stocky bearded gentleman beside whom rode a lady with a fine, picturesque sort of beauty for which I cannot find an adequate word; one of the faces which no one can forget. Breeding, sincerity, cordiality all shone from the bright eyes. The wagon was filled with pretty girls, and one caught glimpses of flying veils and clear complexions and bright tartan cloaks as it dashed up and down James Street. This was the Sedgwick family, from the other side of the hill. Mr. Charles Sedgwick was at once lawyer and farmer, owning broad acres, living in a hospitable and altogether charming dwelling, a low house with jutting wings and many windows, where fine minds came together from far and wide. A large family circle formed the centre of an independent but influential community-within-a-community. Mrs. Sedgwick was a New England woman, one of the Boston Gannetts; her husband a New Yorker, but indigenous to the Onondaga hill-country

At the time of our arrival in Syracuse the second and third of the girls were my sister's age and among her first friends; the youngest of all was a dreamy, studious child, responding with a slow, appreciative smile to advances, a character which was one day to make itself a force in the world about her. What Dora Sedgwick Hazard has meant, and still means, to the life of the City of Syracuse needs no recital. Her unflinching sense of justice and her liberal progressive spirit have made her a leader in every forward movement, whether political, civic, or creative.

There were other old families in Syracuse; some with Dutch blood, some with a Huguenot strain. It was by no means a purely western community in the sense which our parents had imagined from what they heard in Boston. In fact I think it was my brother James who remarked that when his mother and sister particularly liked some new acquaintances they called them "New-England-y."

But our neighbors were by no means only of the privileged sort. One of the nearest was an old Irishman who had a complete farm inside the limits of an ordinary city lot; a tiny house, shed and barn, a diminutive garden with flourishing crops, a horse, cow and pig.

We all recognized Mr. Sullivan as an agriculturist of parts. His cow was pastured largely on the grassy stretches of James Street, between the sidewalk and the highway, and her nibblings kept the turf smooth and green. I don't recollect that we had lawn-mowers; at all events the city was under no obligation to provide them, so the Sullivan cow grazed peacefully in front of our houses, and other streets also boasted a wandering animal here and there. Now and then even a promenading pig would be discovered, or on rare occasions a horse. The neighbors took milk from Mr. Sullivan's farm, with no worries whatever as to its informal handling or the amount of bacteria that it might contain.

Our older sister was soon settled in the midst of a delightful group into which, with her social charm and alert mind, she fitted naturally. It was exciting to have the Sedgwick wagonette stop at our door, the active little horses pulled suddenly to a halt, and the crew of gay young people welcoming her to their midst as she climbed in beside them and the party started off on an excursion. We felt so proud of her. Mother had new friends as well and was busy with them, falling in with some established charity work and helping to make committees for new undertakings which the Bishop had set in motion. Molly had joined a placid group of little girls, who played dolls and had quiet times under the oak-trees.

3

GRANT AND COLFAX!

There was only one experience of political excitement in our Syracuse childhood. It came quite early, after we had been but a few weeks in school. A Presidential election was on, and not only the rival banners, but torchlight parades, newspaper pronouncements and various other signs of campaign activity were in progress. Children were adopting the catchwords, songs and slogans of their elders. All but two of the nice little girls at Miss Jackson's school were Republicans, and very highbrow Republicans at that. The lone Democrats were the daughters of General Peck, who had strong Southern sympathies. The Pecks were our most dearly loved friends, and I was much concerned over the jibes and insults heaped upon them by the opposition. I objected to hearing them called "Irish" and rowdies, and came home to my family one day in a state of extreme indignation.

"Papa," I burst out at the dinner-table, "why do they say that Republicans are better than Democrats? What's the difference?"

The Bishop was not in the mood for giving political definitions. He assured his young daughter that while there were arguments for both parties, the dispute at the moment was in the majority of cases merely a difference of opinion about the candidates, not the theories they represented, and that little girls would do better to leave the quarreling to grown-ups.

But I was not satisfied with any such evasion.

"Yes, but see here, papa. The girls say that all Democrats are on the side of the Irish, and that Seymour just stands for Irish votes, and anybody who votes for him will help to get a lot of dirty micks ruling the country. And they set on the Pecks, and talk horridly to them. *Is* Seymour Irish?"

"Governor Seymour," said the Bishop sonorously, "is a high-minded Christian gentleman. I know him personally, and have stayed at his house in Utica. General Grant is a brave soldier, deserving of credit for his services to his country. The Irish are an industrious people, entitled to their citizenship and their votes. We are all alike in the sight of God, whatever our politics may be. I trust you will never allow yourself to belittle a political rival because he does not share your views."

This put rather a solemn aspect on the controversy, but it settled the mind of the would-be combatant.

"Well," she declared, "I think I shall be a Democrat then; I might just as well, and I want to stand by the Pecks; they're only two against all the rest. If Governor Seymour is as nice as that I might as well be for him."

By recess-time next day feelings had been roused to a high pitch. The school was gathered on the sidewalk, each little girl with her ordinary lunch, a bunch of grapes.

"Yes, I'm a Democrat now," the shrill voice of the Bishop's child announced. "I wouldn't be Republican for anything."

"Grant and Colfax!" shouted an opponent. "Seymour is for the Irish. You're a paddy!"

"Seymour is a high-minded Christian gentleman!"

"He isn't! Grant is!"

"Grant?" I became derisive. "I heard a lady say that somebody went to speak to him in Washington once and found him with his hat on and his feet on the table smoking a cigar, and he didn't know enough to stand up and say how-de-do."

"How can anybody smoke a cigar with his feet?" asked a smart young Republican. Even the Democrats laughed at that. But another girl whose size and muscle equipped her admirably for aggression called out.

"Let's put 'em off the sidewalk! That's what the boys do up at my brother's school. Come on!"

Only a part of the girls joined her, but the mob was double the strength of the Democrats, who rushed for the inside edge of the sidewalk. The Pecks got something to cling to, probably an iron railing, and held fast in spite of attempts to dislodge their fingers. The belligerent Bishop's child, however, clutched with one hand, and with the other, and also feet, laid about her furiously, knocking one girl in the eye and kicking the shins of another. I felt myself a Joan of Arc, a Barbara Frietchie, a Boadicea, all the heroines of history rolled into one. But unfortunately the din of conflict had reached Miss Jackson's ears. She came out just in time to save the self-appointed champion of Democracy from being dragged over to the gutter.

When we came out from lessons, all the children were shocked. The walk was gory and slippery from a mass of crushed grapes.

The fourth child picked her way across the smeary pavement. "Trampling out the vintage where the grapes of wrath are stored," she sang, prancing along the street in the time and tune of the Battle-hymn, and setting her heels down at "God Is Marching On." When she reached home she gave an account of the fight to her shocked parents.

"I am ashamed of you," said the Bishop. "You have entirely misunderstood the whole matter. You must never do anything of the sort again. I am only too glad you did not injure any of your companions."

"Oh, papa!" she insisted, "it was awfully exciting; just a kind of game. We all want to play it again tomorrow."

The Bishop was obdurate. At family devotions the next morning, he prayed that "patience and prayer might prevail over partisanship." His fourth child admired this alliteration, and while still on her knees, she thought of more words beginning with p, which might increase the effect, such as patriotism, petitions, perseverance, and politics. The significance of the actual situation did not dawn upon the children, but their spasms of party spirit continued all through the autumn, until Grant and Colfax at last came out victorious.

4

MUSIC IN SYRACUSE

The Bishop had on his mind a little mission at the Indian Reservation for the Onondaga tribe, not far from the city. There was
a chapel, with services, but at the moment no organist. One of the
chiefs, a Christian, had a young daughter who was fond of music,
and had been able to pick out one or two hymn-tunes by ear. If she
could learn to read notes and use both hands, she might help out at
the chapel later on. With the reserve of his race, the chief gave no
idea whether she would be amenable to lessons, but he nodded
when the representative of the Great Father suggested his bringing
her to town every Saturday morning, and leaving her for an hour
with his own child. I was called into his study, and asked if I would
like to show a little Indian girl how to play the piano, since I had
had such good instruction myself.

I received the idea with enthusiasm. Why, showing-how was
teaching, whether dignified with that name or not. A music-teacher;
like Mademoiselle de la Motte; like Miss Jones, perhaps, only with
no knitting-needles for prodding. And the daughter of an Indian
Chief! Really too delightful. I experienced some slight disappointment at the fact that the Indian wore coats and trousers instead of
war-paint and feathers, but the women of the tribe as they appeared
in Syracuse streets were rather picturesque in their straight skirts of
bright cloth, and the blankets over their heads. They made very
ordinary, unsalable beadwork, and sold bows and arrows, also of
mediocre quality. They had made for Father a strange cane with a
highly colored snake carved about it, emblem of the original subjugation of the serpent. The Reservation itself was wild country, a
tract some miles long, with hills, valleys and a dashing stream; beau-

tiful with a touch of loneliness and aloofness which befitted the home of an isolated people. The Christians came to the Mission Sunday-School; the pagans had barbaric dances and other strange rites, and roasted the meat of animals in their fires. Their habitations were huts in the woods. One or two chiefs had built real homes on the road by the stream, and had pianos or melodeons in their parlors. But many of their customs were still aboriginal, untouched by civilization. They were reputed to be lazy and shiftless, and often dishonest, stigmatized as "no good" by the folk living near their borders. They were exploited by saloon-keepers and Government agents, but not so systematically robbed, perhaps, as some other tribes farther west.

The Indian girl appeared promptly for her lessons. She was tall and lithe, without the gawkiness of thirteen, but with a poise which the white does not develop so early; with long coarse black hair, piercing eyes, and a marvelous complexion nourished by wind and sun, bright brown with something of the lustrous tinge of the horse-chestnut. Undernourishment had not preyed upon her physique. She was so much taller than her ten-year-old teacher that the latter had to stand up in order to have hands level with the keyboard when the pupil was seated on the piano-stool.

Mother had provided a large pink instruction-book with a depiction on its cover of two detached hands on a row of black and white keys. The course was grounded as far as possible on the methods of the Boston music-school. Indians are good imitators, and Mattie Hill—this name was the unromantic translation of a far more striking one—could copy accurately the motions of the grubby hand presented her as a model.

It was a somewhat erratic form of musical education, without doubt; various essentials were overlooked, and I insisted conscientiously on her committing to memory the names of the older composers, written out for her in round hand. There was little conversation between us, yet somehow we managed to understand one another pretty well, and never noticed that members of the family peeped at us from time to time, and came away smiling at our intense seriousness. I have no recollection of how long these lessons lasted, or just what was achieved; but Mattie did actually learn to play the melodeon at the chapel without any other instruction, and kept it up for twenty years. I met her a while ago at an anniversary celebration there; a hale and capable old person in a spotless Hoover apron, serving a delicious lunch with some of her colleagues. She insisted upon calling me "teacher", and beckoned to her grown-up son, an entirely civilized Indian and a United States citizen, saying, "Come here, Joe; I told you I'd show you my teacher today; she taught me to play the organ."

But there was one interesting occasion which transcended all the pleasure of the music-lesson; a day when the old chief, who was apt to make convivial contacts on his visits to town, did not appear to claim his daughter at the appointed time. So Mother cordially invited her to lunch with us—her first meal with a white family, and perhaps her first with a knife and fork. She made not one slip, even under the watchful eye of Harriet, who visibly, though respectfully, disapproved of the necessity for waiting upon a savage, as she would have put it, and confidently expected a jar in the etiquette of the Bishop's dining-room. But barring her utter silence during the meal save for a "yes" or "no" now and then, no smallest breach of manners was discernible. Her bright observant eyes, quietly busy, took in each motion of her hosts in wielding the unfamiliar tools. She copied faithfully, and ate normally of strange food. After lunch her father arrived in the light wagon, himself in a mood of somewhat uncertain gayety, and they went swaying and careening down James Street, the old horse breaking into its usual canter, the typical sure-footed gait of horses used to fitful urging.

My own music lessons were revived under the instruction of an interesting character who had been teaching for years in Syracuse: a German gentleman, then about forty years old. He had a charming wife, American-born but of German lineage. Ernst Held is still revered and loved by the pupils who remember him, and whose musical careers he moulded. Up to the time of our arrival he had been obliged to struggle against a certain amount of popular prejudice with regard to the quality of productions studied by his pupils. That did not become evident until the interview in which my mother arranged for lessons with him, and told him that the condition thereof was his teaching her little daughter only the best music, in the strictest sense. She was to study with him, to be instructed regardless of popular demand in what was then called "classical" composition.

Mother liked to describe the conversation afterwards, telling how, when he had said good-bye and opened the front door, he came back again into the drawing-room to ask, "Are you *sure* you want the best? You will not change your mind?" He afterwards told her, with tears in his eyes, what a relief it was to have had that assurance, and how it had cheered him on his way. I can well remember that it was a trial, however, to be given pieces of a more serious order than my young friends, who at *soirées* performed wonders in the line of *colloratur;* deftly executing the *Maiden's Prayer* or the *Shepherd Boy* or *Silvery Waves,* all of which were favorites with the average audience. But our teacher began with the *Nel Cor Piu* variations of Beethoven, and took me on into Mendelssohn's *Songs without Words,* and those things were looked upon as severe.

Then came to visit the Helds a charming little niece who played with unquestioned talent. And at the next children's musicale her number was a quiet, unaffected rendering of some of the Schumann *Kinderstücke,* which she did with an interpretation that made her the star performer. That attractive child later became Mrs. Philip Hale, wife of the renowned music critic of Boston. She was the little Irene Baumgras who helped convert her uncle's pupils to appreciation of the greater music. She and I had now a bond in common, and our contemporaries began to care for better compositions. Mr. Held always spoke with gratitude of our mother's help in bringing about this change.

He was himself a fascinating teacher. His facility in drawing was often turned to account in amusing ways. I have an old copy of Mozart's sonatas containing a passage in which I stubbornly repeated a wrong note. After he had stopped me several times he said, "I cannot always be telling you of this; I shall have to make a reminder for you." He seized his pencil, and *im Nu* as the Germans say, had sketched on the margin of the page the head of an old-school teacher in a high stock, frowning as he looked over his spectacles at an imaginary pupil.

His contribution to the cultural progress of the city can never be fully realized, but the foundations he laid were solid. He made the study of music a lasting joy to his scholars, and that is certainly the harvest of the really gifted teacher. Music and the love of good music had made real progress by the seventies, and brought about of happy companionships. Ernst Held's pupils were nearly all good sight-readers. We played four-hand, sometimes eight-hand, arrangements of the great symphonies, overtures and quartettes, and familiarized ourselves with them.

We had transcriptions of Bach, Beethoven, Mendelssohn, Schumann, the songs of Schubert, the overtures of Weber, and gained happy associations which to this day make orchestral performances of them a greater joy. I smile involuntarily when the *Vorspiel* to *Rosamunde,* or the Beethoven *Septett,* come over the radio; or when the *Barber of Seville* recalls a species of trio which usually opened a school *soirée,* three girls performing on one keyboard with elbows in uncomfortable proximity, and with a danger of stepping on one's neighbor's slippered toes by mistake in reaching for the pedal. Then we had a club which met and gave performances to itself, now and again inviting a select public. Semi-social music-affairs were frequent in those days when accomplishment was our musical goal.

We had better and better concerts, too, with the years; Theodore Thomas's orchestra, the Mendelssohn Quintet club from Boston, plenty of noted soloists, now and then a good chorus from our own German *Liederkranz,* still a figure in the musical history of the city. Most large towns, east and west, had their local choruses, and sang the oratorios, the *Elijah* and the *Hymn of Praise,* the *Creation* and the *Messiah.*

We played games on warm evenings, in the big back yard under the four oaks, which stood in perfect juxtaposition for Prisoners' Base. The boys in the neighborhood played with us, and while they were better sports, we considered ourselves superior strategists. A slender boy, tall for his twelve years, would race past the oaks, springing lithely between the box-borders in the garden to dodge his breathless opponent who was more familiar with the little twisting paths between the flower-beds, which might not be stepped on, even in dire exigency. But his elastic muscles outstripped mine in the game of Prisoners' Base, just as his mental agility outstripped that of his fellows forty years later when he was the genial Judge before whom the Roosevelt-Barnes case was tried in the Syracuse courts. Judge William Andrews' scholarliness, matching that of the litigant, who ostentatiously buried himself in a volume of Thucydides when not occupied on the witness-stand, came to the fore in some bits of inimitable dialogue which delighted the Court and the public. But we did not dream in those games of Prisoners' Base that one day he and I would be colleagues in grand-parenthood, and share a measure of family pride in another youngster, also slim and fleet-footed and tall for his age, who would be working out an inheritance from bishops and jurists.

While those games we played taught us a much needed coordination and balance, they held none of the dignity of a new undertaking which was begun the year I was twelve. At that time I began to substitute at the afternoon organ playing during Lent. I had practically to stand on the pedals to get enough air into them to sustain the tones. My legs were provokingly short. I must have been a funny little figure, in my red and black plaid cloak, with my gray astrakhan cap, the crown lifted in front. It was interesting to be an organist; I imagined myself a Saint Cecilia. Not the Cecilia of the Raphael variety, but the more modern and sentimental one at the pipe-organ, with cherubs looking down at her. After a few gusty the short-winded efforts from the bellows, I became sure-footed enough to manage the tread-mill motion.

5

RELIEF AND WELFARE

The civic problem in the 70's which most pressed upon Syracuse citizens was one of relief and welfare. For help in its solution the Bishop looked to his older daughter and the friends she had gathered about her. They were of the same calibre—among them the Sedgwicks, Wilkinsons, Burnets, Townsends, Millses, Calthrops; others as well. The girls studied and read together. (They did not all read Mazzini's essays, as my sister did, but it was the age when young people read Carlyle and Browning, and discussed the latter exhaustively in many clubs.)

The Bishop had already begun to experiment with remedies for the door-to-door begging, which was demoralizing both beggars and givers. He made an arrangement with a cheap lodging-house and restaurant to accept tickets given to beggars in lieu of money. These were received with dissatisfaction by the mendicants, sometimes actually refused. It was found before long that they were sold for the price of a drink, on the street, and presented at the eating-houses by respectable people. Meantime a room in the Bishop's house had been opened for the reception of used clothing, which the women of two large Church societies collected or donated. This was a departure from previous charitable methods. When it became known to the householders of the city all manner of donations poured in. People evidently felt it a relief to turn out the contents of attics and wardrobes

The incongruity of some gifts was amusing. Odd rubbers and gloves abounded. A prominent widow innocently disclosed her intention of marrying again by sending her coachman with an armful of boxes which were found to contain seven black crepe bonnets, with heavy mourning-veils attached. We all enjoyed watching for the announcement which followed a few days later in the newspapers. We had thought the offering a somewhat unpractical one, but found it, on the contrary, extremely useful, since deep mourning was so fashionable in those days that the poorest of widows could be consoled by the acquisition of really effective black. We raided the collection occasionally for costumes, when we gave dramatic entertainments.

The first efforts of the newly organized welfare societies were directed toward a separation of the worthy from the unworthy, a difficult matter at all times. No machinery existed for investigation, and no standards of respectability were possible without classification. All work of that sort had to be accomplished by amateurs. The Huntingtons were by no means alone in these beginnings. A number of men and women with real aptitude for social service came to the fore: the time was ripe for progress. Arria Huntington started combining methods already in use. Boards of Health had not been established in some states; the care of the insane was being looked into here and there; there were terrible discoveries made in private institutions of all sorts: lying-in homes, baby farms, orphan asylums. The young reformers were always trying to strike a true balance between patience and consent, necessity and waste, the psychology of reform-movements.

Our sister's activities in all branches of civic work were aided and abetted by the family. But probably the most appealing one, the cause of the "fallen" girl, was more familiar than any other to her younger sisters. She had become interested in a class of women, court cases at the penitentiary. They were mostly drunkards and prostitutes, pathetic when they finished their terms and came out of captivity into a world of old temptations, with no prospect of friends or decent homes. Arria had begun at the most difficult end in an attempt to start them in happy and improved conditions of living, and the work had proved fruitless. They began, with release from their jail terms, to try to reclaim themselves; but habit was too strong for them, and respectable earning too difficult. Gradually the ardent young women began to realize that any enduring work must make its appeal to the young rather than to the middle-aged. Arria Huntington took up the saving of these girls as her life-work. She built a school, *The Shelter*, to which first offenders could be sent, and where they might be trained for a self-supporting, normal existence. There was much difficulty in the enterprise; the opposition of certain political forces, hitherto the protectors of vice; wealthy patrons of the houses of prostitution which crowded certain sections of the city. The work was attacked from within and without. But the girl who had undertaken it met these disheartening conditions with a bravery which won the admiration even of its enemies. The powers which controlled the vice traffic deemed it best to lie low, and leave their henchmen to make what defense they could. They felt a rather unusual confidence in a personality who, with her youthful appearance and her ease of manner would, they knew, pursue her course with discretion and with entire absence of personal ambition.

We younger ones had always taken our sister's superiority for granted, but had never really appreciated it as we came to do in those early days of Syracuse experience. We knew all about that particular work, and it was discussed quite freely in the family; no one could take the time to banish us from general conversation or to practice very much secrecy.

I did a good deal of wondering. I overheard talk of "houses," of court cases, of babies which seemed to have been unlucky, and for which homes had to be found; of "bad" women and girls, of feeble-mindedness, of penitentiaries, of prisons, of prostitution; the last word bothered me. I imagined it as meaning some sort of *in*-stitution. The dictionary got my understanding involved with still more incomprehensible language; *strumpet, harlot, lewdness*; all synonyms for badness apparently. The people I heard talking did not define the words, in fact did not use them very much; they talked more about "lost" and "fallen" women. And yet after all there was some mystery, I felt. Men were connected in some way with the question.

Often we saw a handsomely upholstered carriage and inside it a vacant female face with skin like parchment, eyes staring straight ahead; no youth, no life, no color; a face like a mask, jewels hanging from the tense neck. That solitary figure passed and re-passed the living beings like a wandering ghost, never seeming to move, never heard to speak; let go on her weary way. People whispered; that was Diamond Nell. She was *bad,* they said. Some rich men had given her the horses and the jewels. We did not of course know what that particular brand of bad meant; to us she looked plain lonesome. Why did she always drive by herself? But the horses were lovely, and her jewels glittered if her face did not.

Another little girl had heard things. She imparted the fact that Diamond Nell had a "house"; a girl who sewed for her mother had told her. She knew the street and the number. She and I went there one day. The house was near a big church; it was painted a sort of cream-color, and it had lace curtains, drawn tight, in all the windows; sometimes closed blinds too. But the sewing-woman had said there were lights there all night long, and that men were always there. Both of us felt a little scared and a little guilty. A carriage and pair of horses was standing in front of the house, but it was not Nell's. A coachman in livery sat perfectly still on the box and waited, his face inscrutable. We hurried away, and talked about it all the way home. In one of the heavy, faded old volumes of the *Encyclopedia Britannica* I had seen an article on *zoology*. I continued my research, which led me to the heading *Mammalia,* a department that included cats, dogs, cows and people. I knew about cats and dogs, and partly about cows, but had made only vague guesses about people. It was a fascinating subject. The young Eve ate quite happily some of the fruit of the Tree of Knowledge, and as she ate the feeling of guilt dropped from mind and conscience.

The encyclopedia, in its faded red binding, lay innocently upon the chair-seat, not alluring but revealing. When I had really fathomed its depths of information I did not, it is true, feel that I perfectly understood the whole matter. But there was a dignity and authority about the Latin terms which allayed my impatient curiosity. By and by I closed the book, and thought a bit. There was still something to know. Yet it would not fit into the discussions with other girls; the newly acquired equipment was my personal possession, not to be talked over. I could do my own observing and thinking now. It was not silly kindergarten stuff, either. And it was not romantic, I reflected, perhaps with a slight disappointment—it was *scientific*. And my sister, who knew everything possible to know, undoubtedly knew too. So I waited from that time on, without any sense of hurry, for further information to come to me instead of seeking it. Something or somebody would have to shake the branches of the knowledge-tree. Then I would pick up the fruit.

Later I overheard a conversation which added to my slim knowledge of the matter. An announcement through a half-opened door aroused my attention.

"What do you think. Amelia Hallett has had a baby!"

"A baby? Amelia? Is she married?"

"No; she had made up her mind she wanted a child, even though she could never hope to have a husband, with that scar on her face. She said she had a right to, because she had money enough to bring it up."

"But there must be a man. Who is he?"

"She won't tell. Says it isn't important. She's gone with the baby to a farm in Idaho."

Then I heard a voice say, "But it's awful. She ought to be ashamed." And an answer.

"I think it's better not to judge her. I'm sure she'll make a lovely mother."

From my youthful point of view, it seemed unnatural to prefer a baby to a husband. The world was still very incomprehensible, and I could not ask my parents for an explanation.

There were other projects beside our sister's work, and one of them offered a new opportunity for community-cooperation. Syracuse had but one public hospital, which was much over-crowded. Better care for the sick was imperative. The Bishop had become more and more aware of this need. It was debated and weighed by a group of the more thoughtful minds of the city. Foremost among them was Dr. John Van Duyn, then in the prime of life; young, enthusiastic, tremendously absorbed in his profession, already known as an expert. His fine eyes, keen and penetrating, looked farther than symptoms or megrims. He knew what to do with a nervous patient, a broken bone, a strained back, or a "situation" that was physically upsetting and debilitating. He had science for a weapon, and judgment for a guide. His organizing power was as inherent as his penetration, or his understanding of *materia medica*. His patients adored him, and as one of them when quite a young girl, I can remember how I looked for the cheery and prompt diagnosis which restored confidence in my own physique, and the masterful orders he gave in his bright, brusque fashion for the right maintenance of that physique. Sometimes his prescription would be a tonic, of which he would observe that it had a lot of things in it so that one of them would be sure to "hit"; sometimes he would say to a mother, "That girl needs something to do to keep her nerves busy"; sometimes he would ask "What time do you get to bed?" and follow the answer with, "Now mind, ten hours a night, honor bright, till you get some life in you."

But his professional popularity was the least of it; his scholarly habit, his philanthropy and his progressive spirit were strong factors in starting a hospital with good-will and energy in place of an overflowing treasury. The only possible way was to begin it on a small scale, and let it grow. The courageous promoters, a few physicians and interested citizens, leased and repaired an empty house, furnished it with stores from friends' attics, collecting funds as they went along; and put in charge a good sensible woman who had recommendations as a nurse but no real training. It was before the days of training-schools, antiseptics or dieticians. Everybody turned in, and worked for it. Near neighbors stood in little groups on their porches when an emergency case arrived at its doors, and sometimes ran over with offers of help. Indeed it was a neighborhood affair. That dear, well-meaning, informal, mussy little hospital! It was filled with patients in no time, and more than filled with visitors, till it fairly cried to be delivered from its friends. Clergy, medical students, kind ladies came unannounced at all hours. I can't remember that there was any way of keeping even a single-room patient quiet, nor protecting the four-bed "wards" from Bible-readers and exhorters. There may not have been many dangerously sick cases in those days. The doctors had a hard time to preserve proper precautions; rules were made as need dictated, but there was no one to enforce them. We children also raced in and out irregularly, zealously, to entertain two crippled children, victims probably of infantile paralysis. We must have been hopelessly underfoot, but could be sent on errands, and before the days of telephones it was helpful to have young runners. The evolution of the work was slow, and fraught with many problems. Superintendents of all sorts tried their hand at it; years passed before the training school, vitally necessary, took shape, and with fine women at its head brought the House of the Good Shepherd to strength and completion. It is one of the City hospitals still, now the property of Syracuse University. Started while antiseptics, bacteria, and many of the intricate processes of surgery were unknown to the American physician, it made unbelievable progress. Of course it was following and learning from the hospitals of the larger cities. But I am glad to have learned something of the realities, pain and patience and devotion to the sick and weak, by experience rather than statistics. Dr. Van Duyn lived not only to see his own work grandly fruitful, but taken up and carried on by son and grandson.

6

With the arrival of the teens, and the new dignities to which one finds oneself committed, comes an inevitable change in codes of behavior. Having grown quite tall, I began to take an interest in clothes and hair-arrangements. Molly, at eleven, had had an attack of scarlet fever, and her curls had been shorn, so she was beginning again with a short curly crop like a boy's, and looked like a smaller edition of her brother Jim. But perfectly straight locks, not a twist in them, were discouraging. A long thick braid had to be turned up and tied in a "club" behind. And then came the lengthening of skirts. Spring dresses were more or less of a problem, and there was no influential Miss Balze to decide ahead upon the probable trend of the fashions. Our Syracuse mantua-maker was a young Irish seamstress named Maggie, with black eyes and rosy cheeks, very fond of trimming and furbishing, since it prolonged her days of work. She spent weeks on the family wardrobe, and I grieve to say that our busy mother was obliged to leave the cut of the gowns pretty much to her taste. Our older sister planned her own dresses, but the younger children were at Maggie's mercy. I remember one gown which was a real affliction—a light gray material with two skirts, bound with bright green silk in curious little triangular points. It was begun rather ahead of time, as it was supposed to be necessary to engage the sewing-force early. The combination of green and gray tried me, and I frankly doubted Maggie's assertion that it was the latest Paris touch. But the elders of the family seemed satisfied, so there was nothing to do but accept it, and wear it on an Easter morning in April, when Nature, it is true, was beginning to deck herself in green, but not in *points*. Alas! my joy was dimmed, that happy morning. The skirt was long; at least I had the consolation of looking a little more young-ladyfied than before. But though gray was the prevailing color that season, not one single gown was trimmed with green nor cut in triangles. It was hard to be cheerful under the circumstances. The outcome, however, almost atoned for this affliction. Our parents finally had an inspiration, and began to give me a dress-allowance, with permission to plan my own frocks. From a financial standpoint this was never quite satisfactory; there were deficits, extravagances, and inconsistencies which did not commend the scheme at all in its first years; but I was far more contented. Maggie was obliged to yield, and look up the modes in *Harper's Bazaar,* and I attired myself in garments which were pronounced "old for my age," but I certainly moved with more ease in the sphere which I was supposed to adorn. And then the beginnings of social experience opened up.

Through the winter the Cobleighs, a set of dances named for a popular dancing-master or master-of-ceremonies, met in a downtown hall. They entertained the younger set, reinforced by each year's debutantes—only they were not called by that name, since there were no formal comings-out like the Boston ones. I had now been attending a girls' dancing-class taught by a lovely young lady who was the idol of her pupils. We learned the polka and the schottische, rather jerky steps, and of course the waltz, a gliding and graceful variety, suited to the beautiful waltz-music of the time. One could make it even dreamy, redeemed from dizzy effects by constant reversing, which was difficult for the beginner. Then the square dances, alternating with the round ones, were so like games that they were very popular—the Lancers, the Quadrille, and the Virginia Reel, with which every dance ended.

But musical though I was, I could not manage to keep time with the orchestra. My companions tripped the light fantastic toe with abandon and grace. Perhaps I tried too hard. I was invited now to parties, and was much excited when the invitations came. They were early affairs, at private houses. The girls wore little silk frocks, and the boys were supposed to appear in white cotton gloves, but frequently tore them off. I had some pretty gowns of my sister's, made over.

You sometimes drove to the house in a hired vehicle, which gave you a sense of elegance. You were shown upstairs to take off your wraps, and the girls chattered noisily, giving touches to hair and neck as they had seen their sisters do. You had a card given you for partners to write their names on, with a diminutive pencil attached to it by a colored cord.

The popular girls had their cards filled very quickly; one should have been prepared for that, of course. Only you weren't; and yours was not asked for, probably. Possibly one or two boys, brought up to you by the hostess if she was a thoughtful lady, would put their names down for one dance, but it was quite certain that they would claim it, and it seemed to be always near the end, beyond the time-limit of an early dance. You held your card out of sight, and went and sat down on one of the chairs which were ranged round the wall of the dance-room, getting as far from the chaperons as possible. Then the music began, and the boys came rushing up to the girls on the other chairs, and danced off with them. You thought there might be some boys left over, but there were left-over girls instead; and they, too, came and sat down in the empty chairs. *Wall-flowers.* The hateful epithet ran in your head. The girls were dull company. All of them were absent-minded, somehow. I felt deadened and my muscles were affected by it; they were stiff all over; my head ached dully, and I almost wanted to cry. If a boy finally appeared and asked me to dance, however, I blushed and said:

"Oh, *thank* you! Yes, I'd like to ever so much." But after I was on my feet I realized that it was not one of the best dancers who had sought this honor; they were all dancing with the popular girls. This one was usually knock-kneed and bashful. We hitched along unevenly, not keeping with the music, the boy breathing hard, and perspiring sometimes in the effort to catch up. Toiling once or twice round the room seemed to tire us both out.

"We don't go together very well," I would suggest.

"No," answered the boy. "I can't seem to keep step with you." Then we would mutually succumb and sit down. By that time I found my throat swelling a little in spite of heroic efforts to be cheerful, and my eyes getting damp. There was a horrid feeling that if any better dancer tried to go on with me it would be as a last resort. Why had I come? But why shouldn't I? And why couldn't I chatter and giggle in the fetching way the other girls did? It quenched my usual enthusiasm completely.

After swallowing a good many potential sobs, grinning inanely the while and repeatedly vowing never to go to a party again, I decided that there must be a technique for becoming a ball-room belle. I took close observation of the successful girl. It appeared that one should not jump up with ecstatic thanks when a partner offered himself. Evidently he ought not to be made to think he was desirable. I noted that the girl with real poise just giggled gently—the little simper was clearly a part of the ritual—and if she made any remark at all when approached, it was merely to murmur good-naturedly, "All right," at the same time rising with leisurely acceptance of the honor, or the air of conferring one herself. I practised that at home before a glass, and got into a fit of laughter in imagining the suppliant partner. It was Dickens-y, and my own attempts at smirking and simpering were irresistibly funny. But that was apparently the principal thing to be studied. Real success, however, would not be achieved by artificial methods alone. Yet why worry about success anyway? After all, the dancing-party was only one way of having a good time. The thing was, I decided, to become a jovial wall-flower. Of course it is hard to be jocund when one has just been through that awful waiting-in-the-hall experience; you do get pretty hopeless over it. "But never mind, make the most of what you do have," I admonished myself.

I tried first to get the other wall-flowers interested in observing gowns, or playing games, or just laughing at nothing. This plan fell to earth because they were too occupied in watching for partners to be interested in anything else. Then I had another inspiration. Why not cultivate the bashful boy? It was manifest that he, too, got but little out of parties. At all events I might sound him out. The first victim that came to hand was a somewhat ungainly youth who evidently wanted to ingratiate himself with girls, and who held his head on one side and smiled self-consciously. Odious, I concluded, but maybe not impossible. I began by just simpering at him. After

we had shuffled round the room uncomfortably, I said "Let's sit
down out in the hall and talk; shall we?"

"Oh, yes," he answered; "I'd like it ever so much better than
dancing." So we found a bench from which it was necessary to remove a few hats and coats, and perched upon it. The slightly unso-
cial nature of the move made a sort of bond, and we each confessed
to a sense of boredom at having to sit and look on at the dancing.
Before long we were carrying on quite an animated conversation.
The boy's neck lost its tenseness, and he evidently felt at home with
this new sort of partner. He confided to me that he was in high
school, studying hard because he wanted to be a surgeon. He had
done a little of it, and had some practice with animals; a dog's
broken leg and a couple of weeks with a cousin who was a veter-
inary. I was all interest, having myself treated a dog whose leg was
cut by a mowing machine, in the face of the doctor's prediction that
he would have necrosis. And the dog had recovered. We were in
the midst of detailed though somewhat gruesome description, when
the hostess, an older girl, bore down upon our retreat.

"What are you doing here?" she inquired tartly. "People come
to parties to dance. Clayton, you go right back and take a girl out.
As for you, Ruth Huntington, you ought to be on the floor yourself."

"I will," I answered, turning pert, "if you'll get me a partner.
But don't trouble yourself too much." Whereupon the call came
for the Grand March to the dining-room, and Clayton reappeared
to ask for the honor, his head as one-sided as ever, and the old bashful smirk. At any rate one was assured now of a new name on one's
card at the next party.

It was plain that I was not cut out for a social success. Still I
made up my mind to become a better dancer, and to study the
finesse of party procedure. It was easy enough to get acquainted
with the non-dancing boys, but there was more than that to be
learned. Just then came an invitation to a little club which the
Sedgwicks and Wilkinsons had formed. We met once in two weeks,
I think; we did not dress up, came home early, and had apples and
crackers for refreshment, or sometimes pop-corn. The dances were

at different houses on the hill. There was no band; a tall, lank negro played piano for the dancing. Also no cards nor formalities, but much jollity, and some of the older girls and boys saw to it that everybody had a partner. Hostesses like Mrs. Wilkinson and Mrs. Sedgwick really gave us lessons, by their own hospitable example, in entertaining. One danced without thinking about it, and felt as if one had belonged for years in that friendly, cordial circle. There were boys whom I had not known before. I could not get the general rhythm quite so well as most of the others, but talking was not forbidden, and there was one boy, who liked the authors whom I best loved. It was a pleasant discovery. The foundations of a happy friendship, often silent for months but always congenial, were laid then and there. He was an usher at my wedding years after, and on visits to Syracuse I always enjoyed him; a quiet bachelor, writing sometimes, browsing in a well-stocked library, entertaining a circle of friends with whom he shared his literary treasures.

7

EDUCATIONAL FACILITIES

What are known as "educational facilities" were very good at that stage of Syracuse history. The little school with the bay-window had been enlarged, and had become a boarding-school—in fact a diocesan school with episcopal backing. It was quartered in a commodious building, and its scope amplified. Miss Jackson's methods had fully kept up to the standards of the day, although the equipment of the school was meagre in comparison with that of the twentieth century. But I did not reflect any credit upon the provisions for my acquisition of knowledge. I was a most unsatisfactory student.

In the winter, I was often out of school for weeks at a time with chilblains. Our house on James Street was poorly heated; great Himalaya shawls were hung outside of doorways, to wrap about us when we made trips from one warm spot to another. There was compensation to be had in the fact that Father allowed me to stay in his warm study. The weeks spent there, however, provided no adequate training in application. Still, those delightful long mornings—how I revelled in them! There was a corner at the end of the tall bookcase, to the left of the fireplace, where a warm register, a low, soft chair and a high footstool for disabled feet made a nook unequalled for browsing. And the absorbed cleric who came and went sometimes without so much as a look at his daughter's curled-up figure had no inkling of the arbitrary and un-academic tastes I was indulging. My mother would have been scandalized had she realized; my sister, a student born and bred, guessed nothing of the disorganized methods practiced under the Bishop's very nose. He had been sympathetic with her own scholarly habits, and she supposed he was attending to those of the younger daughters also. The whole household was occupied with social work, and I went undisciplined.

I had been spoiled for steady application. Research delighted me, and every now and then I would trace down assiduously some special phrase or fact and call to my aid the resources of the library. But for the most part the subject of each day's reading was determined by mood or fancy. I remember devouring portions of the *Faerie Queene,* a fat blue volume with thinnish paper and fairly good print; reading until I was saturated with uninterpreted old English text, and had to close my eyes and dream about it all. For history there were Prescott and Motley, Greene's *Short History,* and Parkman once in a while. I did not like reciting in a history class, nor keeping notes and recording contemporary dates. I was utterly lazy about that sort of thing, and preferred a long reading-sojourn in some one country, inhabiting it with my imagination, dipping into its language perhaps, with the linguistic passion which had possessed my forebears.

Our French teacher had drilled her classes thoroughly in the speech and literature of her own country; she was a dominating person, large, red-faced, and with a head of short, loose, Medusa-like ringlets which fairly squirmed at the pupil. I neglected geometry and algebra for an astronomy course, a much-popularized affair, interesting but short. The girls fitted up a small observatory on the roof of the "See House," as we called our James Street edifice, and spent more time in hunting constellations than in calculating distances. Rhetoric was delightful, and also Mental and Moral Philosophy, as they were termed. Moral Philosophy was taught by a clergyman, who introduced a certain amount of theology. Physics, with no school laboratory, only rather dull trips to factories and an occasional half-hour standing round a locomotive with a teacher explaining its possibilities, sometimes getting a little mixed up herself, was not inspiring. Latin was a joy while we were learning the language-structure, the thing I most loved. Caesar we translated without proper reference to grammar or construction, but with merely a species of understanding that the pupil would do that herself—a laxity which once roused the Bishop to unexpected concern over school methods.

I had brought home my Caesar, and was boggling one evening over the strenuous fifth paragraph in the first book, when he asked to look at the text. I begged him to help me, and he took it up with a sudden revival of teaching-instinct. A question revealed the fact that I had been taught nothing of parsing, very little of the application of rules, nor had I memorized either declensions or conjugations any too well. He was horrified.

"Your mother and I," he declared, "would either one of us have died of shame if we had ever been discovered in such a plight as this. In our day we *studied* Latin; we should never have dared to trifle with it as you have done."

He informed me sternly that his help was going to consist of a thorough drilling, with every phrase and noun and verb accounted for. It was a racking experience, lasting until nearly midnight; for once in the swing of constructive activity he would not give up, even though the yawns of a sleepy pupil might appeal to him for mercy. At the end of the lesson I had mastered the translation, but had vowed inwardly never to ask for assistance again. The reaction, however, came in an access of diligence and more systematic study. After a winter of absorption in the military manoeuvres of the famous Roman, I sailed into Virgil with real enthusiasm.

There was one priceless gain for which I bless my good father and his toleration of my presence in his study. He came and went, put me out now and then temporarily when important interviews took place, and let me pretty generally alone, for our mother was his real consultant and confidante, and he took his letters and problems to her, dependent upon her criticism. One summer a slight accident to his right hand resulted in stiff fingers, and his handwriting was ever after illegible. Proof-readers and type-setters were not able to decipher it, so when writing for print he was obliged to have his manuscript copied. It occurred to him finally to dictate as he composed, and for this the round hand of a school girl was as useful as that of a paid copyist. So he made the experiment with the young bookworm who shared his work-room, and to my infinite delight I was installed as a regular secretary when he was preparing material for the press.

It was my happiest task of all. I sat at his own desk with the square sheet of sermon-paper spread out, and the fine inkstand before me, wielding a steel pen which by that time had superseded the squeaking quill. Luckily I was sound on spelling and grammar. To follow the keen mind, the fine literary style, and the argument that was almost too ready and rapid for transcription, was stimulating beyond measure. He was a master of English, the recipient of more honorary degrees than any other dignitary of the Episcopal church at that time; also a stern self-critic, pruning ruthlessly as he wrote, even ridiculing his own rhetorical excesses when on rare occasions the swiftness of a conception momentarily outstripped his power of expression. His fondness for words and his delicacy in determining their fitness for his purpose, gave him an almost human companionship with language. His young amanuensis became accustomed to halt her pen instantly at the call of "Stop! Strike that out!"—followed by a pause, out of which would come a substitution that changed a sentence or perfected a paragraph. Now and then a few words of explanation or the invoking of a rule would add to the treasures tucked away in my memory; points which in a textbook would have been difficult to assimilate.

In rare instances he allowed me to search for a synonym to give me practice. But if I showed him a composition or even an examination-paper of my own, he read it thoroughly, sometimes twice, and handed it back with the remark, "You can do better than that." I like to fancy that I hear him say it now, when the longing comes for his judgment on anything I have done. It was dampening at the moment, but it gave me the assurance that I might one day deserve the praise for which I was working. I learned afterward that a strengthened faith in one's own ability is infinitely better than the passing approbation.

There were claims upon the young person in those days. I was introduced to a new set of interests, wholly apart from music or education, in the early years of my adolescence. I had been helping my older sister with Sunday afternoon work at a mission

Sunday-school in the South part of the city, teaching an infant-class, and sometimes playing the melodeon, when it occurred to the Bishop to start another mission, this time in the picturesque north district, at the foot of Round Top, a wooded hill at the base of which a large population mostly Germans, was settling. Why not let me help, he thought. I was now about fourteen, tall for my age, and outwardly mature. Why not let me do some of the scouting in the neighborhood, and then assist, under direction, with the starting of a little Sunday class? I was enchanted with the idea, especially the prospect of going about the picturesque German neighborhood to gather in scholars.

Mother did not feel quite easy about this entering wedge, as she termed it. She knew how far I could be carried by enthusiasm. Despite my apparent hardiness, I had weak nerves, and lame feet which had not yet been pronounced flat, since broken arches were then undiscovered. My astigmatic eyes, though fitted with glasses, were victims of my carelessness. But downs which sometimes kept one inert on week days, yielded to ups on Saturday and Sunday, and I became a different being when pursuing any of my special interests.

The first steps did not seem to involve undue effort: afternoon walks through the unpaved streets of the Round Top neighborhood, stopping at each story-and-a-half house, and telling its tenants about a Sunday-school which was to be started shortly, and asking them to send their children. The practice in English was an inducement, and the hours would not interfere with the services in the Lutheran church, to which most of the people went on Sunday mornings. Three girls went out on bright October Saturdays, and made calls upon the immigrants' households. Often the mother of the family could not speak English, and her rosy-cheeked youngster would have to act as interpreter. But we struck common ground somehow, and collected a primitive vocabulary in which the word *Schule* played a conspicuous part.

The project advanced, in spite of our parents' concern, into very active work. We founded and furnished a little chapel, made out of a barn, with a small wooden cross over the door, and space inside for the crowds which appeared at our first meeting. Soon afterward someone gave us a melodeon, on which I played hymns that we stencilled on cloth. Later we held evening choir-practice to which I sometimes had young girl-escorts. If I did not, I went alone; the German people respected me as "Miss Hunnikum," the organist and the Bishop's daughter, and did not realize how young I was.

8

REALITIES

My brother George had been married at Emmanuel church in Boston in the spring of 1874. Dressed in a pale blue and white summer silk which came to my ankles, and a white leghorn hat decorated with a large wreath of apple-blossoms, I had felt very important at the wedding. Thereafter my mind became occupied with love-making, but the Harvard boys who came home with my brother James did not give me a great deal of attention, so when they went hunting or fishing, I picked up the books which they had been discussing. Among them were Turgenieff's novels which I found as hard to understand at the time as Russian music. There were Mallock and Hamerton, and two Tauchnitz' volumes of Richard Feverel which I read because I wanted to believe myself clever. I did not learn to enjoy the work of George Meredith until later, but I remember that some of my brother's friends secretly considered themselves highbrow if enthusiastic over him. The boys had a tendency to consider Harvard a stronghold of informed public opinion, and they had many discussions in which the various members of our household took part according to their capacities.

My brother James' hopes for a lifework in his chosen profession now began to crystallize. As soon as he graduated from college, he came home to study in the small divinity school which the Bishop had started in Syracuse and to work in the mission chapel. He was a forceful character, with real gift as an orator. His clear mind was reenforced by wide reading and a phenomenal memory. During his years at Harvard the appearance of a pamphlet entitled *Modern Christianity; A Civilized Heathenism* had stirred thought-

ful men and wide-awake students, especially those who were looking toward the ministry.

It was written in 1873 by an English clergyman named Pullen,
the author also of a book entitled *The Fight at Dame Europa's
School,* and was a biting arraignment of the Christian Church,
questioning "whether there is any creed whatever that is worth reciting; not whether this form of Christianity is preferable to that,
but whether all forms of Christianity pretending to come from God
through Christ, are not gross impositions from beginning to end."
It was actually an arraignment of the hypocrisy, unreality and in-
consistency existing in a so-called Christian world—violently
enunciated half-truths put together with the idea of constructing
from them one complete and unanswerable truth.

It was in its fifth thousand when it reached the young thinkers
at Harvard, and perhaps agitated their ranks more violently than
any book of that generation. James Huntington was deeply affected by it and by the many truths it contained, however crudely
put. A revolt against the easy, comfortable aspect of church life in
America after the reaction from Calvinism, along with the growing
energy of the Oxford Movement in England and its revival of
ritual and reverence, brought about a crisis in the young man's
thinking. Finally, the counsels of his father, a moderate churchman but intensely sympathetic with youth and its questionings,
came to the rescue. "He saved my life," the son admitted afterward.

I felt no theological stirrings whatever, and recoiled from the
belligerent tone of the book; for me the Christian life signified
struggle with temptation, a challenge to sincerity, a sense of accepted authority and a dread of an all-too-common disturbance in
a somewhat complacent faith. I was not aware of the deeper changes
then taking place within my brother's mind. We two, in happy
companionship, carried on the mission work, for older volunteers
untrained in its activities came and went; only the people themselves, who loved it, were permanent and faithful. It was a youth
movement in the fullest sense. I liked the intimacy with the German and English girls, workers mostly, and healthy, eager creatures; my brother loved and captivated the boys. We trained a

boy-choir, led by a whole family which had brought church traditions and beautiful voices from England. We had clubs and entertainments, classes, discussions. At the little parish house, next to the church, life was as animated as in the social gatherings on James Street.

We used to take our young people from the mission for picnics on spring nights, leaving the city after business hours, and driving them ourselves. We made a departure from custom in allowing the girls to invite boys to those parties, but our chaperonage was recognized, apparently, for we had response in good behavior, and the boys were all devoted to their young rector, who kept them busy exploring wood-paths, or making camp-fires. But one night, sitting with him on the driver's seat as we were returning to town, I happened to look around into the body of the "barge," as we called it, to discover that each girl had her head on the shoulder of the accompanying boy, and her hand clasped blissfully in his. The Bishop's daughter was properly scandalized.

"James," she whispered to her brother, "What sort of chaperons are we? Look in there."

"They look very comfortable!" he declared with a chuckle. When the horses stopped, most of the passengers were fast asleep. There was no question that the trip had given perfect satisfaction. It did us an immense amount of good. I think we acknowledged by degrees, the right of every woman, beginning in her youth, to male friendship, love, and marriage. It seemed to me exceptionally pleasant that our friends at the mission chapel should take somewhat franker means of acknowledging these things than were allowed in our own set, especially since many of them were chained to hard work, long hours, and infrequent holidays. But it was only in Little Germany that I could indulge these emancipated ideas. People muttered occasionally at the laxity allowed the Huntington girls, but as they gave no evidence of it in more exalted circles, it was not considered of great moment.

The religious zeal which I believed was my inspiration was not like that of my brother; not the flame that animated Elizabeth of Hungary or Joan of Arc. A love of importance and passion for leadership, a social instinct and joy in imparting, had far more to do with these activities. With my German girls, I was not the neurotic, over-enthusiastic child whose companionship with books and music-makers might have unfitted me for realities. But still my imagination was dominant, and although I was far from maturity, responsibilities at the mission were not then a strain upon me.

9

CONGRESS OF WOMEN

Syracuse continued to be a gay place with many distractions. Public events, advertising schemes, frauds like the Cardiff Giant, an absurd statue, faked, "discovered," and supposed to be an ossified man; a barbecue at which tons of bread were distributed to the public, and oxen roasted whole in a public square; rumors of one description or another, and experiments which came to naught. Things of that sort enlivened the succeeding years of the city's history. Excitement flickered up and died down; but in 1875 came an event really important and definite in its influence: a Women's Congress. Its object was not the furtherance of any one particular cause, but the gathering together of a body of women leaders for the advance of civilization, to exchange ideas, and report opportunities and educational methods.

When it became known that a quantity of "Women's Rights women" were coming to town, there was a great stir. Some people were frankly apprehensive, as they might be today if it were announced that a party of Soviet ladies from Moscow were coming to hold a convention in New York. Others were curious; they were used to the few radicals in our own city, and their doubtful ideas, and rather wanted to know more about the Advanced Woman. A few were frankly inimical. But Miss Jackson, always broad-minded, stimulated her girls to a genuine interest in the meetings, and gave us all permission to attend, even during school hours.

We were tremendously enthusiastic when we heard that Louisa Alcott was coming, and would stay with our friends, the Mills family. Their daughter Harriet Mills was at Cornell, and was looked upon with intense respect by the rest of us. Miss Alcott's father, that quiet and completely unworldly Concord student, had held one of the interesting lecture-discussions which he called "conversations" at our own house, and justified the portrait she had painted of him in *Little Women*; and that book was then, as it has been ever since, a favorite story of growing girls. To see its author in person and hear her talk was a prospect which enlisted feminine interest, old and young, in the Congress itself. Even timorous parents who dreaded "masculinity" in women could not refuse their offspring that boon. And in truth, when we spied her walking up James Street hill with her hostess, one morning, there was nothing conspicuous about the tall, well-poised figure in a gray suit and small black hat of contemporary mould, although we had heard that the Alcotts were as a family somewhat "regardless" when it came to fashions.

The locally conspicuous specimen of independent womanhood had thus far been Dr. Mary Walker, the extremist, who had appeared every now and then on the streets of Syracuse, an odd little figure in masculine attire, very dapper black coat and pants, as I recollect, with a shiny shirt-bosom, high hat and cane. The police of various cities had arrested her frequently, it was said, but had become tired of it, and left her to circulate freely in New York state. Far from averting its countenance, the public stared at her as if she had been a chimpanzee, and went its way with a laugh. She had, however, something to do with the strong community prejudice against feminism.

Now sixteen, I had led far too easy a life to be conscious of the heroism which characterized those early days of woman's struggle for independence. A typical product of the Victorian Age, I believed that the destiny of woman was to rule over a domestic kingdom as queen and mistress; man's guiding star, a beneficent influence, a wise mother, a gifted teacher or writer or musician if possible, but at least, failing more striking attainments, a contented housewife. To do my parents justice, this lofty vision had not been set forth in our own domestic circle, where the elders were absorbed in community life. Our conception of a great woman concerned itself with her attitude quite as much as with her achievement.

The much-anticipated Congress opened on an October day. We settled ourselves upon the back-slanting seats of the Wieting Opera-house with a sense of surrender to the forces of expansion and progress. We were kept busy before the meeting opened in having the celebrities pointed out to us. Foremost was Mrs. Mary A. Livermore, a friend of my mother; an ample figure, who "might be anybody," as one reflected, so far as the effect of a well-fitted black silk gown and a fichu of white net was concerned.

Beside Mrs. Livermore sat Miss Maria Mitchell, whom we had especially desired to see—the woman who had discovered a comet, and was now teaching astronomy at Vassar. She was regarded as one of the most interesting women in America, and through her pupils various descriptions of original teaching methods and principles reached the public. She had exhorted her groups from the graduating class to abstein from sewing and making their own clothes, for example—a most radical piece of advice. She told them that there were plenty of women to do that sort of thing, and that it was taking the bread out of the mouths of the laboring class for privileged students to waste their time in needlework, because the large amount of money spent to fit them for a higher order of employment should be justified by useful activity in the professions.

Elizabeth Cady Stanton, one of the most valiant members of the Equal Suffrage group, had curls as did Miss Mitchell, but they were arranged in even rows upon a very shapely crown, above an attractive face. She was manifestly a woman of the world and an ornament to society. She and Mrs. Gerritt Miller of Geneva, trying to introduce bloomers, had appeared at a New York theatre in bloomers concealed by elegant evening cloaks, which they removed in the box. It had created some sensation, and was coldly received by their society friends, so there were no bifurcated garments visible on the platform at Syracuse. But reform garments were on exhibition in an ante-room, and various matrons were seen going to this exhibit after the meeting.

There were all sorts of live topics. Dr. Antoinette Blackwell, speaking for the medical profession, quoted a French professor who had said that "there was no more danger for a woman in the dissecting-room than the ball-room." A woman agriculturist, Mrs. Thomas of Philadelphia, made a persuasive plea for that occupation, giving pleasant sketches of rural life and achievement. Mrs. Bohn, a Boston watchmaker, surprised the audience by recounting her achievements in manufacture.

Miss Catherine Beecher, a sister of Mrs. Stowe and of Henry Ward Beecher, who was then a sensational Brooklyn pastor, opened the education symposium with a paper entitled *Suggestions and Reminiscences*. Her coming as a delegate to the conference had made some stir in the Bishop's household, because she had been wont to appear at ninety-eight Boylston Street years before, carrying a little black bag and announcing her intention of spending the night. I can hear my older sister saying "Oh dear, there's Miss Catherine Beecher getting out of a hack: now I must go and make the guest-room bed up for her." She did not care for children, was always nervously on edge, and was quite a talker, which perhaps explained our reluctance to entertain her. Some one else spoke on *Unsectarian Schools,* urging that steps be taken to include advantages for Hebrews in the public school system. Mrs. Julia Ward Howe commended preparation in teaching and the familiarizing of parents with educational projects through mothers' clubs and neighborhood associations. We were excited at seeing Mrs. Howe, for her *Battle Hymn of the Republic* had virtually become a National Hymn in wartime. And she was a most attractive personality, in a soft dull-blue gown which set off her red-gold hair. She spoke briefly, but with conviction.

Journalism was represented by Mrs. Jennie Croly, long editor of a newspaper in Newport, Rhode Island, once published by the widow of Benjamin Franklin's brother, whose two daughters set type while their maid worked the press. That example of sheer pluck touched the audience.

It was agreed by the speakers that women lacked financial ability; at all events participation in banking or brokerage was not hinted at. But Mrs. Miller, the charming lady from Geneva, gave a fine paper on *Chemistry in the Kitchen*. Mrs. Phoebe Hanaford, a Baptist preacher, spoke for that profession, and reminded us that

in the seventeenth century the Quakers permitted women to preach
and pray in public, mentioning the name of Lucretia Mott, at which
the whole audience applauded. She also alluded to another Baptist
exhorter who laid her baby on the pulpit stairs while delivering her
sermon. This produced somewhat mixed emotions and murmurs of
"Poor little creature!" Miss Eastman of Tewksbury sounded rather
a belligerent note in making the suggestion that no woman should
give any money to Harvard College because President Eliot had
said that a two-thousand-dollar school was good enough for girls.
Someone else then cited the fact that Oberlin College had opened its
doors not only to women but to Indians and negroes, at which there
was some applause, but no real enthusiasm, from the audience.

Then there was a spicy debate on the subject of distinctive costumes. Miss Swazey, a clever delegate speaking on *The Ethics and
Aesthetics of Dress,* held health, comfort and decency to be the
paramount considerations. Any dress that violated these, she maintained was unbecoming. Mrs. Edna Cheney took issue with Miss
Swazey on the subject of religious dress, and Miss Abby May of
Boston, a fine-looking woman with the rugged features of New England and the plainest of clothes, warned against extravagance in
attire, and felt that economy should have a place on the list of
qualifications.

A recommendation for the formation of art-groups brought out
some interesting comments. The wife of an artist defended cheap
chromos, to the amazement of the high-brows. She pronounced
them a medium, imperfect but useful, for an acquaintance with
treasures of art otherwise impossible to the poorly educated. But
this theory conflicted with the standards of the progressive element,
and met with protest.

Miss Anna Brackett, her voice always authoritative, urged better classical instruction and more complete outfits for scientific research in girls' schools. And Miss Churchill, of Providence, pleaded
for the teaching of political economy to girls as well as boys. But
there was no stressing of special causes or grievances. A local newspaper said that the subject of equal suffrage was "admirably shaded"
during the sessions of the congress. It was not intended to be a

gathering of radicals, but of awakened and intelligent minds; a preparation for the tackling of greater issues to come. Some one did say of women, "The vote is waiting for them just ahead."

The most brilliant speech of all, however, was Mrs. Livermore's address on *Superfluous Women*. That was unforgettable. I can quote only a few of the aphorisms which were applauded by even the conservatives in her audience, but she captured it by the very weight and dignity of her oratory. She considered the various phases of celibacy, both forced and voluntary, going back to the School of Pythagoras and the women to whom it gave inspiration for the sacrifice of life to the virtue of chastity. We youngsters who had absorbed the idea that matrimony was the chief end of feminine existence, and that the "old maid" of history represented failure, if not tragedy, were quite aroused by the reminder that nearly half the girls of gentle birth in medieval England were consecrated from their cradles to religious celibacy, since the monastery offered the sanctity of perfect continence and holy life to tens of thousands. This seemed to us a very large order, but we realized that it was a reaction from the scandalous social conditions of the time and the depletion of the male population by war.

She recounted the achievements of the "social failures," as Henry James called them, in nursing, as attendants in prisons, healers on battle-fields, doctors, priestesses, mothers in orphan homes, and so forth, "carrying civilization to far lands, earning money to put brothers through college and into professions; like the caryatides of architecture, holding the roof over dependent households." She disposed of the expression, "Man is the head of the woman," with the remark, "The head of the woman is the head on her own shoulders."

She made us feel a deep respect for the brave woman who had gone through the fire of ridicule and satire when fighting her first battle for equality and justice to her sex. In fact she convinced us, in our adolescent enthusiasm, that there need be no such thing as a "superfluous" woman, but that the gentler sex could answer completely to the needs of the nation and its men, whether in or out of the matrimonial state. I think we came away with such a heroic enthusiasm for the glorious possibilities of spinsterhood that we almost reached the point of abjuring marriage altogether.

One other high spot was touched when Mrs. Howe recited her Battle Hymn. She put into it all the fire, reverence, and spiritual intensity of the vision to which it had owed its inspiration. The other girls laughed at me for talking about her "intellectual voice"; but one did catch the tones of the scholar and thinker, and her slender figure and delicate features added to the effect. The vivid imagery of the poem never seemed an answer to one's sentiments in later wars, somehow, yet even today I find that its ringing stanzas stir the heart.

The speeches made at the Congress of Women left us with a few suggestive quotations which we schoolgirls discussed among ourselves with special ardor, such as:

"Personal ability is the limit of personal responsibility." Some of us did not think it was; we thought riches, beauty, opportunity had to do with that limitation. One thing we did not quite appreciate—I think Mrs. Howe had said it—that "it is sheer waste of human energy to persuade women that they ought to become superannuated before seventy-five or eighty." I have a much better comprehension of that remark today. Then another statement—"The best mothers are something *more* than mothers"; curiously enough it was a spinster who said that, so we did not get the real force of it.

I had now gone in, head over heels, for the Cause of Woman, and spent the next few weeks debating it with my comrades. I was quite sure I wanted to be a suffragist, and also a big person of one sort or another; I even dreamed of studying law or medicine. But a talk with Mother—a great privilege because it was rare in those busy days—straightened out my vague projects somewhat.

"You will find out in time, you know," Mary Lincoln's daughter said with the same calm judgment which had on many occasions cooled the ardor of the little sea-captain, "just what you are built for. To train for the law, or for medicine, takes years of intensive study. I wonder if you are quite persevering enough for that? I'm glad you have taken Mary Livermore for a model; you know what she said about putting your education into whatever occupation you take up. There are very few women who have achieved greatness without scholarliness. But I do hope you'll be a large-hearted character, no matter what else you are."

Spring brought back, that year and others, more intimate concerns than the Women's Congress. The white violets clustered under the elms in our yard; thickets of snowy trillium blossomed on the east side of Round Top. There were picnics, moonlit nights when our choral club wandered about serenading. Then June warmth, anxious examination-days, and school graduations; heavy odors of syringa and roses; *soirées* on whose programmes appeared gems like the Chopin *Nocturne in G,* Mendelssohn's *Rondo Capriccioso,* Weber's *Invitation to the Dance,* Liszt's transcription of *Hark, hark, the Lark,* even the *Moonlight Sonata* with its ascending broken chords of the *finale* played in rampant and desperate *prestissimo* after days of dogged practice. Boys of a neighboring "prep" school as eager admirers in melting collars; white frocks and bouquets; Mr. Held with a rose in his buttonhole to present to the most successful pianist of the evening; the Bishop giving a stimulating talk on good manners.

Then the year was over, and we packed up and departed, in the limpid dawn of a summer morning, for Hadley.

Forty Acres

1

THE FARM

As far back as I can remember, we went to Forty Acres every summer, and spent the entire vacation there; Father, Mother, five children, Harriet and the cook. It took practically all day to go from Boston then. We enjoyed a stopover in Springfield, with a noon dinner at the Massasoit House. Those journeying days were hot, and I remember the shady coolness of the dining-room, the refreshing clink of ice in our glasses, and the little mounds of ice-cream deposited before us by a colored waiter. We were impressed by the stiff napkins, crimped into plaits and spread out like fans. We were polite for the moment, trying to behave as if we had dined in state all our lives. Mother did not spoil our sense of importance by making corrections. We could even order the Massasoit specialty, waffles, in addition to a full meal. Afterward we sat around in the high-ceilinged parlor, bouncing gently on the springy plush sofas, while she, a little fatigued, would rest and read. The wait always seemed long, because we were bubbling with impatience to collect our baggage again and run to the station.

Then came the last lap of the journey from Springfield to Northampton, by the easy-going four o'clock train. We knew all the stops: Chicopee-Junction, which we pronounced as the conductor did with the greatest possible rapidity, and Willimansett; Holyoke, where the glimpse of the falls, a veritable Niagara to us, gave us a first sight of our river! The mountains, the little green islands, the very sky, were our unquestioned property, only waiting to be recognized by their ecstatic owners.

The train sped along by the waterside, round a curve beyond the South Hadley dam, into the shadow, out again, and there was

Mount Holyoke with the house on top and the steep railway
mounting to it: safe, unchanged, gleaming in the sunshine of late
afternoon. The same ferry-boat at Smith's Ferry; after it Mt. Tom
station, with little Nonotuck rising behind it. More and more excitement. The meadows, Northampton in the distance—hurry,
train! "Hats on!" The shady straws were clapped on above our
moist foreheads and white elastics hastily snapped under our chins.
There we were, and sharp eyes spied three vehicles drawn up by the
platform: two carriages and a wagon for the trunks. We tumbled
down steps and rushed to pat the horses, Major, Max, Dolly, Robin,
and they whinnied a recognition. The baggage was piled on a big
haycart which two men were to drive. Jamie, Arria and the maids
went in one carriage; Father took Mother, Molly and me in his
own special vehicle, an odd little two-seated one with the front seat
folding over toward the dashboard when the occupants of the back
seat got in.

Then came the drive of six miles across the turnpike to Hadley.
Ahead of us went the stage, loaded with big mailbags and drawn by
four galloping horses, carrying a crowd of guests bound for the
Orient Hotel in Amherst. In it were young men in straw hats and
pretty girls with long blue veils floating from their bonnets. Away
it went, the horn sounding, the group on its top swaying as it
rounded the curve below the station. Now then, forward Major,
forward Max, and set us in motion! After one spurt the horses
settled down into the jog-trot of farm custom and we were presently
busy recognizing old landmarks, spotting new barns in the tobacco
fields, nodding our greetings to friends as we passed them.

"Hello, Doctor! Glad to see you back," shouted a farmer from
the edge of his field. The "Doctor" waved his hat. We smiled and
nodded along the way, like parading monarchs. The two-mile turnpike across the meadows was dry and dusty; at our right lay the
Holyoke range stretching eastward; before us old Hadley village
with its broad street, the river at either end of it, and the hotel
made out of a house where our great-great-grandmother's second
husband, Parson Russell, sheltered the regicides, and the meeting-
house which great-grandfather Phelps planned and built, crowned

by a Christopher Wren spire. And now the Post Office, where Mr. Shipman, the postmaster, with a face which recalled our Cruikshank pictures of Mr. Pickwick, beamed benevolently, and handed a pile of mail to Father. Up Middle Street the younger elms grew in graceful promise; beyond it the Connecticut finished its ox-bow.

Finally we passed the buttonwood tree, the limit allowed for horseback rides, to the row of dark, clean-limbed maples along either side of the road, and the white picket-fence of Forty Acres. *Our* House, *our* big gate opening wide, *our* elms stretching their canopies far over the roofs and lawns, *our* south door flung wide open and the figure of Aunt Bethia, erect, serious, but with kindling eyes, standing on the doorstep in her gray gown and white kerchief. We sprang from the wagons and rushed under the lilac-trees to embrace her. Everybody talked at once; the scent of new-mown grass, cut that very morning, blew across the lawn and into the house where we raced from room to room investigating, recognizing, shouting, unearthing old treasures and discovering new ones, until we were called by Aunt Bethia into the cool dining room with its mysterious high cupboards.

We always knew just what Aunt Bethia would have ready for that first supper: thin sliced ham in a long blue platter, raised biscuit, big and light, with pats of fresh butter. There was a bowl of strawberries ripened in the Hadley sun, a pitcher of yellow cream, a harvest-cake of yeast batter sweetened and baked with raisins, and baked custards in old Lowestoft cups, flavored ever so slightly with nutmeg. We drank warm Jersey milk out of our silver mugs and cold water from the depths of the well dug by forefathers.

Supper finished, we continued our rediscovery of the house. We went through the narrow hall, past the oars, walking sticks and guns, into the Long Room on the right, with its graceful wedding arch under which seven brides had been married, and its low spinning-wheel which had been used by the Elizabeths. At the ends of the broad fireplace there were deep cupboards, one for the best china, and the other partly given up to a collection of Indian relics from our own ground. Nearly every summer the plough would turn up some curious implement that had been used by aboriginal warriors or farmers in the meadows west of the house. It was Father's delight to exhibit to visitors the arrow and spear-heads we had found, the mortar and pestle for grinding corn, and the primitive bowl. (The collection, which was given to Amherst College after Father's death, is now in its museum.) The fireplace and these cupboards were fitting background for the Puritan severity of the Long Room furniture, which was created for use, not luxury.

Then came Father's study in which we so often watched him working, his north window open toward the garden, where two rows of brilliant hollyhocks bordered the path to the grape arbor. Beyond his study was the room where he was born, with its portraits of our grandfather and grandmother, Dan and Elizabeth Huntington. This was Aunt Bethia's room, its contents a fitting expression of the deep reserve which overlay her responsiveness to the people she loved. Upstairs the high beds, mirrors, and bureaus in the numerous bedrooms through which our explorations led us, would dazzle the eyes of a collector, as would the spindle-legged desk in a tiny library which held the theological works belonging to our grandfather. Here was a copy of the death warrant of Charles the First, which had been signed by two of our Puritan ancestors, and in the hall hung a portrait of a continental soldier who was painted with that mysterious dot in the eyeball which made his gaze follow us wherever we turned. Often on the first day of our return to Forty Acres we would run to a corner to escape his scrutiny, and shout gleefully, "He's looking at me! He's looking at me *still!*"

Finally we scrambled through a little door into the lower attic, past the chimney closet, where the mellow odor of cured hams blended with the faint scent of herbs, into the "prophet's chamber." There on the window-frame my next older brother, whose sleeping room it was, had copied the familiar quotation from Clough, in whose poems we all had our periods of absorption:

> *And not through Eastern windows only*
> *When daylight comes, comes in the light;*
> *In front the sun climbs slow, how slowly,*
> *But westward look!—the land is bright.*

The little window in the prophet's chamber framed a lovely picture: green meadows in the foreground, then a line of soft willows and bright water, beyond that the peaceful dwellings of Hatfield under trees, and the plain white spire topped by a friendly weathercock; rising behind it all, hills upon hills. When the river-fog enshrouded it on a dog-day morning, the first mists lifted and floated away in long streamers down the valley. Autumn sunrises touched all the roofs of Hatfield village with their glow, giving an old red barn the hue of an American Beauty rose. One could see thunderstorms mass their battalions of cloud to sweep down upon the valley, or catch the first strip of clear blue in the northwest after a shower. Purple windclouds swept across a primrose sky to portend fair weather for tomorrow. Yet the room had plain whitewashed board walls and the furniture of a cell; such a setting befitted him who lifted up his eyes unto the hills.

But we were a joyous returning family, and there was much re-visiting to be done in barn and garden. Father might be seen leading a tour of inspection, with a skipping child holding either hand. The older ones strolled along more slowly across the broad spaces of the farmyard, its turf kept soft by the croppings of cows and sheep, allowed to linger and nibble on their way to and from pasture. The sheds, carriage-houses and granary extended almost to the barn, running to the left as one drove down from the road.

The great barn doors were open on these warm June nights and through them one caught a glimpse of the mountains in the south, with the white spire of Hadley meetinghouse thrown out in relief against its dark background, where the sunset often left a deep rose-colored afterglow on Mount Holyoke.

The barn* was a splendid place. There stood the row of beautiful fawn-like Jerseys, one of the first imported herds in the country. Every cow had her own name; there were always four or five new calves waiting to be named when we reached the farm. We each had an opportunity to bestow these names according to fancy:

---

* The old barn is still intact. It has been moved to Hadley village and made into a museum.

Stella, Cordelia, Jessica, Chloe, Bess, from classical or fictional sources. A heifer with a perfect white heart on her forehead was especially loved. The younger calves were often tied in the yard, and were such ornaments to the landscape that passing strangers remarked upon them. We lingered in the barn, salting each cow and enjoying the tickle of her rough tongue on our hands. Their owner went proudly along the line, greeting each one as if she were a lady of quality.

It is sometimes necessary to revise our childish notions of the bigness of things, but those haymows, reaching to the cobwebbed rafters, are still in recollection vast heights. We scaled them by a ladder of rough pegs driven into an upright beam, and slid down, tumbling deep into a pile of sweet-smelling dry clover and emerging, flushed with the swiftness of descent, ready to do it all over again. The cows raised their heads for a moment to look at us, then plunged their dark nozzles once more into the mangers. The bull lowered in his pen, and sometimes gave a vexed toss of the head but was restrained by his nose-ring; the horses whinnied at us, for they were personal friends. Old Max, a trustworthy brown cob whom we were allowed to harness and ride, turned his long neck around to look at us with a puzzled air, wondering if we planned to make him the victim of our perennial circus.

Finally our tour of rediscovery ended on the stoop, a pre-bedtime haunt. This was a gallery built across the whole western end of the house, where the ground was terraced up from the meadow to be out of reach of spring freshets. The roof of the ell sloped down over it, making a raftered ceiling, and the floor of weathered boards was broad; along the wall ran a narrow wooden bench some fifty feet in length. Here the farm helpers in our father's childhood had eaten their meals in harvest-times when eight yoke of oxen drew the loads of hay and corn from a great acreage. Tables had been spread for thirty or forty, and Father remembered the clatter and the cooking; the old brick oven, from which pies were taken on a long wooden shovel, was still at one end. But in our day the place was used for washing and churning and ice-cream freezing, and at night-fall for watching the sun go down. After a visit to the barn the family could be found there, the boys sitting astride the low railing, the older people leaning on it or ranged on the benches. On Thursday nights the Hatfield bell sounded across the river for prayer-meeting. After the sun had dropped behind the hills and twilight was descending upon us the frogs began their evening concert, and Father told the story of three mean old deacons, who mixed hay from bog-lands with their better quality, and sold it at too high a price. He imitated the frogs, who, after the deacons were in bed one night, roused the suspicions of the village by a loud conversation:

"Who sells bog hay? Who sells bog hay?" pipes the first frog.

"Jeremiah Bogue—Jeremiah Bogue," answers the second in a deep and solemn croak.

"Captain Dyer! Captain Dyer!" comes in on a higher key.

"Elderkin too, Elderkin too," squeaks a little fellow, and the old rascals are supposed to shiver in their beds, while the triumphant frog-chorus keeps on all night with its revelations. We never tired of that recital.

We lingered on the stoop that first happy night, occasionally running into the garden to see if any moths were flying. There were damask roses, spread low, and a yellow rosebush which poured its largess of blossoms across the path. Blue fleur-de-lis stood tall and elegant among the foxgloves; golden June lilies crowded gregariously in a corner where the bees could find them. There was not too much order or clipping of those beds. We could still smell fresh hay and roses, as we dropped asleep in blissful realization that all this summer loveliness was ours to keep for months. We could not have dreamed that after half a century it would all come back to us, preserved during the years of adolescence and maturity, and recalled with a touch of the same enthusiasm.

2

There were enough occupations on the farm to keep everyone busy. Even Father, transformed from prelate into farmer, left his parochial or diocesan cares behind him, and threw himself whole-heartedly into the cultivation of the farm.

We began the summer days at five; the boys and men getting up to go for a swim in the Connecticut. Our brothers had the yearly task of putting the boat into shape, painting and calking it and whittling new thole-pins. It was a flat bottomed craft, made expressly for use on the somewhat treacherous Connecticut River. A keel was unsafe because of invisible snags and sand-bars, so we had it shallow and light and too broad to be overturned. The process of getting it ready for use absorbed the boys for several days, and we hovered about them, occasionally getting a dab of tar or paint on our brown ginghams. Arria, a close comrade of both brothers, could walk or row as many miles as they without fatigue, and shared their outdoor life as well as their literary tastes. I can see her starting for the river in her dark blue flannel boating-dress, a pair of light oars over her shoulder. All three older ones rowed well and taught us, too, to manage a boat.

Our oldest brother George, however, spent many hours in woods and fields, getting botanical specimens or shooting hawks that threatened the chickens. Glorious great birds they were, and in those days natural wings were worn on city hats. He dried and cured them for Arria and the young girls who came to stay with us. He was not only a practised ornithologist, but knew the name and genus of every plant in the county. He had been a pupil and friend of Professor Asa Gray, the well-known botanist at Harvard

College, and his enthusiasm stimulated us all, so that we were constantly on the look-out with him for new varieties of flower and fern. He could find bits of wood of fine grain and color for carving or whittling and was clever with a penknife. His taste was often consulted as to the hanging of a picture or adding to the ornamentation of a room. His studies in Italian, Greek and Hebrew were shared by his younger sister and brother and occupied much of his time when indoors. He found chances also to read to us little ones and taught us chess, of which we played many games in the course of our various summers. One particular summer, we had a series of them, two against two, and kept the board on a small table for a week or so, making about one move a day after private conferences over it in the Long Room.

My father enjoyed the companionship of both sons, with a sympathy and understanding of their point of view, and the confidence between them was never, so far as I can remember, disturbed by any action or decision of theirs. Whether the three were completely in agreement or not, they discussed with him their educational problems and ambitions, their theories and plans and reading.

There were various tasks for women to perform on summer forenoons, in order that the household and farm should be carried on with that smoothness which can be achieved only through good planning. Men and maids must be provided for. In busy seasons like haying or corn-harvesting our brothers groomed and harnessed horses, and washed the carriages with a mammoth sponge. We little girls helped with the harnessing, buckling straps and joining reins. It was the object of our young lives to get the bit smoothly into a horse's mouth, which was only a knack after all, like feeding him with apples on outstretched palms.

During our earliest years food was kept cool by lowering it into the well-shaft through a sort of box which stood covered on the kitchen floor. Pails with meat or butter were let down on ropes. But later on my father built an ice-house, and it was then the boys' duty to bring in cakes of ice to the cheese-room, a shady pantry where the milk, in great shallow pans, stood for cream to rise. There was almost always a breeze blowing through the cheese-room between the slats of the closed blinds, and by night the sheets of cream would skim off in rolls on the spoon. Butter freshly churned and deposited in wooden bowls was set on the ice to wait till it was ready to make into pats and balls.

James was the inventive member of the family, contriving labor-saving devices to help others with their chores. He made playthings for his little sisters also. A primitive wagon of his manufacture, a box on roller-wheels which we thought remarkably easy-running and speedy, is still used for the babies of the family. He invented a box for the garbage-pails, the cover of which lifted up by means of a pulley-weight, so that it did not have to be held open —the cook blessed him for that. And he gave us the realization of one of our dreams by making a playhouse with two stories in the corn-barn in which we could actually mount a staircase—merely a small ladder, but our imagination was quite equal to that—and look out of the "upstairs" window.

After our noon meal, when the shadows of the huge elms stretched over the farmyard, our mother and sister and their guests rested, while Molly and I repaired to our apple trees with books. During hay-time Father worked steadily at this hour. It was his own particular way of resting. Our brothers often helped, running the hay-rake or turning the morning's mowing into hay-cocks.

There were few books at the farm; we reread old ones every summer. I can still repeat many of the verses learned by heart from an old blue volume, *Gleanings from the Poets,* which I carried to the apple tree with me on those summer afternoons. In it were Wordsworth's *We Are Seven,* Pope's *Ulysses' Dog,* and Shelley's *Complaints of the Poor,* which impressed me by its relation to my sister Arria's work, and bits from Henry Vaughn, George Herbert, and Chaucer. There was a volume of Milton in which I read *L'Allegro* and *Il Penseroso,* and dreamed of composing music to both. There were two German fairy tales, *The King of the Golden River,* and *The Goodnatured Bear,* which I read long after fairies ceased to populate the elms and the woods around me.

Many times we carried the good news from Ghent to Aix, repeating Browning's description of the race in rhythmic accord with

Maggie's leaping motion. Black's *Princess of Thule* enchanted us with its description of the Hebrides, and *Lorna Doone*; but it was the Marlitt translations from the German in *The Old Mamsell's Secret* which provided sentiment and mystery for our romantic young minds. The stolid, brutal Teutonic surgeon fascinated us; to have one's affections captured by storm seemed to us wonderful. We bemoaned the impossibility of finding in America a nobleman like the one in *Quits*, and we longed to meet the hero in novels of Mary Cecil Hay, the final pages of which were so touching that they were tattered by repeated perusals. Maggie was brought to the door by an imaginary groom, and I galloped through the green wood, expecting Lord Leaholme to be lurking in the shadow, heartbroken from unreciprocated devotion. But when I returned to look in the glass, I saw not the tiny heroine with tendrils of black hair around a calm forehead, but a solid oval countenance topped by a brown bow surmounting a turned-up plait and an uncompromising bang.

We loved Celia Thaxter's verse because her own history appealed to us. She was the little lighthouse girl on the Isle of Shoals, where her father, defeated candidate for the governorship of New Hampshire, had gone as keeper in bitter reaction. The tutor who came to teach his brilliant little daughter, fell in love with her, and when they were married their house became a meeting place for writers; the romantic circumstances of their life died only when they moved to the mainland, but we never forgot the tender regret in Celia Thaxter's poems.

At four o'clock Mother came downstairs in her cool sprigged lawn and lace cap, when we usually rowed upstream on the shady Hatfield side, or went into the hayfield to "rake after," with the short wooden rakes which Father cut down for us out of old ones. If we worked well we could count on riding triumphantly into the barn on top of the load, high up from the floor on which the horses' hoofs resounded noisily.

But this description of the summer days at Forty Acres might give the impression that we had it wholly to ourselves, when as a matter of fact we were seldom alone. The house was always filled with friends of both generations. Distinguished strangers appeared in our midst occasionally; I remember particularly a call from Harriet Beecher Stowe, because Father had just been reading us *Oldtown Folks*, and the prospect of seeing a living author was very exciting indeed. Guests seemed delighted with the informal, almost casual entertainment which they were given at our house. They were free to swim, row, drive, or sleep without any inconvenience to the simple living in our household.

My brothers brought their college friends, and Arria her intimate schoolmates. Together they lived in what seemed to Molly and me a whirl of delight. They were a carefree lot in the summer, boating and tramping, giving theatrical entertainments, and joking with a mutual abandon that we younger ones could only hope to imitate sometime.

At night we and our friends often climbed to the top of the gambrel roof of the house to watch the chimney-swallows put themselves to bed. Only the chimneys of an old, old house can furnish that entertainment. Ours were full of nests, and the whirring at night and in the early morning sounded like distant thunder. In rainy weather a nest of little birds would occasionally become loosened and fall down into the fireplace, giving frightened cries. Then we had to rescue them, feed them crumbs, re-arrange their queer house of gluey twigs and carry them to the roof to be recovered by the parent birds, who would fly about anxiously in the meantime. Later in the summer they would sometimes come down themselves, and appear in some room, beating their wings against mirrors and windows, so that they had to be assisted in finding a way out. The maids were alarmed by these apparitions and declared that a bird in the house meant death.

The good-night dance of the birds, as we called it, was very curious and fascinating. The whole great family of them from one particular chimney would begin flying over house and garden just after sunset; round and round in circles, now dipping, now soaring —and as the twilight deepened they would return from these flights, and fly across the opening of the chimney, at which moment just one swallow shot downward into its depths. We always wondered how that first bird knew that he must leave his comrades, and go into the dark. They flew around in another big circle, and a second swallow dropped inside, and then another and another, always with their circling regularity, until we could count the number who had gone in and the number left. Sometimes as many as a hundred swallows would pack into a chimney one by one. Finally two birds flew together and came back, and one left his comrade, obedient to some call or law. Then the last solitary swallow, on the edge of darkness, soared high, dipped low, flew over meadow, over garden, over the great elms, loath to join his fellows. We watched him with tense sympathy until he too succumbed and dropped into the silent chimney. *How did he know?* What, and where, was the sign given him? We shall never in this life have an answer to that question. Perhaps Browning guessed:

> Some time—in His good time—I shall arrive.
> He guides me and the bird: in His good time.

NEW ENGLAND PORTRAIT GALLERY

Conditions of labor in rural New England were somewhat unique in the sixties. There was a strong tradition of neighborliness. People "helped" one another rather than hiring out to an assumed superior. Farmers were so accustomed to payments in kind —exchange of products between themselves rather than dollars— that mention of money was avoided except in occasional reference to tying up or laying away. A tactful bargainer for extra farm-work was wise enough to omit discussions of cost. Nobody was employed by the hour; you paid for day-work, and long hours at that. Modestly tendered remuneration was accepted, but it was etiquette to wait for a bill, sent in when the payee was in need of cash and supposed to be paid very promptly. Checks, however, were frequently retained for months before presentation at the Bank, a compliment to the solvency of their signer. It was interesting to be taken along as our father's companion when he went to negotiate for some special form of assistance required at Forty Acres. Sometimes we called on Mr. Matty, a talented person who owned a "cradle" for cutting rye: a broad scythe to which was attached a convex frame that caught the straw and held it together in small masses, cutting and bundling at once. When our rye-field had grown high, and its golden billows blown by a south wind were lovely against the heaven's blue, Father would remark to John Breckenridge, the tall dignified man who presided over our farm-labor-contingent:

"The rye's getting pretty ripe; I guess we'd better have Matty come over in the morning if it's fair."

"Mebbe we had," would be John's terse answer. So that evening, after supper, the master of Forty Acres would drive over to

Mr. Matty's, taking a younger child with him. It was always hot at rye-time; a red sun going down in a hazy sky, a motionless air.

Mr. Matty would be standing inside his gate, his elbows on the top rail. He had a long, slanting face and straight light hair. We children thought him inscrutable.

He made no offer to open the gate as his visitors drove up in their old green express wagon, reining in the horse on the grassy space in front.

"Good evening, Mr. Matty," Father said.

"How d'do?" answered Mr. Matty. "Kind o'warm."

"Yes. Pushes things ahead, doesn't it?"

"Tobacco's hangin' back this year."

"Going to have a good crop?"

"I dunno. We was awful slow gettin' it sot."

"Is your wife pretty well this summer?" Father's voice had a cordial ring, but he wasn't hurrying his objective into consideration yet awhile.

"She ain't complainin'."

"How did that Jersey heifer turn out?" Mr. Matty had bought her from Forty Acres.

"First-rate. Had a calf last month. Givin' sixteen quarts."

"What did you do with the calf?"

"Kep' it." After this laconic answer there was a pause, both parties to the conversation gazing at the landscape.

In due course of time, from Mr. Matty:

"How'd them tomatses come out?"

"Oh, very well. Yes," after a moment's wait, "Very well indeed."

The child would begin to think the subject of the rye might be introduced now, after this successful prelude. Not *too* soon, of course, but before long. The horse was bending his head down and cropping grass. The Rector went into a reverie, and Mr. Matty knocked the ashes from his pipe. Presently the dialogue started up again more auspiciously.

"Have you got much rye this year?"

"Yep—over on the side-hill there"; with a backward jerk of Mr. Matty's lean thumb in the direction of Amherst.

"Cradled it yet?"

"Nope. The edges don't amount to much. Sort o'scatterin'."

"Mine's pretty thick. I've got it on the lower meadow this year."

No reply. Mr. Matty showed by a face devoid of expression that the location of the lower meadow meant nothing to him.

"I thought I'd like to get you to come over and cradle it tomorrow, if it doesn't rain."

More silence, then another question.

"Mr. Matty, who were the people that used to live in the little red house on Porter Pipkin's land? Did they move away?"

"I've heard tell that they did. You know the house was struck by lightnin'."

Then followed a protracted inquiry into the genealogy of the family in the red house. The twilight was gathering; a breath of damp air came across from the river bank. The child was getting sleepy. Was Mr. Matty coming to cradle, or wasn't he?

"There's a nice moon," observed my father, pointing eastward with his whip, at the great clear globe above the Pelham hills. Not a ring round it; no fog or rain in prospect. He gathered up the reins.

"Well, goodnight. See you in the morning." Silence still hovered over the top rail of the gate.

"Father," the child urged. "He didn't say whether he would or not. Will he, do you think?"

"Of course. He'll be there by six o'clock most likely. But it would be beneath his dignity to accept a job too hastily, you see. He's just coming over as any neighbor would, to help out."

"And don't you have to pay him?"

"Certainly. I shall hand him the dollar or so that I know he expects, and he'll pocket it; no questions asked. That's the proper procedure."

So it was. And this was a New England bargain. The children had witnessed many such transactions. That was "all there was *to* it."

By the time the sun was well up next morning, our lovely rye lay prone. Matty-the-Conqueror came up from the lower meadow, the scythe-blade of his cradle gleaming.

With all the buildings at Forty Acres, we had shingling-times nearly every summer. We did it in August, after the haying was over, and that lasted into July, for we cut the hay later than they do nowadays, letting it grow dry and ripe. The farmer in me still objects to the modern method of cutting green hay and leaving it two days to dry; we mowed grass at six in the morning, cocked it after noon dinner, and got it into the barn by supper-time, in normal weather. The July sun was powerful.

After the last hay-mow was filled there was a week or ten days of "straightening up," which might mean reinforcing the stable floor or the barnyard fence, or maybe just hoeing corn; and then Mr. Marsh came with his cohorts to repair the roof. He was tall, broad-shouldered, with a gray beard and bright eyes which could estimate distances and measurements with unchallenged accuracy. A good citizen too; shrewd but tolerant. They called him Mr. "*Ma'sh.*" There was a delicate shading which in this case could not easily have been imitated; not Ma*rr*sh, as enunciated in New York State, nor yet *Mash*, as indicating the cereal product given to horses; but a soft accent just between the two.

Mr. Ma'sh was a King of Builders. Arriving with his fine tools, his assistant or two or three apprentices, he took command of the roofing-operations, and we all bowed to his authority. The shingles would have been previously hauled and piled in the farmyard; a first-rate quality, Mr. Ma'sh said he could *smell* the difference between a good shingle and a poor one. The cheap quality, pale in color and full of knot-holes, such as were used for the roofs of pig-sties or manure-sheds, had but little odor, when fresh, whereas the better ones, fine golden pine-wood, absorbed the sunshine and sent it out again rich and pitchy. The work of nailing was delightful; stripping off the old rotten shingles not quite so attractive. The farm boys and our brothers, sometimes Harvard men who visited us, helped with that. The discarded heaps lay about on the ground with bits of rusty nails in them, of which our elders were somewhat shy, since rumors of death by lockjaw were prevalent in the Valley. As soon as a certain portion of the roof was clear, the men would go up on long ladders and begin the task of fitting the new overlapping shingles exactly in place, setting the slender, short nails and striking them deftly with the hammer, getting five or six feet of achievement ready in no time. The younger men would bring up fresh bundles and knock off the wooden wythes that bound them together. Mr. Marsh's commanding figure moved about in perfect poise on the risky declivities. When he stood up with bared head on the ridge-pole of the barn, he made us think of Columbus on the prow of his vessel discovering America; when he came down the ladder at the close of the day we felt like natives acknowledging his supremacy. He was friendly with the two little girls who scaled the roofs in stockinged feet, to help by handing nails to fill the men's apron pockets, or passing along the fresh shingles. These men worked for the pride of accomplishment of their job, not merely for the wage. If it took till dark to finish a day's allowance, they stayed on and left a completed job behind them. The family went out to bid them goodby when they were done, and paid visits to the new roof, standing back and looking at it in all lights.

Painting was another process which interested us; buildings had to have fresh garments. Various artisans qualified for this task, but for some time it was "Hen" Tailer who made the most satisfactory bids, though it could hardly be said that he was a brilliant business-manager. He had married a woman twice as old as himself—a shrew it was said—and had no children. A wisp of a man, always "sickly," but cheerful and sanguine, with the creative instinct; quite unable, however, to stick at his job for any length of time and frequently dropping out without warning, or pottering unnecessarily long among the paint-cans, mixing dreamily, and letting us children peer into them to watch the colors change. He was always a long time eating his lunch, which was untidily wrapped in a bit of old newspaper and thought by observers to be inadequate. So was the fodder of an old white skeleton of a horse which stood all day long tied to a nail in the shed-doorway.

Poor Hen. His artistic sense made life more bearable, but the doors of his home were barred against it. He was always in some difficulty; his place was mortgaged and his taxes unpaid, and he would come slinking into the study on a rainy evening, a deprecating little figure, trying to borrow money on his one security, an old four-poster mahogany bed which it was rumored had a deficient leg with its crack varnished over. Nobody knew to how many creditors it had been secured already. We always surmised that the Master of Forty Acres did a little gratuitous helping-out on those occasions, for Hen would depart with a more springy gait; but we had nothing to go on; their transactions were strictly private. And our father periodically announced that Henderson Tailer did *not* drink; he was positive that certain hints of bibulous excesses were merely village calumny. One did not want to be suspicious; there was something so childlike and appealing about Hen.

At that time a number of French Canadians had come into the valley, following an earlier deposit of Irish immigrants. The French were thrifty and made excellent farmers; many of them worked at Forty Acres from time to time. They raised broom-corn, for broom-making was a flourishing local industry. I rarely hear the strains of the *Marseillaise* without recalling an old fellow who used to drive past the farm on summer afternoons, with a load of broom-corn on his wagon. He walked his horses all the three miles from Hadley to North Hadley and back, and through the still, hot afternoon air one could hear him, a mile or more away, singing as he lay on his back atop of the corn-stalks. The inexact melody wavered, died down till I fancied he had dropped asleep; then I would hear, perhaps on the wings of some slight breath from the south, a revival of patriotic energy; a shrill, gusty bellow of

> *Aux armes, citoyens!*
> *Formez vos bataillons!*
> *Marchons, marchons.* . . . .

But when he actually approached the fencing at Forty Acres, either slumber or shyness overtook him. The uncertain air died down, and, peeping from the branches of my apple-tree I could see a recumbent figure, a battered straw hat over its face and the thin leather reins grasped in a relaxed hand, while the horses sagaciously found their own path and pursued it at a funereal pace. *Marchons! Marchons!* Sometimes, when I wake after a nap on an August afternoon not quite arrived from the past, I still hear the *Marseillaise* meandering up the road!

No description of Hadley characters would be complete without some mention of our cousins, the Phelpses, who lived a quarter of a mile from us in a big weathered structure guarded by two beautiful tulip trees. The House of Mystery, as we called it, was built by my grandmother's only brother, Charles Porter Phelps, who in 1816 had suddenly determined to give up his legal practice and profitable importing business in Boston and take to farming at Forty Acres. Possibly he may not have intended that the house he built should be more than a summer residence. But after it was built and furnished, the lure to reclaim ancestral ground became irresistible. Apparently he did not consider the implications of this change for his wife, the daughter of Justice Theophilus Parsons, in whose famous office he had studied law, or for his five children. The blow fell hardest upon the oldest son and daughter, Charles the fourth and Sarah, who were already moving in Boston society. The latter, by the death of her mother in 1817, became housekeeper for her father and guardian of the younger children. I remember "Cousin Sarah" as a white-haired old lady in a lilac print gown, moving about her garden, or driving in her hooded chaise wearing a long cloak and little bonnet. Later her father married his first wife's sister, Charlotte Parsons. Five more children came to that union and grew up under the now weathered roof-tree.

At various times Charles Porter Phelps's ten children came back as visitors to their childhood home. I can just remember Susan, a curley-headed, vivacious creature whose heart was broken by the death of her lover; and her less attractive sister, Charlotte, married most unhappily, and practically lost to her family. There was Cousin Francis, a teacher for many years in a Boston school, and his next younger brother, Cousin Arthur, our ideal of a gentleman of the olden time. And finally there was Cousin Caroline, the widowed daughter-in-law of Thomas Bulfinch the historian, who came up from Cambridge with her daughter Ellen. Ellen Bulfinch had all the attributes of a New England spinster, square-built, tall but not angular, a combination of practicality and forethought with creative artistic ability and a shrewd, sympathetic appreciation of the interests which animated her young relatives. I like to call up her sensible face—a little cold the casual observer would say, with a slight cast in one of the gray eyes, but responsive alike to a flash of humor or a daring departure from precedent. I remember I longed for the time to come when I could really claim companionship with Cousin Ellen.

But we children at Forty Acres were naturally most curious about the three peculiar brothers who lived all the year round in the old Phelps Place with Cousin Sarah. The bowed figure of old Cousin Charles was little more than a moving object against a sombre background. Looking across from our house, we used to see his bent old figure driving the cows, wheeling the wheelbarrow, swinging the scythe in his north meadow. He never smiled, never seemed to be holding conversation with his helper, a strong younger man. Even Father had merely an occasional, infrequent word with him, although we believed that a recognition of kinship existed between the two.

Theophilus, the "crazy" brother, whose figure also appeared in the panorama of the gray house, was white-haired, with an uneven short beard which concealed his mouth. His locks had been so long uncut that they had matted themselves into a woven fabric, which hung in a flat sheet at the back of his head. We knew that he had been a college student in his young days, and had broken down, allegedly from overstudy. He wandered about, sometimes by night, and often slept on the coarse grass by the river bank; he had also an appetite for uncommon or forbidden drinks, contents of medicine-chests. He was reported to have swallowed without disaster a whole bottle of "Lixy Pro," a popular physic which every family kept on hand and which was a nauseating mixture of aloes and myrrh. Paregoric he simply slept off, even huge doses of it; he "smacked it down" with a child's love of the sugary taste. It was impossible to keep these potent nostrums from him, till the medicine-chest of green-painted wood was finally hidden on a high shelf. We children felt no fear of Theophilus, but watched him from afar as he came and went with unflagging punctuality in the process of exercising a family of some seventeen or eighteen cats who marched after him in single file. Nature took care of him somehow, and in the end made him into a measurably normal old man who even produced and published a poem before his death in the eighties!

The last of the "uncommon Phelps Brothers," our cousin Billy, was the best known to us. On the road, on the bench in front of the Post-Office, in farm-house kitchens, in our own house or on the stoop, might be seen a strange, and to the uninitiated, frightening apparition: a man with a shaggy beard and vacant eyes, a narrow forehead and a lank, slack figure, which shambled about, its long arms swinging, uttering a jargon of unnatural sounds and syllables; no smile, no direct response, nor sign of observation; without teeth, without palate. Cousin Billy was born in the same year as my father, Frederic Huntington, who became the idol of the handicapped child. He followed him about as they grew older, wistfully watching the progress he made in school, and calling him "Soo'boy" (School-boy). His eternal question, "What Soo'boy say?" was applied to every problem that presented itself to his frustrated intelligence.

He had to make a language for himself, impotent as he was to utter most of the words which he heard spoken around him. Children and natives of the village learned to catch the meaning of his harsh and discordant sounds, and to appreciate the ingenuity with which he made them intelligible. Some of his expressions were poetic. If he arrived in a shower, for instance, he announced it as "high dew hush the dust." Receiving a guest hospitably, that is, giving the right hand of fellowship, was "hold up gee hand and say 'welcome in' to Billy." He knew his "gee hand" from his "haw hand," too. A happy disposition was "cheerful sun in mind"; to talk was "tell idea." Many expressions reflected a Biblical association, as his description of kissing—"Mercy and Truth," taken from the Psalm. Best of all he loved reading aloud, especially Shakespeare ("Billy Bow") and the Bible. He carried in his pocket a little worn

Episcopal Prayerbook which he would shyly hand to some of us children with the request "Read Dust-to-Dust!" There was a mark at the page containing the burial service, which he knew by sight even without power to decipher printed words. Some of us were rather bored by the frequency of this plea, but our brother James never lost patience, and would go over and over the sombre text as often as Billy requested it.

Billy was the village gossip, and wandered into various kitchens, spreading news in his jabbering vernacular. The farmer's wives saved triangles of apple pie for him, his favorite food. At our house he was usually surrounded by a group of young people who took proud satisfaction in discovering the meanings of his phrases, and their shouts of laughter delighted him; it troubled him to be misunderstood when he had anything important to communicate. Every afternoon precisely at four—and there was no striking clock within hearing—Billy repaired to the old red barn and closed its doors tight. Then he walked up and down the aisle between the haymows, "preaching to the spirits." Even when driving by on the road, one could hear the harsh voice raised almost to a scream, then lowered to a mumbling monotone.

4

BEHIND A HORSE

James sometimes took the corn to the North Hadley mill to be ground, and we often rode on the corn-bags beside him. It was amazing how eventful a drive of one mile could be. Our young ears were trained to catch every new note of a bird's song and our eyes to spy a bluebird, scarlet tanager, or oriole as it flashed past or lighted on a near branch. There were flocks of tiny yellow butter-flies which kept just ahead of us all the way and settled in a cloud on the dusty road, waiting till the horses' hoofs nearly reached them before flying saucily up into the air again. Then there was the wa-tering-trough by the roadside, where someone must always climb out and let down the horses' check-reins that they might be free to get deep draughts of cold water. We let them go slowly up the low hill which followed, and in descending held them up well, bracing our feet firmly and pulling with elbows tense if we were allowed to drive. Each child was taught in turn to manage horses, and we were very proud when permitted to hold the reins in one hand. Slapping them up and down on the horses' backs was considered most unscientific, but our steeds were all rather leisurely, because they had been allowed to choose their own gait; and when there was no whip we used now and then in desperation to gather the leather straps into a loop and lean over, holding to the dashboard with one hand while we applied it vigorously to their haunches, the result of which was usually a more or less abrupt start. While it was not supposed to be done in public, it expedited matters.

The road descended steeply as we entered the village, crossing a short bridge beneath which the mill-stream splashed over its peb-bly bed. And then came the mill: such a mill one never finds now, when corn is ground up into ensilage on the farms and meal and "middlings" come already pulverized from the West. Now the ancient stones are lying about idle and moss-covered, or tumbled into streams. But our mill ground all day long, and when the wind was north we heard it a mile away. The miller, powdered white from head to foot, stood at his door as we drove up and backed round. We slipped down from the pile of bags and dashed inside, pursued by the warning, "Keep away from the wheels, children!" That was merely a matter of form; we kept away from nothing and rushed all over the place, watching the golden stream of corn-kernels go into the hopper and the soft yellow meal emerge from below. We were everywhere at once: round the machinery, upstairs into the loft, at the wide dangerous door which stood open above the dam, from which we could watch the falls go roaring over and see people driving across the bridge beyond.

If the corn was long in grinding, we ran across to the village store. Inside it one perceived the composite smell to which cheese, molasses, codfish, onions, fertilizers, vinegar and kerosene contributed. It was apparent on entering, but did not impair our appetites for a kind of large soda-flavored cooky which we considered a rare dainty, as well as the pink or white peppermints, which were occasionally bought and dealt out to us. Our domestic code did not allow us to buy sweets for ourselves, but the paternal principle itself was not proof against those little peppermints, crude of flavor and heartening in times of fatigue, dissolved thriftily against the roof of the mouth. What matter if the jar that contained them was a bit fly-specked? The molasses-barrel diverted the attention of the flies somewhat.

After the store came a visit to the blacksmith. His smithy was close to the pond. Very often the horses were brought over to have a shoe set, which prolonged our stay in the village. The paring of their hoofs delighted us, it made their feet so trim and tidy, and I am conscious at this moment of the strong smell of scorched bone when the red-hot shoe was taken with tongs from a bed of coals and fitted against the foot. Then it was hammered and fitted again, put back, heated more and hammered more, till at last the smith was ready to take the leg between his knees and, bending over, finish nailing the shoe with quick, pertinent strokes, a nail at a time taken from his leather apron-pocket. We loved the moderate, relaxed way with which he swung his arm to pull the handle of the big bellows slowly downward, sending a shower of sparks over the top of the fire. He was not so loquacious or jocose a person as the miller and addressed his conversation chiefly to the horses, as, "Hey! stand over there! Back up!" and so forth. The assistant stood by, swishing a horse-tail brush back and forth over their damp backs to keep teasing flies away. Now and then mysterious signs and syllables passed between the two, too technical for us to understand. Their processes were faithfully reproduced in our play at home on rainy days with a tack-hammer and an old pair of bellows from some fireplace.

As we grew bigger we were given the afternoon duty of going to the Post Office. Three families of neighbors took turns carrying the daily mail. I was taught to ride our little mare Maggie, who superseded old Max, and galloped joyously back and forth with the full mail-bag over my saddle-pommel. We sat on an antique one-pommel saddle, and had brown linsey riding-skirts to wear over our ginghams. Maggie was a clever and lively little horse, who enjoyed our informal way of leaving the road and willingly scrambled up a hillside or jumped a low fence-rail, even forded a brook if necessary.

We liked to see the stage come in from Northampton and dash past our post office, throwing off the letter-bags in its flight. In those days it was the only public conveyance between the towns. It was worth seeing, drawn by four horses with gay groups on its top, a veritable garden-bed of flower-wreathed hats. There was a glimpse, we felt, of the great world outside our Paradise. It roused one's imagination, the vision of those buoyant young females and attendant swains whom we saw afterward on the croquet-grounds of the Orient Hotel when we drove past it up Pelham Hill. I thought as I cantered home with my letter-bag to the simple farm life that perhaps my own future romance would come in that way; maybe some day a handsome person with a brown moustache would alight from that very stage and climb into a phaeton beside me. The phaeton would be like that of a stunning New York girl, Miss Talbot, a friend of my sister Arria, who spent her summer at the old Talbot mansion in Northampton. She had a graceful black horse with white reins and whip, and a footman in the rumble, and she drove her admirers about while they held parasols over her head. *That* was grandeur indeed to the eyes of a tanned country child in a linsey riding-petticoat. She was a princess, we thought, when she rode through the villages. So I put my future lover into that setting, but he reappeared in other picturesque roles at the time when I was reading Mrs. A. T. Whitney's stories for girls.

When Father drove to Northampton, we were sometimes allowed to go with him. We were put at short notice into fresh white stockings with round-toed slippers buttoned at the ankles, and a pique or red cloth "sacque." After the dusty trip across the Hadley meadows, through the long covered bridge on which the horses' feet clattered mechanically on its worn wooden floor, we stopped to pay toll on the Northampton side. The one-armed man who came out to collect it had replaced his arm with a wooden one, which had a kid glove on its rigid hand. We used to speculate on the probable color of that glove, which was perennially new. The year it was dark green, we considered it very handsome. The bridge was finally carried away by a wind-storm, and its successor has never had the same charm.

Northampton was very different from the town of my father's youth. The old canal no longer existed; the Mansion House still remained, but it entertained a less lively public than in former years. Up on Elm Street near the present site of the Hospital stood a water-cure, to which various friends of our family came for a summer stay. There was another cure and hotel on Round Hill from which one obtained a view of the Holyoke range. People tied their horses to posts on Shop Row and we used to watch them and my father as he stopped to chat with one and another on the shady sidewalk. In those days elderly gentlemen wore suits of white linen or striped seersucker with broad-brimmed leghorn hats. The merchants looked cool and leisurely in their doorways, never pressed for time. Mr. Bridgman at the door of his bookshop had always some humorous greeting for his friends, and well-known people from all parts of the world came to buy books of him and were entertained at his house, a gambrel-roofed mansion on Elm Street.

Those visits to town were always long, especially when various members of the family went. Our funny little open carriage would hardly hold the bundles of all kinds packed away under its seats. When it was well filled with paper bags, tin pails, kerosene cans and dry goods bundles, Father might decide to call upon some friend at the Mansion House. We drove up to the hotel entrance and he alighted in his shabby old coat and joined a cordial group on the piazza, making himself genially at home with the city-dwellers. Everyone knew him and paid him respect. It was only when he and his wife went calling in the afternoon that they had the black carryall, a more formal carriage which was polished up and equipped with our best harnesses. The Bishop's *penchant* for old clothes was the subject of mild joking. He wore seersucker coats and trousers long after they had been superseded by other fashions, and a story was told of his call upon a lady in Amherst one day in that costume. She was out, and when she returned home she was told by her maid that she had had a visit from "th'ould gintleman in the calico pants."

5

THUNDER AND LIGHTNING

One of our greatest delights was a drive into the hills on fine days—"northwest days" we called them. There had to be a particular kind of weather for mountain excursions, and thunderstorms were apt to be the precursors of a really perfect one.

A thunderstorm in Hadley was an overwhelming event. I think it brought out more than any other manifestation of nature, the traces of old Puritan beliefs and fears which were inherent in Father's make-up and to some extent our own. Thunder and lightning always seemed to us the direct voice of God, and a storm the visitation of His wrath. Father did not attempt to conceal the fact that he dreaded it. The showers practically always took a fixed course, coming down from the northwest along the line of hills to Sunderland or Hatfield and then crossing the river on a broad line over Mount Toby to the Pelham hills, moving southeast to Belchertown and leaving a cloud behind which the shower pursued its way from Hatfield to Northampton and Holyoke.

We always know when a big thunderstorm was coming. Early in the sultry forenoon great copperheads of cloud, at first dim against the lead-blue sky, would begin to pile up above the northwest hills. They hung there ominous and menacing, always mounting a little higher, till after noonday. Then came faint, sullen rumbles, far away and only discernible at first to the sharpened, anxious ears of fearful souls. Father said little, but dinner was hurried somewhat so that he might get into the hayfield if there was a mowing to be brought in. Afternoon quiet reigned in the house, but down in the meadow the men worked furiously, the boys riding the hayrake, the horses stepping more rapidly than was their wont. The clouds in the northwest began to grow gray, blending into a misty horizon; long, growling rolls of thunder, still subdued, grew more frequent. We could see the Rector standing at the horses' heads, perspiration streaming from his face, looking anxiously at the advancing cloud. By three o'clock a gigantic black monster crossing eastward from the Vermont hills loomed behind Mount Toby. Even with the sun still shining we could see a narrow zigzag of lightning shoot downward from its center. Father pointed toward it with his rake. "That's not coming here, it's going round to the north. But there'll be another one later."

The haymakers were in a hurry. As the cloud grew more dense guests, maids and children would gather on the stoop to see those last loads come up; horses straining, wagon swaying, men tossing the hay frantically into the lofts. Then back again in the rattling, empty rack, the boys jumping from its sides to the ground and plunging forks into the remaining haycocks, the treader on the load manfully stamping down the masses which flew at him from all sides. And all the time more blackness, stronger peals of thunder. The sun seemed to be holding out till the very last moment, sending great rays down athwart the purple vapor. Father's courage seemed to grow stronger as the climax approached. "We can do it!" somebody shouted. Oh, could they? The onlookers shivered. "Hadn't you better come up?" Mother would call at last. Father would wave his hand toward the wagon, almost filled, a purple mist behind him. The sun plunged at last into that thunderous vapor. Then came the final stretch. Groaning, creaking, the hay hanging over its sides, the horses' hoofs gripping the steep bank, the men hastening after, that last load rode triumphantly up into the farmyard and round the elm-tree just as the tempest broke. A roaring of wind and swishing and cracking branches, a sharp rattle of raindrops striking the river, and the shower leaped across it with a crash and bolt over the very spot where five minutes ago the haymakers had been standing. Between big drops everybody hurried to cover and the furies and floods engulfed us all. There was a hasty shutting of windows and banging of shutters; mad whirls of paper, slamming doors.

Mother's room, on the northeast corner, was our gathering-place in those storms. She sat there calmly sewing or knitting till the room grew dark, then laid down her needles. Father always removed his watch, his glasses and any other metal which he had about him and laid them on the dressing-table. The darkness was intense because no lights were lit, and the incessant flashes revealed a circle of awed faces. A few hardy people remained downstairs or sat on the stairway, but we felt that they were tempting Providence. Somebody invariably counted the time that elapsed between flash and crash, guessing at the location of the cloud. Then, bang! would come an unexpected explosion which seemed to split the earth asunder.

Prone on a bed or sofa, hidden under pillows with which I tried to stifle the din, I felt that the vials of God's wrath were being poured out upon us. There seemed to be no world, nothing but the thunders of Omnipotence. After a tremendous crash I could hear some voice saying, "Oh, that *must* have struck!"—and thought, "I shall go next—we all shall." Would it be the head of the family who would be lying there unconscious, or Mother, or my venturesome brothers and sisters who always insisted on going too near the windows? Then even as terror reached its height the rattling would echo a little farther away. "That was in the east," Father would say confidently. "It's gone over; they must be getting it in Belchertown now."

We were sorry for the poor Belchertown people, but how relieved for ourselves! The wind still doubled the trees over, but the next crash certainly *was* in the east; God had spared us from the effect of His wrath after all; He must have heard our prayers for help. And now came a joyful cry from below, "Look out of the west window; it's all bright over the hills!"

I cast away my pillow and ran to see the clearing—a strip of sky flooded with suffused and brilliant light; the last drops still falling, the hills visible in golden mist and the blackness massed over behind Mount Tom and the Holyoke range. Somewhere there would be a burned tree, but our buildings had come through safely and we knew that the bright strip was going to widen and lengthen till the forces of darkness were routed altogether. Soon a rainbow would span with its arch the woods and fields between us and Amherst.

As long as I live I never expect to know—I never have known—anything like the rapture of that clearing-off after a storm. There was the blessed silence after it had died away and the liquid notes of a song-sparrow, as thankful and blissful as we, no doubt. There was the sense of having been spared disaster and the little sounds about the house of return to normal life—safe life without fear or haste. There was that widening strip of clear blue in the northwest out of which fair weather was coming for a morrow full of delight. We went out into the garden and found the flowers less beaten down than we had feared, although much corn was lying prone. A great golden butterfly with black-edged wings floated over the larkspur, lighted on the hollyhocks. The cows came from pasture in leisurely fashion as if nothing had happened, nosing gratefully into the wet clover. Birds soared high above the elms. Father came to the window and held up his hand.

"Hark," he said. "Do you hear the mill-stream?" We did hear it, a mile distant. There was the roar of falling water, the buzz of wheels, the grinding of the great stones, and the rumble of wagon wheels over a bridge with loose planks. *"The wind is in the northwest."* It was called out all over the house. "Hear it? Hear it?" one cried to another. "It's going to be a splendid day tomorrow."

We knew exactly what that meant. Nobody said so but one had only to wait, on tiptoe, for news. At supper everyone was light-hearted, uproarious, expectant. And before it was over Father would say quite casually—he loved to give his invitations so—that he had been wanting for a long time to explore a certain hill-road on the other side of the river, and would we give him our company tomorrow?—finishing with a look at Mother and saying, "What would you think of that, Hannah?" Very often when a choice was put before the household in the same impromptu fashion, it called forth a tremendous discussion, for there was an endless variety of picnic places. We might drive to Pelham or Shutesbury, on the east side of the valley, or Montague, round on the further side of Mount Toby, or to Roaring Brook or Sunderland cave, Whately Glen,

High Ridge, Chestnut Hill, Ashfield, Colrain—or just take a long rambling ride through forgotten roads uphill and down, coming out on unexpected views of Monadnock or Graylock or Wachusett, and finally dropping into our own valley again toward supper-time. But I really think we liked best to have the excursion one of Father's own inspirations, because he planned it so nicely.

After supper we hastened to the stoop, to see the sunset, final prognosticator of tomorrow's perfection. Gold and crimson in the west, the east deep violet with a few last thunderheads just visible as the remains of the storm drifted out to sea. Upper currents were twisting the clouds into fantastic shapes which changed from moment to moment. A doubled-up clown with a peaked cap became a maiden with flowing hair; a mammoth bird floated southward in the changed guise of a friar with cassock and cowl. After sundown came pale, cold greens among the glowing tints; these gave place to a primrose sky and the long, purple cloud-masses, slowly thinning, which foretold our northwest day; a great planet blazed out in solitary grandeur. It was bliss to fall asleep in that cool, crisp stillness, hearing the particular little rattle of the blinds outside our windows which was an assurance of storms past and fair weather on the way. For days there had been a southerly breeze moaning restlessly in the elm-branches by day and dying down at night, leaving sultry, foreboding silence; now breaths of coolness came through those gently clattering slats and lulled us to sleep under our re-appropriated blankets.

On excursion days we made an early start in the morning. The preparations took an hour or so, simple as they were. Mother rose early and superintended lunch-baskets. Harnesses were inspected: traces must be strong and springs reliable for a mountain-climb. Big shawls to sit on, staffs, binoculars, tin botanical cases, drinking-cups, were packed under the seats of the wagons. It was a Huntington custom to take books along on excursions. I remember a certain drive when one of our guests—a young man—took Hamerton's *Intellectual Life*; another had the first volume of Ebers' *Uarda*; a younger girl Kingsley's *Westward Ho,* our older sister *Sordello*; still another *John Halifax, Gentleman.* Shakespeare was occasionally produced out of somebody's pocket as a favorite book of poetry for two friends to enjoy together on a rock after lunch.

The heads of the house led in the little phaeton, while the other two vehicles were loaded with a more youthful freight. If we were travelling westward we turned left down a sandy lane after crossing the little bridge into North Hadley and came to a wire ferry which carried passengers across the Connecticut. That ferry, long since abandoned, was one of the most picturesque things in the valley. The ferryman seemed by some perversity of fate to be always on the opposite bank of the river when wanted, but there was the fun of blowing a long tin horn, tied to a post, to attract his attention, and we could see him, a small figure in perspective, come down the steep little approach and climb into the boat, pushing it off with a large flat oar and taking up a curious affair like a currycomb with which he gripped the wire and pulled long strokes which sent his craft along toward our side, out of the deep channel and over into the shallower river-bed. Often there would be a team standing on the flat, long flooring with low sides and hinged ends that were held in the horizontal by chains and let down for vehicles to drive on and off. The ferryman always had a greeting for us as he pulled in; for many years it was an old Canadian Frenchman, who knew each child and its history somehow and kept track of family changes. Careful driving was necessary to get the wagons all on to the boat properly. Some of our horses never became entirely reconciled to ferrying and tried to back us off into the water; big blocks of wood were put behind the wheels and Father stood by their heads, patting them and saying slowly, "Whe-e-y Major, whe-e-ey, Maggie—gently, gently, now Jamie, George, hold them in when the boat stops!"—for at that moment they were ready to make a spring which would have interlocked wheels hopelessly. Father would drive off first, then the next restive horse was curbed firmly by his driver—the ferryman officiously assisting now and then—and at the signal, "All right, let go!" would bound forward, up the bank, the third wagon following.

Now came the gradual, uphill drive for many miles. We missed none of the exquisite details; the intense blue overhead and the fleecey little clouds—*Schäfchen*—as the Germans call them—floating so low and close and casting shadows which changed from moment to moment the tints of brown pasturelands; a gray farmhouse on a rocky ledge under a pair of huge maples, with a row of crimson hollyhocks set off by its weather-beaten clapboards; a shaggy colt peering over a stone wall, or a half-dozen wild steers tossing their horns inimically out of a clump of sweet-fern and laurel among the rocks. Sometimes we drove for miles with the branches meeting over our heads and great brakes and maidenhair by the roadsides, brightened by clumps of jewel-weed; now and again when we came to a stony climb the boys walked to save the horses, who were, however, sturdy little beasts and used to scrambling up steep pitches. When we came to a clearing, a superb view of the mountains was disclosed, and we would hear the cry, "Monadnock." No view could ever be quite supreme to us children without this mountain in it.

The choice of a noonday resting-place was our great concern on a mountain-trip. We must satisfy a mighty hunger, give the horses rest, and ourselves a chance to read or nap. Sometimes we camped by one of the streams which accompanies almost every New England hill-road, with its cold pools for chilling watermelons or making pats of butter hard and firm while the coffee boils. Or again it would be on a clean brown hillside with flannelly mulleins, pale yellow and gray-green, among the boulders, and miles on miles of hill-country spread before us. Royal mountains towered on the horizon. The horses would be taken to a near-by farmhouse, or fed with provender brought from home in the wagons. Then sometimes our father invited us to dine at a country hotel, an invitation which we found extremely jolly, taking possession of a rural hostelry for the time being and admiring the curious old prints on the wall of its little parlor. Usually we enjoyed a dinner of savory chicken, pies of many varieties which the waitresses enumerated glibly for our choice, five kinds at a time, and fresh brown bread which everybody thought would be nice to make at home but for which the recipe could never be obtained. Now and then we surprised a landlord, who then gave us just what his immediate resources could offer, a grand platter of "ham'n eggs."

Once we had a horrible disappointment, when, having counted on dining at a particular inn and regaling ourselves on its far-famed blueberry pie, we found the inn had been burned down during the winter. I well remember our gloom as we investigated the village store, finding only moist crackers and stale cookies, with root beer to wash them down. What were they to a starving multitude after a thirty mile drive? But a scouting party discovered two old ladies in a charming house who agreed to have a hearty meal ready in forty minutes and invited us to make ourselves at home in their large living-room. We sank into comfortable seats and got out our book-companions. Such a long silence ensued that one of our hostesses left her preparations in the kitchen and came to see what had become of us. When she saw us, she pattered back to her sister, and said, "Well, if they ain't the queerest people! They've all set down and gone to readin'!" She discovered later that we were quite normal when it came to disposing of her delectable cold beef and fresh rolls, huge roast potatoes and pickled apples with cloves stuck into them like pincushions, not to mention a generous triangle of custard pie. We forgot about the blueberries.

After dinner and rest came the descent into the valley, always by a different road from the ascending one. That was fully as interesting as our morning's climb. Down, down through the canopied wood-roads, over steep pitches where the horses must be held firmly and reined in a bit at every "thank-you ma'am"; smooth, shady plateaux where we found rows of tall maples and passed prosperous farm-acres, the farmers' wives gossiping on their broad verandas, the children waving to us as we passed. The mountain stream led the way through winding wood-roads again, coming out on clearings with saw-mill or cider-mill to give us a chance to check the horses, wild in their descent, and pick flowers. We gathered great bunches of fern, cardinal-flowers, later in the season rare fringed gentians which grew in places remembered from former summers.

And then the return at dusk; dropping farther down into the valley and re-crossing our own broad river, with Sugarloaf and Toby and Mount Warner welcoming us back to the level again.

Never was the ferry more lovely than in sunset light, the boat slipping through water with reflections of the hills deep, deep below—pledges of peacefulness and safety. The northerly breeze that was companion to us all day was hushed. Frosty airs freshened us as we drove in under the familiar elms and found doors thrown wide, supper spread and fires of big logs in the chimney-places. The mountain air which we had stored in our bodies once more invaded the house, identifying it with the hills which surrounded it, and its occupants with the secret of happiness.

6

AN ALTAR IN THE HAYMOW

In spite of all the formal expression of religion around me, I felt the need of a personal religion. So I set up an altar of my own— on the topmost haymow of the barn; a refuge to which I fled when it seemed impossible to resist crying. I would run out, hot and hurt after some sharp correction or outburst of temper, and scale the old beam-ladder, digging hands and feet under the haystalks to get a grip on its pegs. I made the ascent as hastily as if there were blood-hounds on my trail, instead of indignant relatives whose anger was undoubtedly justified. I crept across the haystacks which crackled under my feet, until I found a deep hollow of dry, sweet-smelling clover, where I lay back with the relaxed abandon of a young animal. The pent-up sobs would burst forth, shaking me from head to foot, bringing immense relief to an overwrought spirit. After-wards came the bliss of seclusion, there with the cobwebby rafters overhead and the little square window under the ridgepole, letting in a slant of dust-blurred sunshine.

It was so deliciously still; just the odd, thin snappings of the hay-stalks bent by an occasional grasshopper or beetle, or again the cosy chirp of a big, black cricket who had climbed laboriously out of the depths of the big mow, after having been buried since haying-time. And if I raised myself on my elbow and listened intently to the rustling in a farther corner, I might spy a scarlet scrap among the fuzzy ends of timothy or redtop, and see a yellow bill and two beady eyes below the touch of color. An old hen who had come off into solitude also! Perhaps she would get up by and by, cackling if urged, and disclose a whole nestful of dilapidated, unfertile eggs— or nothing at all. "Just settin', the old fool," the farmer would have said. But she never disturbed my sense of possession and privacy. Somehow I got the feeling of being near to a God of my very own, Who understood me and to Whom I was not in the least afraid to talk. I felt Him there on the haymow. Moses' burning bush itself could not more surely have brought the Almighty to a place of worship, the worship which, when all the creeds and theologies and philosophies and sacerdotal systems have had their sway, is offered directly, without intervention, from the soul to its Maker.

The queer petitions that I made were not preceded by any orderly confession, for I had confidence that my requests would be heard and graciously considered. They came spontaneously; that there mightn't be a thunderstorm; or if there had to be, that it wouldn't be near enough to strike anything; that it hadn't been any harm to eat a green apple, even if the seeds weren't wholly black; that the boys shouldn't get drowned going in bathing; that George wouldn't shoot any more squirrels; that I might find my lost hair-ribbon; that I should have a chance to ride horseback tomorrow morning; that I should beat at croquet. This was a frequent prayer, often ejaculated on the ground. "Oh Lord, please let me hit the stake!" would be fervently breathed at the last moment, and as I was not such a bad shot it usually seemed to be answered. I began to feel that perhaps I was taking an unfair advantage of my fellow-players. One day an admiring masculine partner had said to sister Arria as she shot her ball triumphantly across the lawn and hit that of a distant enemy,

"You have an unerring eye, Mademoiselle."
This gave me an idea. How much more dignified and legitimate it would be to pray for skill than for immediate victory, and then leave the outcome to chance! So after that I carried to my orisons in the haymow the fervent request, "Oh God, give me an unerring eye."

Gradually the process of refining my manner of address made these devotions more reverent. I got the idea that to add "if it be Thy will" was to make one's case more deserving of consideration. I even added the improved, "Thy holy, heavenly will." Now and then if they were ill or in need, I made intercessions for family or

friends. Like church-members, armies and governments, I prayed
first and foremost for my own particular wants.

I sometimes planned to stay on in the haymow till the family
was moved to search for me and I relished it when someone called
out my name from the barn floor or the yard. I held myself tense
and still, and never moved till I heard the footsteps die away. No
one should suspect that safe place of refuge. But toward supper-
time it began to seem advisable to return to civilization. And I
must make my exit before the milkers came into the barn. That
meant waiting for a propitious moment, then sliding down into a
heap of soft hay and slipping out through the back door behind
the horses. I always returned to the family circle with a rein-
forcement of good resolutions and with that sense of superiority to
the rest of mankind which follows an experience of special religious privilege. If a person carried out his good impulses he was
bound to be better than the people who had not had any. So I
moved about for the evening with my soul on a high plane, keeping
aloof from the crowd and cuddling up to Mother, to whom I felt
nearer when consciously good.

It was not possible, however, for a Bishop's child to live a solitary religious life in the haymow, for there were constant visitors
to remind her of the existence of the church. I remember a visitation from seven bishops, who came to us because father was chairman of a committee appointed to construct a hymnal for use in the
Episcopal church, and the summer season had been selected for
their work. In order to facilitate the undertaking, he conceived the
idea of inviting them all to spend a fortnight at Forty Acres, and
accomplish the task under its elms. Our mother and sister were kept
busy with preparations and the necessity of supplementing the
services of the small staff of domestics, represented by Harriet and
the cook. So we children were left more or less to our own devices
each forenoon while the right reverend gentlemen discussed and
weighed the merits of the poems under selection, having already
decided that only those containing a direct address to the Deity
should be classed as hymns and considered suitable as a form of
worship.

It was very pleasant to listen to these discussions from underneath the syringa bush outside the long room, and hear fine verse read aloud by sonorous voices; I enjoyed that kind of eaves-dropping. One morning while we were swinging listlessly on the gate we evolved a plan of driving to North Hadley with old Max to purchase some candy as the basis of a store at which the bishops might be persuaded to be purchasers. It was accomplished, by an expenditure of thirty cents and the arrangement of two barrels and a board in the yard, just before the committee emerged from the meeting for their noon recess. Much amused by the children's venture, the bishops bought at usurious prices, and doubled our original investment in a few moments, to the guilty delight of the principals in the transaction. The portly bishop of Rhode Island, grinning broadly, paced the farmyard with a red-striped peppermint stick held cigar-wise between his lips, while the bishop of Ohio, a lean little person, nibbled a chocolate mouse. They were all in high humor when our parents arrived on the scene in a state of visible mortification. Apologies were received with laughter by the delighted prelates, who interceded in our behalf. The offense had never found its way into any code of behavior, so we could not be logically punished. Father had the discernment not to propose giving the profits to missions, so the matter stood as a humorous interlude of the compilation-committee's meeting. . . . . Not long ago I met a charming gentleman from Rhode Island, who asked, on hearing my name, if I was "the little girl who kept the candy-store for the bishops."

7

VICTORIAN SUNDAY

When the old Hatfield bell tolled for Sunday morning service it took no prodding to get the horses to start the procession of three Huntington carriages toward the gray stone church in Amherst common. Attendance was never urged on anyone, but it was the thing to do, and none of us considered it an imposition. We sang hymns and listened to chapters about the lilies of the field and husbandmen and fruitful vines; sometimes we children watched a spray of woodbine swing across the outside of a stain-glassed window, and thought that it must be lovely outdoors. We read passages in our Prayerbook and made too much noise turning the leaves perhaps, but when Father preached the sermon we listened quite intently until church was over, when there were handshakings and introductions on the steps.

We drove back to Forty Acres for a bountiful cold dinner, after which all of us took long naps, the boys under the trees in the farmyard, where the horses had been turned in to nibble grass as a Sunday treat. At five o'clock there was evensong in the long room, where all of the many guests who stayed with us, joined us and sometimes witnessed a baptism of some country baby whose parents wanted the Bishop to baptise it at Forty Acres. We children helped make a wreath of flowers for the christening bowl, and watched the performance narrowly to see how individual babies took it. Afterwards we all took a walk along the brook, where we found cardinal-flower and the delicate Indian pipe or picked the partridge berries which carpeted the path. From a clearing in the pine woods we could see the northwestern hills outlined against the sunset, and we felt that even the hills and the valley shared our observance of Sunday at Hadley. Through the years we never lost our sense of thankfulness for those days of withdrawal from the pressure of everyday life.

Now and then I had a Sunday of quite a different sort, when Father was asked to go to some distant hill-village and preach to old friends in "orthodox" meetinghouses. He took me with him, a sun-burned child in a clean white frock, my short legs dangling from the seat of an old-fashioned wagon, my white-cotton-gloved fingers ec-statically interlaced, beside a middle-aged clergyman alive to every bit of light or shadow, every birdsong every mountaintop or hillside along that twenty or thirty mile drive. The start was usually made in one of those morning fogs which are a feature of Connecticut Valley weather through August and early September, a season chosen for our drives together. We got up at six and breakfast was solemn, partly because of the enormous delight which was held in suspension, and partly because of the dark and the need to keep quiet in order not to wake the household. There were several miles made in the gray mist, so thick that we could scarcely see the fence-posts. Up to North Hadley, over the plains to Sunderland, talking a good deal because there was nothing to divert our attention. Then maybe, when we crossed Sunderland bridge close to Sugarloaf, about the time when the family would be getting up at home, we could see a little patch of sandstone with a crimson tinge. It was a deep, smouldering red in that light, coming from a sun-ray in the east which had penetrated the fog and disclosed the mountaintop. *Day*; that was the signal. And then the cloud lifted, parted, floated away down the straight line of the river and when we turned into the up-hill road leading westward we began to see farmhouses and barns, and cows going out to pasture, then the tops of the encircling hills against a clear sky.

"The mountains shall bring peace," Father would say, "and the little hills righteousness to the people." Somehow his rhythmic way of repeating Bible texts never jarred upon his companions; it fitted in quite perfectly with the state of mind to which the glories of nature brought one. He was so entirely human a being himself and so at one with the processes of life that it seemed quite fitting to have him use the words of men who had, like him, recognized and lived by the same kind of inspiration. It sounded entirely different, too, on New England byways; unlike church and the emanations from chancels and surplices and Prayer-books with embroidered bookmarks. I privately thought it much more the real thing, but it wouldn't have occurred to me to say so. When he repeated passages from Job or Moses or Isaiah, religious ladies would murmur an assent and say, "How wonderfully he quotes the Scriptures!" But I know that he did it better still when those bits of the Psalms burst forth on a mountain ride and expressed a gladness like that which the seers of centuries past had felt.

The horse worked his way slowly upward, tacking from side to side, and stopping for breath on the "thank you ma'ams." And then after a four hours' ride our road would open unexpectedly into a village street, decorous in Sunday inaction. We drew up in front of a white parsonage near the meetinghouse. The pastor and his wife would come out to meet us and say how glad they were that the preacher had brought his little girl. When I went into the pew belonging to the minister's wife and when she covered her eyes with her hand, sitting upright, I felt I ought to kneel down to show that I was an Episcopalian. Harriet had given me the suggestion. It was much easier to do, too, and less conspicuous in the big pew, so I got down on the carpet and said the Lord's Prayer to myself as being something familiar to everybody and fitting in well.

The hymns were mostly long-metre and sung out of oblong green singing-books in which the four voices were printed in single notes on separate lines. *Antioch* was a well-known tune. There was seldom an organ in those days, so one heard the clang of a tuning-fork and then a subdued, nasal *m-m-m-m-m-* on different notes as the choir-leader felt for his pitch. Then they burst out, securely, on the familiar high note and descending major scale, in good old musical form, back again to the triumphant tonic:

> *Joy to the world! the Lord is come,*
> *Let earth receive her King. . . . .*

I joined heartily in this chant of praise and nodded my head as others did, swaying gently, in time to the beats. Enthusiasm lifted the flat soles of my "ankle-ties" off the ground with toes firm, bearing me upward in accompaniment to the chorus. The short blue ribbon streamers on the back of my straw hat flapped to emphasizing nods. I joined in as fervently as if the hymn were sung by the cross-bearing processional choir in the Church of the Advent in Boston. Nothing beautiful in the line of accessories to worship except one vase of many-colored garden flowers; no genuflexions but those dignified, time-marking nods. And yet their God—the God loved by simple New England folk; by pious, shrewd old deacons, by sober women who had lived on lonely hill-farms and worked in the fields, by open-faced young men and girls whose lives would be more eventful than those of their forerunners—*that* God was immanent and real. In my childhood I made no comparisons but took every variety of worship for granted. Later on it was explained to me that vestments and bending knees, candles and incense, typified the heavenly obeisance to the God of cherubim and seraphim and the saints who rest not day and night singing *Holy, Holy, Holy*. I understood by the aid of my imagination and paid homage accordingly. But when I was caught up and transported to the village meeting-house on the hills and nodded and swayed to the tune of *Antioch,* my heart leaped in firm conviction to that Lord: the God of the gentians and the asters, the sunlight above the fogs of earth, the square pew and the tuning-fork.

When there was an extempore prayer, Father was sometimes asked to give it. He made beautiful ones, as long as anybody else's, even if he was a 'piscopalian and accustomed to liturgies. The petitions covered a great deal of ground and all the avenues of Grace. By that time I did not feel any more need of impressing my apostolic upbringing on the minister's wife, so I sat up beside her to look at him as he prayed.

The sermon which followed was listened to intently by the country audience, because they were inured to long discourses. The minister's wife left promptly to attend to the dinner to which we had been invited. Once in a while, when Father had come a great many miles to preach, the people gave him a collation at the parsonage. That was nice; cold hams and jellied meats, spiced cake and sponge cake, pies, preserves, pickles of every variety. It was the largess of rural storerooms and pantries, donated no doubt to symbolize loaves and fishes.

Many of those little New England villages to which we went were miniature seats of culture, with good libraries; one found *The Atlantic* and *Harper's* and *The North American Review* on the tables in their big living rooms with shining floors and braided rugs. The people who gathered there spoke the language of informed minds. I heard phrases to which I was accustomed, even if they were beyond my comprehension.

Father, the responsibility of his sermon over, talked freely to me as the horse took us easily from the hills from the high moments in the uplands we came back to the quiet and content of daily living at Forty Acres."

8

EXPERIMENTS IN EDUCATION

Our interest in colleges had centred largely about the Harvard traditions of the family. Grandparents and great-grandparents, uncles and great-uncles, cousins, our brothers and father, had been students or professors there, and we had the sense of proprietorship to which many New Englanders still confess. But a new horizon was opening, and in the neighborhood of Forty Acres itself. For several years people had talked about the will of Sophia Smith, and we had known that the old bridge of which only the pile of boulders in mid-river was left, had crossed directly from the Phelps acres to her father's lands in Hatfield. The white spire of the meetinghouse, beyond which lay the western hills, was a reminder of her Sunday church-observances. Uncle Phelps, the father of the queer sons and builder of the gray house, had drawn up the famous Oliver Smith will, a charity-foundation bequest made by Sophia's uncle. The two men had been neighbors, and crossed the bridge to visit one another. Sophia had longed for an education and left her fortune to make that possible to other girls by the founding of a college.

In that summer of 1875, its first building was being put up, and the architect, Robert Peabody of Boston, was a good friend of our family, having married my older sister's friend and next-door neighbor of Boylston Street days. Mr. Peabody, a tall man with a great charm for young people, stayed at Forty Acres with us while supervising building-operations. There was much interesting debate on the subject of women's colleges. President Seelye and the Bishop were also friends, and I think some of my father's antipathy to the college idea was dissipated that summer.

Robert Peabody was anxious to hear more of the prospects and plans for Smith College courses, and our evenings were much enlivened by discussions as to the need for the higher education of women. As all the older women of our family had pursued advanced courses of study themselves, it was hard for them to understand that there could be any possible opposition to that; but by conservatives it was apparently regarded as the right of the privileged only. The danger of allowing women of the middle and lower classes—and even in our time those social designations were considered arbitrary by the more democratic element—to be taught the classics or advanced science and economics, not to mention civil government, was pointed out by a large conservative element. What it might lead to was prophesied grimly, but the beauty of College Hall and the Smith campus won over the inhabitants of the town at least.

We were keenly alive to all the questionings. We had ourselves great curiosity regarding the new college. The conception of Tennyson's *Princess* was the basis of our imagination when we pictured it all, as the green lawns would look, with beautiful dignified women moving about beneath the spreading elms, followed by young disciples in graceful gowns and mortar-boards. It was an intriguing vision. All that women, as queens and saints and writers, had contributed to the world, entered into its prophetic spirit.

There was, however, little discussion of public affairs at Forty Acres. The adults made comments on the daily news as it came in by post, but it seems to me we were on the whole strangely indifferent. Happenings in our own country, barring outright disaster, did not touch us much in summer time. Contemporary English history made a greater appeal than that of America, during those particular summers of the seventies. Trollope was somewhat responsible for this. We lived in his England for weeks at a time, through our forenoon gatherings at the East door, and in the political novels of other writers which could be discussed and compared very much as long letters from abroad would have been. Not only Trollope's clerical sketches but the parliamentary ones, each as it was published, made their characters and backgrounds extremely vivid, and my father's informal, colloquial fashion of reading aloud, pausing here and there to enjoy some especially amusing bit, kept our minds occupied with affairs across the sea.

The *Springfield Republican* supplied the best of material about our own county, and its editor, Samuel Bowles, was a friend of our family; but girls did not read the daily journals regularly then, unless some very special happenings attracted them. It was looked upon as worse than bad taste to read accounts of crime, unless some prominent trial had stirred general sympathy. We "took in" *The Guardian* and one or two other British periodicals, and my sister and brother kept track of parliamentary developments. They all held with Cobden and Bright and the Free Trade principle and admired the great minds of Queen Victoria's court. Gladstone and Bismarck each in his own field, were revered as statesmen with whom America's political scramblers were not to be mentioned in the same breath. The summer of the Franco-Prussian war had been intensely interesting to them, and I recollect that even as a small girl I had caught echoes of that and knew the names of the Generals on both sides, and had felt the horrors of the siege of Strasbourg.

Somehow I think, as I look back, that in Hadley we have always had a more instinctive international *sympathy* than in the city; it may be that the closer one gets to elemental processes and beauties, the more deeply one realizes the eternal oneness which brings us under the law that governs them both: an inescapable and universal dependence. Be that as it may, our world had broadened in the early seventies, for 1875 was the year of the Women's Congress at Syracuse, and the still more marked mental and social expansion spurred by its meetings.

I realized, that summer that I needed occupation. My brother James, who had graduated from college, was in Scotland on a walking tour, and I found that purely bucolic forms of entertainment now seemed a little dull to the friends who visited me or my sisters. I had always longed for the career of a country schoolmarm, and my little sister was not averse to an experiment. A visit to the haunted room in the south wing gave us an idea; it was just the place for our undertaking. An outside staircase led up to it from the pillared woodshed. There was a row of hooks behind the door, and a little platform for a teacher's desk; somebody had left a flat wooden picture-case there. A dormer window let in the morning sun. At one side was a sort of alcove, where an old washbench could be set to accommodate Molly's classes; she was to be the assistant.

We had ambitious plans. The idea was to make every course so interesting that the children would not know they were studying. Having no text-books, we invented various expedients. For one thing, reading was to be taught through learning by vote; we were to begin with poetry and teach each child a different poem, making her read it and then memorize it and finally write it out. No pains were to be spared to give each individual the kind of verse which most attracted him or her. We also fitted out a low table for writing-lessons and worked up a grand system of penmanship intended to supersede the tiresome copy-books of the moment, with their endless pothooks and slants and loops. We made copies in our own not too elegant round hand, on sermon-paper, and presented these to our eager pupils, who worked away at them with tongues out and long indrawings of breath. They were left free to hold their pencils as they chose, I recall; results were the important thing. Apparently we were really ahead of our time in some of these academic methods, to judge from the similar latitude allowed our grandchildren today.

There were nine or ten youngsters, four boys and five or six girls. They came rambling along the road, a picturesque group, every bright morning. When it rained, we harnessed up a farm-horse to the big carryall and fetched them, crowding them in impossibly. We thought their minds remarkable, and taught them poetry and elocution after our own taste, which was flexible enough to meet theirs; not to mention mathematics, undertaken, I believe, on a system of guesswork!

My creative urge during this period was boundless. Ideas came to me and clamored for expression. I longed to write. I brought out my great-grandmother's journal and pored over the bundle of yellowed sheets written in cramped characters by Betsey Porter when she had been so profoundly stirred by the confession of a young man who had seduced one of the girls in her community.

The parson's discourse on the subject appeared to have been a solemn one, and the opening roused my interest keenly. I wondered what had brought about the girl's lapse from virtue and yearned to know why the word "fornacation," as Betsey spelled it, was applicable to the "malloncoly instance." I knew, or thought I knew, more about fornication than my great-grandmother. My sister's work in Syracuse had brought many such offenders to the fore, but the details were lacking. Elizabeth Porter, too, had been reserved with regard to her own experiences in love. My own chronicle should be a more personal history of my emotions.

It was intriguing to lay out a schedule for the narration of my own life-history. I invented a form in which to clothe it—a series of letters to an imaginary friend, who would become a real personality in this form of "pretend." This ficticious friend was supposed to be a girl older and more staid than the chronicler, living in a retired village and with no excitements except those that came to her through the mails. She should be a person of infinite good sense and conscientious habit, something of a mentor but rarely severe. Her name, decided upon in a whimsical mood, was Turnip, expressing the homely virtues by which she was known. To this innocuous personality a series of epistles, always phrased as answers to communications from her, were to be written. For some time I firmly believed them to be true pictures of my life and actual self. They usually presupposed a lecture or censure in a mild form of some behavior which needed defense or apology. A large part of their content had to do with affairs of the heart; not of my own heart apparently, but the reactions of that organ and my brain to the influence of sundry admirers whose secret passion was mostly a figment of the imagination! It was all very good exercise in composition, written mostly in the style of the late eighteenth-century novel.

9

YEAR BY YEAR

One annual experience always brought a special touch of romance into the last days of summer. The old elm at the farm and the great tulip tree at the Phelps Place have been for a century past, guest-houses for the birds on their way south. We are on some heavenly aerial route which they take unfailingly in September, and have never watched in vain for the visits they made us. They arrive in late afternoon, making the halt in time for settling in and getting an hour's recreation before bedtime. There is a soft whirr, a scattering black cloud which descends in winged precision from the heights, and in an instant the huge tree is alive with twittering, chattering little figures. For all the world like a party of human tourists, they make a grand to-do over the occupation of their quarters, picking out comfortable apartments, no doubt with an eye to the view and the eligibility of certain places for trips to the farmyard which is their principal restaurant. Sometimes the crowd is so great than annexes have to be opened in neighboring maples. A delicious clamor fills the air, with no attempt at bringing order out of chaos. After disposing of their invisible baggage, parties go out for supper and one sees small flocks of them visiting the granaries or even flying as far as the cow-pasture, dipping their thirsty bills in the horse-trough and splashing in the pools left from recent rains. We often tried unsuccessfully to count them, and always took account of their species, which was usually the same, the bobolinks of June going away to turn themselves into rice-birds in the swamps of Florida. We wondered if any of them crossed the Caribbean, and loved to imagine their several destinations.

They came back from little trips to see the town, and went to bed with the punctuality of chimney-swifts. By dark the great tree was silent, and all night one had the consciousness of tiny feathered things cuddled among the leaves. In the morning they wakened with more joyous twittering. There was a half-hour granted for excursions out to breakfast and plenty of time to collect phantom belongings and dicker with an imaginary landlord. Finally after a quiet moment, there was a simultaneous upward flight. A dark wing-shaped cloud soared, a shadow swept across the dewy grass, then in magnificent flight the company sped southward, leaving us clumsy humans with feet clinging to earth, and spirits, we may believe, crying out in the poet's own ecstasy of longing to follow,

Des ailes! Des ailes! Des ailes!

It was always a disappointment that just as the autumn beauty of the Connecticut Valley was coming to its height, we should be obliged to return to city life.

There had been two Octobers, however, when I stayed at Forty Acres, and of these I must speak. The first was in the summer of 1870, when I had been taken ill with an intestinal disease, and was unable to return with my family to Syracuse. My mother and George stayed with me, and weak as I was, I enjoyed the cold, clear days, and the fall nights when the stars blazed in unearthly splendor, and the mornings when a thin frosty fog covered the valley. George would bring in big logs for the fireplace, and Dr. Bonney would make his daily call, chatting with us for nearly an hour.

The old doctor believed that my disordered digestion could be cured by keeping nourishment at a minimum, so that I lived on a few tablespoons of milk a day, and a beverage called "crust-coffee," made by soaking pieces of toast in hot water and draining them off. On such scanty rations I was sustained until I thought of nothing but eating, and could be diverted only by reading about it. *Little Dorrit* contained a good many allusions to English relishes and I went over them each day with comfort, from Monsieur Rigaud's veal in savoury jelly, and the little white loaves to the three "kidney ones" with hot gravy poured out of a tin spout for Flora and Mr. F's aunt to consume at the pastry-cook's. I begged bright ribbon-ends from the family piece-bag and put them in between the pages to mark those filling descriptions. When hunger became unbearable I would go and dine with the Casbys on soup, fried soles, a butter-boat of shrimp sauce and some potatoes. Toward supper-time the ham and bread and butter which Young John brought in a cabbage leaf to the imprisoned Arthur would seem a royal banquet to my famished imagination. Even the piece of toast—anchovy toast sounded so mysteriously toothsome—which Mr. F's aunt handed to Arthur, saying, "None of your eyes on me! Take that!" was more satisfying in fancy than crust coffee in the concrete.

My mother finally decided that these Barmecide feasts were making me actually morbid and told the doctor that she felt I could not gain strength without tangible nourishment. So he permitted the hazardous experiment of letting me have a little bird for my dinner. George, who knew just where to find the right sort, went off into the woods with his gun, shot a tiny creature and plucked and dressed it, bringing it up to me himself on a piece of thin buttered toast which was Mother's risk and tasted as if it had been imported from an English fireside. I devoured it with the avidity of a cat eating a mouse, crunching its diminutive bones. That was the beginning of better things. I began to gain and was even pre-sented with a mould of jellied rice made in a wine-glass by the doc-tor's own housekeeper, on which he allowed a few drops of maple syrup. Every morning thereafter my brother went off with his gun, and I learned to tolerate that instrument, listening for the distant shots which assured me my bird. There were lovely partridges scud-ding about in the woods, and now and then golden pheasants would come down near the house and trail their beautiful tail-feathers among the dead leaves. But we could not let them be shot. Finally I was moved into a big chair by the east window in the autumn sun-shine, watching the post-wagon drive the school children to Hadley Academy. One fine day I was wrapped up to take a little drive, and soon, but not too soon for us to finish *Little Dorrit,* we left the old house to return to the city.

Some years passed before we had a second October holiday in the Connecticut Valley, but it was one of the happiest experiences of our older girhood. We drove around the woodroads, gorgeous in all the richness of color that New England air can produce—crimson maples, yellow elms, dark backgrounds of firs, white birch-trunks from which bronze leaves hung and trembled. We climbed up hill, singing as we went, and crowded our swaying wagon with branches of brilliant leaves. There was a pile of orange pumpkins against the gray wall of an old farmhouse, an apple-orchard with heaps of red fruit on its green carpet, a red school-house guarded by two straight, spreading maples, and children smiling from its windows as we drove by. On rainy days we sat by a great fire in the Long Room, and read aloud *Evelina* from a fat little leather volume, reflecting that there were many young women like the feckless heroine.

In the afternoons, undaunted by a tramp over the high hill, a group of Amherst students came to climb with us to the old quarry, where we found polished chestnuts to roast by the evening fire. They were splendid fellows, every one of whom made his mark in the professional and literary world; Howard Bliss, and Lawrence Abbott were two of them.

There was one delightful day in Amherst, when our two groups met at the Dickinson house. Austin Dickinson was then Treasurer of the college, and his son Ned, a boy of our own age, was living, while his sister Martha, later their Aunt Emily's biographer, was then a schoolgirl. Mrs. Dickinson had the same happy faculty as a hostess that had characterized the entertainers in the family for years; a way of drawing out each guest, making him feel himself not only at home in her house but a contributor to the general enjoyment. One might go with one's sole talent in the shape of a well-worn anecdote or joke wrapped as it were in a napkin of oblivion; but it would be called for and somehow the owner would find himself bringing out in quite fresh form to a sympathetic audience the feeblest wit. The rare test of that sense of humor which can appreciate a joke on one's self, was also applied at times, and even sensitive people measured goodnaturedly up to it.

We heard many stories of Aunt Emily and Aunt Lavinia, who were then old ladies living in the mansion next door. Their niece and nephew enjoyed them both; Lavinia was spicy and entertaining in everyday fashion; Emily, all unconscious of her coming fame, recluse and mystic, still piling up her wondrous undiscovered harvest of poetry, was the rarer spirit. Of both figures, under the great trees which shaded the common ground of an uncommon family, we had occasional views. Miss Lavinia came to the farm during our summer stays, driving in her little carriage, for all the world like a figure in one of Thackeray's original illustrations; pendant curls, lace shawl falling from her shoulder-blades by some remarkable arrangement with the force of gravitation which balanced it impossibly and kept its place only through the poise of the old-time "lady of leisure"; those of us who knew that genus knew that the term did not imply wasted hours nor limited capability. Ladies of leisure invariably took time to draw on their gloves with that meticulous fitting of each separate finger which brought about perfect smoothness—no flap at the tip—and to tie the bonnet-strings without the suggestion of a knot—loops broad, ends unwrinkled. Emily's white gowns gave her distinction as one dedicated to the spiritual and immortal, but never the air of perpetual mourning; her youthful romance was garlanded with asphodel, not buried under a weeping willow. Ned, an invalid, shut in sometimes for weeks, had something of his Aunt Emily's imaginative intellect, along with the blunt, but kindly critical faculty of his father. Martha, mature beyond her years, was companionable to old and young, and extremely amusing to her aunts.

Final days of that October were mournful. Even the animals sensed it; the great Leonberg would steal off when the hour of departure came, and hide till the carriages had driven away. It was a sad moment when the wagons full of people and trunks stood at the horseblock, while someone, left behind to fasten the great south door, slid the bar of oak, smooth as a paper-knife from long use, in between the irons of its latch.

We said always, "Next summer we shall come back again." We go on saying it, year by year, knowing that, like the chimney swallows we may be called to take our turn and go fearlessly down into the dark. The hills and the sunsets, the meadows and the river, will stay on with their eternal welcome.

End of Childhood

1

The many summers at Forty Acres had made a peaceful pattern of life for childhood and adolescence. The place teems with vital associations, with history and character; an inheritance which every descendant feels when he crosses the threshold of the old house. We absorbed it unconsciously in our early days, and carried it with us into the busier life to which growing experience brought us. One by one, the older and then the younger, met the claims of an impatient world, and broke in upon the summer stillness by temporary flittings.

A departure from custom came to me in my sixteenth year, when a depleted nervous system had called for change of air and sea-bathing. "Salt and tan," prescribed Dr. Van Duyn. After much deliberation my family decided that I should be sent to Hingham, the home of our Lincoln ancestors, and live at a pleasant boarding-house where my young married cousin Clara Bryant could act as my chaperon. To go away quite by myself was a thrilling prospect. Although I had visited friends in Central New York, the Hadley life had been my only background in the summer. I wondered whether the people at the boarding-house would think me too much of a westerner to fit in well, or guess that I was only sixteen. My mother and older sister took an active share in preparations. A suitable wardrobe was provided. Skirts were let down to young-lady length, close to the floor. I was tall and large for my age, and must live up to my proportions. I had fresh white lawns for mornings, and what now would be called a "sport dress" of creamy flannel, tight-fitting. Flummery had been prevalent in the middle of the century; hoop-skirts, for instance; but these were out now and bustles had not yet come in, so the human form was left more to it-self than the mantua-makers were wont to allow. Hats were not striking either; my best one was a turban of white chip that perched with a forward slant on the top of my head, with long black velvet streamers which curled unmanageably at the ends and had to be cut off gradually. These clothes and more were packed in a brand new trunk, which made me feel especially responsible.

The journey to Hingham was broken by a visit to Cedar Square, where my two uncles, James and Epes Sargent, made it particularly pleasant. Uncle Epes was at that time greatly interested in spirit-ualistic manifestations, and was going to many *seances,* of which he had surprising tales to relate. He was fond of his nieces, and an in-vitation to dine with him and our aunt brought out various disclo-sures of magic achievements, beside his collection of written com-munications from departed friends. These were not especially thrilling, however. Either through the fault of the medium, or perhaps his or her inferiority as a transmitter, they were expressed in extremely poor English, totally unlike the style of those bright and particular spirits who were supposed to have sent them back to earth. My uncle had entertained the famous Madame Blavatsky at his house during her visit to this country, however, and she had per-formed a few miraculous feats and captivated a good many people. Exclusive Boston groups were given over to the entertainment of titled orientals and studies in occultism, so the lady had been warmly received and though a little strange and wild, according to accounts, was a magnetic personality. Uncle Epes had written sev-eral books on esoterics and theosophy, as well as an essay entitled *Planchette; The Despair of Science.* Planchette, the forerunner of the Ouija-board, had been a pastime at Forty Acres, so I became fas-cinated with these works for the moment, perusing them in Grand-mother's cool, dark, drawing-room.

The place had a decided atmosphere, made slightly foreign by its touches of European art and treasures from the far East. I loved to be alone there with the old square piano whose yellow keys and thin strings sent out sounds like a harpsichord and suited certain stately bits of Handel, Gluck and the old Italians, which Grandmother Sargent loved and listened to from her sewing-chair. One day I got a bawdy old English novel from the library shelves, probably *Tom Jones*. The Fielding and Smollett type of fiction had not appeared among our virtuous volumes at Forty Acres. I recollect that I was absorbed by the novelty of it and felt quite superior and emancipated, not to say surprised at being able to assimilate that particular variety of realistic literature. It was with just a shade of disappointment that I found my grandmother did not consider it pernicious for youth, as I had thought she might. I remember her remarking that it was an excellent picture of certain phases of English life at that time, and that gentlemen were accustomed to curse quite frankly in her own youthful days, even in the presence of ladies, and make jokes which savored of the stables.

"It was the fashion of some young men to be *horsey*, you know," she explained; "In England there was a great deal of that." I was beginning to realize that in spite of the freedom of our Syracuse life and pursuits, I had enjoyed a "sheltered" youth, and that now I was called upon to contemplate the follies of the past and present world without being shocked. I longed to try out for myself the code which prevailed in my immediate social circle, and I found my Grandmother Sargent, the product of an earlier and simpler culture, very keen and understanding.

"What are known as advantages," she said, "include travel and a knowledge of the world through meeting many people. Your father and mother will want you to have them so far as they can afford it. For my own part, I hope it will give you a broader outlook and teach you to understand people who have been brought up differently from yourself. But you are not hide-bound as it is, and not prim, I hope. That would be a pity."

Prim!—no. Almost better be ordinary than that. "But do you think I shall get along all right, Grandma? You know in Syracuse we *do* meet all kinds of people. There's much more freedom there; I'll probably show it."

"I don't know why you shouldn't," said Mary Lincoln. "Enjoy yourself as much as you can. And be sure to go to the old Lincoln house. Your great-great-grandfather was a brave soldier and, more than that, a statesman." With this and still more advice as ballast, I parted next day from my grandmother and from Cedar Square.

It was exciting to embark, in charge of my uncle, on the *Rose Standish,* an old steamer which plied for many years between Boston and Nantasket. We made the trip on a bright afternoon from the very port whence my grandfather Sargent had set sail again and again. We glided gently into old Hingham Harbor, coming nearer to quaint spires and narrow streets, with low hills beyond and pretty country houses overlooking the bay. Here, in this sedate setting, I felt, destiny and adventure awaited me. My lovely cousin was a part of it. I had never seen her before; she was a Lincoln, a direct descendant of Grandfather General, brought up in the old family mansion there at Hingham. She was a girl not so much older than myself, married at seventeen and already the mother of two babies. Such a sweet, and shrewd, young woman she was, perfectly competent to assume the duties of chaperonage, but with a fund of sympathetic understanding and a sense of humor which helped to make us friends at once. The big white house kept by two typical New England spinsters was as solid and dignified as Hingham itself. My little upper window looked off toward the sea. Nantasket beach was over there, its long, glorious roll of surf breaking upon sands then unmarred by tawdry sheds and advertisements.

The inhabitants of the boarding-house were typical Bostonians; most of them good old stock with familiar names, comfortable couples with young children, who liked to spend their summers out of town where their husbands could go to and from their offices daily. Knowing my family connections, these matrons were very sympathetic about our having to live in Syracuse—such a Western sort of place, they had heard—and thought my manners had borne up well. They had a strict code of behavior for young girls, but I found the question with regard to any particular departure from it was not so much whether it was proper as whether it was Boston. Since I never could look forward to "coming out," the indispensable finish to a young lady's breeding, they apparently thought it less necessary to preserve me for appearance in society by extra limitations, and gave me various unconventional privileges.

One of the matrons' husbands asked me to drive him to the boat every morning in his wife's phaeton, a stunning carriage with a rumble behind. She did not like horses, and was quite amenable to this arrangement, so I had all the joys of the gay scene at the pier. At that time I was somebody else; not the erstwhile tomboy, but a young lady in a crisp white gown, with a beautiful black horse following every lead of the white webbing reins in my hand, and a whip so long and tapering that one could almost have threaded a needle with its silken tip. I had in a week's time become absolutely at home with these luxuries—things never even dreamed of on a New England farm.

I found myself tossing repartee like the other young women, waving a jaunty farewell as the men lifted their hats from the deck of the *Rose Standish,* sniffing the refined cigar-smoke which lingered in the air, and feeling easy, with a coming sense of power, as I drove back to the feminine group at the boarding-house.

In the weeks that passed, I amused myself by taking the boarding-house children to the beach in the pretty rig which was mine for six weeks, or driving my new friends along the Jerusalem Road to Cohasset. When cold fog dropped upon us, we sat at home and read aloud Trevelyan's *Life of Lord Macaulay,* which had just been published. On many afternoons I rode with my married cousins and John A. Mitchell, who was later editor of *Life,* behind a distinguished looking animal who had a trick of stopping to stretch his long neck, with legs braced, refusing to move. Mr. Mitchell would get out to argue with him solemnly until logic took effect, and we would finish the drive, helpless with laughter at Mr. Mitchell's verbal handling of the horse. The four of us made an intimate quartet.

During the conversations with my cousin Clara, while she was caring for her babies in the nursery, I found that I could ask questions that had long seethed in my mind. She answered them so cannily that mysteries turned into commonplaces, and the long-feared serpent of Adamic legend became harmless as a dove. As we grew more confidential I ventured to ask the thing that was most personal.

"Would you be willing to tell me just exactly the truth about something?" I ventured. "Can one be pretty, really beautiful, you know, without knowing it? I want so awfully to be beautiful; I've wanted it ever since I was a little child, and sometimes I've hoped that maybe I didn't look to other people as I did to myself in the glass. Am I pretty, or is there any way to make myself so? Enough so that men would fall in love with me?"

She hesitated, smiling with a little embarrassment. "I think you're going to make a fine-looking woman when you grow up, my dear. As to the men, you have a perfectly good knack with them; you'll get on with them all right."

"But that's not it," I persisted. "You've made me brush my hair back and coil it behind, because you say it's more becoming; does that mean that it is one way of being pretty?"

"Now I'll tell you," the wise person continued. "You need not expect compliments. Now and then you will get one; everybody does. Someone will tell you you have nice eyes, another person that they like your smile; another that your complexion is clear; another that you look best in brown or blue or some other color. That is all the average person can reasonably expect. If people like you they like to look at you. Don't try to be attractive and don't worry about the looking-glass except to get your hair or your collar straight. You're going to have a good time because you like all sorts of people; that's the secret of getting on with them. One doesn't *have* to be beautiful." That was all that came of my probing.

It was hard to part with them all when the end of that visit came. The train journey was a jumble of images which passed and re-passed before me all day long. My thoughts were incoherent, but I lived over again, to the rhythm of the rolling train-wheels, every hour of the six weeks. The simple life at the farm was a bleak prospect; nothing ahead, no coming drives or dances or strolls along the beach, no plunges into the surf, no companions to draw out one's best points.

The train slowed down, stopped. There in the dark in the queer little open carriage, my father sat waiting for me, wondering to himself if his child had returned to him unaltered. I forgot everyone else as I climbed happily in beside him, knowing instinctively what would appeal to him most in my outpourings of experience. The meetings with his earlier friends, the Old Ship church, the Lincoln house and letters from Washington to Grandfather General, the rocks at Cohasset and the thunder of the waters at Nantasket; these were the things we talked about during our drive across the Hadley meadows.

2

A MARK AND A MEANING

It was a more sophisticated young woman who came back to
Forty Acres that night. I had grown up during the six weeks. Not
only had I played at being another person and thereby found a
hitherto undiscovered side to my own personality, but I had gained
in power and poise. No doubt my family realized it to some extent,
but they did not make it apparent. They were only politely interested in information about the life in Hingham or the special
events that had made it interesting. Even Molly asked few questions.

My feeling of mental isolation was at first very strong, and probably my relatives tacitly concluded to let me indulge it in peace.
Perhaps they had had similar experiences, and knew the adjustment
that must take place after a separation from the accustomed family
pattern. I felt that I must get away alone and face up squarely with
the situation. A chance came to climb Mount Warner one September afternoon, with the dog for company. It was the high hill east
of the farm, beyond the woods, so I rambled up through clumps
of sweet fern and huckleberry bushes and patches of yellow grass,
to "John's Rock" where I could get a view of the valley and its
encircling hills. There was a cool, even gray sky, neither damp nor
dark; a "brooding day" the Bishop would call it. The river, catch-
ing every point of soft light, was brighter than the sky; a smooth
surface curving and twisting as it passed on and out through the
village lands from which late crops had been gathered, between
Mount Holyoke and Mount Tom to the busy cities beyond.

To eastward the Amherst College buildings stood out sharply
against their background of wooded hills; the old chapel with its

tower and clock, and a cluster of dormitories. The Agricultural College, much younger, had already made its impress on acres of surrounding field and forest through scientific cultivation. Across the valley, to westward, Northampton was just beginning her venture in the higher education of women, and girls from the towns of New Hampshire and Vermont and Massachusetts were at that moment arriving, eager and ready to enter classes at Smith College and find homes in the old houses of the town. Mount Holyoke Seminary was just out of sight behind the southern range.

I leaned back against the rock, looking off. The stillness was profound, save the sharp tap of a carpenter's hammer below. From a pasture on a slope came the dull, continuous tinkle of a cow-bell. The dog sat up beside me, ears alert. He let his forefeet slide down along the slippery grass, and laid his head between them, near enough to be patted. It was calming to be up there again, among the soft browns and olive-greens, gazing at the outlines of the hills, and getting once more a sense of limitless horizons. This was reality; the past weeks away from it were already becoming blurred. . . . . But something was left to be gathered up.

What *could* be done with experience? Surely those weeks at Hingham had been more than just pleasurable. Responsibility, freedom, people—all of these must have left a meaning and a mark on me. What had my cousin meant when she spoke of "liking all sorts of people"? Did that require a flat good nature and a lack of discrimination? It was the person who had well-defined likes and dislikes who was more often considered strong, and that seemed infinitely better than the dead level of acquiescence.

Perhaps, I thought, there might be a way of liking all sorts of people without sharing their views or habits. There might be something in the "fine art of liking people," if done advisedly by finding out the things one had in common with others and letting these point the way. It would be less easy to slip into the habit of liking or disliking if one understood "all sorts of people," and interpreted *their* likes and dislikes.

It was a new idea to the sixteen year old girl who had thought it more elegant to have a few, selected "loved ones"; it was worth-while as a principle, if nothing more.

I moved, and the dog started to his feet. I took one more long look, north, south, east and west, while I breathed the crushed sweet-fern that was in my hand. We climbed down over the slippery rock, through pine thickets to the pasture, below which the Hadley millpond lay. I came upon a group of blind gentians in a hollow; they were the last flowers in the wood.

I went in by the farmyard gate, along with the loitering cows. Harriet was pottering over the supper-table, putting china cups into saucers with gentle clicks; Arria was coming up from the river, the oars over her shoulder. And the mail bag was full of letters.

Just before bedtime the kitchen was shut up, dark and still. The old settle stood there, its seat worn but still strong enough for potential 'Zekels and Huldys. The tavern table stretched along under the windows, and on it a great pan of bread-dough had been set to raise against tomorrow's baking, covered with a warm cloth and sending out a yeasty, nourishing smell. The great skillet hung beside the fireplace by the ring in its three-foot handle. The brass saucer-candlestick stood on the shelf by the wooden clock. In the stove lay a remaining bit of burning wood. I lifted the lid and tucked in two thick blank-books, their covers wedged apart by many dried flowers, programmes and other mementoes. The little flame caught a dry corner, and blazed, sending out a red glow across the room. The *Letters to Turnip* had vanished from sight. Only a little heap of white ashes was left for posterity. The fourth-child-grown-older had begun to put away childish things.

3

Partisanship ran higher and higher after 1876; at every election federal or municipal scandals were revealed, vituperation raged; cautious promises of reform were used as incentives to win the ballots of the better class of voters. President Hayes, succeeding Grant at the White House, had not the hearty support of either party, a fact which actually produced a slightly calming effect upon the country. Silver had gone out and come in again; greenbackers controlled a large popular vote; the question of pensions for veterans was still, ten years after the war, perennially under discussion. And national issues, brought continually before both parties, interfered more or less with a citizen's contemplation of affairs in his home town.

Some of us read of the doings of Arnold Toynbee, the dawn of Socialism, the growth of the trades-unions. In the large cities, beginnings were being made in organization and research. We younger ones read the works and speeches of European statesmen, even when we neglected the daily bulletin. With the avidity of youth for mental stimulation unaccompanied by hard work, we absorbed the idealism of Ruskin, the pungent, restless gloom of Carlyle, the quiet philosophy of our own Emerson; we discussed Browning; we raved over Matthew Arnold's poetry.

We were enthusiastic over each of these writers in turn, taking on new views as young chameleons change their color.

The Hingham visit had succeeded in putting an end to my idea that an exciting love-affair was the aim of life, but in spite of an interest in politics, church work and music, my life in Syracuse during the following years was not devoid of the normal number of acquaintances among young men. Mr. Andrew D. White and his family had gone to Ithaca to live, since he was now President of Cornell University, and his daughter, a merry comrade of our childhood, often invited her friends there.

Those visits to a man's college were very exciting to us. The fun of getting off; the reenforcement of one's wardrobe to meet special requirements; the arrival just in time to dress and whisk off to a dinner or dance; the eager partners; the assumption that one would be popular and gay; the boxes of flowers; the repartée; and the certainty that one's actual social value would be augmented after one's return.

After one of my gayest visits at Cornell, I returned from Ithaca to find that my father was away, and I gave my glowing account to the rest of the family. A few days later Mother handed me a letter that the Bishop had sent on receipt of their report, in which he said,

"From all accounts R's visit in Ithaca was a very gay one. I have no doubt she enjoyed it, but with her weakness for admiration and pleasure, to which such experiences pander, I fear it may not have been a helpful influence."

I was furious. Father had always given sympathetic attention to any account of his children's pleasures, and it was disconcerting to be put in such an unfavorable light. When I suggested that Father liked praise and admiration himself, Mother smiled and said,

"We all do. It's only when people *compete* for admiration that there's any harm done."

"But it spoils everything when it's called a *weakness* to enjoy being liked." My hitherto assertive voice shook with wounded pride.

"Some people have *pet* weaknesses which they enjoy confessing. I don't think your father was seriously disturbed about you. Remember that there's still a little of the Puritan in him. It will take at least one more generation to eradicate it. His mother had much more of it, and you know how Aunt Bethia seems sometimes almost afraid to have a good time."

Like Grandmother Sargent, mother could preserve an *entente* with a person of any age.

In spite of Father's verbal check on my enthusiasm, nothing less than presentation at the Court of St. James could have assumed so great a social importance as an invitation to the Cornell Commencement ball. I spent two months' dress allowance for my ball gown and gloves and fan, and stayed at the home of a charming woman of the world who was interested in the young men and my prospect of a social success.

The ball itself was a blur; I recollect only lights and music and men; men dancing, men fanning, men bringing ice cream; a sheaf of pink roses to be carried on one arm while the other hand held up a train; and the unworthy little triumph of knowing that one of the Syracuse belles who carried all before her at home was not having quite so much attention, or half as attractive a partner, as I.

My hostess assured me the next morning that my partner was not only rich, but clean-cut and clever, and quite wild over me. I looked forward to our dinner engagement at an inn a good many miles from town, chosen because we were likely to be alone there, my partner said, looking directly into my eyes. When we started, I was appalled at the young man's handling of the horse, and once I expostulated, "You really *must* hold him in when you're going down hill, you know; he might stumble and fall down any time." What would Maggie have done under such a lax hand? I wanted desperately to take the reins, but according to buggy-driving etiquette, that would have invited the encircling idle arm of the driver. I was immeasurably relieved to drive up at last in front of the hotel. But where was the easy, confidential attitude of the last twenty-four hours? Instead there were two embarrassed young people, the man puzzled, and the girl mortified at her own obdurate impatience.

When we returned to Ithaca my chaperon extended her arms. "Was it a perfect day, dear?"

"N-no, I'm afraid it wasn't, exactly. We—, you see it was very disappointing. *He can't drive.*"

Disillusionment was complete.

180   SIXTY-ODD

I was now headed for a life of single-blessedness, so far as my attitude toward matrimony was concerned. It seemed to me that the prospect for usefulness in the community was broader on that basis than to devote my strength to the management of a house, not to say a husband and children. While visiting in Utica I had met a girl four years older than myself for whom I had conceived a fervent admiration. She was the daughter of my father's friend, Dr. Watson. We were drawn together first by church interests, I think, but we had in common an appreciation of the possibilities of usefulness to the community, and our comradeship grew into a deep affection. Her passion for social justice was tempered by humor, and her influence was steadying to my less evenly-balanced temperament.

Notwithstanding my absorption in my friendship with Lucy Watson, and my conviction that matrimony was an unimportant aim in life, a closer observation the courting around me, the many subtle expedients for expressing devotion to a lady-love, fascinated me. An interesting example of this intellectual type of wooing was before us in our own household during a winter in the late seventies. We had a particularly attractive young woman, a friend of Arria, staying with us, whose admirers were legion. Two of them were conspicuously in love with her, and their rival approaches amused the younger members of our family. One of them kept ahead in the race; every pursuing ingenious device for prosecuting his suit. He had a glorious bass voice, and sang in concerts as well as parlor musicales; I had the supreme delight of playing his accompaniments at times. When he sang the love-songs of Schubert or Schumann, or old English airs like *Drink to Me Only with Thine Eyes,* he did not need to look at his lady-love in order to let the world know that he was addressing himself to her and her only. In fact, observers felt that even his choice of programmes was influenced more or less by moods of exaltation or despair. No one could have put more convincing expression into the famous aria from the *Elijah,* one of his masterpieces;

It is enough; O Lord, now take away my life
For I am not better than my fathers.

All the humiliation of defeat, of misused inheritance, of weariness and fear, was brought out in this cry of the prophet under the juniper-tree. But sentimental young admirers, watching for developments in the singer's love-affair, were wont to ascribe his dramatic rendering to the result of a rebuff at the hands of his idol. When he sang a popular favorite, *Down the Shadowy Lane She Goes,* winding up in the last verse with

> *Surely every living thing*
> *That has seen, must love her, must love her,*

we watched Jeannie Dows, the most downright and unaffected of beings, for all the masculine adoration bestowed upon her, as she sat apparently unmoved by the tribute.

During her visit at our house we made many observations. We noticed—and felt very proud of our perspicacity—that when other admirers called to take her to the theatre or a dance she came down already wrapped in her evening cloak; but it was hanging over her arm when the particularly favored escort appeared, and he folded it about her with such tenderness that our maiden bosoms fluttered in sympathy. Once, leaving the drawing-room after a call, he lifted a rose (which he had sent her) out of a vase, and touched it lightly to her lips before putting it into his button-hole. Oh, to be the recipient of delicate overtures like that! Implications so exquisite could not be long ignored.

Then there were daily deliveries of notes or offerings; once a sheet of paper with a marvelous illuminated monogram, nine letters entwined in soft colors with touches of gold. He was as facile in the use of brush and pen as of his voice. I wish I could remember the word the cypher represented; it was *devotion, adoration* or some other expression of his sentiments, and his sweetheart took some time to unravel it.

We had also an interest in the rival lover, who was handsomer, but not so keen nor talented. One day he made a long afternoon visit, with the drawing-room doors closed; an interview which we felt was final, especially when we saw him depart with drooping shoulders. Our mother and sister were not at home, else I think we should have been denied the chance of spying from an upper window; and of course no hint of the proceedings reached us. Arria and her friend probably had it out in the midnight hours.

A few days after, the engagement of Jane Dows to Edward Westcott was announced. The successful suitor was the author of *David Harum,* one of the "best sellers" of late nineteenth-century fiction. Their house became the center of a cultural, and preeminently musical, circle, into which I entered in following years.

This example of Victorian courtship was not uncommon, as we know; the facts verify those descriptions which fiction has given us. Stark sex-impulse was not the first consideration either in the man or the method; a gradual approach of the lover occupied his ingenuity and captivated the lady; there was no open public encouragement to hurry matters, save impassioned drama, occasional distinctly "sensual" literature and a measurable amount of heated interpretation. I do not know that wedded bliss was any more certain as the result of this calculated courtship, but I like to think that reaction came somewhat more slowly and that marriages were contracted with a narrower margin of uncertainty and allowance for the fading of attraction.

4

The fifteenth of August, 1879, was a clear bright day after a thunderstorm. Coming home from an early row with Cousin Ellen, the Bishop's fourth child heard voices in the Long Room, and slipped upstairs to doff her boating-dress. Molly heard her and followed.

"Who do you suppose is here?" she asked. "Grace, 'our girl-cousin,' and Fred and Will from the West, and a quiet one from Brooklyn, Cousin Lizzie Sessions' son. He's awfully good-looking but he doesn't say much."

"I don't care about meeting him: he's his sisters' pet. The others are jollier. Give me my brown gingham, Molly, will you? I suppose I'll have to go down."

She set her feet on the stair-treads as firmly as if she had been Elizabeth Huntington going to meet the deacons. Behind the two nice Western boys stood a brown-eyed lad of nineteen. Yes, rather handsome, she said to herself.

"This is our cousin Archie."

"Our cousin once-removed. We're a generation ahead of you," the girl laughed. So this was the boy with a name like an English curate. She had heard it before.

They were all invited to stay to dinner, so in the meantime, the young people went to the croquet-ground. The "unerring eye" was vouchsafed to the fourth child as she sent a ball flying from long range to hit that of her silent cousin, just in time to prevent him from carrying his partner to victory. Down went her square-toed shoe, and a hammer-stroke dispatched the ball into exile.

"You play splendidly," he said; "I choose you for the next

game." And before dinner he had been invited to stay on for a few days at Forty Acres. The Bishop was pleased to learn that his mother, the fifth Elizabeth, who had been a close friend and bridesmaid at the time of his wedding and always a favorite cousin, had sent Archie to see the old family house because of her happy associations with it. That evening he was especially genial with his young kinsman, and told story after story of the old times, with snatches of song and bits of legend.

"They get on wonderfully, don't they?" said Molly.

"Yes, he's really quite nice," admitted her sister.

But the clear day had been a weather-breeder, and next morning the farm was enveloped in rain and mist, shutting us off from the outside world. The western cousins had gone back to Amherst, so there was nothing to do but find entertainment in the house. Exploring the attics was an appropriate pastime, and to this the boy and girl betook themselves, hunting out spinning-wheels and trundle-beds, looking from the window of the prophet's chamber across the rain-drenched meadow, finally squeezing into a tight little niche in the library to look at a black-letter volume of Fox's *Book of Martyrs,* with its grewsome illustrations; it was a rather protracted session and amusing withal. Now and then they wandered off the subject of the martyrs, and discussed mutual likings, one of which was music. The boy had enjoyed fine concerts, and had inherited his mother's lovely voice. The Damrosch and Sessions family were friends, and Theodore Thomas, the great conductor, had been intimate with them. Walter and Frank Damrosch were about our age and were planning to follow their father's profession.

"We can take you to hear some wonderful music if you'll come to visit us," he said. But he said nothing of his own favorite pursuit, and when the girl came downstairs that afternoon, having exchanged the brown gingham for more becoming garments, she found him deep in a rather faded book, of whose title she gained a fleeting glance. Newman's *Grammar of Assent*; most extraordinary reading for a college boy. Was he going to be a minister? Hardly, one would think, and yet she had certainly seen the book in her father's theological library. He had been taken ill at Harvard the winter before, and was now returning, in the class of 1883. He put the book down when she came in.

The next day was Sunday, and the rain had not abated. Just how the day was spent, I cannot remember, but in the evening the two walked over to make a call on Cousin Ellen at the Phelps house. The walk comes clearly to mind, for on the way along the muddy road, the girl's foot slipped, and her cousin caught her wrist to pull her to her feet. His face was turned away; of a sudden a thrill passed from his finger-ends to her shoulder, a light, but disturbing touch, such as she had never felt before. It was gone in an instant; they drew a little further apart. Had he felt it too, she wondered. The east wind blew fine raindrops into their faces, and they fell into a rhythmic step, keeping pace with fresh energy.

Cousin Ellen, welcomed them in her plain, hearty fashion, and so did little Cousin Sarah, lovely in her soft laces and pearl brooch. When it came to a genealogical straightening-out of family relations, the younger woman observed, "So you are 'once removed,' you see, Archie."

He smiled; "The further removed, the better." Cousin Ellen's gray eyes met the brown ones squarely, with instant understanding. But the girl was irritated; she had not caught the implication, and felt suddenly disappointed. Nevertheless, a certain bond had been acknowledged; something new, something of a stimulus to the quiet, augmenting affection of the last three days. After an evening of Cousin Ellen's delightful tales, chiefly relating to a recalcitrant great-great-grandfather in Vermont who had been cast into prison for his objection to the expansionists there who had seized his New Hampshire grants and appropriated them to the interest of the new State, a tale to which our cousin could do full justice, we tramped back to the old house bubbling with merriment, swinging along in the fog, thrilled when hands touched, cheeks burning as we sat by the woodfire later.

Then followed a week of marvelous weather, and a series of excursions; the house filled up with young people, the cordial, cousinly western boys and their sister, more Amherst friends. We two were not often alone, but little secret signals, as one took a pencil from the other, or was helped from a carriage, were multiplied. Outwardly there was reserve, almost shyness.

Somehow the Fates managed to give us a long afternoon to ourselves at the very end of that blissful week, in the old hay-mow, the fourth child's special fastness. Archie had promised to read aloud some Shakespeare sonnets, which he had quoted once or twice when we were looking over the same poetry-book by the long room table, an occupation pursued under cover of general conversation. But we went out to the barn for the ostensible purpose of letter-writing, and were a bit breathless and embarrassed as we sank into the soft, sun-warmed hay. The solitude, the familiar crackling of brittle haystalks, the chirp of a cricket, were momentous. The boy plunged at once into the faded *Grammer of Assent,* not Shakespeare. Disappointing, that. But one had pen and paper and could keep busy at letter-writing. Presently, however, the girl was piqued into asking bluntly,

"Why do you read that? It can't be interesting."

"Well," Archie said, thoughtfully, "when I went to college last year I was a comfortable Unitarian, but when I was sick, I began to think I wasn't satisfied. A man has to have some basis of faith if he is going to accomplish anything, and know what he believes and why. I made up my mind to watch other people's religion, so I came up here to do it. I knew that my mother's grandmother had come over to Unitarianism from a much more positive theology, and that my great-uncle had changed his faith and gone into the Episcopal church. Mother was disappointed about that, but she is fond of your father, and thinks he is not bigoted. In the meantime, I have a friend who is Catholic, and he lent me the *Grammar of Assent.* I wish you would read it, but what I've got by being here has meant more to me than any argument."

"What *have* you got by being here?" I asked.

"Well, I expected you'd all be dreadfully pious. I didn't dream that Uncle Frederic was the kind of person he is. The family life is so perfect, yet you are all so alive to spiritual things."

"I'm glad you think so, but I don't imagine we'll settle your religious views one way or another. But somehow it would be incongruous for one of our tribe to go over to Rome, after all the other departures!"

"I don't know. I wish you would tell me just what you do believe—what your faith rests on. Maybe it *is* true that what our fathers fought out, makes a background for our own beliefs. The question is whether we can be satisfied to let them carry us. I suppose that was in Newman's mind; an inherited faith, passed on by the Church. The church that has the longest and strongest history will naturally claim the authority, of course."

"Yes, and that is the easiest way. Authority is what *each* church claims. Newman is settling it in the Catholic way."

"One would think assent was more important than prayer, even."

"Have you gotten anything out of family prayers?" I asked irrelevantly. "Doesn't it pall on you to have a thing like that every morning? I've wondered how it strikes an outsider. I sometimes think there's a sameness about it. There's no liturgy and Father mostly makes up the prayers as he goes along, to be frank. It's a part of his early training; his background, you know; from years and years back, like most New England customs."

"I like it. I'm not very religious myself, so far. But I'd like to be, I think."

It was late afternoon before the talk ended. He had told me about himself, his home, his hope to study law and go into his father's office. He could be a help in that way, and the family thought it his best course. But he loved literature better; he had always loved it. He was nineteen; the youngest of four. His mother and uncles had been educated in France. He had spent a good deal of time by himself and thought things out.

When it was finally time to descend from the haymow, Archie gave me his hand, and we slid over the edge of the mow and were still holding hands when we plunged into the dry clover below.

I wanted to be alone to think. This person for whom I was coming to care intensely, had challenged my carefree spirituality. I reproached myself for a weak parasite, and my merriment of the preceding days was checked. This sudden thing, so unlike my imagination or experience, fascinated me. I was convinced that the boy wanted help which I might give, and that I must try to meet his need. But the significance of that magnetic touch, made the need a desire, not a duty.

Sunday, the last day. . . . . The Bishop and his lady drove to the Amherst church in the little black carryall, and the rest of us followed in the open wagon. To the pair of us who sat sharing one book in that little gray stone church, there seemed to be divine intent in its words, and the message of the preacher was intensely significant in the light of our discussion the day before.

In the afternoon Cousin Ellen shared our walk over the farm. There was a cardinal flower in bud beside the brook, and we stopped to admire it. I found it difficult to get an opportunity for something I wanted to say to Archie. I was carrying, out of sight, a worn copy of *The Imitation of Christ* which my older brother had given me years ago.

"I want to lend you a book of mine," I said simply when a chance came. "You see, I have absolutely no theology to fall back upon; I'm ashamed to say that I never seemed to need it, with such a large supply in the family. But Thomas à Kempis is different. He's helped me to *live* what I couldn't understand. I believe that's the thing to do; you may wait forever to be entirely settled, and meanwhile one gets a chance to see how faith works out. Anyway, when you feel you've got what you're looking for, just send this back some day. I'll know then that it proved to be what you wanted. It's my only way of giving you any real help."

He took it and my hand with it. Molly's voice called from the woodshed arch close by.

"Come out on the stoop, you two! There's a wonderful Aurora; great streams of color going up."

Half a dozen people stood together watching the north. The flickering waves of color reached almost to the zenith. A shaft of light shaped like a great bird's wing moved above us. It was a supernatural seal on our unspoken pledge.

In the morning there was a bustle of preparation for departure; thanks for a splendid visit; handshakes; people not finishing their boiled eggs at breakfast; a list of commissions for the Northampton grocery store and a hunt for the big oil-can; an address scribbled on the back of an envelope; somebody wanting to borrow a stamp and somebody else forgetting to put the whip in its socket. Merciful trivialities blunted the keenness of the parting moment. As the carriage drove away, life sank suddenly to a dead level.

5

DECISION

The last September days at the farm were quiet ones. I was much by myself, but my family did not notice it; they were used to my love of solitude. When the return to Syracuse put an end to my dreaming, some of the brightness of the ten days' enchantment faded. Someone had suggested that James should have as his assistant in his church work, a person more mature than I (there was something grotesque in having Mothers' meetings conducted by a nineteen-year-old girl, and a Bible-class for grown boys in charge of a teacher only three or four years their senior) so I gave up my work in that capacity and spent the winter in active dislike of the substitute who had been imported for the purpose, and who lived at our house. In May, however, she left, perhaps for the reason that some of the working-men's wives had not been properly grateful for their husbands' conversions. In any event, our family was happier after her departure, and when summer came, I was invited to Berkshire, where Archie was staying with his family. It was a happy visit, but not quite like the glowing week of the summer before. Archie's family had no inkling of the affection between us, so a forced gaiety covered up our real feelings, and since we were never alone together, I returned to Syracuse puzzled, and slightly embittered at our failure to regain and continue the charm of the intimacy we had begun.

I took up my music and practised fitfully, accompanied singers at concerts, raved over the Pre-Raphaelites, memorized poems of the Rossettis, Morris and Swinburne. I did crewel embroidery, stitching sulphurous flowers on dull green backgrounds. But life was jaundiced. My friends remarked on my sallow skin, the dark rings under my eyes and my nervous habit of twitching. In November I went to Cedar Square, dreading the visit because of Grandmother Sargent's death the year before. But Aunt Kate was there, and she too, was concerned about my indolence, and lack of initiative.

"I wish," she said one day, "that you could see Dr. Zakrzewska. She is the one person, I believe, who could find out what is the matter with you. She's a very dear friend of mine: I'm sure she would take an interest."

"What's she like?" I inquired. John Van Duyn was the only physician whose opinion I respected, just then, and even his advice I had not followed.

"Marie Zakrzewska is an unusual person. She's about fifty now. She's a descendant of a Polish family. Her great-great-grandfather was an army surgeon all through the Seven Years' War, and his daughter was his assistant. Then in some way the profession was handed down, and her father, too, was an army surgeon, but was dismissed from his post because of revolutionary tendencies. Marie is rather proud of that I think. Her mother became a midwife afterward, studying for it as a profession. Marie herself was the eldest of five sisters and brothers and had the family mania for surgery. She was once taken to a dissecting-room to see the decomposed corpse of a young man, as a matter of interest apparently, and was forgotten and locked in there for hours. That was when she was eleven; she had read the History of Surgery and Midwifery before she was thirteen, at which time she left school."

These biographical facts, less concisely stated, interested me. More followed. Marie had assisted her mother in a large practice, and at twenty was admitted to the Berlin School of Midwifery, but only through an appeal to the King by a powerful intermediary—and was met with any amount of opposition, some if it treacherous. That was in '49, Aunt Kate said. Then, discouraged, she determined to go to America, where she had heard there were medical courses for women. She came over to Boston with her sister, but of course met with more discouragement; women physicians were ranked as low in the United States as in Germany. It was humiliating to acknowledge defeat even before the struggle, and to piece out the scanty sum she had brought from Europe by keeping an embroidery-shop. But she had thirty girls in her establishment before long, and incidentally learned enough of their handicaps to become a champion of the laboring woman and her cause; the cause of morality under deadening conditions. Then Dr. Elizabeth Blackwell, herself a pioneer in the medical profession found the valiant girl and took her into her dispensary, taught her English and brought her a practice. She was later given the chair of Obstetrics in a Boston medical school and resigned from it later to found a hospital for women and children. It was incorporated in 1863—quick work,—and began on a basis of funds to the amount of over a million dollars. Ever since, she had had a warm interest in working-women, girls of all sorts, and reformers or revolutionists.

"I'd rather like to meet Dr. Zakrzewska, if she's as interested in girls as you say she is."

In a few days I found myself face to face with a remarkable woman sitting in a straight arm-chair by a wood fire, a dynamic person with irregular features and bright eyes; hair carelessly, but becomingly, twisted; beautiful brown hands, made for skilled activity.

"I'm glad to see you," she began. "I'm so fond of your aunt. Lovely old house, that. I've only seen the lower story, but I want to go over it some day."

"Oh, it *is* lovely. Only of course we miss my grandmother. Did you know her?"

"Met her just once; a strong personality and much poise. Is your mother like her?"

"Yes, the same calm, I think; not demonstrative but tremendously sympathetic."

"Do you think you have anything of her make up? Your mother's, I mean."

"Something, maybe, but she hasn't got nerves, and I have. Of course it may be that I wasn't meant to have them." I was anxious to get in the story of the cannon-shock. It was so interesting to talk about oneself. But Marie Zakrzewska did not follow up this lead.

"What do you enjoy most in your visits here?"

"Oh, the old house, and the library, and my uncles, but most of all the concerts, of course. Music is the one thing that means the most to me!"

"*What* does it mean?"

A somewhat disconcerting question. I faltered.

"Why—it takes me out of myself, and my surroundings. It lures one on. Sometimes I can't keep away from the piano."

"Oh, so you play?" A bright understanding glance flashed from the keen eyes. "How many hours a day do you practice?"

"I'm afraid I don't work very hard; not more than an hour some days. But I get so much out of it—out of life. Art too, and books. And people. All kinds of people." (The Fine Art of Liking—I thought of that unexpectedly. I had not consciously practised it, but believed it to be one of my principles.)

"I can see that you like them. I imagine it's one of your strong points."

"But I haven't any strong points." One could not help but be honest with this sort of person. "I'm *swayed* by music, but I've never accomplished anything with it—I've been satisfied to be thought talented, but haven't done any work. It's the same with religion. I expected to be a church worker for life, but I—didn't succeed in that."

"How do you know you didn't succeed? Did you find out you had not cared for it after all?"

"Not that—and I worked. But"—and the thought evoked a dampness about the eyes, "I was supplanted; put out of it; and it has proved that I wasn't strong enough anyway. I seem to have no endurance at all. It began with chilblains—"

But the doctor still sheered off from any contemplation of physical woes.

"You say you like people. What people have you known, outside of your own circle?"

Before I knew it, I was describing the German immigrants, the New England farm-friends, even my own ancestors; the people in books, the members of my immediate family. My tongue was loosened, and the doctor listened intently.

"You have had a great deal in your lifetime, so far," she pronounced. "Plenty of opportunity to be strong, and to be contributive, if you know what that means. You've lived in a sort of fairy wood and obeyed your impulses and the call of beauty in many forms. It is like the children who followed the Pied Piper, to put it very simply. You haven't been lured into a cave, it's true, and you have had far more freedom than one would expect. Everything has come to you easily, and you've been satisfied to let it come. But the great things—" and here I detected just a slight foreign accent—"are not achieved passively. Music, for instance, is not merely an escape, not just a means of forgetting what is sordid and disagreeable in our environment. Art is not; literature is not. They are elements of life and governed by the laws of life. You can't pick your soul out for special coddling and keep it inactive. Furthermore you may not turn back after defeat, not even admit defeat. Who can measure defeat, or success either?"

"And religion?"

"Religion is the highest. But that, too, is not separable from life, not a thing apart. All the other things, nature and art, lead up to it. Music will be merged in it; work will be deepened by it. The Spirit *gives* Life. You and I may not have the same faith or the same expression of faith, but we both live by what we believe."

Then she went on:

"I make a proposition to you. I want you to get out into a broader world. You have had much freedom, but even so, there are limits of circumstance and of experience. By getting out of those limits one makes one's life bigger. I want you to go to Europe for three years, and study there."

"What do you mean?" I asked. "How can I go?" My brain reeled.

"I think you can go. Your father and mother will do anything in the world to help you. Your aunt has told me about you; I know more of your history than I have seemed to know, and you have given me a still better clue. You must go this winter if you consent to the plan. You have always longed to study music in Germany, haven't you?"

"Always—for years and years! But—I don't want them to think that I'm willing to leave them except for the sake of bringing back some results to them. You see the others—my sister and brother,— have been a help; they've made it worth while to do for them. They'll think I just want to get away!"

"Haven't you sometimes wanted to get away?"

"Yes, every once in a while, ever since I was very little. But not because I don't love my own home—it's an impulse; a sort of thing from outside one."

"No, from inside one. It is the impulse of progress; of climbing higher; 'leaving one's outgrown shell,' as your poet says. Remember, I'm not sending you for a *cure*; you must understand that. You are going for a definite purpose and going alone; you will study music to teach it; study it as an art, not an accomplishment. And you will study language. Also you will meet people—human beings who have a likeness to yourself—but are working out their lives in other conditions and with other backgrounds. Your own failures and shortcomings must be left behind in America; your ailments you will forget. It's a serious thing that I am proposing to you. Will you promise me that if you go you will work to prepare youself for paying back what you are taking from your parents by supporting yourself for three years—for as long a time as you will have spent in Europe? That should be the agreement."

I was ready to promise anything. Life had taken on a new and solemn meaning; it was beyond me to plan, even to realize so profound a purpose as this which was put before me. But I would set myself to the task.

I came out from the interview with a surprising sense of energy. Such a stupendous issue had been raised by the talk that mere physical ailments seemed unimportant. I had already begun to wonder what Archie would think about it. He had acquired the habit of running over from Cambridge in late afternoon for a walk or talk with me. We were no longer on the footing of the year before; we had grown perceptibly since the week in Hadley. Through letters our intimacy had finally increased, and we understood each other far better. We had not discussed religion, nor books; the happenings of the moment presented more immediate interest. On the very afternoon of my talk with Dr. Zakrzewska, I poured out my enthusiasm. We were tramping along with unwonted rapidity, toward the hill on which the reservoir stand-pipe stood, commanding a view of Brookline and the distant city, lit up by a winter sunset blazing in deep orange below late November grays.

"She's splendid. I had known of course that I wasn't accomplishing anything but even so, I was far more satisfied than I had any right to be, and what was more, I was getting peevish whenever anything I had set my heart on failed to turn out as I expected. I was just drifting along uselessly."

"Don't say that. One can't tell what one is accomplishing." His tone was quiet and steady. "What does she want you to do?"

I faltered. "I—something that will be hard. I begin to see that already. It means going away, Archie—for three years. To Germany."

"Three—years?" His voice was low and unexcited, but his face whitened. I looked full at him, knowing now something I had not been able to guess.

"Yes, three years. Six years for that matter. We shall both be busy anyway, you know, that long. Two more years at college for you, and then studying law, and getting a practice, and so on. But years go so fast."

"I know it. We have got to show what we are, I suppose, in that time. It looks very long just now, though, doesn't it? Is it certain that you will go so far?"

"I imagine so. I think it has been talked over at home, although it came unexpectedly to me. I—she wants me to go in January."

"Then you have plans to make. We're not likely to see each other many times more, I'm afraid."

As we returned to Cedar Square there was a crowd of homecoming people, hurrying along the sidewalks in the winter twilight. We did not walk arm-in-arm; it was not improper in those days, but by daylight it would have been considered "marked," and had slight implications. Archie's hand was eager, nevertheless, at every crossing, every downward step. I looked around at him as we talked. He was a person to be noticed in his new and becoming overcoat, and the small moustache which he had cultivated since the beginning of the year.

Meanwhile plans matured with astonishing speed. The Bishop had taken kindly to Dr. Zakrzewska's proposition, and my days at Cedar Square were numbered. Archie asked to have the very last evening, suggesting that we go to hear *Carmen* sung. As the evening approached, however, a weight descended on me. It occurred to me that we two had been moving toward a settled understanding. It might not be a spoken one, but within my own heart it was a certainty. Three years of separation would put a tremendous burden on our faithfulness, and so, to myself, I made an heroic resolution.

That night when the carriage drew up, I felt more than an ordinary thrill of anticipation. Archie arrived in evening clothes, white shirt-fronted and studded, with a large bunch of violets in a box.

I felt a wild desire to call off the European trip and see the *City of Brussels* sunk at her dock. I too had dressed myself in full regalia, and I was glad that I had even kept my handkerchief in orris powder, the nearest approach to perfumery for girls of my circle.

We listened to Bizet's enchanting opera that night, even forgetting the name of the *prima donna,* in our delight at sitting there, the two of us, listening to the singing which was made for lovers' ears. And we were lovers that night, not losing a moment's delight, nor a single thrill of physical closeness.

But when I sank back into the carriage after it was all over I was forced to think of my resolution. Their consciences never let them alone, those ancient Puritan zealots, even when happiness was at its height, I thought. There was only a short time for my proposed declaration on the drive to Cedar Square.

"Our last evening together for months," whispered Archie.

"For years. It has been perfect tonight, more perfect than it can be ever again, perhaps. You see, it won't do for us to let it mean too much. I want you to feel free these next three years. You may see some girl you care for a great deal more than you do for me. It would be dreadful for you to feel that you are bound in any way—" But here I recoiled at my own daring. I was offering myself to him, instead of refusing him, when he had not even proposed.

"I don't mean that there's anything, *really*," I hastened to add. "Only just that we've had such a very happy time, and you might think that you mean more than you do. We're both pretty young, and we ought to feel free to fall in love with anyone we want to." I felt tremendously magnanimous and prudent.

"*You* can be as free as you like. I should never think of hampering you," said the steady voice out of the darkness. He had drawn away a little.

"Oh, but it's not for *my* sake." I was horrified. "Please don't misunderstand me on this last night. You'll always be so much to me. And I hope you'll keep on writing till the very last minute."

His laugh expressed relief. "I will; it'll be a long correspondence, I guess, but you must, too."

"Of course. Only I'm going to be an old maid; somebody's jolly aunt."

We were climbing the hill at Cedar Square. The gravel crunched under our carriage wheels; the sharp cedar points stood out in black relief against the moonlight. The driver was paid and drove away. We stood shivering on the steps in the frosty air, tense with the keenness of parting, longing to give each other the seal of the fidelity on which we were counting. But we set it away from us with all the bravery of our young hearts. To me, with my Victorian romanticism, a kiss was a pledge, when it was exchanged by lovers.

"It's been so beautiful tonight. I'm glad we had it together. We won't forget it."

"Never. No matter what happens."

"Don't *let* anything happen!" Archie's voice was positive. He clung to the hand he held, and for an instant he wavered. Then with a last desperate "Good-bye" he ran down the steps.

Music in Germany

1

The *City of Brussels* lay at her dock, enveloped in thick fog. Two girls in brown ulsters, an older woman beside them, followed with wistful eyes the retreating figure of a cleric. He looked back once, and raised a hand in a parting salute; then disappeared in the drizzling rain.

The cables which bound the ship to the pier were loosened. The signal boomed from her mournful horn, and The *City of Brussels,* drawn by an impatient tug through ferry boats and vessels, was off to sea. Really off!

I was leaving my native land with few misgivings. I should be alone for two years, but my sister, Arria, and an older friend, Miss Hamilton, and I were to travel together before I was left in Leipzig. And then, armed with letters of introduction to some thirty distinguished Germans, I should never be really alone. Besides I had more than two years work ahead of me, studying German and music.

I had scarcely prepared for a new life in the one short month before sailing, and had certainly not carried out my noble resolution of a year before to study theology, and catch up with Archie's investigations. Whether it was sheer cowardice, a fear of finding shallows in the stream of my own thinking, or the old willingness to identify the joy of living with life itself, was hard to tell. But the conviction had grown strong within me that Christianity was first of all a Way of Life in which dogma had its function and beauty its significance. It must be followed without delay or doubt with strength and youth as part of the equipment. I knew I had made confessions of faith, and taken on obligations which I had not understood, but I realized, and found solace, in Dr. Zakrzewska's profound truth: one lives by what one at heart believes, whether translated into a creed, or sub-consciously interpreted.

The ten-day voyage was not lacking in interest. A passenger who had kept to himself for the first three days, came into the cabin one evening while a concert was being arranged, and was presented to us by the Captain as "Leftenant" Bell of the Royal Navy, a man with a fine voice. I was importuned to play accompaniments, and found it good fun to follow the Englishman's rolling baritone. He sang *Who is Sylvia?* and *Twickenham Ferry* our old favorites with gusto.

That was the beginning of a pleasant acquaintance. He was a mine of information about London. I asked question after question, and betrayed my own book-learned familiarity with its topography.

"What parts of London do you want to see?" he asked.

"Oh, all kinds of Londons: the London of Dickens, of Thackeray, of Trollope and Meredith, the London of St. James, the East End and the docks, and of course the Tower. I want to stroll along Piccadilly, buy things in Regent Street, drive in Hyde Park, go to the National Gallery, walk around Trafalgar Square, stand at Charing Cross, and hunt out corners like Tom-all-alone's and Mr. Venus's—I'm sure one could find them—, and see the lodgings of the poets in Grub Street. Think of all the memories to be dug up! And I'd just like to *look* at Mr. Gladstone, and hear John Bright on Free Trade, and lunch on penny buns, and ride in hansoms, and watch Ellen Terry and Irving do Shakespeare, and go to afternoon service at Westminster Abbey because the choir sings so beautifully then, and look at the monuments, only I like living things better than dead ones, and hear Canon Farrar preach at St. Paul's." I paused from sheer lack of breath.

The Lieutenant broke his British calm.

"I swear, you know more about London than I do myself! I had no idea that American girls were so beautifully-educated and well-read. Pardon me, but aren't you an exception?"

This was inexcusable. The compliment passed unheeded as I flew to the defense of my compatriots.

That made clear, I went on, "Besides, I need to hear more English music. We hear mostly Church composers: Elvey and Barnby and Stainer and Dykes. Think what we owe to Dykes! Then you do such wonderful things of Purcell's, and the Messiah is sung more superbly in England than anywhere else. I hope I shall hear it."

He was alert at once.

"I've sung in that. But the last time we gave it in Windsor, where I live, I wasn't allowed to be in the chorus; that's one reason I made the trip to America."

I wondered what he meant. Later I was to know. We spent a good deal of time pacing the deck together, and when he would rest, stretched out in his steamer-chair, we discussed, not music alone, but favorite books and personal experiences. He was a retired naval officer of a Conservative family. He had little interest in politics beyond a strong disapproval of Parnell and a lack of patience with Ireland and Gladstone's actions in its favor. He had, like all British subjects, unbounded admiration for the Queen, and a supreme indifference to the affairs of other countries.

The day before we landed, the gray sky and sea gave place to a radiant day: a powdering of snow froze on the masts before dawn, and sparkled in brilliant sunshine. Then came a moonlight night, and we two sat on deck till late, which brought down a protest from Arria and Miss Hamilton. The lieutenant invited us to visit him at Windsor on a Sunday afternoon, so that we might hear Sir George Elvey play the organ at the Royal Chapel, and meet his sister.

"I'm sure we should love to come; I'll ask my sister and Miss Hamilton."

I hastened with all speed to the cabin. Alack! the invitation was received with coldness by the older lady.

"I certainly should not want to accept a proposal of that sort," she said firmly. "We know nothing whatever about this man. American girls unfortunately have the reputation of being easily taken in, and he probably just wants to flatter you. You might go to Windsor, and find there was no such person in the town. As to the talk of his being a *naval knight,* who knows whether there is such a thing, after all? *I* never heard of one, I must say." She seemed unnecessarily peevish.

"Whatever he is or isn't," I declared, "he's a thorough gentle-man, if I know one when I see him, and I'm sure I do. He's so *very* nice, Miss Hamilton. I do wish you'd let me accept the invitation for us all."

But it was of no avail to coax or sulk. Chagrined, I returned to my new acquaintance.

"I'm ashamed to tell you that we can't come to Windsor after all. Our friend is frightfully obstinate, and insists that you may be—that we don't know anything about you! She doesn't even know what a naval knight is!"

"Oh, that's quite all right," said the Lieutenant easily. "One really can't be too careful. But I've quite set my heart on your com-ing, and if you'll give me leave, I think I can convince her of my respectability."

We had our first sight of land next morning, Sunday. The Cap-tain, in lieu of a Chaplain, read service in the saloon, and the First Officer led the choir with a cornet. The Lieutenant had joined actively in the preparations: moving chairs, putting English prayer-books about, perfecting a programme of hymns and chants with our assistance. He had mentioned that one of his brothers was a clergyman. Miss Hamilton was plainly impressed, but had made no comment. At the dinner table he inquired:

"Am I still *mal vu*?"

"I haven't found out. But I presume she is partly mollified; she's an ardent Churchwoman."

"Ah! Tomorrow I shall play my trump card."

I wondered what that would be. We were coming nearer and nearer shore; there wasn't much time.

Next morning there were signs of preparation for landing. We were being drawn up the harbor of Liverpool by a tug. Yellow mist enveloped the ship; through it we could descry outlines of tall buildings. There was neither sound nor conscious motion; we seemed to be moving in a dream. Below, in the stillness of the saloon, sitting at a long table, the three Americans were finishing letters to send home. Lieutenant Bell appeared, and sat down opposite us, a neat purple morocco paper-case in his hand. I wondered vaguely what his next move would be. Presently he drew out a sheet of paper. Casually he passed it across the table to me.

"Are you interested in autographs? You might like to see this one; it's a very good hand, I think."

There was a coronet embossed at the top of the page, and a few lines written or engraved, possibly in circular form, with names filled in. But the importance of the document lay in the short statement, conferring knighthood on a commissioned officer in Her Majesty's service. And underneath, a single proud word, written in bold characters by her own hand, VICTORIA.

I played my part in the little drama with a presence of mind over which I gloated ever after. I handed the sheet to my sister, saying only:

"It *is* a fine hand. Very interesting, isn't it?" I appeared to be already familiar with the handwriting of Royalty. Arria Huntington was equally calm, and made some appropriate comment. Our chaperon colored up to her ears, and murmured something about the honor of possessing such a treasure. The paper floated gently back to the Lieutenant's portfolio. Pens scratched on.

When we all stood on the wharf that afternoon, the young officer offered his hand to Miss Hamilton as if to an old acquaintance.

"So virry pleased to have met you, Madam. We shall look for you next Sunday afternoon by the two o'clock train from Paddington station if you please. My sister and I will meet you when you get off at Windsor." And, bowing to Arria and me, he disappeared in the crowd.

"I really am very agreeably disappointed in that young man," observed our chaperon.

2

LONDON

The Adelphi Hotel in Liverpool was then a hospitable, spacious mansion. I found my room like the guest-room at Cedar Square: the high bed was curtained with flowered chintz, and before an open fire was a deep armchair. Into this I sank for a reverie and a review of the voyage. I still felt the motion of the steamer, and smelled the salt air in my nostrils. Out of my hand-bag, an un-business-like affair of sage-green plush with gilt mountings, I took a photograph of Archie, which had come to me the morning of my departure from Syracuse. I studied the fine profile—the nose clean-cut and as sensitive as the mouth which a college-grown moustache had hidden, the broad brow. These were features in which I had always taken pride, and this likeness, taken especially for me, should be a talisman, a pledge of loyalty. Nominally we had set each other free, but there could be no real freedom from abiding love. We might doubt ourselves, one another's constancy; yet faithful or unfaithful, in the depths of our hearts that love would remain. Let it be itself the holding-power! I assured myself once more of this love—the strongest thread in the pattern life was weaving for me, and then fell asleep, as usual expecting a joyous to-morrow.

We two sisters realized what congenial companions we were as we travelled together on land. Getting into London was a matter of, "*Why*, that's Charing Cross! *Here's* Trafalgar Square and the lions! That little bookstore must surely be a Dickens landmark." Everything was familiar; omnibuses, housefronts, hucksters, sign-boards, criers were sights long seen by the inner eye. Our faces at the windows of the cab were alight with discovery all the way to Albany

Street where we were to stay with relatives of old Boston friends.

We arrived in time to dress for dinner. When we descended the household was already assembled: Mr. and Mrs. Yardley, their daughters and two other guests, one of them a fine-looking, middle-aged woman, her hair tinged with gray. She was describing a visit to Mrs. Ritchie, Thackeray's daughter, where Robert Browning had been present, and interrupted her narrative to nod pleasantly to us as we took our seats. English hostesses did not introduce guests to one another at their tables, so conversation was general. We learned that the lady was an American, on her way home after a journey on the continent with the quiet gentleman, whom we supposed was her husband, called Oscar. Moncure Conway was coming that evening to take her to the theatre or elsewhere. We realized that she was a highly privileged, if not also a celebrated personage.

After dinner when we gathered in the drawing-room upstairs, she brought out photographs collected in France and Italy, especially in Florence. I, who had already made an idol of her, as Cousin Ellen used to say, noticed that these were not just buildings or landscapes, but oftener some human scene with a personal association: an open doorway; a picturesque donkey, a group of peasants; or a young mother with the face of a Madonna.

"You found something *lovable* wherever you went!" I ventured shyly.

"Of course I did. Isn't that what one travels for? I can't tell you anything about belated trains, or bad food, or poor accommodations—those are the things one forgets, or ought to forget. People are the real thing—the near thing."

The words brought a glow into her listener's face. Here was a person who was seeing lands and people as parts of the world, not just as nations and nationalities. There was something about her that suggested an unusual background and great experience. Mr. Conway was announced presently, and the new acquaintance went off, calling "Goodnight, Oscar; don't sit up too late." Oscar was called Mr. Laighton by the Yardley girls. *Oscar Laighton*: we could not think where we had heard the name before, but it was familiar. We were hurrying off ourselves, however, having just learned that Mendelssohn's oratorio, *St. Paul,* was to be sung at St. Paul's Cathedral that evening in honor of St. Paul's day, January twenty-fifth. Our London visit was beginning gloriously.

When we reached home later, Miss May Yardley was sitting up for us.

"It's not so very late," she said. "Mrs. Thaxter has not come in yet."

Thaxter—Thaxter—and Oscar Laighton! Memory supplied a sudden realization.

"Not *Celia* Thaxter," I cried. "It can't be she! Why, I've wanted all my life to meet her!"

"It certainly is, her very self. She's been travelling about Europe on her brother's account; he's had rather a hard experience and been very blue."

Yes, we knew about that, curiously enough. His sister had taken him abroad in order to distract him from an unhappy romance, it was said. One never knew how true such rumors were, but I had the popular sympathy for parted lovers, and was of course concerned. From that evening on I took every opportunity of talking to Mrs. Thaxter and casting surreptitious glances at the sphinx-like brother. I was asked to the poet's room, and allowed to help her dress for festivities, even to choose the brooch she wore when with Browning and other celebrities.

"Pick out the jewel you think prettiest," Celia Thaxter said, pushing a little tray toward me. Uppermost was a boat of silver filigree—a gondola in fact, but significant as a symbol—with a great green aquamarine crystal hanging from it.

"Oh, *that* is the thing!" I cried, "the boat and the crystallized seawater. It just suits you, in that dress!" And when Mrs. Thaxter let me fasten it on, and stood up to be admired, my satisfaction was complete.

That week in London passed all too quickly. The glimpses of English life and the people we constantly encountered delighted us both.

We have seen, one of us wrote, Cheapside, Piccadilly, Paternoster
Row, the palaces, the Temple, the parks and parades . . . . and all the
appropriate characters which fit into those backgrounds; seen Oliver
Twist holding out his hand, whether for more or not one does not know
—Sam Weller, Noah Claypole, Smike, Major Pendennis, Lady Glencora,
Mr. Casaubon—we met him in the British Museum! As a matter of fact,
Cruikshank's pictures themselves don't really exaggerate—it's all in the
way you look. But books give no idea of the effect of deep stone archways,
queer alleys, mounted motionless guards with bright uniforms and the
most eccentric little round caps set on the side of their heads. We've
poked all over London and seen a thousand and one things that are not
even portrayed in fiction. Imagine milkwomen with poles across their
shoulders and pails at the ends, like our early imaginings of Mary Epes!
And forlorn wisps of crossing-sweepers who hold out one hand and pull
their forelocks with the other!

More of these ravings appear in the correspondence, and serve
to show that the London of sixty-odd years ago had not lost its
flavor of antiquity. As for us, we nearly lost ourselves in a genuine
fog; got indigestion from a late supper of cold roast pork and bread
and cheese and porter; had a pleasant interview with Mr. Lowell,
then our Ambassador, at the American Legation, and a talk about
old Cambridge days when he knew Arria as a school-girl and saw me
in my cradle. That same evening we saw Ellen Terry and Henry
Irving in *Much Ado,* a performance to be remembered all our lives.
When the celebrated pair came to the United States their acting
did not eclipse that first hearing. We could not decide whether it
was more wonderful to play Benedict to Terry's Beatrice, or Beatrice to Irving's Benedict.

I spent every spare moment at the National Gallery, determined
to understand Turner because of a devotion to Ruskin. The *Tém-
éraire* did begin to creep out of the fog, but I preferred the traditional painters. I explained in letters that I hadn't *got* to Alma
Tadema and Burne-Jones and the others yet.

The Sunday afternoon at Windsor was all I had hoped for.
We left behind the Sunday stillness of London. All along the way
as the train made its stops at little stations, we could hear church
bells ringing for afternoon services; chimes of eight bells playing

the familiar *Change*. That chime rang itself vividly into my memory: the forceful leap to the octave and the descending scale which followed; then another mounting and descending. A hymn of certitude in key-tones and dominants, like the security of an Established Church:

I got as I listened an impression of universality, of faith and worship as the habit of the whole people. The footsteps of old and young on sidewalks, through churchyards, up flights of stone stairways; bent knees, clasped hands, all this made me feel one of the up-surgings of conviction which occasionally possessed me. Yes, the Church was a tremendous thing, not resting on the shoulders of the last generation, but on the foundations of the centuries: immovable, though battered by dissensions; just, but less inexorable than other systems. It had made mistakes, had become de-spiritualized here and there, yet great minds and faithful souls had kept guard over its deposits of sacred truth. It stood behind the Church of America,—always had stood behind it. What place had dissenters, after all? I thought. What right had the Puritans to destroy its landmarks, to tear down its altars, to rob it of its beauty and symmetry? Did it still need to be cleared of old idolatries and superstitions and made an actual *Via Media*? (I had had a glimpse of Newman's *Apologia* since the days of my introduction to the *Grammar of Assent,* and had thought I understood why the latter argument had been presented to Archie.)

But the train stopped suddenly at Windsor and put an end to these reflections. There stood Lieutenant Bell and his attractive sister. Before we knew it we were all rambling along a narrow street, going through the gate of Henry the Eighth and feeling for the moment some of its sinister associations; then into a shady quadrangle with ivy-covered walls, into which the windows of the military knight's apartments looked out. We knew about the knights by this time; we had learned from our friends that the honor was conferred by Her Majesty for distinguished acts of bravery which had resulted in permanent disablement. Some of them thought they could remember hearing that our friend the Lieutenant had rescued some men from the wreck of a burning collier, and that fatal damage had been done thereby to his lungs and heart; but we were never able to verify it. The young fellow who had been travelling with him had really been a doctor, then; and he joined our party that afternoon. A handsome older man was detailed as *galant* for Miss Hamilton, who was a woman of parts even if somewhat over-conscientious. Arria Huntington at once found common ground with the fine women.

It was a glorious day, and our wanderings about the castle and its grounds gave us something to remember vividly. I was more drawn to my companion since the story of his valor had been told me. We stopped once to lean against a wall, or gate, and look over toward Eton, on an opposite declivity. The buildings were dignified, and across the broad grounds we could see moving figures of boys, slim figures in black jackets and white collars.

We walked on through a door which he unlocked, into the Dean's Yard, and across to the knights' apartments. Miss Bell and another sister were waiting for us in the Lieutenant's drawing-room, where we had our first experience of afternoon tea. That had not then become a settled American custom, and it was fascinating to us. We relished the thin-bread-and-butter which only English slicing, it appeared, could achieve, and the plummy pound-cake and short-bread served on beautiful china like that of our own family.

Then came Evening Prayer at the Royal chapel, across the quadrangle, just at five o'clock. There we met Sir George Elvey, a "nice quiet old gentleman with a churchly air," I wrote. The provisions for royal worship were impressive: the Queen's stall done up in purple and gold, the beautiful carved backgrounds of the chairs where the ladies of the court, only two of them present that day, were already seated. Apparently the knights had their places opposite these; at all events we were in them, looking across at the ladies, one of them a very beautiful blonde in the deepest of mourning, her golden curls set off by a heavy crepe veil. Her Majesty was not at Windsor nor in London. An accident to one foot had kept her out of town, but we gathered that her little phaeton was a familiar object in the palace grounds. I took in, dreamily, the effect of the shaded chapel, the candles burning in great brass candlesticks, the fair lady-in-waiting, the perfection of the organ-music and clear high voices of the choir, said to be the finest in England.

Awake! Awake! Put on thy strength, O Zion! I forgot that I had heard that stirring call sung by an American quartette; it was hardly recognizable. The choral chanting of the Psalms reminded us of Calvary chapel, and we wished its untrained singers might have listened with us. Elvey's dramatic accompaniments, the thunders of the organ intensifying "wind and storm fulfilling His Word," tones of trumpet and harp, brought out by the stops of that remarkable instrument lifted us to the Hebrew poet's own exaltation. And this was all just as beautiful every day in the year! What need to poke about in theological backgrounds when music itself echoed, reverberated, overwhelming certitude?

When we returned to the Yardleys' that night there was time for one last session with Celia Thaxter, who had been visiting at the studios of Millais and Sir Frederick Leighton, and had much to report. She was to leave next morning. We had got better acquainted with brother Oscar, and made him talk a bit; he had told me that he was the author of a "cunning," as we should have described it in those days, little love-song printed among Mrs. Thaxter's own poems:

> *The clover-blossoms kiss her feet,*
> *She is so sweet;*
> *While I, who may not kiss her hand,*
> *Bless all the wildflowers in the land.*

This had an appeal of its own to one member of the Albany Street public, and naturally started the suggestion that it might have been written to the lost sweetheart. At any rate it did no harm to fancy that. But the poet's parting salute was characteristic; he merely put his head in at the door of the drawing-room where we were reading our letters, and called out, "Good-by, you nice girls."

3

THE CHANNEL

The next night we sailed from Queensboro to cross the Channel. We found on the deck of the steamer a pleasant-looking trio of voyagers; two of them young women in tailored suits, modish little bonnets with short black lace veils, and heavy coachmen's capes of dark fur. They were the princesses Victoria and Matilda of Schleswig-Holstein-Sonderburg-Augustenburg, daughters of Duke Frederick, the late defeated aspirant to the Duchy of Holstein. Accompanying the pair, whose luggage was put on board by an unconscionable number of lackeys was an elderly man of impressive appearance. We learned later from a garrulous stewardess who seemed to be in possession of many royal secrets that he was Prince Christian of Sweden, younger brother of Frederick and husband of Queen Victoria's daughter Helena. We had seen his house, Cumberland Lodge, at Windsor, and had been told that he was one of the most biddable and beloved of Her Majesty's sons-in-law.

As a tight little crowd packed the top of the hatchway, I was jostled against the Princess Victoria, and eagerly begged pardon for the sake of speaking to her. We did not see each other. "Not at all," was the courteous answer. Later the stewardess and a maid were gossiping below in the lavatory over a huge bridal bouquet of gardenias, lilies of the valley and white roses, which was being sprinkled. It appeared that the older girl was on her way to Berlin to marry William, son of the Crown Prince of Prussia, and grandson of the German Emperor, as well as of Queen Victoria. The two had become secretly engaged at a countryhouse the summer before; a real love-affair apparently, for there could be no diplomatic incentive to such a match. The wedding was supposed to

be coming off immediately; as a matter of fact, however, it was post-
poned for three or four weeks. I begged for a flower or leaf from the
bouquet, and picked up a bit of maiden-hair from the floor to send
home. Then I was accorded a tuberose, I believe, which had become detached from its wiring. I thrust it into my Baedeker; it
proved to be one of the useless little mementoes which one carries
about and makes into a fetish.

The two Danish sisters were gone next morning when we left
the boat, but we thought about them on our journey over the monotonous stretches of snowy Dutch country, among the windmills
and dykes and ponds with skating children. Already England and
its joys had begun to seem like a dream; the Cathedral of Cologne
replaced Westminster, and a strange tongue assailed our ears.

4

Fräulein Isidora Herrnsdorf of Leipzig was a teacher of German to foreigners, largely Americans, who came to study at the University or the Conservatorium. She imparted more than a mere knowledge of the language; she was a humanitarian and a philosopher. College professors and budding diplomats had entered her precincts, and returned to their native land enriched. Pupils sought advice for the conduct of their lives from this shrewd, typically German yet internationally minded woman. Plain, unassuming, clear-eyed and discerning, she could kindle ambition or infuse a sense of justice into the mind of a partisan, and when there was need, evoke a wholesome shame without the use of sarcasm. Above all she could encourage self-confidence and perseverance.

The little apartment was dreary in its flat simplicity. Brownness and grayness had been absorbed into the threadbare carpets and the spare upholstery of chairs and sofa. Monotonous walls were hung with one or two stern engravings and a couple of family miniatures; a bookcase of leather-bound volumes represented the entire library; the whole background gave an impression of arid and straitened living. There was a plump sister, Fräulein Fanny, who represented the practical end of the establishment, and was cumbered with much serving, since they had usually a male lodger-pupil who shared the boiled beef and sauerkraut.

Fräulein Doris, in a gown of a previous period, its texture thinned and like a late autumn leaf in color, had just finished correcting a pile of exercises on the afternoon of February 7, 1881. Twilight had set in at three o'clock, although there was a bright sky somewhere behind the chimney-pots. The sun never sent any direct rays into the apartment, wedged as it was between tall houses. But there was no more writing to do, for a letter of introduction had been sent that morning, signed by a Cambridge man, an erstwhile pupil, commending a couple of American girls to her attention.

Just then the bell tinkled, and she went out into the dark hall. Two young women with eager manners and a sparing equipment of language, mounted the staircase somewhat breathlessly.

The older girl, she noticed, was handsome, with the face of a Teutonic heroine: blue eyes and dark lashes, calm brow, a more mature bearing than the average German girl at her age, for Fräulein Doris, like the rest of the world, believed her as youthful as the sister who accompanied her, a more animated, nervous person.

Over the Saxon coffee which she offered us, our errand was explained in unpretentious accents by Arria who was leaving Leipzig presently and wanted to find lodging for me in some pleasant family where "good" German was spoken, near the Conservatory and Gewandhaus.

The outlook was apparently discouraging; Fraulein Doris explained in halting English that a perfect accent was difficult to find, except among some of the more aristocratic burgher families who did not take boarders. But she favored the acceptance of a plan proposed by the American Consul that for the remainder of the year I should go out to Plagwitz, a suburb within walking distance of the city, and take a room in the house where he and his wife were living, a *villa* so-called, with a pleasant garden; the landlord and his wife had lived in America and understood cooking for foreigners, and there was a family of attractive children, all ages. As I was arranging for music-lessons with Coccius, one of the Conservatory men who could give me special instruction and fit me for entrance there in the course of a few months, she felt this arrangement would be convenient, and meantime I could devote myself to concentrated study of the language and gradually develop plans for a more complete experience of German life in the autumn. The consul's association with important personages and contacts would undoubtedly lead to some excellent arrangement by that time.

This plan was a bit disappointing, but offered some advantages which I could well understand. The dreary aspect of the Herrnsdorf flat discouraged me; average German family life took its color therefrom in my imagination, and the odors of cabbage and stale tobacco had assaulted my nostrils on the staircase. I decided rapidly in favor of the proposed settlement, and passed on more enthusiastically to the plan for study.

Lessons were soon scheduled. I was supposed to purchase a copy of Otto's Grammar, and a book into which treasures of literature could be copied. An intensive study-course was mapped out with amazing rapidity and comprehensiveness; the teacher knew her subject. I must use every opportunity for conversation, even with Saxons, and remember that in the theatre one could hear a standard German accent, and that the exchange of simple phrases with young children promoted fluency while their incorrectness would be offset by the studies in construction. Did I want to devote myself to a special practice of pronunciation? Some pupils had no interest in that, or perhaps no aptitude for it. But I was most anxious to become perfect in that very respect; Fraulein Doris would please be very strict with me. A good understanding was developed between us, and as we walked back to our hotel in the Rossplatz, we agreed that a satisfactory contract was under way.

The next thing was to introduce ourselves to the Herr Doktor Erb, a mild, blonde gentleman whose modest office seemed hardly representative of his worldwide fame. He had received a special letter from Dr. Seguin, and asked very few questions of his prospective patient, but had a certain regimen all ready to put before me, its main recommendation being that I should have plenty of fresh air and motion. He approved of living two miles out of town, and when told that my future dwelling was probably to be in Plagwitz, suggested that I make it my business to walk into town each morning for my lessons, returning by tram at noon. He peered into my eyes through a glass which produced the effect of boring into them, and made me hold one arm outstretched, seemingly for the purpose of testing its steadiness. His serious *"Gut!"* after these experiments, was heartening.

It was a somewhat melancholy parting, when I came to say good-by to my sister, after our congenial traveling and a greater measure of intimacy than we had ever known. The twelve years dividing our ages had been forgotten.

But I had already attained some fortitude and arrived courageously expectant at the Plagwitz villa. This was a large, country-like mansion, with a beautiful garden on a side-street at the end of the long two-or-three-mile turnpike stretching out from town. The top floor of the house, with pointed windows for all the world like Richter's pen-and-ink sketches, was inhabited by a blissful young married pair, of whom the other lodgers saw little. The second floor was given up to the consul and his wife and their young niece from New York, Annie Dexter. Colonel Montgomery was a hundred-per-cent American, intensely patriotic, and very scornful of the Germans, since he had been transferred to the Leipzig consulate from a much more congenial position in Brussels. His wife was very pretty, musical, and entertaining, but she, too, disliked the Leipzig environment. They were kind to me, however, and we discovered many friends in common.

On the ground floor of the house were the apartments of the *Familie Poetsch*, for such was the name of our corpulent—and indolent—landlord, whose hard-working wife carried on the menage with real talent. The man had lived in America for ten years, and as a baker had accumulated sufficient property to come back to his native land and live comfortably without labor, it was rumored, by the aid of certain successful German investments. He was also an American citizen, which gave him some privileges. He spent his days smoking and pacing the garden, guarded by a large mastiff called Pluto, and his evenings at a *Kneipe* where he consorted with a mysterious group of which I shall speak later. They had four enchanting children; Gustav, a boy of thirteen, the prim, regimented product of the German educational system; Olga, a fanciful but housewifely little maid of ten; and two smaller ones, Fränzchen and 'Nando, who attached themselves at once to me and became my inseparable companions out of study-hours. They were the saving of me during some of the desperate accesses of homesickness which came upon me in those first weeks.

My room, when fitted with a piano and the various pictures and other *penates* brought from America, was extremely pleasant, but lonely; partly because of the fact that my meals were served to me in solitude. The Montgomerys had their own dining-room, barely large enough for themselves, and the Poetsch family slept and ate in a mysterious background which I did not penetrate. There was another lodger whose apartment was next door, but propriety forbade one's eating in a gentleman's bedroom or entertaining him in one's own. He was an American student at the University, a long-legged, solemn-looking youth with eyeglasses, whose name, as I heard it, reminded me of a letter I had received just before sailing.

"If you are going to Leipzig," it had read, "maybe you will meet Dick N. He's studying there this winter and is really very nice, but a woman-hater—can't abide girls, they say. Maybe you can wake him up."

This was of course an interesting idea. He looked more indifferent than inimical. He happened to have had a letter also, it developed, whose contents he did not divulge till long after. It had said:

"Ruth H., your brother-in-law's friend, is going to Leipzig. Don't fall in love with her, or you may be sorry. She's not susceptible, but she's good fun."

The brother-in-law was much older than either of us, a clergyman who had married the young man's sister. The effect of these communications, was naturally to make us interested, and also amused, at finding ourselves housemates. Nevertheless, I had plunged too deeply into my studies to take account of personalities at first. I concluded also that my fellow-lodger was lazy, and careless of his privileges, as he practised very little, and though he went to town each morning did not seem to have engagements at any special hour.

I swallowed my lonesome meals with a lack of appetite and an occasional salty flavor from overflowing eyelids, and worked day and night at the intricacies of the German tongue. My music course had also begun. I was to have private lessons from Herr Coccius, one of the Conservatory professors, in order to be prepared for entrance there a few months later. Fräulein Herrnsdorf had recommended this arrangement as being the most satisfactory. Since his test of my piano performance, I had not ventured to play him anything more brilliant than a Schumann sketch. That had brought a verdict of good *Vortrag*, but much need of a carefully built-up technique. I knew it all too well; our beloved Ernst Held had not wanted to disturb the joy of an acquaintance with the great Masters and their works by over much drudgery, so the pipes of Pan had led the way and the pupil had followed at her will.

I mapped out a definite division of work. Each morning at eight came a walk through the great Johanna-Park, a short cut to the Nürnbergerstrasse, where Fräulein Doris awaited me three days in the week; then on the other two days to Herr Coccius's house for a lesson. He began at once to give me finger-exercises, for the construction of which I took notes, beginning with very simple ones played chromatically in all the keys. Coccius was called the Apostle of the fourth finger, and his methods included the development of that particular digit by putting extra tasks upon it and building up its efficiency. I was started on a Beethoven sonata, some variations of Schubert and a bit of Bach. The task seemed too heavy for one week's work, but there was no help for it; my hours lengthened and drudgery began. The teacher cared not a whit for sentimental interpretation or shading; in fact he scorned anything of the sort. A smooth, firm, mechanical rendering of the notes, a dead level of correctness only broken by the variations of phrasing were the objectives, and most necessary discipline it was. The days were leaden-gray; I braced myself upon the stiff piano-stool and followed the black notes with desperate persistence but not a ray of hope. Those were my first reactions, and they were gloomy ones.

With the language-lessons it was different; they were festivals. I climbed the stiff staircase to Fräulein Doris's apartment with an

elastic tread, even after a long walk. The teacher had always some
surprise ready. With her secret divining-rod she had learned that
her pupil would respond to a dramatization of the task laid out
for her, and pursue it all the more heartily for the sake of offsetting
the more mechanical drill at the piano. She made a rapid review
of the exercises I had written, picking out from their imperfections
my special weak points, and this she followed with pronunciation
exercises which I even practised, to the curiosity of passers-by, on
my way home.

There were rewards for assiduity. By the second week, the accumulation of a vocabulary was under way, and it was in late February, when there were hints of spring in soft afternoon light, in
moist earth and in the appearance of potted daffodils and tulips at
windows, that the brown-clad oracle in the Nürnbergerstrasse produced a bit of poetry as a special treat, to be read and memorized.
The sight of that precious possession, copied into my faded old
red blankbook in the stiff, slowly-executed German writing of a
tense pen, brings the day to mind with luminous clarity. It was
the *Lob des Frühlings* of Ludwig Uhland, and I dare not attempt
to translate it into English verse:

> *Saatin-grün, Veilchen-duft,*
> *Lerchenwirbel, Amselschlag,*
> *Sonnenregen, linde Luft!*
> *Wenn ich solche Worte singe*
> *Braucht es dann noch grösser Dinge*
> *Dich zu preisen, Frühlingstag?*

It was dictated, first, so that as one wrote the words their meaning
might possibly begin to penetrate. Somehow I caught the soft
moist breath, the misty sky left after winter's withdrawal, and felt
my consciousness melt into tender emotion with a quick reminder
of the happy past, of spring's "first flutes and drums," of the twilight orchestra of frogs in the meadows at Forty Acres, of Cole-
ridge's "dilating soul, enrapt, transfused," at dawn. A strange
tongue had intimated a bit of eternal truth and a finite mind had

grasped it. I could understand, could understand! The rapturous discovery of childish days was renewed; it did itself.

After that day each lesson provided a poem for memorizing and repeating in the park. I find copied in the old blank-book Lenau's *Schilflieder*, Heine's *Fichtenbaum steht einsam*, Rückert's *Aus Der Jugendzeit*, Uhland's *Schäfer's Sonntagslied*—all short, descriptive bits which gave distinct pictures to the imagination, and were easily memorized. The German script, labored and tensely correct at first, grows more pliable later on, as longer poems like Geibel's *Freundschaft und Liebe*, which fitted in with accesses of exuberant sentimentality, and his *Minnelied*, were undertaken, and Goethe's *Mailied*, and more Heine. Love-songs appealed to one mightily.

5

NIHILISTS IN LEIPZIG

On the first day of March, the Consul came in with an account of the royal wedding in Berlin on February 27th, to which our minister, Mr. Andrew White, had been bidden. We heard that the sedate young girl of the Channel trip was now the bride of a potential emperor, the erratic and physically handicapped Prince William. It had been a very gorgeous affair, but not nearly such a magnificent and impressive demonstration as that of his father and mother, for a cold indifference on the part of Bismarck and the military clique was evident.

We heard much gossip concerning strained relations of the Crown Princess, who was now in rather an equivocal position, with the old Emperor still in power and the young princes, her sons, in the hands of an element which was working to nullify her influence over them, under Bismarck's dictatorship. One of the stories which Doris Herrnsdorf imparted to her American pupil has never appeared, so far as I know, in any biography published, and may have been merely a malicious fiction, but it was whispered that in trying to keep her boys' education in her own hands the Crown Princess had followed the example of her mother Queen Victoria, who had succeeded in getting the Prince of Wales out of the clutches of the English army and direct military dominion. William was destined by German sanction to be reared a soldier, and the younger son, Henry, was claimed for the navy and sent on a long cruise at Bismarck's orders in spite of her frantic plea that such a little fellow, only thirteen, should not be taken from his devoted mother. After he had actually been carried off, and the steamer had docked for diplomatic reasons at a port in the Orient, the captain, it was said, received a telegram ordering that Prince Henry be sent back to Germany at once by special transport, signed by Crown Prince Frederick; a command which could not be disobeyed. The inference that his wife had really sent it, and used his name was of course to be deduced from this tale. It was also reported that in consequence of her insubordination the Crown Princess was known to have made a stay of several months in Switzerland—a species of exile. Naturally there was no way of verifying the report, but foreigners believed it and trusted in the benign influence of Anglo-German marriages. These unpleasant aspects were probably not serious, I concluded. But the story of the Schleswig-Holstein-Denmark usurpations as told by my teacher, who was of an independent mind and had no sympathy with the Austro-Prussian combination and its repercussions, gave me doubts and conflicts of a mild nature, which when talked over with the consul, and my new acquaintance, Richard, produced a nationalistic manifestation from the former, who detested the German government and all its works.

With the young man it was different. He had been frequenting, to improve his German, the already mentioned *Kneipe,* or beer-room where a small group, to which Herr Poetsch, our landlord, belonged, met every evening. The discussions there were conducted in a vernacular different from that of the University lecture-halls, naturally, and were rather difficult for a foreigner to understand. But he found them exciting enough and vehement enough to make him suspect that the men represented a revolutionary group, and he had even picked up hints of impending disaster, although it was only through facial distortions, oaths and sinkings of voice that this could be recognized. We had all discussed it, and Colonel Montgomery had warned the young man that he might get into some unpleasant complications if the police learned of the place and its associates, but had not succeeded in frightening him.

We two young people had had little to do with one another during our first fortnight under one roof, for I was altogether too much occupied with my lessons to have time for any more social contacts than an occasional half hour upstairs in the consul's flat. But it was presently suggested by the long-legged Richard that as he was due in classes every morning it would be pleasant to join forces with his next-room neighbor on her walk to town, instead of going alone over the long *Plagwitzerchaussee.* I was not pleased to have my solitude interrupted, but he proved quite adjustable, as I wrote my friend Lucy, and tramped along silently, smoking a short brown pipe, while I declaimed German poetry and gurgled, now quite easily, the *ra re ro.* One morning toward the middle of March, we encountered a curiously changed condition of things. The avenues in the Park, usually empty at that hour, held a stream of moving *droschken,* small one-horse carriages crowded with men who were to all appearances fugitives bound for the country districts. They were an unshaven, rather wild-looking crowd, most of them; there was something terrifying about the procession and the type of humanity it represented. The two Americans spoke of it and wondered what had occasioned the stampede. We parted at the gates of the Park and I walked on toward the Nürnbergerstrasse with a somewhat uneasy, though vague sense of disturbance. I met no women; usually early marketers with baskets were to be seen, but few female laborers. The pavements were deserted, only here and there a small crowd stood in front of some drug-store or newspaper-stand, trying to decipher a printed statement on a small sheet which had been pasted to its window.

I reached my destination, and climbed the stairs. Fraulein Doris was standing in the hallway, looking white and frightened.

"Was ist los, Fräulein?" she cried. "They are calling extras in the street. Something terrible must have occurred; that only happens when the Reichstag opens, or some great battle is fought. I am afraid for Bismarck, for the Kaiser; there are many nihilists in Leipzig!"

I could not tell her, but volunteered to try to find out something. I descended to the street, and joined the crowd in front of a nearby pharmacy. The Emperor of Russia, Alexander the Second had been murdered by a bomb, thrown at his carriage in the street, not far from the Palace, as he returned from some sort of military gathering. A nihilist plot was suspected. He had not regained consciousness before he died a few hours after.

It was frightful, frightful, said Fräulein Doris. This tragedy
was of enormous significance to Germany as well as Russia. Maybe
Bismarck would go next, or the Kaiser. The Social Democrats, it
was true, were strongly intrenched, and nihilism did not exist
within their ranks, but it was a menace, an incalculable sort of
thing. The police would undoubtedly act. It threw out our lesson,
for Fräulein Doris became voluble and spent the rest of the time
explaining what had led up to this turn of events, beginning in
purely feminine fashion with family history. As the tale unfolded
it appeared that Alexander II had endeavored to do justice to his
mistress the Princess by marrying her in an indecently short time
after his wife's death and bestowing upon her a high rank and a new
name, Princess Youriewski, to which restitution his two legitimate
children were said to have agreed. He was, in fact, we learned
afterward, about to sign a species of will giving her ample means
of support in the event of his death. One could not show any definite reason for the terrorists' attack at that particular point, for
he was returning peaceably from a military review.

I had known so little of contemporary Russian history that this
tragedy stood out against a vague background. But my teacher enlightened me. And at the end of the lesson, an hour-and-a-half, we
came upon Goethe's *Wanderer's Nachtlied,* I remember, after
Fräulein had quieted down. The words gave one the sense of
majesty in mountain-summits and blessed stillness in tree-tops, and
I was grateful for its calming influence on that disturbing day.

On our way back to Plagwitz, however, the pressure of mass-ex-
citement and fear was still perceptible in the atmosphere. The
sinister line of *droschken* with threatening passengers was still out-
ward-bound across the Johanna-Park; it was as if all the underground dens of criminality had disgorged their inhabitants. I had
never seen human beings with so menacing an aspect. It was a relief to get back to the Poetsch villa with its calm garden-shade. The
consul was very late that night and arrived in much excitement. A
small mob had torn down the flag outside the consulate. Leipzig
was declared to be in a state of siege, with the army in command;
the police, acting under it, had notified our landlord to collect the

passports of his American lodgers and deposit them at once at the Central Bureau, or *Amt,* since every foreign resident was in effect under arrest, unable to leave the city without permission. Hence the prompt exodus of many suspicious characters that morning. Richard, going that evening to the *Kneipe,* found it completely deserted, and the host more reserved than usual. Herr Poetsch also had discreetly remained at home.

There was apparently a political house-cleaning carried on for a number of weeks. Crowds of emigrants from all directions arrived at the railroad stations, especially by Bavarian trains, and crossed to another depot whence those heading for America would be dispatched to Hamburg or Bremen. Even Plagwitz, a small country village where peasants were accustomed to dance of an evening on the green in front of a peaceful little inn, had its quota of fleeing families. The nihilist ranks had been temporarily diminished, but there were disturbing elements in the population which must be suppressed, it appeared. Somehow one did not feel altogether safe, and even the courageous consul admitted that foreigners, official or not, were kept very much in the dark about governmental activities.

6

MUSIC IN LEIPZIG

Music and musical opportunities were as rich as ever. The two young people at No. 5 Lindenauerstrasse, Leipzig, were making all kinds of discoveries in one another's company. I joined the choir of the English chapel in the old *Bachschule* in the Thomasplatz in order to be clear of any suspicion of narrowness. Colonel Montgomery was an ardent churchman from his point of view—a wholly American one, however, and virulently opposed to the English Prayerbook.

The choir itself was unpromising. The English girls were shy and stiff and their weekly rehearsals, followed by tea and biscuit at one of the boarding-houses, were not yet productive of any friendships. But we two young people at the Poetsch villa went together on Saturday noons to hear the Bach *Motetten* sung in the *Thomaskirche,* the grand old church where Johann Sebastian Bach had been organist and choirmaster. From the building of his old school near by, undernourished lads in faded green caps came across the cobblestone pavement of the square and sang like young larks from the upper gallery, rendering the dignified anthems and chorales. The bells of the *Thomaskirche* came to be part and power of my Leipzig life. As the English chimes had expressed a sort of slogan of continuity and security, so these German bells grew—while I worked next door to them for two years—to stimulate a rhythm in my daily habit and study.

I went by myself, one day soon after my arrival in Leipzig, to explore the tall belfry, towering above the little square and its surrounding houses. Entering through a low door at the foot of the tower, there came a long climb up winding stairs past the huge

festival bell which could be rung only at Christmas, Easter or
Pfingsten by four men standing on a hinged platform like a see-saw.
At the top of the staircase three children's faces looked down at
me through a trap-door—the family who lived like birds in the summit of the tower, with a father, a man long since retired from the
world because of a terrible scar on his face, and a mother who
cooked and washed, let down baskets for bread and coal, and
received the many tourists who climbed to look at the view. All five
became my warm friends. In their company I explored the rough-
boarded space above the organ loft and learned how to reach that
sanctum by descending some sort of ladder leading to various
galleries and corners. I was introduced to Bach's own organ and allowed to play a chorale on its yellow keys, with little Hermann serving manfully as blower and Clara Elizabeth and Olga Martha dangling their thin legs from either end of the bench, while their father
grinned contentedly, a bunch of dusty rags in hand. The royal pew,
an arched niche perched on high, commanding a view of the whole
interior, was hung with faded emblems and worn banners, and the
family offered to smuggle me into it when the *Hohe Messe* was
sung, or the Passion-music.

Evidently they regarded themselves as leading performers, with
their command of the bellows; and why not, I thought. In that capacity one had the joy of being organist, chorus, and cantor; everything depended on one's brawn. Music as an element of life, I said
to myself, is the interpreter of revelation, a winged ministry like that
of the angels. I came down the winding stairs that day with a deeper
respect for the old faith of Martin Luther and its perpetuity, and
for the family life which could plainly keep its integrity and unity
even in the restriction of the gloomy old tower, far above the rabble
in the narrow square below. The children's content, the parents'
pride, brought a new peace into my soul.

There was other music. We heard many operas at that last end
of the season. One went at six o'clock, after a cup of tea or other
light refreshment, and returned for a late supper at nine or there-
abouts. The first opera of the Leipzig experience was *Fidelio,* the
great favorite of the people. Merely to see the audience thrill, weep,

utter bravos, recall the singers, was more than satisfaction. And the second was Gluck's *Alceste* which introduced me to old-time ballet and rather ludicrous attempts at classic effects but wonderful orchestral achievements. After that the *Barber of Seville* struck a popular note, and then when Mozart's *Magic Flute* came on, the opera reached its highest point for me.

Richard, my housemate, made a very good escort on these occasions, and sometimes an attractive Boston man joined us. I found that going to the opera with two men was not especially thrilling, for I took it as the Germans did. It was a genuine rest, I concluded, to find oneself out of an atmosphere where every young man one met was regarded as a potential husband. Our trio, very congenial, came and went quite freely, each too much interested in his own pursuits to think of other people except as incidental participants.

We were all anxious to hear *Tristan und Isolde* when that came, and the young men had been studying the motives and text enthusiastically. I myself was merely curious. I was still musically conservative, intolerantly retentive of first impressions, determined to stand out against the "sensuality" of the music, and impatient with the long-drawn out passages in the love-scenes. I could not resist the cry of the *Walküre,* however, nor the dash of the horses across the stage, not to mention the mechanical splashing of the Rhine maidens against blue gauze billows. And as for the "hoots and squeals," as I would then have called them, inside the Venusberg, they were most intriguing when offset by the address to the Evening Star and the exuberance of the Tannhäuser March. It was not my fault if a thirst for heroic harmony and flowing melody had been created in me, as in most nineteenth century music lovers, and in truth those first months in Germany brought me enough enchantment to endanger my deeper purposes, had it not been for the pledge that lay behind them. There was rich reaping in the harvest of that year's musical production. Two great Masses were sung: the *Hohe Messe* of Bach, and the *Missa Solemnis* of Beethoven; either one of these enough in itself for a whole season's glory. I had never dreamed that a *Miserere* could be written through which one might listen to the cry of a world of sinners, not merely a pious congregation; had never felt the solemnity and massed authority of a *Credo*; had never been swept up into the heights by a *Resurrexit* like Bach's. More irresistible waves of conviction swept over me, and lifted me beyond mere assent, beyond the stated truth of my religious experience, and the acknowledgment of belief.

7

GERMAN EASTER

On the great day of Holy Week, Good Friday, the singing of
the Bach Passion-music was truly a national event, and nowhere
more devotional and significant than in the Leipzig *Thomaskirche*.
First came the rehearsal, on the night of Maundy Thursday. The
old church was so flooded with moonlight that a few groups of
people slipped quietly in and felt their way into the pews; only dim
lights shone in the organ-gallery over our heads, where the members
of the *Bach-Verein,* a chorus which ran back in the history of its
membership to the Master's time, was assembled. The effect was
solemn, hallowed; yet that does not express the spirit which moved
through the music. One of the most moving of the arias was *Ach,
Golgotha! unsel'ge Golgotha*! At the very end, there was a sense of
peace. Then slowly, one by one, the listeners stole away. Lights
were put out, the doors closed, and the old church left in its moonlit
solitude.

One woke Good Friday morning with a sense of world-tragedy.
Through the long forenoon there was quiet in the business-streets;
even the battalions of soldiers who usually marched to gay music,
refrained. Before two o'clock people began to come to the *Thomaskirche,* first by twos and threes, then in crowds. For an hour the
throng poured in; they filled the long auditorium, the galleries, the
canopied balconies where royalty had sat in state. All ages, all
races: the clergy, the city officials, the helmeted soldiers, merchants,
servants, a crowd like that at the foot of the Cross on Calvary. I cannot remember whether a great bell tolled, although memory suggests it, but I do know that neither of the two young Americans who
found place in the assemblage had ever seen so universal a spirit of

reverence and mourning. That first Good Friday was a revelation of the power and intensity of the Lutheran faith. I looked upon the scene of the Crucifixion with the inner eye, and heard with the ear something as truly a voice from among the voices which are neither speech nor language. I came out in the awed and silent procession, and was grateful that my companion, also, remained speechless and left me to my own thoughts as we walked out across the long stretch of highway to Plagwitz.

There was work to be done before and after supper, for I had made plans to go to Dresden by the morning train. I had also to consult with Mr. and Mrs. Montgomery for Richard had asked that he be allowed to make the trip also.

"I don't see why I can't," he maintained, "when I go about with you here every day. If I'm sailing for home next month, I must see Dresden before I leave Germany.

"Well, we'll ask the consul," I said rather grudgingly. "It would be nice, but I don't know what he'll think."

To our amazement, both elders agreed at once that there was no harm whatever in his going, and admitted that they would feel far easier to have him "along" for the trip. So next morning we two made the two-hour journey quite peacefully.

In Dresden we proceeded to the attractive *pension* kept by Fräulein von Germar, a lady of aristocratic birth whose German had been recommended as perfect. She was a woman of dignity, and welcomed us into her beautiful apartment, filled with treasures of furniture and painting. She gave a keen glance at Richard as he put down my bags in the pleasant room assigned me.

"And where do you go, young man?" she inquired.

He smiled, "To the hotel, I suppose. I am the Fräulein's fellow-boarder in Leipzig, but she won't let me stay in this house."

"Why"—in energetic German, "if you live in the same house in Leipzig, can you not do so here? Am I not a chaperon? I assure you I'm very strict!"

He looked at his companion. "If you say you think it's all right," he began, "I might—."

"I don't dare impugn Fräulein von Germar's efficiency," I

laughed. "Make your bargain with her; she's letting her rooms, not I."

So he stayed without further ado, and the question of propriety was dropped.

We went to the theatre, to the great Gallery, to the environs of Dresden by way of the Elbe pleasure-boats. Easter was a gloriously bright day, and we were wakened before sunrise by the heavy booming of cannon, a ceremony which symbolized the rolling of the stone from the Saviour's tomb. There was one tremendous report, and in the silence which followed it began the soft twitter of waking birds. Then came detachments of soldiers, the blue Hussars of the Royal Guard first, in bright festival-uniforms marching through the streets to bands playing chorales and joyful hymns. The two comrades went to early service at the beautiful English Church and heard our own familiar carols, with full ritual—Easter would not have been complete without that, we both agreed. The young man had presented me with a bunch of violets that made me think of Archie and wonder what kind of an Easter Day he was having; just how much the significance of the Festival would mean to him in America. His photograph, in a small velvet frame, had been taken from the top of my piano in Leipzig and was set up on Fräulein von Germar's little dressing-table.

We took a long walk that afternoon, and absorbed the atmosphere of the typical German festival-holiday. We saw *das Volk* at its best, alive with color and self-abandonment, nationalism forgotten; the spirit of the joyous child. All Dresden was thrown open to a moving mass with color, light and *rhythm*, no harsh or cheap sounds but always a strain of music in the distance; behind it all the celebration of an event of deep significance. The performances of Faust which were held on the two successive nights were interesting but grotesque, because the astounding perfection of detail in the scenery overpowered one's emotional response to the poetry.

The week passed rapidly. We visited the Gallery daily. I was systematic in my study of the different schools. One Dutch landscape, Ruysdael's *Sandy Road on a Summer Day,* was a reminder of Hadley by-ways, and I visited it every day for a moment before leaving. There were pleasant social contacts also: garden-parties, steam-er-excursions on the *Elbe,* and one delightful dinner-party given by the American wife of a German general.

I returned to the routine of study mentally refreshed. Already the German language was becoming fluent and familiar. The jour-ney back to Leipzig took us through lovely country, with the new-sown fields in their fresh green and symmetrical lines, in compari-son with which our American agriculture seemed rough and un-tidy.

Archie's letters had not been communicative. His first one, answering my account of the sea-voyage, was studiously matter-of-fact. I had re-read it many times, trying to wring out some evidence of sentiment. He had said:

You must have had a glorious time on the voyage over, with all the novelties of an ocean journey and its attractions on board ship, which include, I presume, the young Englishmen, the officers, the naval knight, etc. I hope you didn't flirt too desperately with them.

The mild sarcasm was disquieting. Had my vaunted conquests suggested the application of that dismal fallacy, so frequently ac-cepted by young women, that the way to hold a man's affections is to keep him jealous? While there might be nothing to hope for, I could hardly wish to destroy what was hitherto so natural and spon-taneous, so in answering a long and far less reserved epistle which was waiting on my return from Dresden, I refrained from any similar allusions. One's correspondence was selective and a trifle complicated anyway. Different people wanted to hear about differ-ent things. To one's parents one described churches and concerts and fine landscapes and lessons and impressions; young women heard of social contacts, and handsome officers and operas and cele-brated buildings; the man of one's heart would be glad to know what constituted one's chief happiness, and have just a little assur-ance that . . . . well, one must be careful not to take too much for granted, of course, but one need not keep one's own heart and its promptings under lock and key exactly, even though one might not carry it on one's sleeve! I sighed over the heavy responsibility and now and then tore up a too-sentimental passage.

In a letter to my brother, I had written of a military parade, and in contrast to the disturbing effect of those witnessed on Boston Common, I found myself enthusiastic over brass bands. The glamour of the uniform, the helmet and the sword had no connection with slaughter in the peaceful Germany of 1881, and the official march of the Leipzig regiments was the Carmen *Toreador,* which evoked happy recollections of the night when Archie and I had gone to the opera in Boston.

In May Richard sailed for America, his year of study over. The Poetsch family, to whom he had endeared himself greatly, children and all, parted from him in tears, and the great mastiff, Pluto, refused to leave his kennel for twenty-four hours.

8

REASSURANCE

July had hardly come in when a public tragedy shattered the composure of the American colony. On the morning of the third, the consul wakened me with a terrifying knock and called:

"Bad news from America! President Garfield shot; this world is too wicked to go on any longer. Listen"—and he read a telegram just received from Washington. It was a severe shock to everyone; dispatches poured in all day at the Consulate, reporters besieged house and office, the American flag hung at half mast; a mist of doubt brooded over the foreign community. A grand Independence Day dinner was in preparation, and as Mr. Montgomery was especially happy in presiding at functions of the sort, we were hoping it might take place after all and be turned into a sort of consolation-gathering; but Mr. White telegraphed from Berlin that all festivities must be called off.

Just as my spirits seemed to reach their lowest point, however, Dr. Zakrzewska wrote that she had arrived in Dresden. It was precisely the moment for a reassuring figure to appear on my horizon. I went to Dresden immediately.

When we were alone she asked "Are you amused?"

"Very much."

"Are you in love? I forgot to ask that last year."

"Not with anyone in Germany."

"I see," the keen eyes softened. "Is he patient?"

"He must be. But need I stay three whole years?"

"Let me count. You were to teach when you go home, were you not? I think we might say till a year from next May; that will have given you two and a half seasons."

"I've learned one thing and another already," I volunteered. "You were right about music. It's no escape from the vicissitudes of life; it's woven into life, through and through. It's the rhythm of all growth; religion, science. The study of it has to do with the making of character and steadying of one's emotions, not running away from them. I realized that. You don't get terribly excited about it, over here, you just *go in for it*. I can't express it, but you'll understand. I never thought that digging at piano-technique would be actually a creative thing, but it is."

"Certainly it is. You gain power, too, by thoroughness; and that is something you can learn in Germany. And power means self-control, or ought to. Go on drudging, and keep yourself well."

In those two and a half seasons that followed, my studies were interrupted first by a trip to Thuringia in the capacity of chaperon for Mrs. Montgomery's thirteen year old niece, Annie Dexter. I was, to be sure, rather young for that role, so I made my costume as duenna-like as possible, but I do not think I should have deceived the Germans we visited, even if my young charge had not given me away in a confidential moment. In any case, it was a delightful experience, and after I met American friends in Weimar, I joined Arria in Switzerland, and went to the Bernese Oberland for a month. From there, I traveled with three students. We were a hilarious group and I realize with mortification that our disregard of public opinion, or public convenience, for that matter, must have made a horrible impression on the beholder. At Frankfurt I embarked for Leipzig, but not to the Plagwitz villa, for the Poetsch family had moved into small city quarters; the consul and his wife to a hotel.

The right kind of German family, however, had been found through the ministrations of Miss Doris and an astounding advertisement which she had published in the *Tageblatt,* mentioning her pupil as a *höchstgebildete Amerikanerin*! In less than a week I settled in the old stone house which belonged to Herr Pastor Valentiner, the Archdeacon of the Thomas Church, with the *Bachschule* and its green-capped family of boys opposite, the great tower next door, and the short alley leading to the military fortress, the *Pleissenburg,* whence a glittering regiment emerged triumphantly.

Once or twice a week the tread of marching feet sounded in the Burggasse at sunrise, and a band trumpeted the Carmen *Toreador*. Looking down from my window I saw serried ranks of helmeted men moving as one, without even the suggestion of a break in their strenuous lines or a single bayonet out of place.

I settled down to a steady routine, continuing my lessons with Fräulein Herrnsdorf, and at the Conservatory of which I had become a member. Coccius was my teacher of piano, and Dr. Rust of harmony and counterpoint. On Wednesdays I went with my fellow students to the last rehearsal of the *Gewandhaus* concert, and every afternoon I studied until tea-time, when Minna the maid would announce that the Frau Pastor was serving tea. Fresh *Zwieback,* or sweet cakes were served on a plate with a twisted border, like the plate Cousin Sarah Phelps had used for her caraway cookies in our childhood. To the children who sometimes came, I told fairy tales. Or if there were a real afternoon party, or *Kaffee-Klatsch,* I was prim and proper, being anxious to learn the rules of German etiquette that I might be considered a well-brought-up *Mädchen* at the more formal dinner parties where the American girl's idea of entertaining her partner was considered bad form by German matrons. More than once that was curbed by means of a reproving glance from the opposite side of the table.

On Sundays the Archdeacon came out in his full black gown, and marched to the Thomaskirche, where he made an impressive figure in the pulpit. At the jovial Sunday noon gathering, wine was served instead of beer. In the afternoon, the women got out their embroidery, and although I was accustomed to the easy ways of our Forty Acres Sundays, an illogical conscience bothered me. I wrote to the Bishop, thinking it might amuse him to justify this breach of the Fourth Commandment in the Archdeacon's house, and he answered that I could safely join in the occupations of the family if I sewed something useful for others' benefit. Oddly enough, I curled feathers to decorate the hats of the Valentiner family! I had learned to do it at home, so I went to work with a silver knife, curling up the ostrich plumes which the Leipzig climate flattened, and thus dismissed conscience from sentinel duty.

During those autumn weeks, however, a sobering piece of news from home made me feel inwardly solitary. It came first in an affectionate, but short letter from my brother James. He had made a momentous decision; he was leaving home and his work in Syracuse to join, or practically found, a monastic order, living in the slums of New York and devoting his life henceforth to poverty, celibacy and labor among the people of the tenement regions. It meant not only a party which I knew would be agonizing to his father, but a change to the extreme Anglican position, and a reversion to primitive forms of doctrine and sacramental practice. I knew his intense interest in the Oxford movement and its fruits. Sometimes I had thought it would be the Church of Rome to which he would turn, and had wondered whether that was destined to be the next move in the religious history of the family. But I felt sure that his sweetness of spirit would make the disclosure as gentle as possible, and that there would be no break in the harmony of the household. Father's letter, and one from my older brother, full of affection and solicitude, were reassuring. We had lost him, in one sense— his bodily presence would be terribly missed in the household— but it was to be expected that a son would sometime leave his father's house for a new field of labor and a greater independence, and the Bishop's sympathy with that move would be ready. The sisters knew none the less that to his mind the revival of a monastic system meant return to outworn medieval practices and mystical beliefs. He would be somewhat in the position of his old Unitarian friends at Harvard, when he left them to go into the Episcopal Church. Yet not quite that; his confidence in his son was too strong to leave room for doubts that the change would bring an opportunity for greater usefulness. He wrote:

How could I hold him back—knowing his heart, seeing what he has done for me, and fully believing with him that the Church sorely needs both a standard of holy living in the Ministry and a leaven of evangelization supplementing our miserable, halting, half-secular parochial system. . . . . They live in poverty, chastity and obedience—with bare floors, no tablecloths, scanty furniture, plain food, and seem content.

I went and celebrated with them one morning, slept there in a cot, and we consecrated the different rooms with prayers. . . . . Pray for them.

A Way to Life. That was what they were trying for, before all else. More life, and fuller. What matter if doctrines differed? The Bishop's daughter thought of Luther, battling against pernicious practices, holding his own as witness to the Faith before the judgment-seat of an emperor and a crowd of judges, praying in the solitude of his cell in the Wartburg, bravely defying evil, yet breaking in the end over a dispute regarding the nature of a sacrament. Music, learning, fighting, expounding, the founding of a great church. His life a warrior's combat. But St. Francis, the saint of all others who most appealed to her in his choice of the Way—our brother had followed him in holy poverty. This was the transition of the third successive generation. Archie was in the fourth. I wondered how his quest—the search nearest to my heart—was coming on. And I was confident, with the hopefulness of youth, that whatever faith he came to embrace, were it that of the oriental or the Catholic or the man of science ever groping and analysing, there would be no shadow between our souls. I attacked the history of monastic orders, in my late evening hours, and also began Ekkehart. The contribution of the monks to literature, to agriculture, to art, hitherto only dreamily comprehended, took hold of my imagination for the time, and with my old impulsive habit, I centred my attention upon past conditions, gloating over the fact that my very dwelling made an appropriate setting for the picture.

9

SIX TOGETHER

Friendship, however—the one thing needed to give reality and interpretation to the experiences of that remarkable winter, was coming into the pattern. I cannot remember just how the power of social gravitation drew six of us into one another's company and held us united during the rest of our stay in Germany. I believe three of us met at a tea given by the Fräuleins Bohm, to whom I had been introduced by letter. The other two were brother and sister, James and Annie Muirhead.

Jim was a lanky Scotchman, with auburn hair, a much more approachable personality than many of the Britons we had met, and evidence of a culture that plainly fitted him for his position as compiler of a German *Baedeker*, the indispensable guide-book of foreigners. It required constant and up-to-date research to keep abreast of changing conditions, as well as a cosmopolitan outlook and a thorough knowledge of business, banks and exchanges, so he was in permanent residence at Leipzig for most of the year, and was more socially stabilized than any other *Ausländer*. His sister Annie was the genuine Scotch lassie, demure but with a sparkle of fun and a clever brain; they kept house together in a small apartment. We were very good friends, going to classes and concerts together. We even undertook to read aloud an English book now and then in short sessions, when two New Englanders, accompanied by their mother, arrived in Leipzig. The three were members of the Cabot family of Boston, on their father's side; their mother was a cousin of my grandmother Sargent. They fraternized with the Scotch couple, and the four fitted admirably.

The Bostonians I shall call Peter and Nora and the sixth, Felix.

Felix had a knack of getting on with difficult people, particularly Germans. He was medical, not musical, but said very little about his profession; he had been brought up among Philadelphia Quakers, and absorbed something of their shrewdness. He and the Cabots had mutual friends, and it was through them that he became attached to our group.

We fell into the habit of doing things together a good deal; going to concerts or operas in twos or threes, or all six at once, men and girls separately or in a mixed company, often including other acquaintances, and if transient visitors needed to be entertained, taking them about or getting up parties for the theatre or lunching at the *Café Francais*, or going for supper to Bonorand's—the popular beer garden in the Rosenthal Park, where there was always lovely music. We ordered favorite German dishes which we had learned to like: *Häringsalat, Schmierkäse, Sauerkraut, Rehbraten,* Saxon coffee, of which one could drink any amount without disturbance, since, as Dr. Erb observed, it was loaded with chicory. We drank beer or red wine. The men smoked pipes if they smoked at all; we were enveloped at any rate in clouds of tobacco. (A Weber Overture always makes me smell cigar-smoke and taste *Wurst*.)

James Muirhead, as a permanent resident, knew all the ropes— and ran a set of dances those two winters, getting hold of new arrivals from London or America, hunting up obscure students with a social bent, and introducing some German officers who were always available for the gayeties of foreigners. Those dances in the winter of 1881-2, usually ended with a cotillion for which the girls made up figures and favors. Peter Cabot or the tall Scotchman led the cotillion usually, and we all became inured to the queer twirling waltz step of the Germans, which was somewhat dizzying. They had indefatigable legs and were never tired; the uninitated were always ready to drop after the first round.

After a Tuesday night dance we used to stumble over to the *Gewandhaus* more dead than alive in the dark next morning, and talk it over as we ate our *Brödchen* in the concert-seats. The concerts themselves were always a fresh surprise. Some of the great musicians of the world came; Sarasate with his Spanish violin and his passionate, tense features and graceful bowing. He was young then and achieved a far greater sensation in Leipzig than he afterward did in this country; Moskowski and Scharwenka made great "hits." Rubinstein as conductor and soloist, came leading his Ocean Symphony with such *éclat* that the whole orchestra broke out incontinently, playing every instrument at once with wild shrieks and thumping of drums, and Reinecke embraced him in public, so to speak, while the audience shouted bravos and encores.

There was much excitement when Hans Von Bulow appeared in the *Gewandhaus* with his Saxe-Meiningen orchestra, the Grand Duke's favorite art-trophy. The musicians wore a uniform of red-and-silver, and brought their own equipment of seats and *pulte* to match, not to mention the most superior of instruments. Bülow was himself in a nervous condition at that period. Fifteen years before he had taken heroically the elopement of his wife Cosima, daughter of Liszt and Madame d'Agoult, with Wagner, and kept the sincere friendship of her father, who deplored the match. But it had been a terrific strain on his sensibilities, had left him a neurotic, and on occasions he betrayed sharp irritability. One climax during the rehearsal-concert of the Meiningen orchestra made a lasting impression on the Leipzig gathering. The first movement of a Beethoven symphony—the fifth I think—was under way with the audience holding its breath in wonder, when three or four unlucky late-comers somehow got into the hall and were trying to find their seats. Bülow heard the slight stir, turned his head, caught a glimpse of them and struck his baton sharply against metal; the players stopped in the middle of a bar, with the finality of a lightning-flash. The scared interrupters, their faces as white as the leader's stumbled into the midst of the waiting audience, his glance piercing their souls, no doubt, with its malignity. The horrible moment lasted until they had dropped into place, and then in another flash he turned, raised his baton, and the instruments took up instantly the beat at which they had paused, and continued the symphony in triumph. It was a feat so amazing that a storm of applause followed. Many ventured an opinion that the whole thing was done to show off his power over the players; but whether or not, Bülow earned preeminence as an interpreter of Beethoven through the achievements of the Meiningen orchestra, and no one who can remember his conducting will ever be able to satisfy himself completely by listening to the conductors of today; the subtle rendering of tone-values, the reserve, the stateliness, which the music demands, was brought to its peak in that era, and I believe has never reached such perfection since.

Clara Schumann came to play Mendelssohn's G Minor concerto, with the orchestra, and a Beethoven sonata, *Les Adieux,* Opus 81A at the *Gewandhaus* concert, and take the piano part in her husband's quintette at the chamber music on Saturday night. Nora Cabot and I were on the scent, the day after her arrival in town. Nora had a forenoon practice-hour in the conservatory building; the old janitor was susceptible to small attentions and promised his aid. He was sure Madame Schumann would come to try the piano. About eleven o'clock he appeared in the practice-room, and laid one finger aside of his nose, pointing with the other in the direction of the Concert-room. *"Angekommen!"* he whispered.

We slipped out of the door, up the mysterious little staircase which came out into the gallery just above the stage. We crawled on hands and knees, afraid to let our heads be seen above the seat-backs. A furtive peep showed us two figures in front of the piano; a white-haired old lady of sixty-three and her daughter, a fine-looking, dark-haired woman. There was a little discussion over chairs; it was hard to find one of the right height, among the orchestra-seats. Finally when a satisfactory one was discovered, Madame Schumann said:

"Now, how shall I know which this is, at the concert? I *must* be able to find it. We'll mark it; *was?*"

"Oh yes, I know. See: this way." The daughter produced from her silk knitting-bag a ball of red yarn, and broke off a long piece. "So; *'rum und 'rum;'*" she wound it about one of the rungs of the chair-back and made it fast. "Now you will be able to pick it out." Then her mother sat upon it and began to practice the sonata.

The musician struck the piano, played a part of the lovely slow movement of the concerto. There was one passage, a descending scale, that did not please her. She played it over and over—it must have been at least fifty times; just that one bit. By and by she went back to the beginning and played the whole movement, letting the difficult run take its place naturally. And just before the very last bars, at the end, something made her look up and catch sight of the two girls' faces, and she gave us a smile all for ourselves, which sent shivers of delight down our spines. We hardly dared breathe till she had left the hall. All the rest of the day was spent in telling of our adventure.

Of course Madame Schumann played even more beautifully at the concert itself, and the Leipzigers applauded almost hysterically. On Saturday evening some old friends, members of the *Kränzchen* of her young days but now dear old ladies in caps and soft shawls, sat with her on the stage, their knitting in their hands. She looked younger than any of them; there was a freshness of youth about her, for all her silver hair. When she rose to take her place at the piano and walked past the row, each one grasped her hand in turn, with a smile of encouragement, as if to assure her that she would acquit herself successfully. And when the Quintette was finished, she consented to play some of the *Davidsbündler,* and then the *Warum?* with a wistful, lingering touch and a tender recollection, one could feel, of her husband and lover. I ventured to go and see her next day, taking a photograph under which she wrote her name.

By this time, Fräulein Doris and I were reading *Faust.* It had been promised me that I should begin it when my understanding of the German language had reached the requisite point, so the sweetness of reward was added to the zest of literary adventure. And by good luck, that winter was productive of all varieties of Faust-music. There was the Gounod opera of course. The Liszt Faust Symphony was played two winters, and stood out from some less worthy productions of the great composer. The Schumann Faust-music was one of the most beautiful performances of the winter, and was given on the same programme as the Ninth Symphony; a stupendous event in my experience.

10

After the Christmas holiday with its trees and chorales and carols and typical German celebrations, in the pastor's family, I returned to the special pattern of recreation which the six of us had developed. Three of us actually gave a ball, and invited all the young English-speaking residents, and a few Germans, mostly officers, to give color to the occasion. Jim Muirhead and Peter Cabot were Masters of Ceremony, and helped us to carry out our determination that everyone should have an equal amount of attention, and every dancer be kept moving. It was most certainly a success, but no hint of the ball was ever given in letters to my parents. Perhaps the fatal "weakness for admiration" which the Bishop had noted after a visit to Cornell, might have accounted for the failure to record this important occasion. My letters were, in any case, decidedly selective.

For the Easter holiday, the six of us travelled to Dresden, with Mrs. Cabot to chaperon us. The performance of *Faust* which was given that season meant infinitely more to me, with my better knowledge of German, than the performance I had seen the year before. But even more than the music I enjoyed intensely the common adventures with my five friends; we were responsible to nobody but ourselves, and developed a congenial intimacy which had implications no deeper than that of pleasant companionship. During that time lessons were interrupted often by the many diversions around us, and I had to make up my work late at night, but somehow did not miss the sleep.

In the spring, life at the Thomas-parsonage was transferred to the Johannesgarten, a great tract of land outside the city where hundreds of little gardens were laid out, each surrounded by a wall high enough to insure the privacy of the family who used it. Every pleasant afternoon, when lessons were over, we took the tram and travelled thither, proceeding down the long central avenue to a little gate with a number on it, letting ourselves in with a special key. The Valentiner-Bruhns garden was at least a quarter-of-an-acre in size, two or three great trees at one end shading a small *Garten-haus* which could hold a dozen people in case of a shower, and had a tiny kitchen with a stove and cooking utensils. Minna, laden with a heavy market-basket, preceded us thither. By four o'clock the family was assembled; the Herr Pastor in the shade, his wife beside him, and a table in front of them set out with coffee-cups. The boys studied in another corner usually, the little children playing by themselves in a sand-pile; the two girls, with Willi when he was free, played croquet. After our coffee, pretzels and Zwieback there was a half-hour of chatting, and at eight a supper of cold meat and salad in the long-lingering twilight.

The maids went home, taking the little children; the rest of us sat on, on the cool ground, and talked, listened to mingled sounds of music and hilarity which rose from the adjoining gardens; last of all a bowl of *Maitrank,* kept cool by being buried in the earth, was brought out and glasses filled. It was white wine, filled with fresh green sprigs of *Waldmeister*, a wood-plant which gave it a delicately pungent flavor, and was consummately refreshing. The great warm moon came up, and flooded the garden with light; we sat on and on sometimes till the bells of the city sounded their midnight stroke. Those tranquil evenings have a place in memory like the gatherings on the old stoop at Forty Acres; shut away from the weariness and restlessness of humanity, and from the problems of past and future; the quiet heart of that strenuous Leipzig life.

In July came a journey to Heidelberg, where I went to await the arrival of my friend Lucy, and go, at Dr. Watson's invitation, a month later on a drive through Switzerland and the Engadine. The Cabots and Muirheads went thither also; Felix had gone with his family to travel among the Alps. It was a month of excursions, boating on the Neckar, spending long afternoons in the Castle grounds. Old friends turned up and augmented our group. Then came the summons to join the Watsons at Lucerne, leaving Heidelberg by night just after a dance, with a jovial group in slippers and muslin gowns and evening suits at the station. The next morning, at the *Beau Rivage,* with the blue lake sparkling and the half circle of hotels, drawn up in line, as it were, to receive the trainfuls of arriving tourists, we had a joyful meeting.

Our drive from Lucerne through Andermatt, Ilanz, Tiefenkasten, above the St. Gothard tunnel which was then begun, was an interlude of pure happiness. Dr. Watson, Lucy, and a young cousin, Helen Choate of Boston and a rather dolorous French maid, completed the party which set off from Fluelen on Monday morning in a large travelling-carriage drawn by four horses, their harness decorated with red tassels and hung with gentle bells. The departure from our lodging-places each morning were moments of intense anticipation; the packing of rugs and alpenstocks, the basket of juicy fruits, the bag of books—we had *John Inglesant,* I remember, and a couple of French novels and Charles Kingsley's Life, and *Yeast,* in Tauchnitz paper editions.

Socialism, and the stirrings of labor unrest had had their repercussions in America. Letters from my brother in New York had kept me in touch with this, and he was at that moment deeply interested in the founding of the Knights of Labor, one of the earlier unions. He had instigated a sympathetic association in the Episcopal Church, small but valiant, and we were keen for a knowledge of its forerunners in Great Britain, where Charles Kingsley's interest in the Chartists had had its influence also. We had both wanted to read his *Yeast,* published some years earlier, and brought it out in the evenings, discussing as we read.

We arrived, after crossing the Albula Pass in wind and snow-squalls, at the Hotel Roseg, Pontresina.

Prince and Princess Christian had come to Pontresina in order to be present at the consecration of a newly-finished English Church to which they had contributed, and a choir was in process of formation for the service, with Joseph Barnby himself to train it. The Barnbys immediately became our friends. We were asked to join the class, and sang lustily on the great day, August 19, which we always commemorate as being an outstanding event in our history. *Barnby in E* was one of our favorite chants already, and we persuaded the composer to train us in it that we might use it with greater devotion in time to come.

One night when I was playing the piano for a dance, and running into Chopin polonaises in the intermission, an old gentleman came and leaned on the piano, and asked me where I had studied. After a while he announced himself as the husband of the late Jenny Lind; he was Otto Goldschmidt, who was traveling as tutor for the little sons of Prince and Princess Christian. When in America, he had stayed for a time in Northampton, so this common bond resulted in a pleasant supper at his hotel.

11

COUNTRY OF SAINTS

From the land of avalanches and glaciers and deep cold lakes, we went on over the sombre Bernina Pass and dropped down into Italy. Now we were in Catholic country; the country of the saints, of hierarchies, of monasteries and mystics, of miracles, of sacred art. All along our road we came upon wayside reminders of the faith. The crucifixes were poorly carved, and we were sometimes more shocked than moved at their crude pretensions. But here and there a great stark cross, with crown of thorns and nails and hammer, standing back on some lone hill-top in relief against the sky, brought to mind the Divine Figure, and we bowed our heads while the driver made a devout sign upon his breast as he held the lines in his left hand. When we had reached the end of a day's journey and came out into the twilight, we often saw the outline of an old village church against the fading sky, and a dim light burning above the head of the priest in the doorway, as he stood holding the bell-rope, while his peasant flock came up the stony path in twos and threes. The three girls would join the kneeling figures within and sometimes wait for the chanting and the Latin petitions and the benediction.

I felt that of the three great European churches I had known, it was the Church of Rome that touched the hearts of humble people by the simplest and most constant reminders of the Holy Presence in their midst. Ever since the early prayers in the haymow, I had been seized at moments with a longing to get out of the ordered, active church life and its obligations, its liturgies, the catechisms to be learned or taught to others, the sermons to be listened to, the truths to be accepted, and the doubts to be com-

batted, and have a religious holiday among unprivileged people—
people for whose spiritual safety one need feel no responsibility.

But then there was Archie, shaming me by his steady persistence
in searching for a fundamental truth underlying all faiths, as he
expressed it, before accepting the doctrine of one body as yet. He
spoke of it as a "weary struggle" and I felt that a study of comparative religions such as he was apparently contemplating, would be
a matter of years. I had not written to my cousin for some months;
I was not sure that I could help him in the best way just then. But
if he had been with me in Italy, and Austria, I thought, he would
have seen the beauty, and perhaps absorbed the significance, of
shrine and symbol, which was needed to offset heavier studies. He
had a steady hand, however, on the helm of his own spiritual craft.

We returned to Germany by way of the Austrian Tyrol, penetrating romantic valleys off the beaten track. Somewhere along the
road we came unexpectedly upon Felix and his pretty sister Fanny.
It was a pleasant surprise, and Felix was excellent at surprises; always amused, never thrown out of plumb or embarrassed.

I dreaded the return to Leipzig and lessons, after such a luxurious summer.

The morning after my arrival there, with a gray sky and sodden
brown leaves crushed into the muddy sidewalks, was dreary enough;
no glowing October foliage, no light and no vision. But at the Bank,
"a queer little tomb of a place," as I had once written, was a pile of
letters. The first one opened came from Father, written on a late
August Sunday at Forty Acres:

Your vivid and stirring descriptions of the Swiss mountains, dear-
est Ruth, have awakened my first real longing to see that part of the
world, I believe. Very glorious they must be! But, after all, I don't know
that I would exchange for all there is in Europe the half-sad and tender
joy that comes into my heart in one such day as this, here: a day between
summer and autumn; a few faint touches of change on the trees and
hills; the splendor of the forenoon tempered now by some soft bars of
white cloud and fleecy cornucopias in the West; the pale blue of the
northern sky kept clear by a light breath of moist East wind; the ridges
of Holyoke so distinct that one can count the pines:—now and then the

note of a woodpecker and a blue jay and the cawing of a crow; the river still, and the cows, with their pathetic eyes, feeding in the yard! I have just been through the pasture and around behind the hill by the spring, and down to the river-bank. Mary was sitting at the little old library window, Arria in her room; James in the attic overhead. I put in the last "Mayflower" as I used to call it, which I found in the pasture—with love. It would be better if you were here; so much better!

I turned and apostrophized my waiting piano, still shrouded in its summer cover.

"*Du*," I said sharply, "Thou and I must go to work now, and make all this worth while. I have a debt to pay."

It was now quite settled that I should return to the United States in May, leaving Leipzig at Easter-time. There was much to be done meanwhile; I plunged into my work with turbulent energy. Music came first, and I set to reinforcing my lessons in harmony by means of tutoring, in order to finish the year's work in four months instead of six. With Nan Muirhead and a Swedish girl, I went to ask for organ lessons. Although women had not been allowed in that department, the directorate of the Conservatorium finally yielded, and arranged a class for us under Carl Piutti. I continued my study of *Vortrag* with Reinecke, and reluctantly gave up my readings with Fräulein Herrnsdorf.

The year 1882 went out with comparative peace in central Europe. For the last time our group of six gathered for a party. At midnight we sang the *Sylvesterlied,* and drank one another's health in strong punch; then the windows of the apartment were thrown open, and we sat and listened to the choir-boys of the *Thomaskirche* singing on the balcony of the *Rathaus* in the square.

On one of the foggiest January days, I received a package from America. It was my purple-bound copy, worn and faded by four years' use, of *The Imitation of Christ.* Archie had sent it back, as I had asked him to do, to show me that he had found the answer to his questionings in learning and practising the Way of Life that led to Christian faith. I had almost given up expecting that the news would come. He had let me know, a year before, that the doubts he thought banished, had returned. Now he had lived his way through them. He said nothing of doctrine, but he told me in a simple, almost blunt phraseology, that it was I, and our talk in the haymow at Hadley, which had given him courage to persevere in his honest quest for a basis of belief. "I hardly dare think," he wrote, "where, or what I should have been but for that. What I know of some men here in college and their state of mind, makes me doubly thankful . . . ."

Was it unmixed gladness that I experienced in reading this letter? Else why did I go on hastily to the end, reading over and over its controlled, conventional signature, "With much love I am affectionately yours?" It occurred to me that perhaps he was really the honest one, expressing gratitude but trying to make it clear that that was the limit of his feeling for me. Considerate, of course, but not what I longed for. Could I be certain how much that mutual stirring of emotion four years ago had actually meant? But I glanced down at the old book, and opened it at a page which held a pressed four-leaved clover. Without doubt that was the leaf we had found at our feet on the last Sunday afternoon of our memorable week, walking with Cousin Ellen. It lay between the leaves, and a passage had been marked by a line on the margin.

Nothing is sweeter than love, nothing more courageous, nothing higher, nothing wider, nothing more pleasant, nothing fuller nor better in heaven and earth; because love is born of God, and cannot rest but in God, above all created things. . . . . Love oftentimes knoweth no bounds, but is fervent beyond all measure.

One stroke of a pencil had written the message, after all. The old saint had not known that he was putting words into the mouths of human lovers.

In February Wagner died. In every shop window appeared his portrait, decorated and hung with purple, or busts and memorials and bas-reliefs; sometimes actual effigies. Commemorative services, great masses, finally operas in *Zyklus*, were given. The musical life of Germany was for a time absorbed in honoring the great composer.

It was the last month, now, of my work. I had cut down my social activities as much as possible, and so had the two other girls, Nan and Nora. Our party of six held to its Saturday afternoon tramps, and luckily it was a warm spring. The last walks, through the woods beside the *Pleisse* to suburban villages, with supper at some little inn and possibly a return by boat, were as congenial as ever; other students joined us occasionally. Easter was the twenty-fifth of March that year, and I planned to leave the Tuesday after. Good Friday was as always the solemn day of mourning, with the Passion-music as intense an expression as ever of the people's devotion; hundreds in the *Thomaskirche,* quiet in the streets. Easter at the little chapel in the *Bach-schule* was a bright day; the group of English and American girls had became endeared to one another and parting with them would be sorrowful, but that last Sunday service was hearty and the flowers lovely. One hated the kind of goodbyes that came after church, and the sense that most of them were final leave-taking.

The evening was very quiet, and we did not read our usual play. Willi and Helene, the oldest grandchildren, stayed on for a final talk that night. Willi, the tall young *Freiwilliger,* had been studying English with me and was able to discuss his plans in that language. He was to enter the University, and Helene hoped to teach, but was growing handsome and housewifely and was likely to make a good marriage. The family life had been so interesting and promising that one longed to be able to follow it. The Herr Pastor and his wife were loving in their farewell greetings. They asked for my agreement that I should cable them one word—*glückselig* was the word agreed upon—when I had arrived in my home and was with my parents again. The picture of their fine old figures standing at the foot of the little winding stairway that night, is still clear, and has kept my faith in the highest type of German character, through any attempt to destroy it.

The thought of home-going made a rhythmic background of joy for my sorrow at leaving Germany, just as the joy of motion in the Mendelssohn violin concerto, which little Geraldine Morgan was practising that week to play at the big spring *Prüfung* in the *Gewandhaus,* gave place to a motif of poignant regret.

All of my new friends were at the train; they had filled my compartment with flowers, books and trinkets, and the jollity which followed was a merciful distraction. *Auf Wiedersehen! Komm bald wieder!* The train moved out, and a guard shut me in among the roses and green garlands.

New York

1

ENGAGEMENT

Almost two years later on a winter night a young man and woman were sitting in the parlor of a Young Ladies' Seminary where the Bishop's fourth child had been fulfilling her pledge to teach. It was a spacious room, designed to contribute to the uplift of young-womanhood, with the heavily-upholstered furniture of the period, and long portières hanging from dark wooden rods. Some good old portraits hung upon the walls, with photographs of pillared ruins in Rome and Athens, a color-print of one of Alma Tadema's gems and a few etchings. On an easel stood a tall engraving of *The Huguenot Lovers,* depicting two young people, a soldier and his sweetheart in a chaste parting embrace. A Morris chair stood near the centre-table; a rich Japanese screen partly concealed the two figures seated before an open fire. Ten o'clock had struck; silence reigned in the upper stories of the house.

"I can't believe I'm here," said the young man. "Curious that letters had to do it after all."

"Yes; I always felt it would be at Forty Acres."

"And *it* hasn't happened even yet. We're still saving up."

"I know. How we have kept apart!—and just because we were so shy of one another; shy and sure at the same time, only we didn't realize it."

"Mighty shy, but not consciously sure. We didn't know what to expect of ourselves or of anybody else. We're more or less tied up by conventions."

"It was partly the delay of the boat. In spite of arguing with myself that you mightn't be there, I was sub-consciously expecting you. I never dreamed you were so near me, that evening."

"I know that, but when I had to go back to Cambridge without seeing you I was horribly cut up, and got more and more doubtful as to what your attitude would be. If I'd only seen you then and there I'd have known in a moment how we stood."

"Naturally! So should I. One can depend upon one's impulses, if nothing else."

"And then you didn't come to Commencement, the dream I'd lived on for four years."

"How could I? No one at home would have seen the slightest excuse for my going away again after just getting home. And it was the same about getting you to Forty Acres; I racked my brain for an excuse, and flunked it out of pure cowardice."

"Then when I came here to see you, with my heart in my mouth, and it was all so formal—like your letters; they had become more and more so."

"Oh, we were absurd! Why do people in love do such things? We didn't even know what to talk about."

"It was really an interposition of Providence that I had to go to the concert in New York. Music has always directed the great events of my life! But you see I only needed a touch or a glance to realize that things were coming right, eventually."

"I had that sense too; it dragged me up from despair a good many times. And when they asked me to meet you at the train that night—actually asked me if I'd *mind* going over—I had a presentiment that the hour had struck. The moment I saw you I knew it. After that, every magnetic exchange was an assurance."

"I know. How jocund we were, without a word of explanation!"

"One thing; I've had enough, please note, of 'due, respective thrift.' I shall spend recklessly hereafter." We both laughed, remembering the long room and the poetry-book.

"We were infants then. But Father thinks we still are. He's a trifle staggered because he thought I should go farther afield for my love-affairs. It's rather a relief to have it all on a familiar basis like this. Only—those pesky Puritan implications. He sees things in the light of fifty years ago. And somehow he can't disabuse himself of the idea that we're precipitate."

"*Precipitate*! When we've waited five whole years to be alone together for even a few minutes! Didn't you tell him that?"

"Of course I did."

"And what did he say?"

"Archie, it was too much. He reminded me that Jacob had served *seven* years for Rachel."

"Jacob be hanged. We won't let the Old Testament regulate *our* lives; we're not afraid to be happy! What are the actual conditions? I suppose he thought we should expect him to make some."

"Just this. He knows that if we're engaged we shall have to keep it from the public as well as the family till our prospects are a little more settled, and if we wait a little longer you'll actually be in the firm and have plans to announce, which everybody looks for."

"Of course. I suppose practical considerations have to come in, more's the pity. It's a sordid age."

"And you know what a nuisance it is to have to conceal things, maybe lie outright. It would be different if they had any idea how much we cared, of course."

"Could they have any idea how much? I doubt it, myself."

"They could if they looked back to their own love-affair, but I don't think parents ever do, in these cases. Of course it doesn't seem as if Father did, for he suggests that we wait six months, till you're all started, and then get "betrothed," as he says and publish the fact. Of course that's the conventional method of procedure. We can have the romance to ourselves meantime."

"Having romance to one's self isn't very filling. What is our mutual status supposed to be during the probation?"

"That's amusing too; an *understanding*! You know—what lots of people have, and carry it through. He says a 'cousinly relation.' "

He groaned. "Whatever that is, I repudiate it. We neither of us have the slightest responsibility for our common ancestors. I hope our children won't either."

"I asked him about letters. He's evidently not anxious to be mandatory, but I thought it might please him to be consulted. He proposed that we 'avoid extreme expressions of love' while still not confessedly engaged."

We shook with silent laughter.

"His note to me was all one could ask. I'd love him for it even if he weren't your father. He's doing his part. But he thinks of us as mere children."

"I know it. And we're not; not the boy and girl who were so thrilled over our love that summer. It's riper and deeper now. And you are a lawyer, I'm a teacher. We have big separate obligations."

"Of course; life undertook us for years and now we're undertaking it."

"And I've one year of my pledge to fulfil. But I can help, you know, when it comes to making a living. I've got the power to teach; it possesses me. I shall never be able to give it up entirely. The girls are absorbing, splendid creatures when you really know them and watch them. They'd be out of their beds leaning over the stair-rail if they knew what is going on down here, romantic to the last degree. Do you know, I've given a recital this month and am arranging for a series of chamber-music concerts here in the school hall next term; quartettes with soloists. We've got to make America far more understanding, and more progressive in musical matters than she has been. I realized abroad how fearfully superficial we are, over here."

"We'll have lots to do together and put our love into it."

"Yes," I flashed. *"Yoked in all exercise of noble end."*

He reached for my hand. There was much more than surrender in its warm vigor.

"Are you as keen as ever on contemporary poetry?"

"Pretty much, yes. Tennyson and Browning and Matthew Arnold keep up my morale. But when are you going to read me the rest of the Shakespeare sonnets?"

"When we get back to the haymow!"

"There'll be chances to be alone again at Forty Acres! I shall have to give Cousin Ellen an inkling of this. But as to the writing— need there be any bother about those regulations, after all? Lovers have had to do this kind of thing ever since the world began. We can say anything we want in a dialect of our own. Intimations! Begin tomorrow."

"Tonight even; on the train." He sprang up, pulling out his watch. "The express leaves at eleven-twenty; I must be off."

The Bishop's fourth child was caught up suddenly and crushed by two arms. Speechless, indignant, rapturous, her eyes closed to shut out the blinding light.

Eleven portentous strokes sounded from the stern clock in the hall. The arms loosened, lingered, dropped.

"Now!" in the sturdy but shaken voice of a runner who has grasped the guerdon, "I think I can manage to be your affectionate cousin for six months more, possibly."

The heavy entrance-door was opened and closed gently, as befitted the place, the hour, and the proprieties.

The probation was not long, as things turned out. Six months' outpourings on paper deepened our knowledge of one another, and the sense of a pledge, implicit though unacknowledged, grew stronger as we came nearer to its fulfillment. When my father felt we had met his test, he himself was eager to have us announce our engagement. Neither family suspected anything, and at Hadley all but the observant Molly were duly amazed. She said that when a girl had been pocketing thick letters out of the mail all summer without even a glance at the postmark, she needn't expect her friends to be surprised by anything. Molly had independent ideas on marriage, which had no attraction for her. But being a loyal sister she had told nobody of her suspicions. The family circle was pleased, and the engagement doubled our family connections.

We were betrothed with little hope of a speedy marriage, but like all lovers we considered true love immortal. We belonged to a romantic generation, and were believed to have been "made for each other." But we did not look realistically upon our prospects; I think we might have considered that kind of contemplation sordid. The difficulties of a young lawyer's career presented themselves vaguely as a romantic adventure. Trusting in talent and compromise, we undertook to solve life-problems with the cheerfulness of ignorance. I fancy the children of this generation would smile at the simplicity of their grandparents' expectations.

Two successful years of teaching at Mrs. Piatt's Seminary at Utica, New York, had passed by that time. The school was of the old "finishing" type, an improvement on the boarding academies of an earlier date. Its principal combined common sense with progressive methods. These provided social training, and good instruction in English, mathematics, Latin, and modern languages. I cannot remember that the sciences were so well represented. In private schools there was still very little laboratory work. The curriculum was rather less comprehensive than that of a half-century before in the best Boston schools, which my mother and older sister had attended. Each year, however, Mrs. Piatt had added to her equipment, broadened her aims, and acquired more flexibility in methods. Though the women's colleges were by that time requiring organized preparatory work, the finishing schools stuck to a so-called general culture which gave much leeway to teachers. Outside of the mathematical and classical courses there was no prescribed system. The young head of the German department was free to work out a plan of her own, based on the Leipzig courses, and for the first year was limited to classes of beginners.

Before the end of the year, however, the principal proposed that I take over the music department, with authority to reconstruct the system and chose my own assistants. My salary was to be raised from four hundred and fifty dollars, which Mrs. Piatt had offered as an experimental stipend, to the really dazzling sum of fifteen hundred. I left her warm study quite breathless. I was glad to be free of routine activities with the one exception of occasional chaperonage. The task seemed tremendous, but I wanted to widen my musical experience and to be able to train younger instructors on German lines, with classes for technique and individual studies in *Vortrag*.

The Seminary, as it was called by Uticans, was modelled to some extent after Miss Porter's well known school at Farmington, Connecticut, where Mrs. Piatt had been assistant to the Principal. We teachers were expected to fall in with her policy, which implied friendly and confidential relations between teacher and pupil. She did not want informers or mediators on her staff, nor did she equip us for direct discipline except in our classes. We were to be companions of the girls, upholding the standards of the school, but reporting mischief only when it threatened disaster. As a matter of fact we received a good many confessions, and were able to persuade offenders to own up voluntarily. Mrs. Piatt had an unusually sympathetic point of view toward the perpetrations of youngsters who came to her with the usual notions of boarding-school life, and who enjoyed midnight adventures and secret flirtations.

"It would be positively cruel," she maintained, "to cut them off entirely from mere pranks at first. Most of them are basically harmless, and can be part of their development."

One night she came to my room to tell me she had heard from a maid that in one of the recitation rooms there was to be a twelve-o'clock supper, for which fifteen girls had made elaborate plans. She had a little fun herself, I imagine, hearing the whispering, the stealthy steps, the stifled giggles. By and by she went down with the intention of surprising them. She had waited till the banquet was well under way and there was noise enough for her to open the door just a crack without their hearing her.

"And I came away without a word," she added. "I let them carry the thing out, and go back to their rooms. For some of them it would have marred the whole year's experience to have been caught and disciplined, and it would have made martyrs of them. I'm going to let them have the triumph and enthusiasm before I let them know I was there. It was likely to be a useful bit of development if I wait, and let them grow out of it a bit before I speak."

After the vacation, which was then imminent, she had a talk with the whole group. What she said to them I don't know, but they became her warm supporters. Outside affairs were handled differently, but with good results. It was a pleasant way of living, but all too absorbing. Perhaps a less smooth-running household would have let in more stimulating influences from without.

The girls took a wistful interest in the younger teachers' gaieties, acted as ladies' maids when we went to parties, and supplied us with flowers, which we wore on evening occasions in those days.

Dramatics interested them mightily, and they were allowed to go to some German plays which we gave in the winter season. There was in the school faculty one specially interesting woman, Emily Griffith, a Vassar graduate, with whom I had much in common, and whose courses in English literature were attended, as were some of the German classes, by town women. Mrs. Piatt welcomed the older students, whose presence was stimulating to the teachers, but they were obliged to follow school rules as to attendance, and to work at their tasks.

The Vassar girl and I did a good deal of reading, and discussed our common interests, one of which was English politics. President Cleveland's government was somehow not so interesting as Parliament. Since we had no status and no responsibility as citizens, we had no reason to concern ourselves with internal affairs as we do today.

We subscribed for English journals, and exchanged them. Speeches like John Bright's bitter attack on the House of Lords, as "the spawn of the plunder and the wars" excited us. Being a pacifist by inheritance I always found Bright's impetuous utterances heartening, and shared his Free Trade principles. We followed Gladstone's career with enthusiasm. With American history behind us we became Home Rulers ourselves. In 1885 the fall of Khartoum and General Gordon's death had aroused the world. While we ourselves could not sympathize with the military side of Gordon's cause, we admired his personal bravery and his religious faith, and felt that he had been wronged by his own government. At election times we took sides vigorously, and supported or opposed Lord Hartington, Chamberlain, Trevelyan and the rest, according to their activities in the Opposition.

Some of my old notebooks contain impetuous comments and quotations. When Bryce's *American Commonwealth* came out, it took a great hold on the American public and inspired us with new interest in our own country. We still had our argumentative seasons, however, and worked ourselves up over African, German and English protectorates and the might-makes-right assumptions of the great countries. My Yankee blood always revolted against colonial policies.

I have since felt that Emily Griffith, whose college-trained mind was far superior to mine, contributed most to my development during those years of teaching. But no one dreamed of keeping school-girls informed of contemporary history. They read and recited what was prescribed for them; fiction was their chief delight outside of classes. Now we were getting Turgenieff and a little of Tolstoi, and George Meredith had brought out *Diana of the Crossways,* which delighted us especially with its British political setting. I loved to reread it, along with *Anna Karenina, A Princess of Thule, Sir Gibbie* and more of George McDonald's stories, and the later Trollope novels. There was no overwhelming annual influx of current literature such as that which floods the reading world of today. We had time to return to our standbys, our Dickens and Thackeray and Browning and Charlotte Brontë and Hawthorne and Miss Yonge and Miss Martineau, and later to the charming biographies and letters of great women like George Eliot and Jane Welsh Carlyle. These were only a few of the influences which pervaded the late-Victorian years, a few of the books which young teachers read and reread in the midst of their work. Much of my academic work I did in the early morning hours because of the lure of study-lamp and easy chair after the house was quiet at night.

I loved teaching more than ever by the end of my four years in Utica, and valued the friendships I had made; but I found myself glad to leave it for a freer existence. When Archie wrote that he was able to set a time for our wedding on the strength of some new legal openings, my joy counterbalanced a heartfelt regret. I hated to relinquish a task which showed greater possibilities each year, but I realized that there would be opportunities for teaching, in one way or another, all through my life. I was not parting from my beloved profession altogether.

I do not think I matured during our engagement. With all that can be said of the boarding-school as a cultural institution, I believe its teachers and scholars need constant broadening to offset too-balanced schedules. I know I might have been a keener instructor and a far more useful wife if I had had fuller experience with the outside world during the years before my marriage—happy years though they were, with long letters from the man I loved.

2

MRS. SESSIONS

It made no difference to those most intimately concerned that our wedding day in mid-November was dark and gloomy. The church was brilliantly lighted at eleven in the forenoon; its seats were packed with a representative assembly, as the papers had it. It was indeed representative of all classes, and the ushers had orders to seat all but the wedding party in order of arrival. We had sent out fifteen hundred invitations, and took the consequences.

Looking back on that congregation I feel like apologizing to it for the bigness of the affair. After all we were avowedly embracing poverty in marrying, and we might well have pledged our troth in quiet and modesty. But we were indifferent to any such implications. We wanted all our friends to be with us, and my father's wide acquaintance called for many invitations. Anyway we felt that the sixteenth of November, 1887, was to be the greatest, holiest, and most joyous day of our lives, and nothing should be omitted from its celebration.

We carried the idea to its limit, and made our morning wedding as perfect as possible—and as conventional. There were six or eight vested clergy. The bride, in trailing white gown and voluminous veil, went up the aisle with her arm linked in the Bishop's full lawn sleeve; the groom followed with her mother. The ushers and bridesmaids preceded us, and the vested choir of men and boys sang *Love Divine, All Love Excelling*, while the congregation joined in. The boys had not been supposed to march, but begged for it so hard that I yielded at the last moment. My two brothers in their priestly vestments met us at the top of the chancel steps, and read the service; we made our pledges from memory instead of repeating them at dictation. The Bishop passed on to the altar, and turned to give us the benediction, which the choir followed, as we knelt, with soft singing of an old English marriage hymn. Then we came proudly down the aisle to the echoes of

Treulich gefuhrt, ziehet dahin
Wo Euch der Segen der Liebe bewahr!

It was all perfect, except that my mother, having laid out a glossy new suit for the Bishop to wear that day, was horrified to find him smilingly receiving the guests at the wedding breakfast in his shabby old one. That was quite characteristic, however, and was relished accordingly.

The wedding was a typical affair of the time, and an auspicious beginning, said Society, for married life. We sped eastward in a Pullman compartment, and not until the shadows of late afternoon had gathered, and the porters were lighting dim lamps, did we begin to recognize the real meaning of the festivities. Not that we thought of anything but the immediate future, not of responsibilities or deprivations; those things were in pale distance. All we felt was the exciting present, our flawless joy after long waiting, and the union now expressed in every touch and glance. As I look back at my own wedding-day, I cannot bring myself to believe that any memories are quite as satisfying as the reminiscence of a marriage backed by friendly witnesses. With all that may be said for the efficacy of civil or secret ceremonies, consummated by the impromptu joining of hands by a chance justice or clergymen, I believe, nevertheless in weddings and consecration.

We spent the next two weeks in New England, first at a spot not far from Forty Acres, whither we were irresistibly drawn. The place was bare and brown, little frozen pools in the meadowland and round the tree-roots. The big white house with its long reach of sheds had still a welcoming aspect; the old Phelps mansion stood aloof, gray and lonely, under its tall pines. Cousin Ellen was away, at her Cambridge house; a good industrious German couple was caring for Cousin Charles and Thophy; sister Sarah had died and was buried in the North Hadley cemetery beside old Billy.

We got out one of the farm vehicles, and drove about the country lanes, in warm coats, the horse's willing hoofs clopping rapidly over hard road-beds, autumn air invigorating us after the more languorous moments of the honeymoon. We visited at the firesides of friends, real farmers who made us feel with pride our kinship by inheritance with tillers of the soil.

And as we drove, crowded together on a narrow seat, we came to a few resolutions and plans for our married life, rather vague it is true, but infused with sincere desire to make it worth something. I remember Archie's remark when one day a doubt was expressed as to whether we ourselves were big enough for the program we were suggesting.

"Well," he observed helpfully, "if we find we don't amount to much ourselves, let's make our contribution by having lots of worth-while children."

And I have no doubt I blushed, because in that day the highly protected maiden turned shy even during her wedding journey at any such hint.

EXCITING MONTHS

We began housekeeping in the expected attic. It was uptown, and up three flights—a tiny flat with a sitting-room fireplace (I mention the fireplace because it took up most of one wall), two diminutive bedrooms beyond it, then a dark dining-room beyond that, and a bathroom. The kitchen consisted of pantry shelves and a small coal range, with about a square yard of space between them and a dumbwaiter in the corner, which we shared, as we did the hall, with another family.

To tell the truth, we did not particularly notice this suite. Our attention was entirely taken up by the view from the front windows, and that was what we rented on sight. It looked out upon the wooded upper end of Central Park, from a corner in the neighborhood of Ninety-second Street, and on an October afternoon, when the oaks were like burnished copper and the young elms golden, with bright straight young evergreens standing among them, we had felt that nothing else really mattered if we could look forward to such a setting for the sunrise every morning, at the price of twenty-seven dollars a month. Had we not a thousand dollars—a vast sum it seemed—to start on? It did not occur to us that our treasured chest-sofa and our large armchairs and square tea-table would so fill the parlor that its door could never be closed save by moving something into the hall, nor that the sole furnishing of the second bedroom would consist of a folding bed which when let down filled the entire space between wall and window. What matter? We unpacked the barrels and barrels of wedding-presents, and blithely crowded their contents together, the better to see them, as the wolf said to Red-Riding-Hood. And then we knelt on our big sofa and gazed into the tree branches of the Park by daylight; at evening we lighted a pile of logs on our new andirons, and sat on a white fur rug before the fire, with knees drawn up.

We had an interesting prospect for spring; among our gifts had been a two-year lease of a house in Englewood, on the Palisades, given us by its owners, a friend of our childhood and her husband. They had just built a larger mansion at the top of a cliff on the road to Fort Lee, and were about to move into it; they were anxious for companionship. The two husbands planned to go back and forth to town together; Mrs. Allison was a little younger than I, and very congenial; the cottage on the edge of a wood was ideal. With this alluring prospect, we could enjoy a city winter all the more.

It was a glowing winter. Relatives and friends of the family entertained us, and I had my experience of the formal New York hospitality of the Four Hundred behind the brown-stone fronts. My years abroad and my teaching had prevented any actual society adventuring except in Syracuse, and this new life was awesome. Archie, a born and bred New Yorker, took it with modest ease, but I can remember how I shivered over our first invitation. The only way was to dramatize it, as I had done since childhood with every difficult undertaking, and that carried me through.

Formalities were tremendous in those days. I felt as if we were bound for one of Trollope's London dinner parties, as the door was opened to us by a man-servant with the face of the Archbishop of Greenwich on Bella Wilfer's wedding day. Entering the drawing-room, and being introduced to various magnificences, was an ordeal, but being apt at imitation we fell into line quite simply as a young couple who were living somewhere uptown outside the pale, in a top apartment; we were something of a curiosity.

The dining-table was impressive and formal, spread with exquisite china and lengths of fine damask. I thought with satisfaction that the cut glass, though sparkling and elegant, was no finer than that which stood among my own wedding gifts, and the napery was matched by grandmother's long tablecloths at Cedar Square. The cluster of wine-glasses beside each plate, however, outdid my previous experiences.

We admired the poise of our hostess and the patience with which she applauded her husband's well-worn jokes, but the most-dreaded feature of the evening came when the ladies filed out of the supper-room, leaving the gentlemen behind with their special drinks and cigars. We mounted to the drawing-room, which then was apt to be cluttered with small tables loaded with ornaments. To be left alone wtih those august matrons was terrifying. They asked polite, occasionally searching questions, some of which made me feel like a freak, although they did not really penetrate to the conditions of life in a fourth-floor flat. Being one's own housemaid was one of the things that was not done, and for the sake of one's relatives one let it alone. So we talked of the lovely view in the upper Park, and joined in mild society gossip, or acknowledged kindly references to the Bishop, for these were mostly Episcopal folk who had entertained him in their own houses.

After we reached home, we threw the dinner-gown and the dress suit into our tiny spare room, and betook ourselves to the fur rug before an open fire to talk it over. After that we had no terror of Old New York dinner-parties. At later ones there were sometimes literary lights among the guests, but it was a little disappointing to be put next to them at dinner, for their conversational powers were seldom equal to their writings.

There were diversions more interesting than society. We used to meet downtown after office hours, quite as twentieth-century couples do, and have supper at queer little restaurants. One we particularly loved was on Seventeenth Street, I think, decorated with scenes from Scheffel's *Trompeter,* with Hiddigeigei, the black cat, frisking about in a frieze of grapevines. Then we would go to the theatre, the opera, or to a concert, sitting in the topmost gallery and sharing the score. We could see our former hostesses, bejeweled and low-necked, with marvelous coiffures, in boxes far below. The Sessions family numbered many musicians among its acquaintance, so we were apt to meet enthusiastic friends at the concerts, and sup with them afterwards.

We visited picture-galleries and exhibitions, or occasionally a museum, but we heard no lectures; our minds went unimproved during those exciting months. We made our little circle of friends, however. It turned out that Felix was living only a few blocks away from us; he was a practising physician, and had a pleasant house and a charming wife, the girl he had returned from Germany to marry. He and Archie took to one another, and Felix partially converted us to the Single-Tax theory of Henry George, who was a friend of his. We found that my brother James, who was then working on the East Side, living with a fellow-priest in a tenement house, was also converted to the Single Tax. He and Henry George had been in England together. When he came to supper with us, climbing our stairs now and then, we had our first realization of the appalling social contrasts of New York: the wretched poor, the reeking slums, the pawn-shops and saloons among which he was working day and night. To us it was only a vivid picture then, I am afraid, though we shuddered over it; but it was not completely buried after all, and we were destined to recall it poignantly before many years.

The great blizzard came on the twelfth of March, 1888. Archie had left for his office in Pine Street, that morning, by the elevated train. It was snowing and blowing, but after Syracuse the weather did not seem to me unusual. I was shut in at home all the forenoon, and never noticed the swirling snow.

I finished my luncheon without a thought of the whirlwind outside. But by afternoon snow had piled thick on the window-sills, and even sifted in here and there. It was hard to see the elevated railway through the swirling flakes. I suddenly became aware that there were no trains running, no vehicles, no moving figures in the streets, save an occasional man struggling through the drifts to a nearby house. No snow ploughs, no sleighs; no attempt at shoveling till late in the afternoon. I became anxious about my husband. How could he get home? Would he have to give it up, and spend the night down town, more than a hundred blocks away? But we had no telephone, and I knew he would make every effort he could to come back.

Finally, in a strange mixture of twilight and snow-darkness, after useless attempts to see through the clouded windows, I heard his step on the stair. He came in cheerful, but said he was chilled, and wanted a hot bath. The garments he had on were wringing with perspiration; his coat was stiff with ice. He had walked all the way from Pine Street to Ninety-second Street against the heavy freezing wind, and had kept straight on, not stopping, as other walkers did, to reinforce himself. He was, of course, spent, and did not go to his office for two days, but we never dreamed of permanent harm as a result. Thereafter he had always an abnormally slow pulse, and though he was told that this often went with longevity, we learned in time that his heart could not stand strain.

In the spring we moved to Englewood. With surprise we discovered that a few miles from the northern end of New York there existed a spot where woodland solitude, grand cliffs, and an outlook on rolling country across the broad river quite isolated us from the city. The little house was charming. The main part had low rooms, steps up and down in narrow halls, and a steep staircase; there was an addition of two large six-windowed rooms. The living-room was ample, and our bedroom above it delightfully airy; its back windows looked out into the woods, and in each room was an open fireplace. There was a garden and a barn; a broad lawn separated the house from the road. A few steps brought us to the Palisades, and we could look across and over, and down at the tiny fishing-hamlet at their base, to which a descending path along the rocky ledges offered an interesting walk.

The woods were full of birds, and twilight brought notes of thrushes; other notes in the daytime set us studying. There were raccoons, too, in the forest which stretched north of us for miles. Now and then at night the barking of dogs and men's voices announced an exciting coon-hunt: otherwise the nocturnal stillness gave absolute rest to a tired brain. Here we could be completely out of the world which even in our sky-suite had been too much with us, we thought.

The life at Englewood was more than satisfying. We found friends, were most hospitably taken into clubs and groups, and especially enjoyed a musical circle among our nearer neighbors on the hill. Our families visited us, and we took long drives, and made explorations in old Jersey towns, where we found interesting traces of the earlier Dutch settlers.

To our great joy we learned early in the summer that we were to have a child. Now there was a deeper purpose in life—a new reason for living, and living intensely. I wanted at first to be near my mother, and to revisit the scenes of my own earliest childhood; I remember that just then prenatal influence was discussed and much written about. After a blissful month at Forty Acres, Archie joined me there for a visit, and a part of our time was spent at Ashfield, Massachusetts, for it would not have been a complete summer's happiness without our older brother George, who was there with his six children.

In the autumn we returned to the charming Englewood community. I had my own piano there, and devoted a good deal of time to practising, or playing accompaniments to my husband's fine baritone voice, all with the hope that our child might be musical. And by the autumn fire, I made small garments while he read aloud. With perfect health and with a strong horse to carry us about, we kept up a pretty continuous social activity.

4

HANNAH

One blustering February day, when a business-like nurse drove up to the door, she found her patient performing a Chopin waltz in which she was so absorbed that the young woman went upstairs by herself, got into a uniform, and descended to call the expectant mother's attention to the job in hand. Our little girl was born that night into a stormy world; the light of a log fire in our chimney-place, reinforced by James at midnight, flickered on her crib. We had my mother's name, Hannah Sargent, waiting for her.

That was a happy time. The cold gave place to softer airs. There were intimations of coming spring: supernaturally lovely yellow light at dawn and in late afternoon, and when my nurse returned from her daily walk along the cliffs, she would bring back tiny green shoots, already starting from the ground, for spring is early on the heights of Englewood; the spot seems to have a climate of its own.

Sometimes my brother came out to sit with me; his accounts of the Order's activities were always picturesque and compelling. My big room let in generous light, and I came to love it during the weeks of confinement and to keep up friendly converse with the few special books on the table by my bedside; Plato's *Republic,* a little worn from its trip to Germany, and a similarly shabby copy of *Faust,* the first volume more thumbed than the second. Companioning them was a borrowed copy of Herbert Spencer, and from the bag which James always carried about with him, he would pour out especially interesting books of the moment. At that moment there was much interest in the Higher Criticism, so-called, of the Bible, a matter of profound scholarly research. The conservatives decried it bitterly; fundamentalism gnashed its teeth. My father was one of the first bishops to interest himself in the movement, and to appreciate its value.

Archie and I had long abandoned theological research; he had been baptized in the Episcopal Church during my years abroad, and later confirmed, satisfied that it was the communion in which his religious life could best be developed. We had never discussed the matter, but simply accepted our faith as mutual and helpful and not dependent on dogma. In spiritual end and aim we were at one; we said our prayers together and made our weekly Communions side by side.

My nurse read aloud to me Barrie's *Little Minister*, just published, and we found it enchanting. The spring days lengthened, mild airs blew in at open windows. Life was full of quiet joys and hopes. But before little Nan was quite three weeks old there came a disturbing telegram to Miss C. from the mother of the baby she had nursed just before coming to Englewood, saying that he had developed pneumonia, and would she please return to their household at once to take care of him? It was quite evident that she was keen to go; the family was wealthy, their house luxurious, and my health unquestionable. Before I knew it I had agreed to let her off, and within an hour she had packed her things, called a cab, and sped to the afternoon train, leaving me somewhat stunned, overcome with the realization that I had learned nothing as yet of the care of a young baby. My husband, arriving a half-hour later, wanted to recall her at once; but it was too late, and we telegraphed my mother, who came next day and took charge of her grandchild's rearing with great delight.

The nurse was, I understand, disciplined by her hospital for having broken its rules. But whenever I see the name of Mr. Hamilton Fish, just now in political circles, I recollect the episode, since he was the infant involved.

5

THE BUTCHER, THE BAKER

The next summer and winter were uneventful, but very happy. Nothing seemed wanting; the child throve apace, our families made us long pleasant visits; in the warm months we went back to Forty Acres. But nevertheless there was a cloud on our horizon. Certain principles observed in our early training, principles which held us aloof from reality, were partly responsible. I have already mentioned that we married without a proper understanding of ways and means. In the 'sixties and 'seventies and 'eighties we had learned that it was not nice to talk about money. Only the sordid, the *nouveaux riches,* or sycophantic insolvents would make it a subject of discussion. Our thrifty forefathers had accumulated it unobtrusively. The Bishop and his wife had lived comfortably on a salary of four thousand dollars, and made generous contributions to churches and charities. Our mother kept house with touches of comfort and beauty which never made a shoe pinch. Maids were paid about three dollars a week, and sent much of it home to Ireland; their wardrobes were standardized, and at Christmas they were pleased with aprons and lengths of calico. As children we had our longings, and would willingly have spent money on trinkets and fine raiment, but were after all as well provided for as our mates. The family code absolutely required that all bills should be paid the first of the month; no younger member of the family might buy on account. After being given an allowance I was supposed to plan before purchasing, but our parents were indulgent, and often helped out when funds were low and desires strong.

If a girl in a privileged family married, however, and her husband failed to keep up with the spending standards of her people, the common remark of observers was that he "didn't amount to much." One had more dread of that than of the old word *ordinary*; in fact that damning adjective was already losing its sting because the majority outside of Old New York and Boston and Philadelphia defied classification.

The children of professional men could not generally aspire to anything like a substantial income. Clients did not pay promptly, and young lawyers dared not urge settlement of their bills. The practice of law could not hold people to obligations, apparently, as did the ministry. But realization did not come at once. Some months of our satisfying Englewood experience had passed before a day of awakening dawned. Every morning Archie took from his wife the orders for grocer and butcher, when he drove to the station, and sent back the provender by James. And he had also taken charge of the monthly bills; smaller payments we made in cash. One day a fatal item, *Bill rendered, $30.00* came by post. It was from the grocer, and brought the current charge up to something like fifty dollars. Another such item swelled the butcher's bill to alarming proportions.

I remember that I sat down on the nearest chair, which happened to be a stiff one against the dining-room wall, and stared straight ahead of me for a long time. Last month's bills, then, had not been paid. The foundations of our economic structure were crumbling; the future was problematical. *Behind* with our accounts! Money to be raised (saved it could not be), perhaps even another such notice next month. I remembered the rumor in our Syracuse days that a certain family, always rather down at heel, could not buy in any of the stores without paying cash for things; it seemed very terrible, for the man had a position that paid him a fair salary, but they had "gone into real estate," some people said, and the wife had been extravagant, and their speculations had not succeeded. Should we get like that, and be alternately pitied and scorned by our friends?

I dreaded to see my husband that night. It seemed to me he must be weighed down by anxiety too. I set to work to cut down the provision bills; a most unsatisfactory effort. One *had* to have sugar and butter and flour and yeast and such things. No one knew about calories and vitamins and proteins in those days. Our garden kept us in vegetables. But certain fruits, preserving-stuffs, maple syrup, sweets, lined up in the attack on my system of economics, and I reminded myself painfully of Meg, Miss Alcott's heroine, when she became aware of her domestic extravagance, and had to present her husband with the "demd total"; a recollection which was followed by pictures of Dickens debtors. Were we to become Mantalinis or Micawbers? Then the upkeep of the house, the horse and carriage and James and the cook, and the more serious expenses ahead for which we had begun to plan in unpractical and vague fashion. A dreadful conviction came with the staring mental struggle there on the dining-room chair. *We were living beyond our means.*

It takes very little to turn a naturally buoyant outlook from despair to hope. When Archie got off the train that night his bearing did not reflect any trace of the anguish which had tormented his wife. I myself was able to dissemble, after a nap and a change of gowns, and to keep the conversation upon a sociable level. But after dinner I showed him the bills. To my amazement he took them quite calmly.

"Yes, dear, I did have to let those charges go over. Nothing to speak of has come in this last month, but I have a hundred dollars owing me. The worst of it is that we've spent our money sometimes before we get it!"

"Oh, but bills *have* to be paid, Archie! We simply mustn't let them go over. It's so wrong, so *futile!*" The sense of my own futility made me fairly tearful. This was vital and yet I was not convincing. He kept calm and steadfast as ever.

"You know," he said, "all professional men have to go through this sort of thing. That's the worst of it; you can't look ahead. My mother and father have had to live that way for years, sometimes getting quite a large payment, sometimes waiting and letting bills run up. Even experienced lawyers have to let their charges go."

"We mustn't have to"; I repeated it obstinately. I have recalled many times since how quietly he took what must have been one of his first disappointments in the woman he had married: her evident inability to understand the financial difficulties ahead for them both. If she had accepted the situation, if they had both put their minds to work on it, it would have helped him so much. But at that moment the one thing to do, as he saw it, was to keep her from worrying. She must not have any more surprises.

He reached out his hand for the unlucky papers. "I'll take care of these," he said gently. "You know I don't mean to have any bothers come to you. Don't think about it any more. You won't get bills in the mail after this. And we'll just go ahead and forget the money part." It ended with a love-scene, and anxiety was shelved for the moment. But the shadow was there. Recovery came after that first taste of debt. Bills rendered were paid, I never knew how.

Then there came prosperous times when we were extravagant to some degree, and regretted it later; when the baby came there were more expenses than ever; debts began to pile up, and we could not conceal the knowledge of them from one another. I was still obdurate, I remember; but there was now no money left of my own, though the families remembered us often with presents. Our happiness in having a child forced financial cares into the background. The first months of her life were spring and summer; velvety grass under the wheels of her chariot, flowers in her little hands. In August, when she was six months old and beginning to creep, I had a sort of nervous breakdown; she was a heavy baby, and I had overdone a little in taking care of her. The doctor ordered me to bed, and my room was turned into a nursery, in which she played and slept, and I managed for a while longer without help, but finally it became impossible to do justice to the task. Kind friends urged that I could not recover my strength unless the nursing were taken off my hands. The one thing to do was to have a good care-taker, and for that position there was a perfect specimen available, Melissa—a little old woman who had brought up the babies of the first families in Englewood, year in and year out, and who just now, luckily, was free to take a place. We didn't think we could afford her, but it was a necessity, and proved an immense relief; the whole tone of the household came up after she was once settled in the nursery. She was a diminutive creature, reminding one of a blackbird, and with a slight quiver of the upper lip when much in earnest. Her long thin arms were incredibly strong for lifting, and once gathered into them, seven-months-old Nan wanted no better resting-place.

I cannot leave Melissa out of this chronicle, for all in all she spent years with us, and was a wise adviser and friend of young mothers. The peace that fell upon our household with her arrival remained, but stability did not come at once, for it was the day of Mary Calligan, the immigrant in the kitchen, and I had grown anxious about affairs below stairs during my weeks in bed. Mary gave her own reports, kneeling by my bedside in an attitude of confession, but framing her activities in a self-constituted halo which was suspiciously decorative. I could not quite believe her accounts of housecleaning and economies. Melissa pounced at once upon a mass of deficiencies, and brought up fearful hints of conditions in kitchen and pantry. The climax came when she appeared one forenoon with lip trembling like a rabbit's, and announced the worst break of all.

"I hate to tell you, Mrs. Sessions, for you won't believe me; it doesn't sound possible. But Mary's boiling the diapers and the dish-towels together in the soup-kettle!"

That finished it. Mary was given her *congé* gently, since she was so manifestly a child, and received it with a distressed wail, "But I dawn't knaw the rawd to Bruiklyn!" She had to be personally conducted thither, betraying no remorse and no anger.

But meantime, a far more heart-breaking departure was imminent. That summer we had begun to realize that our happy Englewood life must come to an end. Debts were mounting, even though a measurable amount of business had raised our hopes from time to time; we had never caught up. It would not do to embark on another season there. Not only was it too far from the law-office in Pine Street, curtailing business hours, but our whole establishment, the railroad fares to and fro, the impracticability of transportation to the village, and even the hospitality which had been our delight, implied far greater financial resources than we could hope to command for several years yet, and should never have been undertaken. Even though we must leave debts behind, there was absolutely no way but to sever what we felt to be strong ties of friendship and obligation before our liabilities swamped us completely. Our friends the Allisons, who had been absent from home a good deal during that last year, and were again going away, offered to let us store our furniture in the little house which they had so generously considered our own while there. I went to Syracuse, with Melissa and Nan, and made a long visit, returning in December to new quarters in a boarding-house on Brooklyn Heights.

6

CHRISTIANITY AND ANARCHY

The two years following are not happy to recall, so far as living conditions were concerned. We knew we must live most economically in order to clear up the Englewood liabilities even partially, and so long as the baby could be made comfortable it did not matter so much about ourselves. We had a kind landlady, and a typical collection of fellow-boarders. Our friends, old families on the waterfront, the Lows, the Lymans, Pierponts, Coltons, Hunters, Bensons, Whites, were all very near; my husband's family not far off with the beloved grandmother, whose advice and affection were a strong backing. There were hard times, foggy days and weeks, much discouragement, but we were happy in one another and in our child.

It was during those years that we came to know certain characters in a world different from our own, yet not unknown. While I was in Germany my brother had brought to our family a new friend, a girl whose visit to Forty Acres was her first experience of the real country, for she had never been out of sight of the chimneys of New York City. He had met her in his work on the East Side, and her name was Leonora O'Reilly. She and her mother were of pure Irish stock, and on the father's side some of her uncles had been priests, men of brains and learning. But the father had died, and the two now lived together in a top-tenement, both working by day and educating themselves by night. Leonora had had only elementary education, for she had begun very early in life—as a twelve-year-old, in fact—to work in the sweat-shops which were then a blot on the city. She sewed in an uptown shirt-factory, a one-room establishment with some twenty sewing-machines crowded together, the girls underpaid and kept for long hours at work. Mrs. O'Reilly worked also, I think at some kind of home-labor. At night, as soon as they had eaten their supper, it was their habit to read aloud, one reading while the other washed the dishes. They had accomplished an incredible amount of study, and an astonishing familiarity with the great writers, both of history and economics. On holidays they went to the museums, and made themselves familiar with art and the history of art.

In the midst of their tenement environment they were solitary, but they had found kindred spirits outside, and one of Leonora's advisers from youth up (she called him uncle) was an old man, a handworker and furniture-maker, born in Italy, and a friend of Mazzini, with many stories to tell of the great Italian patriot whose adventures and escapes he had to some extent shared, and whose principles he impressed upon the adoring child. It was through him that Leonora had acquired a cultivation which later made a place for her among the intellectuals then coming to the struggle for better social conditions and equality. They were cropping out here and there, some of them students working out their courses at Columbia or studying in spare moments at night like the O'Reillys, some of them men or women who had seen a problem and stepped out of their own privileged circles.

My brother James was active in bringing these people together. He had written to his family in the summer of 1882 that he would like, as his birthday present, to be enabled to send a young girl in whom he was sure they would be interested, for a visit to Forty Acres. So Leo, as we came to call her for her courage, became one of the most congenial guests who had ever been welcomed there. To show its beauties to a human being who actually did not know what woods and meadows and a clear river, wild-flowers and hills were like, was an unmitigated delight. And to find her intellectually capable of making common ground with her hosts, and giving as well as greeting new points of view, made her visit an event in the history of that summer. She came again from time to time, and I was able to share the friendship during the rest of her life. She had a passion—more than a passion—for truth. The recoil from even a prevarication, the horror of a lie, the deep sting of social injustice, all this was so marked in her that I think she was able to combat deceit more effectively, in her work with individuals, than anyone I have ever known. Her confidence was irresistible. I vividly remember her figure as it was originally described to me in one of Molly's letters, standing for the first time on a hill-top looking off over a fertile valley dotted with farmhouses and barns and harvest fields; her slender figure (she must have been nineteen then) with the proud little head erect, and her rapt face; an interesting face with quick changes of expression.

"Think of it!" she exclaimed. "Living in this place years and years, these people; born here and working here, always with sunrises over those hills, and sunsets, and northwest winds, and a sky like *that* every few days, why, how *good* they must be! Do New England people ever do anything wrong, or cheat, or hurt their neighbors?" And she meant it. It was difficult to convince her that all wrong-doing did not come from overcrowding and competition and the selfishness of wealth. She called herself an anarchist; there were no communists, then, as I have said, but anarchy was the word for dangerous elements; anarchy, we were taught, meant assassinations and plots and the overthrow of government. The Haymarket bombing in Chicago had touched off a train of revenge. But Leonora was not that kind.

"Yes, I am an anarchist," she always explained patiently. "I believe in having no government; in doing away with governments. They are at the bottom of all evils in society."

And why, it would be asked, should government be in itself an evil? There were bad governments of course, but certainly society could not get on without some laws.

"We believe it could. If everyone would simply follow the Christian law, doing unto others as we would have them do to us, there would be no need of government. Abolish the system of forcing people to do right, and they will measure up. Anarchy is not meant to be lawlessness and riot, and the true anarchist will not promote that. We want to do away with government slowly, not by violently overthrowing it. Terrorism is quite another thing."

Leonora was true to that principle to the end of her days. Although not belonging to any religious body, she maintained, and I think my brother never took issue with her on that point, that it was the attitude of the early Christians.

We were kept in touch with various interesting people during our life on Brooklyn Heights. Now and then we tried to bring two extremes of society a little nearer together, but without much success.

My brother was a great comfort to us in those two winters. He came over to us often, and set our minds working on interests which kept us alert. It was his last year in New York, for the Order was about to leave its habitation, on the East side, where they had worked for ten years, and move to a monastery of its own in Maryland; a small building given by a woman for its use, set in exquisite country and soft climate, where it was thought the broader object of the Order and the ideals of monastic life could be better furthered. The closing months of his New York service, however, involved intense labor. We were grateful for his confidence, and for the inspiration he brought with him.

He brought to us some of his friends who strengthened the link we already had with the world of labor. One of them was a young German in whom he had become interested. It was a year of depression. The man was a painter by trade, and had been for some time out of work. He came to tell us, at my brother's request, his experience of his search for a job. I shall give it as nearly as possible in his own words, written out at that time to be used in a meeting of "privileged" women.

"You don't think at first that it means so much to lose your place. You think you could get bigger wages, or better hours, somewhere else. And the fellows who are in the unions believe they'll be taken care of anyway. You go out to look for a new one, and first you go to the regular big places to see if they've lost a man. You know maybe that there are streets where a lot of shops of one trade are near each other; wholesale ones maybe. So you get a good many at once, and you go from one to another, and they tell you there's nothing for you. The first day you cover quite a lot, but the next day you have to try a little further off; you take one awful long street, or one of the avenues. You can't spend money on cars, so you leg it. You have the same bad luck, and feel pretty used up at the end of the day. But still you don't get discouraged, there are hundreds more places to try. And you have a little bit ahead to give in at home. Some fellows don't let their families know; they just go off in the morning and come home on time at night. But then they find it out. Well, it just goes on like that for days and weeks. Maybe there's a strike in the trade; that don't help any. By and by the women folks ask questions; they say why don't you get work, if you're doing all you say you are. They don't believe you're trying very hard. You get pretty hungry because you don't like to take a lunch when you aren't earning anything, so you go all day without, and you get home starved and find they ate up all the solid stuff at noon because of the children. Pretty soon the home gets to be a kind of a small hell, everybody blaming everybody else. Then, when you've tramped round all day, you don't dare go home any more with bad news. Maybe you sit down in the park and just stare ahead of you. Sometimes you sit there till a policeman shakes you up and tells you to get a move on. You can't shave, and I guess that makes you more likely to be turned back. You get a drink offered you sometimes, and it isn't surprising if you take it; I just happen to hate the stuff, but I don't grudge it to the other fellow. So it goes on, and on. And when you do get a job, at last, maybe it's at something you hate, and you haven't any backbone by that time anyway. You may get on at it, but after all your home is pretty well spoiled; it takes years to get it back to where it was."

I have been reminded of that story hundreds of times, and of the insight it gave us. It lent strength to a conviction which I hold yet, that in order to understand the labor question one must have known, and cared for, some working man or woman who has suffered under wrong conditions; only affection or loyal friendship can make us see clearly and feel intensely, when it comes to taking the side of an oppressed people. Pity alone is moving, disturbing, but we can help only when our hearts are actually in the cause of justice.

My brother discovered that this lad was full of artistic instinct and talent. He had been in the habit of sketching, on any surface he could find, faces, animals, trees, spires, on his way to work, starting early enough to give a moment to making an outline and finishing it later. It was possible to get him instruction, and an eventual situation in a church-furnishing business in which he worked for years. Every human being with whom James Huntington came in contact, no matter when and where they met, was instantly an object of vivid interest to him.

I remember once his answer to a woman who had been arguing that young people should not be allowed to go to the theatre, because of the bad plays which were produced. "Yes," he said, "Theatres are misused. But churches are misused too. And crimes are committed out of doors; yet boys and girls cannot be kept shut up in churches or houses. The point is that the drama rises to great heights of beauty; we must look to that, and try to prevent its debasement, not abolish it. And we must be sure that our own personal moral standards are a matter of *living* rather than criticizing."

Women were somewhat of a mystery to him in the earlier days of his ministry. He did not know how to handle sentimental penitents who came to him with personal tangles to be smoothed out. Now and then he remanded them to his sister in Brooklyn with the message; "I'm sending you a girl who really needs the advice of a sensible woman much more than the prescriptions of a priest; you reason with her and I'll pray for her." The specimens he sent were for the most part impenetrable to common sense or any kind of practical recommendations; but I recollect one very charming girl whose conscience had reproached her for leading a dual life: she was trying to keep up a connection with aristocratic relatives who had helped her and her mother financially, and were anxious to promote her social status, and bring about a good match for her, while she concealed the fact that she was working in a downtown office, and using all sorts of means to avoid meeting by day any of the society men with whom she danced at night. Her adventures were amusing, if somewhat pathetic, and I found it hard to blame her, for she had a very healthy conscience and a real honesty beneath her somewhat unworthy (as they seemed to me) ambitions. I could only urge that friends to whom one dare not admit that one was earning one's living were not worth the sacrifices she had made; but I think she found it hard to agree with me, and would rather have consoled herself with spiritual abstractions and the practice of penitential ritual. She had that kind of a mind, as I told my brother, and I thought it likely that in time her social aspirations would be sublimated through the making of altar-cloths under the tutelage of a good Sister, the occupation which she pursued on her afternoons out. He was not shocked at these sentiments of mine, and accepted her back from me with a kindly spirit; I never saw her again, but a few years later learned that she had left New York, and had met and married a young fellow with money and a finer attitude than that of the society set in which she had been ambitiously moving.

There were compensations, during that gray foggy season: we made the acquaintance of new and interesting people. One of them was Dr. Eliza Mosher, a physician to whom my footsteps seemed to have been guided one winter night when the influenza plague first broke out in America. My husband and baby were both ill; I was desperate, and rushed out into the fog, hardly knowing where I went. A brightly lighted window made me halt before her door, and though it was long after office hours I found there a remarkable woman whose sympathy and poise brought instant confidence that she could help us. After she had accompanied me home, had put a glycerine jacket-poultice over little Hannah's lungs, and given Archie a dose of phenacetine, then one of the prevalent remedies for grippe, all with a bright reassuring diagnosis which braced him for quick recovery, we felt her not only a ministering angel, but a strong friend. She became for me, as for thousands of other women, a counselor and teacher and backer.

7

LOSS AND HOPE

But the dreary boarding-house life came suddenly to an end. In the summer of 1891 we had a season of prosperity; it came after anxious months, since a wave of malaria along the Connecticut River had given Nan chills and fever. They cropped out every now and then, finally forcing us to go to Ashfield to escape the Valley mists and mosquitoes, dangerous at Forty Acres. Rather suddenly Archie wrote from Brooklyn that he had leased a small apartment uptown. He was going to bring our furniture down from Englewood, and have it ready for my home-coming in the month of September. It was good news. A home of our own again, on a broad airy street, where our child could develop and the new baby expected at Christmas-time could have its own nursery. We made a very happy journey, the three of us, and climbed easy stairs to find a charmingly arranged suite of rooms absolutely ready for occupation. In the dining-room stood a tall, capable English girl, to whom small Hannah ran instinctively.

"You're going to be my friend, aren't you?" she said, and was gathered into the friend's embrace at once. Edith never forgot that greeting, and never swerved from the friendship. She bore it out as a matter of fact, through the changes and chances of forty years; the embodiment of loyalty, unselfish service, and above all, good sense and abundant humor. Our basis for comfortable family living was complete, we two felt; and the next three months were completely happy ones.

Our second daughter came in December, a Christmas baby. We named her Mary, after my sister. She was unusually lovely, for a new-born infant, with eyes that were soft like her father's, blue eyes with a tinge of coming brown. Her arrival was so quick and easy that it hardly interrupted the natural order of events; she seemed perfectly healthy except for a little darkness of the skin, over which the doctor did not seem to worry, although she spoke of it. Our much-loved Dr. Mosher had been called away for a few days, but had hoped to return for the birth. The substitute physician was also a woman, but had not had so large an experience.

We had a radiantly happy Christmas, on a Friday that year; but two days after, the baby wakened very early, and did not seem quite right, the young nurse thought. She could not eat, was breathing too rapidly, and lay back on my arm with eyes wide open, gazing into mine with a strange depth of expression, quite unlike the look of so young a child. Dr. Mosher had returned the night before, and had sent word that she was coming up the first thing to see us. We waited in suspense, longing to have her get there, for every moment increased our anxiety. Finally she came in with her breezy greeting, and I heard her in the hall saying to Archie, "I couldn't wait a minute to see that baby." I found myself unable to speak; I could only point to the child with a smile which trembling lips belied. She gathered it eagerly into her arms, and I saw her face change instantly.

"Has she been as dark as this from the first?" she asked, "So blue?"

"Not quite," the nurse answered. "But a little. And we had an accident yesterday; some people built a fire in a flat below us, and there was a leak in the chimney somewhere; a lot of soft-coal smoke came into these rooms, and we had to open the windows to let it out; it was a fearfully cold night. I took the baby back into the kitchen and kept her there, but I think there was still smoke, and cold air, when I brought her back. I was afraid—" but the doctor did not stop to hear more.

"We'll take her back by the kitchen stove," she said. And to me, "Don't worry, child; I shall take off my things and stay right on here; we'll fight for her life."

She came back in a half hour. "It's an affection of the bronchial tubes," she said. "And her heart isn't quite right, I think. But we have had her in a hot bath, and she's improved; we may pull her through. She's lying in the lap of a big chair, close to the open oven."

I don't know just what we did, all that day. Edith was sent down with Nan to Grandmother's, but my husband would not leave me. I remember saying over a short prayer that ended, "Save us and help us, O Lord God." I had never prayed like that before. But when, in the middle of the afternoon, the doctor came in saying that at last the little thing was breathing naturally, and there was really hope for her, she did not see the nurse, who had run in to call her back. Just as she had left the baby, its breath had stopped. She came back holding it in her arms.

"You must have her now to hold," she said, "warm and pink from her bath and like a little rose. But think of the brightness that 'eye hath not seen nor ear heard, neither hath entered into the heart of man.' "

I could not have borne to hear anyone else quote Scripture at that moment; I know of no one who could have done it as she did. But it lifted us up in that moment of supreme anguish. We realized the flight of an immortal soul from the tiny body; no narrow doctrine could ever have taken that conviction from us. It took all the strength we had, but our mourning drew us still closer to one another. Neither of us felt for an instant that the littleness of our baby, her short stay with us, or the suddenness of her passing would minimize that sorrow; it was destined to last for many years, and to remind us at each birthday anniversary of what she might have been if she had lived and grown. And for us both it was the first immediate experience of death. We felt that it had come to us with a heavenly vision.

Another trouble followed six weeks after the baby's death. Nan came down suddenly with scarlet fever, and we were quarantined in our apartment at the top of the house. The young nurse who had been with us at baby Mary's birth came back; she had made me promise to send for her in case of need; she felt that perhaps her lack of experience might have caused the disaster. We were kept very busy for the following month; Edith, our good young helper, caught the fever, and was quite ill. When the spring came, she moved with her family to Connecticut, and for a time I managed the housekeeping myself; I was very strong and ready in those days, and glad to be busy. But we had a warm May, and in June extreme weather; both Nan and I began to wilt. It was terribly close in the little apartment, and through open windows the nearness of the elevated railway, a crash and rush every ten minutes, was frightfully disturbing.

Weariness and another slump in finances brought a discouragement which we would not own even to one another, but we were losing sleep and hope. We were trying to plan in the stifling atmosphere of our tiny rooms for a visit to Forty Acres, but it did not look hopeful.

One morning Archie was solicitous about the mail; a letter arrived just before he left for the office. It was from my father, as follows:

"I have a piece of news for you; I have leased the old Phelps house from the Bulfinches, who are not going there this summer, and have had it put in complete order. The furniture is all there, so you can take possession of it at any time. I want you to leave Brooklyn on Thursday prepared to spend the whole summer. You will take the forenoon train and reach the Hadley station in the middle of the afternoon; you will find my man there with a carriage and a boy with a wagon for the trunks. They will give you the key to the house-door, and you can open it and enter in. Archie knows all about it, and promises to send you off; he will join you later, and we shall be there in about three weeks."

We obeyed these orders to the letter. Archie was never troubled by city heat and noise, although he loved to get away into the country for visits. He could not leave an important case to go with us, but agreed to go to his parents, who were delighted to have him at home. And little Hannah and I were breathing the freshness of a northwest breeze from the hills by the time our train crossed the Connecticut River. We found the man at the station, were given a great hand-wrought iron key, and drove in at the gate of the old Phelps house to find heaps of fragrant hay under the pines, and a gleam of yellow June lilies in the garden beyond. Branches of an ancient trumpet-vine had become twisted in the long closed blinds.

As we opened the door and entered in, it was like being suddenly touched with the spirit of the old Phelps ancestors, and finding unseen personalities waiting for us with a welcome. The house was swept and garnished, every piece of furniture left where the departing inmates had placed it three years before. The long north parlor had its stiff chairs and sofa; against the wall stood the two rounding table-ends of the grand old square inlaid Chippendale dining-table; the tall ugly blue glass vases stood on the mantelpiece beside the curious lamps, the original student-lamps in which former generations had burned sperm oil. With that room we associated our summer-evening visits to Cousin Sarah and Cousin Caroline and Cousin Ellen; Archie and I would always hold it in sacred memory. Had it not a pair of hearts cut into each shutter? There was the little room at the foot of the stairs, which was once Uncle Phelps' office, where he and Oliver Smith drew up the famous Smith Will, contested by Rufus Choate and defended successfully by Daniel Webster. We passed on up the stairs, at the head of which I found Cousin Sarah's bedroom, with the high bed in which she was lying when she received Archie and me and gave our engagement her blessing, not long before her death. I knew that was destined to be my own room, and that the southwest chamber where stood a great four-poster bed and chintz hangings with giant flowers, would remain a guest-room. And that the east bedroom adjoining mine, which was papered in a close-covered design of shaded green maple leaves, would be the place for Nan's small bed. Then there were other bedrooms, giving on a small side-hall, and the back stairs descended steeply into a winter dining-room, with a huge fireplace and Dutch oven and crane, and hooks in the ceiling for hams to hang from. There was a fine kitchen in the ell, into which one stepped down; we remembered the old wooden pump in the center of the room, and its long trough underneath, in which ancient householders were said to have washed dishes, apparently on their knees—a tradition which we could not believe. But a towering clothes-bar structure folded against the wall gave a hint of the enormous washings which 'Liza West, the little old woman who lived to be ninety in the service of the family and had called all the eleven grown sons and daughters of two wives by their first names, must have put through.

I could not sleep that first night; it was too exciting. After midnight, when the moon was shining on Nan's counterpane, lighting up the meadows and reflected in pools left by recent rain, I escaped into the garden, and walked about among the lilies in a sort of trance. One could catch the sounds of tiny feet; three years of solitude had made the old place a home for all kinds of animals.

I sat a while on the doorstep, then flung myself on a pile of fresh hay beneath the pines. After a time, the laugh of a fox sounded from the woods, to which a little lane ascended gently; I strolled across the farm-yard, and let down the bars into the lane. By and by the moon vanished; then came the unearthly rose of dawn. My eyes must have closed. The next conscious moment found me with my head against a porch pillar, and a bright sun coming up over the edge of the hill, between two broad-branched elms, with rosy clouds in attendance—the beginning of another perfect June day. I ran upstairs, to make sure that I should hear Nan's waking cry of "Mother!"

It was a summer that stands out in memory. There was time, to begin with, to lay aside worries. Archie came often for week-ends, and it was good to see him rest; at the end he spent ten days with us. My father saw to it that there were no expenses beyond what we should have spent in town; delicious fruits and vegetables came from his garden, as well as milk and cream, and butter of Mother's churning. Our friend Edith, who had been with her family in Connecticut for some months after the scarlet fever, returned to us accompanied by her younger sister Tessie. We repacked chestsful of old linen, creamy homespun blankets, marvelous quilts and damask tablecloths, all in perfect condition. We might have written a history of eighteen- and nineteenth-century fancy-work, on the basis of further discoveries in crewels, crocheted tidies, pine-cone frames, spatterwork (which consisted in running a brush saturated with ink through a small screen, over a sheet of drawing-paper to which pressed ferns had been applied in designs, leaving white impressions of their shapes when these were removed). A great part of these treasures had to be discarded because of decay; others we packed in empty trunks which we found under the eaves, and there they still remain.

Hospitality was one of the joys of that summer. Leonora O'Reilly came, with her friend Mary Dreier. As a result I resolved to throw myself into reform activities again when we came back to the city. My friend Lucy Watson came, and we lived over again our joys of previous years. Cousin Ellen herself also came, happy in the thought that the old house could be filled with young life again. She sold the whole estate the next year to my father, who wanted to make it our permanent summer home, and left in it most of the furnishings. Forty Acres was by this time alive with children. Little Hannah now had playmates of her own age, beside the chivalrous boy cousins. The Bishop still read aloud delightfully, still had daily morning prayers, still tilled the soil with his own hands in vacation-time, and took friends into the woods. His devotion to his little grand-daughter was lovely to see. Yet no more young men listened, stretched on the grass or gathered in the stoop. It was not quite like the life of our earlier days; after all, the world had changed.

8

THE EIGHTEEN NINETIES

We went back to Brooklyn from that experience with fresh zest for the world. The last years of the century were to some degree a preparation for stupendous advances in human affairs. The face of metropolitan life had been altered; there were strange apparitions in our midst. One day a carriage with wheels but no shafts, no horses, no visible propelling force, came up Fulton Street in Brooklyn, and turned into Washington Avenue under our windows. People stopped, gazed, a few boys tried to run after it. I can remember the thrill the later appearance of the first trolley car gave us as it moved, a dark-colored monster, crowds beholding it from the sidewalk. One felt a sudden swelling of the throat; not so much the excitement of the thing itself, but from a sense of the change for which it stood. Before long the horse-cars that had threaded the city streets for the better part of a century began to disappear. The bicycle, which for some time had amused the man on the sidewalk with the spectacle of one high wheel and a man on top of it guiding a tiny one, had come down to lesser proportions and more speed, and was offering attraction to women riders. The cinema was becoming a source of amusement. Electric lighting had replaced gas in many houses, and gas stoves too were making their way. The telephone was by that time available to smaller householders.

And now, with these and an infinite number of minor changes, there came beginnings of increased social consciousness, manifest in the body politic and the ranks of labor. Reform movements were gaining influence in legislatures, and in New York City the fight against Tammany and its enormities was renewed with fresh vigor.

It was astonishing and revealing, however, to realize with what passivity that huge institution, already nearly a hundred years old, had been taken for granted by the public. It had been making itself gradually impregnable, consolidating its defenses, reaping millions of dollars, and reaching into fields where there could be practically no effective opposition, with more or less backing from the Catholic Church, and the support of an ignorant and bribed public. The arch-villain Tweed was gone, but his successor, Richard Croker, had followed the same course, and was now spending his millions on the race-tracks of England and his luxurious country-house there, while henchmen carried on gallantly in America. He held the whip-hand over the Democratic party, and worst of all, the equally iniquitous but perhaps not quite so lavishly outrageous Republican boss, Tom Platt, was actually his partner whenever that turned out to be for their common advantage.

My husband had joined the Young Men's Democratic Club of Brooklyn, one of the local reform groups which had furthered the attacks on Tammany rule and the attempt to elect better leaders. It was, like other groups of its kind, sincere and valorous, and out against corruption in public office. At that time the agitation for Civil Service reform was also becoming strong, and some of our friends were prominent in that movement; both of the Lows, Seth and William, a half-brother, were working with unremitting zeal in its cause. They had married sisters, Annie and Lois Curtis of Boston, who were friends of my older sister and myself. Seth Low had been President of Columbia College and had served a term as Mayor of Greater New York in the early nineties.

And now Theodore Roosevelt had galloped out on the political stage; I find myself using the word "galloped" as a matter of association, probably; one envisaged him in those days astride a horse, his favorite position, and his horse was not always the familiar quadruped of natural history, but a hobby, the moving spirit of a political race, or a reform, as the case might be; he galloped at all events, and had become a prominent figure in the political arena; a picturesque and challenging personality with remarkable energy and aggressive power, making friends, scorning foes, and pursuing his own boundless activity with indifference to both. He had thrown himself into the Civil Service Reform movement, and President Harrison made him one of the three commissioners who were put in control. But neither Harrison nor Cleveland had given it especially strong backing; perhaps its objective—impartiality and freedom from politics—was better promoted for that reason. Roosevelt was supremely resourceful and good at meeting opposition, hitting out relentlessly on behalf of his cause, an effective weapon against the spoils system. His boldness, his ungloved attack on the flagrant abuses of power, and his impetuous aggression, stimulated weaker movements. When he became Police Commissioner, and started his personal investigations of the New York force, he was already a hero to some extent, though there were plenty of enemies on his trail. Of his bravery there was no question, and the daily accounts of his accomplishments became almost a romance.

My brother, who brought to us his enthusiasms as well as some of the difficulties which we could share at least by sympathy, was then much interested in the Knights of Labor, and had, I believe, become a member of the organization. They were, then, the foremost labor organization in the country. There had been associations of working-men, craft unions mainly, ever since the Civil War, but no centralization or actual coordination since 1874, when they were organized as a national body. From the very first they had excluded unskilled labor. The Knights had started out a few years later, on a broader basis, and with greater idealism. Their order was to some extent a matter of religion, and initiations were attended with ritual, apparently of a slightly mystic character. Their aim was to keep the organization non-political, but they became involved in a measure of church opposition, for the Catholic Church was against them, at first mildly, later more seriously. There was a little infusion of socialism in their creed: it stood for public ownership of railways and utilities. Their president, Terence V. Powderly, was a friend of my brother, who became interested in the movement through his close association with the working-people. He was a person of refined appearance, some education, and perhaps more idealism than wisdom. He had an oratorical gift which gave him some power. He passed out of office in 1893, but meanwhile my brother's interest in the movement, which made some stir in the industrial world, had spread to a certain extent in the Episcopal church. The prestige of the Knights was declining then, although its losses were not generally realized. They had attempted too much and had changed their organization too often; it was top-heavy with a mass of unskilled workers who did not fit into any clear-cut policy, and whose ranks were recruited through immigration—Poles, Swedes, French, Bohemians. The more conservative unions, under Samuel Gompers, a cigar-maker, a shrewd, limited, but very aggressive leader, brought about a split which in the end led to the formation of the American Federation of Labor. The strike and even the boycott became a more frequent resort.

The Knights gradually shrank to small numbers from a membership claimed to have reached a hundred thousand. But my brother had already made many converts to its ideas, and we were greatly interested in the formation of the Church Association for the Advancement of the Interests of Labor, or the C. A. I. L., familiarly known as *Cail*.

My father was, I think, the first Bishop to join in starting this association which made good progress among the clergy in the East. Its work from the outset was bringing better knowledge of industrial conditions to the people of the churches. The Brotherhood of Man was a fine sentiment, to those privileged and religious people who acknowledged it, but actually its significance needed to be brought home to the individual conscience. A very formidable opposition to organized labor, partly because of the weaknesses of that body, particularly of the younger unions, had been growing up. Not only the manufacturing element, which dealt directly with union labor, but the intellectual and rational, were inimical to it. Its methods were questioned, and often held in contempt. It concerned itself solely with the craft wage-earners; there was no hope in it for sweated or unskilled labor. The Cail was not actually militant in its character, but it championed the cause of the helpless, and brought an appeal through religion to the social conscience as far as was possible.

In connection with its work I may perhaps recall a personal incident to which I still look back with amusement. I had been writing a little, off and on, for two or three years, beginning with a serial in *The Churchman,* a story of which I am anything but proud today. I had written stories for children in that periodical, and also in *The Youth's Companion,* which paid very well, and accepted everything I sent in; also an occasional story or article for the Saturday literary column of the *New York Times,* and the Saturday issue of the *New York Post.* And at the moment Henry George's paper, *The Standard,* was a large daily sheet, the organ of the Single Tax. Mr. George was then a public figure as well as the writer of a book which was translated into forty languages, and wielded a strong influence. We were warmly interested in the doctrine propounded in *Progress and Poverty,* and my husband and I were among the friends and visitors who enjoyed Mr. George's hospitality. His house was thrown open every week to a crowd of guests and adherents, and it was possible to get talks with him there, beside his public utterances. He asked me now and then to write an article for *The Standard,* and finally he and my brother came to me with a proposition which sounded like an adventure, to say the least. The General Conventions of the Episcopal Church had never taken up the matter of social abuses; its time was given instead to discussions of canons, proposed innovations or alterations of the Liturgy, matters of ritual and their theological implications, and a host of routine questions carried over and resurrected each year with no prospect of settlement.

My father was openly impatient, as were many others. There was a crying need for more knowledge of, and sympathy with the great questions then confronting Church and State. Dr. Parkhurst was launching his famous attack upon the houses of vice in New York city, and the sensational details were published daily. All manner of civic house-cleanings were going on. But the church fought shy of it. Bishops were shepherds, and only the care of their own particular flocks concerned them. Something was wanted, it appeared, to force the great problems of the moment upon their consciousness.

The plan was that an article should be written, and sent to all the clergy, pointing out this need, and delating upon the influence which might be exerted by strong leaders both in the Convention itself and through its assemblage of delegates, upon the church at large. I remember discussing it with Mr. George in a corner at one of his Sunday afternoons at home, when people streamed in and out of the house, finding acquaintances, or making friends of other land-taxers without the formality of an introduction. The host was invariably busy with one or two people at a time, and had to be seized upon summarily or inveigled back to his station as welcomer. He would dash up to one unexpectedly, and begin where he last left off in the midst of an interrupted discussion, getting as far along with it as he might, but very likely borne off before it was well under way. He was no respecter of persons, however, and had not the accustomed group of satellites who preempt a great man's attention on all occasions.

That day, I recollect, he said to my husband, "Come along, and we'll talk about that article. You've got to see that she does it." Between us we settled on a sort of allegory, a tale of a mysterious stranger going into a meeting of a convention and telling the door-keeper that he was charged with a message to the church from the oppressed people in the tenements and sweat-shops, dens of vice, and so forth, and would like an opportunity to speak. The refusal of this privilege, on the ground of ecclesiastical exigencies and important projects before the House, was the gist of the story. Mr. George decided that this was what he particularly wanted, and gave me but a short time to get it finished for *The Standard*. He sent a copy of it, I believe, to every bishop, and most of the clergy, of the Episcopal Church, at the time of the meeting of the House of Bishops. I signed it with the name *Jacob Armitage,* under which I had written other articles.

The paper received between thirty and forty letters in reply, some of them favorable, some voicing great disapproval. One especially dear friend, the Reverend William Reed Huntington of Grace Church, who had been an inmate of our family in the old Boston days when assisting my father, and was then my little daughter's godfather, wrote one of the most severe arraignments, taking me apparently for a clergyman and deprecating my disloyalty, as he termed it. Naturally he never knew to whom he had been writing. I had not told my father who was responsible for the article, for I wanted his unbiased criticism. I was so thrilled by his warm approval, expressed when he was visiting us, that even then I did not reveal to him that he was praising his daughter's work. Years passed before world issues and evils were taken before the tribunal of bishops, but work went on, nevertheless, among the individual clergy. By and by the Church League for Industrial Democracy, of which such women as Vida Scudder and Mary Simkhovitch were leaders and founders, took up the work of the Cail to a large extent.

9

A PART IN POLITICS

With the ignorant prejudice of the ordinary nineteenth-century woman against political influence, I began by hating to have my husband mix himself up with politics and partisanship, though I was a partisan myself. It was the era that might be called pre-citizenship for women; they were gradually becoming cognizant of social evils, and I had certainly had training enough in early Syracuse days to be ready for reform interests. But then, as in the nineties, the whole field of political activity was seething with corruption, a slough in which few outsiders had ventured to set their feet. Equal suffrage was just visible on the horizon, a vision kept bright by the very women I had seen in my girlhood at their early convention in the seventies. Among my older sister's friends it was in the prophetic stage. Better knowledge of women's possibilities was disseminated through many channels. They were coming into their own in new fields.

But failing a right to equality in the business or political world, the average woman looked upon party affiliations as beneath the dignity, if not the respectability of the enlightened citizen. When Archie joined the Young Men's Democratic Club I was sure he would meet with corrupting influences. Nevertheless I had a great curiosity to see just how they worked. We were too congenial a pair to have separate mental compartments for particular interests; we discussed every sort of encounter or enthusiasm. It was the beginning of my own civic interests. After a political meeting we talked far into the night; he was always ready to describe the evening's adventures.

His friend Frederick Hinrichs, a somewhat older man, and the moving spirit of the Young Democrats group, looked to him for active support. He was a leading influence in the club through some of its exciting crises; once after a dissension he was almost dislodged from the chairman's seat on the platform, and I swelled with pride at his heroism.

Seth Low, who had championed the cause of Civil Service reform, had become a leader of one of the campaigning clubs. He was a scion of the old Low family of Brooklyn, and as my father had said of Governor Seymour in our old Syracuse days, a high-minded Christian gentleman. That described him; a man of the nineteenth century, not politically strong, but discerning and sympathetic with reform. Horace Deming, an ambitious Republican, had a large following in the membership of the Young Republican Club; the Young Men's Democratic Club had organized soon after the first Cleveland campaign in 1884, with the object of restoring Jeffersonian ideals to the Democratic party, and furthering specifically a reform in city government. In that field of course they competed with Tammany. Edward M. Shepard, a prominent and wealthy politician, by inheritance a Tammany adherent but a rebel against the iniquities of that organization, was an early president of the Young Men's Democratic Club, and was followed by Frederick Hinrichs of Brooklyn, a fine speaker and independent thinker.

Hinrichs was a Free Trader, as were various prominent Brooklyn men, like Henry Ward Beecher and Thomas G. Sherman; they were already regarded as dangerous radicals by certain large business interests, almost as communists are today but came from higher social ranks. Cleveland had made it a matter of special presidential policy, and after his defeat by Harrison in 1888 had still adhered to his creed.

In 1892 David B. Hill, the boss of the regular Democratic party, aspired to candidacy for its nomination, and gathered seventy-two delegates to represent him at the national convention in Chicago. This was a menace to the reform contingent. The Young Men Democrats were determined to oppose him, and my husband was at the head and front, with Hinrichs, of a move to frustrate the scheme. A few days after the State Convention had elected the

Hill delegates, he had an inspiration, and decided to see Hinrichs and Shepard, and try to initiate a movement for Cleveland's re-election if the latter could be persuaded to run. He would be the salvation of the party. Archie started forth with a friend, remarking that Hinrichs had courage enough for anything. He came back with good news.

"Fred thinks it's a pretty heavy contract," he said, "and we'll have to have the club back of him, but he's agreed to go and see Cleveland tomorrow, and ask what the chances would be of his con-senting to run. He's the one man that can save the situation, and beat Hill."

We were in suspense for twenty-four hours and more. Then word came that Cleveland was interested, and had asked just one question; *"What are the people going to do about it?"* He was re-nominated at a special convention in Syracuse. The independent delegates were not allowed seats on the platform, but sat at the front of the audience. Hinrichs made a capital speech for the protesting body, and his ringing declaration as he pointed to these delegates, *"We are the People!"* was one of the slogans of the campaign. Many leading men also became Mugwumps, as they were scornfully desig-nated—Mr. Kernan of Utica and Mayor Grace of New York, Fred-erick Coudert, Thomas Mott Osborn, who later became an out-standing fighter for prison reform, and Charles Fairchild of Cazenovia; the last two Central New York men, and friends of my father, who was also deeply interested in the campaign. Mr. Fair-child was made Secretary of the Treasury in Cleveland's cabinet, and Mr. Hinrichs became a friend and associate of Senator Bayard of Delaware, at that time Secretary of State, and later our Ambas-sador to the Court of St. James. Mr. Hinrichs' own account of that victory, consummated over the unanimous opposition of the reg-ular Democratic organization, is stirring. The Young Men's Demo-cratic Club was triumphant, and during following years my hus-band was twice its president.

Election days were curiously solemn, in our neighborhood at any rate; I don't know what took place in Tammany territory. They were not like Sunday, with cheerful bells and best clothes. Business was suspended, and all day the streets of Brooklyn remained quiet. Men walked off to the polls from early morning on. The polling-places were usually at saloons, which was later urged against woman-suffrage. Children were taken to dine with their grandparents, the father of the family perhaps being absent. They did not play in the streets. Offices were closed. Liquor was plentiful, and was used as a medium of exchange in bribery, though mostly under cover. Especially on days of national elections these conditions prevailed, but even when mayors and other local officials were up it was perceptible. My husband used to run in of an afternoon, sometimes reporting close votes or possible disturbances in parts of the city. We grew more and more restive as the hours wore on before the closing of the polls.

When the lamps were lighted, however, the scene changed, and a holiday tempo reigned; the working people and the young betook themselves to places of amusement, the business men to their offices or to windows, whence the returns, thrown upon screens at the top of the newspaper buildings or high towers, could be seen. The theaters also reported to excited audiences. Crowds watched from the sidewalks; figures were received with groans or huzzas. Till after midnight the frenzy kept up. The successful candidates were escorted to, or visited at their homes by joyful crowds and made speeches from balconies. The streets echoed with trumpetings from bands or the humbler horns of the proletariat, and the police went about watching bonfires.

For us two, the night of that election which put Frederick Hinrichs into office—a political "spoil" it might have been called, as Commissioner of Tax Arrears, was the harbinger of a couple of fortunate years. He appointed Archie his deputy, which meant a good salary, a larger apartment, the settlement of debts and freedom from worry so long as that particular party remained in power. Now I had what my somewhat battered New England conscience pronounced a sinful elation. Relief at last from financial insecurity; help in the housekeeping, something put away for illness or emergency, and a release of new energy with the prospect of time for outside work as well as for the writing which had become more than a mere resource, were the results of a political appointment, an interruption in my husband's profession, and an involvement, no doubt, in obligations which might at any moment become threatening.

I went through a considerable mental revolt against this involuntary satisfaction, and was annoyed to think that my husband could take it as complacently as he did. Diplomacy was a new word, an addition to our virtuous vocabulary, and one fraught with alarm. But the two tax-collectors looked upon their accession to office seriously, apparently confident of their fitness for the job, and with the goal of recovering some millions of dollars for the city in the shape of old unpaid taxes on large tracts of land. They became so absorbed in this undertaking that I found myself grumpily jealous of their unwonted ardor. I made truce with my own qualms at last, coming to the old conclusion that this experience would teach us something in any case, and give us a chance to understand the political life of a great city.

Experience, experience; that solemn fowl, as Oliver Wendell Holmes puts it, that cackles a great deal more than she lays eggs. We all cackle with her, of course, and return to sit on our own nests, expecting great results. I must record, however, that it made us jubilant when Archie was tended a bribe by a man who wanted to forestall the assessment and sale of a piece of property on which he had not paid taxes for years. The man laid a large roll of bills on the office desk with the remark,

"Of course you won't put up those lots, Sessions; you're a good friend of mine."

"An annual ceremony," Archie wagered grimly.

The bills were "left lay" till surreptitiously removed by their owner, and the sale expedited. Apollyon had been laid low, and we had been in at the death. What a shame that such opportunities were not open to the weaker sex!

10

THE CONSUMERS' LEAGUE

Politics however, were not the whole of my husband's public activities. He was busy in the service of the Municipal League. He was delegate from Brooklyn to the Conference at Philadelphia in 1894, and again at Cleveland the next year, and delivered addresses before various political organizations on the burning question of municipal government reform. I remember feeling terribly helpless and futile now and then, when we were discussing those things. Being a mere female, going to church societies and Girls' Friendly meetings, writing articles, mending stockings, and making over other people's clothes to fit my child and myself or trying out economical menus, seemed to offer so very little contribution to the community. And then quite suddenly there came the chance for a real responsibility.

I was a member of the large and active Brooklyn Woman's Club, and as nearly as I can remember it was through that club that I received a proposal to take the presidency of a Long Island branch of the Consumers' League, then well started in New York with Mrs. Maud Nathan at its head. The history of that association has been so well described by Mrs. Nathan in her book, *The Story of an Epochmaking Movement,* that I do not need to explain how great an opportunity this opened up.

Information regarding conditions of working-women in New York City alone needed to be brought home to the purchasers and the general public. In every branch of business and industry, from sweatshops to fashionable tailors' establishments and dry-goods stores, investigation was challenged. The New York League, which had gained its inspiration from a woman who had herself known the worst evils at first hand, was at work trying to make consumers realize the menace to the entire public, not only from the point of view of humanity, but from actual threat of disease and poison. Voluntary inspection had been begun in New York City, but Long Island was still untouched through lack of workers. It needed an organization which could work hand in hand with the present one, first of all helping to spread the knowledge of its needs and objects.

I don't know how I ever came to accept that proposal so quickly and impetuously, but it carried such persuasive force that I had agreed almost before I knew it. I who had thought a broken leg interesting, was still impetuously ready to set sail for unknown shores in a fog, without even studying a chart. But it was put to me as a job in which I should have strong backing. I was to have twelve vice-presidents, each of them the head of a separate organization, so that the scheme would be spread at once before a large public. All I should have to do would be—we all know how the duties of an official are minimized when people are urging one to shoulder them. The truth is, however, that eyes are dazzled by the sight of a new field for exploration, particularly when one has been looking at all life and action from a quiet corner. So I agreed, blindly or unadvisedly if you like, to take the job.

There were interesting preliminary meetings. I was glad to meet my sister's friend Mrs. Josephine Shaw Lowell, the founder of the Charity Organization, and Mrs. Florence Kelley, with whom I was destined to come into closer touch in later years. She was the head of the Chicago branch of the League, and was living at Hull House. We had Jane Addams and Ellen Starr as guests at Forty Acres the summer before, and had heard much of Mrs. Kelley from them. Then there was Miss Watmough of Philadelphia, who had started a branch of the League there. One special departure projected that year was a plan for getting hold of consumers, and utilizing their power by means of a label to supplement the White List of fair dealers which was already circulated in New York. A black list was of course illegal, and the New York League had been publishing the names of stores in which good conditions, wages and hours prevailed. Even that was attacked, of course, and I remember certain comments from other than business circles. Economists sniffed at this procedure. But it had very clearly demonstrated the power of the consumer in a capitalistic regime, and as that was the power on which the League had laid hands, it was now organized for use.

I was somewhat divided in my mind, and at those preliminary gatherings we had difficulty in coming to a conclusion regarding the label which it was now proposed that the League should persuade manufacturers to affix to goods made under proper conditions. The White List was not sufficiently far-reaching to be a sweeping force, and beside that it was in continual danger of suppression through the forces of competition, a power which has been defended by the constitution and the courts of our country throughout its legislative history. But labelled goods would go out all over the country and be a valuable advertisement for the firms who consented to earn them by reforming the conditions of their stores and factories.

There was already a Trade Union label, and some of us felt that the Consumers' League should act definitely in support of the unions, either by standing by them in some way or by backing their labels. The President of the Philadelphia League, Miss Watmough, and I both felt strongly that this would be the more helpful course. But Mrs. Nathan and Mrs. Kelley, infinitely better informed and experienced, did not hold with us, and the latter, who was in keen sympathy with union labor, and knew its difficulties better than any of us, brought the meeting round to her point of view, which was that since workers were not then in a position to wage so intensive a battle against low living-standards as against long hours and insufficient pay, their label was not making great headway, and did not confine itself to women's work. So we were convinced as to the nature, as well as the magnitude, of our task, and I came back to Brooklyn with a mingled enthusiasm and terror, at the prospect of facing those twelve vice-presidents, any one of whom would be a far more thoroughly equipped leader for the new movement than myself.

Women were then taking up parliamentary procedure at all their clubs. It would never do for a novice to attempt an organizing job without preparation. Teachers gave courses in parliamentary law, but at the moment there was none available for me; I must study the thing out by myself. I procured three booklets, all with directions for the conduct of meetings. The dreaded gathering, although large, proved less formidable than imagination had painted it, and went off very well; only once did a voice interrupt proceedings with the crisp correction, "Madam Chairman, there is already a motion before the House." The answer "Of course—I beg pardon" sounded more calm than the chairman actually felt, but I remembered Mrs. Lowell's occasional remonstrances at our New York conferences when we fell into discussions; "Ladies, ladies, would you *please* address the Chair?" and knew that there were worse difficulties to be met at times.

We started off well as a Long Island League, with many members but a tremendous task. There was no authorized mercantile inspection then, though we were working for it through representatives at Albany. So we had before us the whole field of investigation to cover, going to stores and factories and finding out for ourselves the conditions under which women and girls were working. Few of our new executives could get out for the work needed; a half-dozen faithful members, giving all the time they could, were able to accomplish only a part of it. I managed to take most of my forenoons, for Nan was a collected little person of six, going to school every day at the Adelphi Academy, and our good friend Edith was with us. I could get off early, and be home by twelve o'clock.

We went from one store to another, interviewing managers, seeing the employees' dressing-rooms, where we found dampness, defective plumbing, lack of any provision for sudden illness, or space for lunch; sometimes a fainting girl laid out on a wooden bench or on a dirty floor. There were seats in some stores, but an employee found sitting lost her place at once; we dared not ask too many questions over the counter, however, for we were assiduously dogged by floor-walkers, and encouraged to move away. The greatest tact was needed in order to get satisfactory reports. As I happened to be an associate of the Girls' Friendly Society, it was sometimes possible to collect information outside from its younger members; but only girls in desperate need of money were able to maintain their positions in the stores. It was refreshing to find a small business, now and then, with better conditions; the larger ones were pretty hopeless. Still we possessed ourselves of plenty of sensational facts. And the factories, at which we made only a beginning in those years, were worse; the moral as well as physical welfare of the workers was at stake, and the pitifully low wages in both shops and stores were actually expected to be eked out by shameful means in many instances.

The investigation, however, was not one's only business. I found I was expected to speak, the winter through, at meetings of the various bodies over which our vice-presidents presided. Both in and out of town, often at suburban clubs, sometimes at forenoon or again at afternoon meetings, one went to try and make women realize to how serious an undertaking the Consumers' League had pledged itself.

Could I ever forget those meetings? At that moment in the history of feminine fashions, middle-aged dames did their hair *à la Pompadour,* and wore black satin gowns with colored vests of the same material, or of plush; the prevailing color that particular year was yellow. So I addressed myself to rows of rolling gray and white coiffures, and gold-colored corseted busts. Sometimes they met in private drawing-rooms, sometimes in club-house parlors, but the general effect was the same, formal and forbidding. One can talk to any sort of audience if a rapid survey of it discloses some promise, be it ever so slight, of a response to one's perorations; but I rarely found it possible to hope for that spark of encouragement. Middle age and conservatism made a more or less stubborn wall against which one battered one's conclusions futilely. Not that there were not individual sympathizers, but as a phalanx the line was impenetrable, it seemed. I made a point of reporting only what I had actually seen, and the tale was lurid enough; yet it seldom roused interest. After its completion there would almost always be some powerful dame who would arise majestically, saying, "Madam chairman, will Mrs. Sessions tell us *why,* if conditions in stores and factories are what she describes them to be, it is impossible to get maids to work in families,

where they can have every comfort and a perfectly good wage beside—six dollars a week and room and board?"

I would answer this question as gently as I could, knowing that to
impugn the sanctity of the HOME by suggesting any possible ground
for objection to it on the part of a working-girl would be more or
less fatal. I usually turned the argument in another direction by
assuming modestly that young girls were inclined to want to be with
their families at night, and so forth; also that of course if there were
no factory workers or salesladies to be had, in case all young women
went into housework, the wheels of industry could not revolve. But
this was always considered a weak defense, and the lady would sit
down again with an injured air.

Once I made an utterly foolish break; my tact was worn down,
and I admitted that girls had sometimes been subjected to disre-
spect, if not immoral advances, by the young men in households
where they had worked. I could have bitten my tongue the next
moment, for it raised a storm. Another lady leaped to her feet
declaring that it was a mother's duty to keep such horrible influences out of her family, intimating that most general houseworkers
were liable to demoralize virtuous sons, and of all things could not
be trusted with young children. The meeting ended, as alas! it
often did in spite of all one's efforts, in a heated discussion of the
servant-girl and the working-class, with presumptuous trades-
unions and persecuted employers thrown in. The pompadours
moved about indignantly, and the poor chairman even had to apol-
ogize for them now and then. But after the meeting, there were
always a few really interested women who remained to ask intelligent questions of the speaker, and show their sympathy with the
movement. One opened up gratefully when face-to-face with plain
tailored suits or even shabby ulsters like one's own, and came away
feeling a little less futile.

Then came a special exigency. There were two large stores,
cheap stores, over in the east part of Brooklyn, which had insisted on
keeping open every night in the week, and were paying their employees shamefully low wages, without allowance for the long hours.
Every sort of pressure had been put upon them—we had no early-

closing law—and the whole community was in sympathy with the over-worked girls. Finally a big meeting was arranged, to take place within the district, and make a public demonstration. Mr. Edward King (a prominent labor-man and socialist), a member of the legislature, and one of the high city officials, were scheduled to address it, and I was asked to speak also as president of the Long Island League. My husband and I went over rather early and found the scene extremely lively; a huge rink, or something of the sort, a long wooden building, already half full of people, a crowd outside blocking the narrow street, and two bands, one playing inside, the other out, with an impossible musical effect, also sellers of pop-corn balls and peanuts, and distributors of flyers. It was a typical proletarian crowd, good-natured, enthusiastic, full of boosters and boo-ers, the sort of audience with which I felt most at home. The platform was narrow, and so high above the crowd that it seemed a dizzy eminence to speak from. Archie got terribly nervous. "You can't possibly throw your voice from that perch," he declared.

"Yes I can; I never mind speaking to a crowd. Don't worry at all." But he was so worried that he went out and walked restlessly up and down the sidewalk, just looking in now and then to see if I had begun. As a matter of fact the acoustics were not so bad; why, I don't know. At all events I found myself warming up easily when it came my turn, for my predecessor was rather perfunctory and weary. And the crowd applauded with delightful abandon, having themselves warmed up by that time. My husband glanced in at the back, found he could hear perfectly, and was relieved. The meeting went off very well, but whether it did any good I don't know.

The stores did finally agree to close on all but two nights of the week. And mercantile inspection came about, though not satisfactorily. It was put under the direction of the Board of Health—not a strong arm to lean upon in those days, for the head thereof was invariably a politician. Mrs. Nathan was at one time appointed a special inspector, with authority; but the appointment was fought with bitterness by heads of large stores and other industrial institutions; her influence was by that time actually feared. A fairly good bill was passed in 1896, but even then there were never enough inspectors to do the necessary work. There was one year when a man was appointed as Health Commissioner who, though he had the reputation of being a philanthropist, and certainly was extremely generous, had a connection with the management of two or more large dry-goods stores. He remained in office only twelve months, I believe and during that time managed to dismiss the mercantile inspectors, an action which put us back just where we were before.

I have often felt that it is difficult to place the activities of the Consumers' League in line with other forward movements of the time. Its accomplishment was greater than all of them; action, and direct action, rather than theory, was its motive power, and its scheme corrective rather than progressive, although some of the legislation backed by its influence contributed largely to enlightenment of the people and better knowledge of conditions. Fought as it was, and bitterly, by powerful interests, it was carried even as far west as Oregon, where the struggle for reasonable working-hours and wages was assisted by the League; there, later on, an appeal to the Supreme Court of the United States was ably advocated by Felix Frankfurter, in connection with the famous case of the laundry-workers. The Supreme Court eventually annulled the minimum wage law in the District of Columbia, but in other states useful legislation was carried successfully through. But the battle is not yet wholly won, as the Supreme Court's 1936 nullification of the New York law shows.

The record of the League's achievements in America and its extension of the work in Europe is imposing to a degree. But, to borrow an expression of Vincent Sheehan's in describing some present-day forces, it was "the old, jerky rhythm of capitalism" and philanthropy; capital, keeping up with the strides of discovery and industrial prosperity, forced to turn and repair its own ravages and rehabilitate a crushed humanity left in their wake, by the aid of such adjustment as could be obtained through courts and statutes— a process that has been going on and on in the history of America, and shows little sign of abatement for all the sharp penalties.

11

THE SOCIAL REFORM CLUB

But there was much to take up our attention in the city during the last years of the century beside the Consumers' League or the politics of Greater New York. In 1893 the Social Reform Club had been founded by Felix Adler. It was an association of men and women who hoped for a reconstruction of society and a progressive study of ills and remedies. Mornay Williams and his brother Ernest Crosby, a fine commanding figure whose handsome head stood out above his fellows in any assembly, and who had the faculty of making an audience enthusiastic for whatever cause he represented; Edward King, a Labor man who had educated himself, and taken courses at Columbia, and was one of the inner circle of reformers; Miss Jean Fine, who afterward became the wife of Charles Spahr; James Reynolds, Mary Kingsbury, who later married Professor Simkhovitch, and many others well known as students and workers in settlements or social reform—a membership of some two hundred. Mrs. Annie Winsor Allen was for seven years its secretary before her marriage. Leonora O'Reilly, I think, was responsible for our membership in the association. She had by that time gone on from her position as forelady in the shirt-shop to a cooperative shirt-factory at the Nurses' Settlement, in Henry Street, under Lillian Wald, one of the early S. R. C. members.

The structure of the club was unique. Its membership must consist of one-half genuine wage-earners, said the charter, and one-half interested people from other walks of life. That gave an effective combination, and worked during the earlier years of its history. But not more than one-third could be women! I was thankful to be in that third and go with my husband to meetings.

The meetings were held in an old house on Fourth Street, once a residence, its two parlors barely large enough to accommodate the eager audience. I revive the impression of hard wooden chairs crowded together, of swarthy skins beside clean-shaven ones, and harsh voices raised in debate from time to time; lights dim and air smoky, feeling now and then high, but subdued by the sense of common interest which many of the members had not known in their solitary lives—workers, students and thinkers brought together for common ends and understanding. They came from every variety of background, but backgrounds were ignored in meetings, although there was no escaping the fact that they accounted for the many approaches to the question of liberty and solidarity. There was a genuine desire for enlightenment, a mutual distrust of the gradual tightening of restraints and accumulation of power through a capitalistic system.

We did not talk of the "profit motive" in those days, but we did make ourselves a part of the struggle for ownership of natural resources by the people, and deliverance through union of workers in all industries from party political rule and subjugation of the laboring masses.

Charles M. Spahr, the Club's second president bore out in his daily life the belief that every man should not only support, but serve himself in minor details like blacking his own shoes, and carrying home his family supplies without accepting the help of the less privileged. Some people considered his ideas and practices fantastic, but he insisted that the only possible way of making his beliefs clear was to practice them with rigid sincerity, which was also necessary for self-discipline. Medieval or not, fanatic or pragmatist, that practice gave him power and leadership, and made him a gentle, perhaps too gentle, judge of others' methods.

I don't remember whether Henry George belonged to the Club or not; he may have doubted the wisdom of excluding specific reforms from discussion at meetings; but he was admired and quoted, for *Progress and Poverty* stood unassailed as an exposition of existing defects in our economic system. I had a little paper copy of it for lending, with the main argument underlined, a few sentences at a time, for the very busy or lazy people who could not or would not take trouble to read all its reasoning. Sometimes it arrested their attention, and made them look further; sometimes even the underlinings went unheeded; but more and more readers bought and perused it, and at least expressed a desire to see the Single Tax tried.

As to socialism, I think practically all the leading members of the club were in sympathy with its faith, if not actually committed to it. Most of my English friends were Fabians, and through them I had become interested in that organization and in its aims at spreading the socialist doctrines. The two Muirheads, of our former Leipzig group, had both come to this country; James to marry my Boston cousin, Helen Quincy, and his sister Annie to teach music; she was often at our house. From them we heard personal reports of Sydney and Beatrice Webb, of Bernard Shaw, of Annie Besant. The Fabians were intellectuals, and their fellowship was enlivened by Shaw's potent wit, which flashed through the whole circle, and was brought across the water in repetition and writing.

We heard much, also, of the Independent Labor party under Keir Hardie's leadership, but not yet much of Marx. There was a tendency in England to find greater value in the associations of the more educated socialists, it seemed to us, than in this country; and while we were heartened and inspired by the Fabian group, we felt that the American Socialist party should be openly inclusive of Labor and its aims. None the less, while our Socialist Labor party itself had broken sharply with any anarchistic connections, the whole movement had shifted from time to time, and split up into groups, which looked to energetic but vague leadership. There were western leaders, like Eugene Debs and Victor Berger, with followings of their own; then there were eastern sectional rivals. Hillquit and Spargo published expositions of their philosophies; in those years at the end of the century there was no strong position held, but the desire for the ownership by the people of natural resources, the struggle of the working classes to overcome exploitation, and the hope of a socialized industrial world, waxed strong in spite of disparities among its supporters. We called it a class struggle, and perhaps there was more actual class-consciousness than there is at the present time; but more education was needed by the workers, and there was a bitter element of ignorant aristocracy, or rather plutocracy. Amalgamation of these antagonists seemed impossible.

It was the rule that no panacea or *'ism* could be urged at meetings. Any speaker might discuss the problem in hand from his own point of view, but might not advocate special schemes or groups nor try to proselyte in connection with the meetings. This brought together a marked variety of thinkers. There was also a long list of causes to which the contemplation of the assembly was directed, and some of the changes which in the course of years have come to fruition were conceived and furthered during the years of the Club's activity. Mrs. Allen, whose children have grown into leadership along its lines, writes most interestingly of its incipient years; she says in one of her letters:

It started not long after the publication of *How the Other Half Lives,* and attracted people who had become used to the surprising facts in that book. Trade Unions, strikes and all the rest were anathema to most of one's acquaintance. When I had begun to be a little important in the Club, my Brearly head (she was teaching in the Brearly School) approached me one day and asked gently if it was perhaps not a club to which a lady should not belong. I answered by naming some of the people in it and then said; "Anyway, I have never thought of myself as a lady. I am not sure I am one." That amused him and he never suggested any opposition to my activities in it. Most people of one's acquaintance held definite views on all the points which the Club treated as moot, at the very least. When I went back for my vacations to Boston, I knew I should not meet one single person who thought the subjects seething in the Club were interesting.

From my own experience I can attest the truth of these statements. Trade unions and strikes, socialistic theories, public ownership, representations of the workers in government, and movers for better wages, were indeed anathema to the privileged. Those of us who had personal familiarity with the laboring classes (we all struggled to eliminate that particular expression, but had not yet substituted the more explicit *proletariat*) were looked upon as cranks or renegades.

The Social Reform Club was thus a centre where many eager reform-hopes were brought into the open. *Propaganda,* however, a word which is now nearly ready for decent burial, was unrecognized in argument.

We all remember how well our tactful chairman steered discussion. It was an arena in which cranks and long-winded orators were bound to seize chances to advertise their specialties, and his courtesy was strained almost to breaking at times, but never failed.

A weird old gentleman secured the floor and held it, one night, by a long speech, setting forth the consumption of brown bread as a panacea for all human ills, and a specific for the maintenance of peace and economic security. It was quite impossible to suppress him without open rudeness, and Mr. Spahr listened so politely that the audience became restive. Finally the speaker, who was deaf in addition to his other limitations, was prevailed upon to stop talking. It was the only occasion I can remember when interest really weakened; there were too many burning questions to let the meetings drag. The club was not destined to have a long life nor a conspicuous career; but through its members it made a distinct contribution to reform. I think it established the legal aid association to which my husband belonged for years, for helping the unprivileged by voluntary legal action and hastening delayed cases to a solution.

12

My husband's specifically political activities ended, as we had expected with the incoming of a new party in 1894, and he was obliged to return to his law practice. He longed for an opening in literary work, for he had never really loved his chosen vocation. His father was an old man with many ideals shattered; the necessary diplomacy and what he considered chicanery in legal procedure, the political rivalry and the legislative complications, had embittered his later years, and his attitude toward the profession was no longer one of such reverence and confidence as it had been when he had urged a legal career upon his son. But Fate seemed to ordain that Archie should return to it after all.

A college friend, a young fellow whose talent and cleverness were unquestioned, but whose inherited fortune had been a handicap to solid work, was about to open a law-office, and wanted a partner who would shoulder the court-work as his share of the business. It was a tempting offer, with good pecuniary returns, and taking it up meant assurance of comfortable living conditions for ourselves. We had looked down from our third-story windows in Washington Avenue at a quaint little house which had just enough antiquity for our idea of homeliness; a good back yard, a grand old peach-tree at one side, a sturdy maple between porch and sidewalk, and a roomy nursery in the ell with a step down into it and a fireplace. Neighbors called it the "Bird House," and its latest occupants had been artistic and had restored it inside without overlooking its claim to antiquity, taking account of low ceilings and broad-boarded floors. They were moving now to a new house and were glad to rent it for a sum which did not exceed the price of our apartment, though with the characteristic unthrift which had marked our business transactions thus far, we did not stop to calculate the many new expenses: lighting and heating, carpeting of stairs, water-rates, window-curtains, woodshed and laundry and cellar.

Our families warned us apprehensively, but our vision of a warm inclusive family life outshone the gloomier picture. We had learned some economies, enough to give us ideas for reducing living costs; in our personal financial management we could rob luxurious Peter, even if we could not always pay fact-facing Paul. We moved in the first of May, and settled down, as usual, with all the confidence in the world.

But even in the process of transition a test came. I was put to bed, for six weeks and perhaps more. The child we had longed for since our baby's death in 1892 was on its way.

It was an ordeal, that. So much to be done, and yet such an impossible weakness and weariness. The spring was abnormally hot, and we were longing to get off early to Forty Acres. Meetings were over for the season, but I was editing a little paper for girls—unsalaried work of course—the *Girls' Friendly Magazine,* and had counted on helping out expenses by some stories for the *Youth's Companion,* which paid well and promptly. I finished a couple of articles on *Fine Women* for the first small sheet, the beginning of a series, writing on a cutting board at a level with my face, not seeing the letters, but keeping the lines straight somehow. I was living chiefly on hard-boiled eggs and chipped beef at the moment, one of the fantastic menus which land-seasickness could invent and endure.

By way of forgetting disagreeable sensations, one could indulge in dreams. With half-closed eyes I fancied I saw a rose-branch, bearing one great open flower on its tip, watching it sway to and fro outside the windows of Uncle Phelps' study as it had done the June before. And I pictured glorious sunsets, smelled new-mown hay, heard the wind in the pines. The deep green boughs of the maple tree outside my windows, a unit of spring life, became a small world. It shut out some of the city noise and dust; it held a nest and a pair of sparrows whose domestic joys and difficulties suggested parallels with our own experience; only the little mother was very comfortable in her woven setting, and not obliged to leave it often. Every soft twitter, even the hum of an occasional big bee among the maple leaves, was welcome to my ears; and then when twilight, or closed shades, gave eyes a rest, they could listen again to the orchestra in the Leipzig Gewandhaus. I heard Beethoven symphonies, note by note, heard Joachim, Sarasate, the Wagner operas, the Bach *Passionmusik*.

Archie would come home at night bringing books from the library, some of them for me to read by day, others for our common enjoyment. We discovered that neither of us had known much of Dumas, strange to say, and he read aloud *The Three Musketeers,* its excitement giving a much-needed distraction of mind.

We got to Forty Acres in time, and had a lovely summer. I stayed on into October, waiting for Archie, who could not get his vacation earlier. We let our maid go home, and at night Cleve, the Bishop's dog, a big straw-colored Leonberg, who had watched beside the family babies for five years, came over and slept at our house, a faithful sentinel. We never locked the doors. Nan used to go over to the old house, and bring him back with her after supper; I would see them coming along the road in the twilight, the child's hand holding to his collar.

After her father arrived, and the family had gone back to Syracuse, Cleve came to live with us, and we had a glorious fortnight, cooking our meals over a wood fire in the long parlor, which served as dining-room and lounging-place. We roamed the woods, and drove over the hill-roads, and brought back apples and pumpkins from upland farms. Next summer we should not be by ourselves, so there was a certain last-time flavor to our enjoyment; but not less looking-forward, with a special joy and expectation which had taken its place among our visions of the future. Somehow it seemed to have been decided that the coming child was a boy, although we had no expert advice on the subject. He would love Forty Acres as we all loved it, and would fish and hunt and swim; perhaps would till the soil, and live as his forbears had lived, we said.

When we got back to town, however, dreams no longer occupied our minds. We must buckle down to work, and provide ways of meeting the heavy outlay ahead. I had an opportunity for some teaching, and took on a number of music pupils in our own neighborhood. Then there was writing to be done in spare minutes, and the editing of the little magazine; the Woman's Club, the Social Reform Club, and the meetings of the Consumers' League, public and private. We expected our baby just after Christmas, and it became rather a problem to get time off for bringing him into the world; all sorts of civic activities and obligations piled up. The League had developed, and there was now a small corps of investigators in our Brooklyn membership. But there was still speaking to be done, sometimes in suburban districts, and as the holiday season approached we returned to the task of persuading the large dry-goods firms to do a little better by their employees, who were forced to work extra long hours during the Christmas shopping-time, with no extra pay for the suppers which they snatched in grudged moments.

The year before we had compiled a White List of stores who served regular suppers in their lunch-rooms without charge to the girls, and had published it in the larger Brooklyn papers. It had apparently proved a satisfactory advertisement, and in the winter of 1896 we found practically all of them willing to continue the free suppers. A few more had been added. I went down to the newspaper offices the week before Christmas, to arrange for publication of it, on the editorial page. The *Brooklyn Eagle* men had been particularly gracious. But when I reached their offices that day, a certain reserve of manner alarmed me. The man I found looked dubiously at the list and said that he couldn't really say just what they were able to do about printing it. He thought I would better negotiate with the advertising manager, who understood the situation better than the rest of the staff. A pleasant looking man was summoned from the pressroom. He appeared embarrassed.

"I'm awfully sorry," he murmured, "but I'm afraid we can't get that in this time. You see our advertisers have made a fuss about it; it would mean an awful money loss if they should withdraw their columns, and some of them are very big firms who aren't giving suppers. They complain that it's discrimination if we print the names of the others. I really don't know what to do about this, but I'm afraid I must give it to them; we can't afford, you know, to get 'em down on us. Every paper has to look out for its advertising business."

"But I've promised to have this list published. They've got our word as a league that we'll have it in tomorrow's issue. What can I do? I can't back out on it now, and you didn't give me any warning, either. You were so perfectly willing last year that I didn't dream of any trouble."

"Perhaps the firms themselves would be willing to pay to have it go in as a regular advertisement," suggested the man.

"No, they wouldn't; they're supposed to be philanthropists; don't you see? Even I know enough about advertising to realize that a notice on the editorial page is much more conspicuous than the ordinary columns. Why I can't give it up; I mustn't. We've agreed to it."

The manager was genuinely regretful. He explained regretfully that the Press was anything but free when it came to business influences. After some dickering and coaxing, however, he made a sally into the pressrooms, and came back with a hopeful suggestion. If I could get about twice as many names on that list, not all dry-goods people, but stores of other kinds, they could consent to print it. Could I do that, did I think? I felt sure that he counted on my not being able to accomplish such a feat at the last minute. But it was a desperate situation, and I resolved to go to work.

They lent me a little office, with a desk and telephone. I got two of our investigators who were up to their ears in Christmas preparations, but magnanimously threw themselves into the breach. They agreed to go out at once, and to call up results. Then I telephoned to one store after another, some of them small business men who, I knew, were probably in the habit of giving the employees supper money. There were corset-shops, tailor shops and book-stores, which employed only a few people; men as well as women. Many were not interested, but I kept at it, and after the first half hour paused between my entreaties to receive the investigators' report. By twelve o'clock there were only two new names. But in the noon hour we had better luck. Slowly the list grew. Even some people who had refused us the week before became interested. From then on I had no idea of the flight of time, but at last when the required number of names was really filled out, and the advertising man had timidly but graciously agreed to yield, just for that one year as he stipulated, I found I had been out four hours, and the clock had struck two before there was an opportunity to start for home. I landed at our corner at half-past two, and met Archie pacing up and down the sidewalk.

"I was just advising your husband to telephone round to the hospitals," said Mrs. Shepard, our next door neighbor, and we all shook with the hysterical mirth of reaction. "Now you've *got* to settle down; the neighborhood can't stand these moments of anxiety."

I was glad to do that, I must say. During the next few days there were more last bits of business to be put through, but we got the Christmas stockings filled and packages mailed. And on the morning of the twenty-seventh, just in time to be welcomed by daylight, our oldest son appeared; a funny little baby, all mouth, as the nurse observed, and with eyes as dark as the proverbial fruit of the blackthorn.

The doctor breakfasted with Archie, and while Miss H., a fine combination of hospital training and old-fashioned family nursing, was getting the newcomer bathed and dressed, the maid came up and handed me my mail. It contained a package of proof which ought to have arrived the day before, and should be sent back at once to the printer. I took a pencil out of the drawer of my bedside table, and went to work at it unobserved, getting it finished just as the two men came upstairs again from the dining-room. Miss H.'s horrified exclamation brought only a laugh from the doctor.

"That's all right," he said. "She's tough. Now, Madam, breakfast off a chop if you like." I gladly accepted the permission, and my husband undertook to mail the proof. Activities really did let up a little thereafter. In two weeks I began slipping down-stairs to give music lessons, and while sitting up I made pretty good headway feather-stitching a set of flannel baby garments ordered by a wealthy lady through the nurse; expenses had to be met somehow.

The child throve apace. My sister Arria came to stay with me, and was godmother at his baptism. We had settled on naming him Roger—Roger Pitkin, I had planned to call him, after a collateral ancestor in England. I was ashamed to give him a purely arbitrary fancy name. The other two saw no sense in bringing in the Pitkin, so they made a plan of their own, and at the service, when Arria was asked to "name this child" as she handed him to the clergyman, I was somewhat amazed to hear her say, quite positively, "Roger Huntington." I had no chance to protest, and we promised with mutual stoutness that he should fight manfully against the world, the flesh and the devil, name or no name.

He was a strong young fellow, very sleepy and hungry, but awakened suddenly one cold night when the tinny jangle of a hurdy-gurdy started up under our window, ground out by a forlorn man who appeared to have been moved by desperation to attempt an out-of-season performance. I have never been able to remember the melody he produced, probably some rattling jig, for the baby claimed our attention. His eyes opened wide, his face grew pink, his hands moved excitedly. Evidently he was listening.

"That child's going to be musical," cried the nurse. "Look at him; he's all stirred up."

We rewarded the hurdy-gurdy man lavishly, and suggested politely that he should move on, the instrument not being suited for a lullaby, but he insisted on giving us an encore, which Roger quite appreciated. The incident was duly recorded, and we found our surmise was correct; the infant's diminutive ear was sensitive to tonal vibrations, and his whole nerve-system responded to them.

Later, when we tried to take him downstairs, he developed a terror of descending motion. We made an attempt to cure it by having him carried in his father's arm, while I played on the piano below. A Bach gavotte from the *French Suite* seemed to suit the down-stepping rhythm excellently, and took his mind off his fears so effectively that we kept up the method till he began to intimate in baby fashion that he wanted to make a musical flight.

Now, with a baby in it, our little old house really began to function as the kind of home we had planned and longed for. I had every excuse to drop outside activities for the time being. Mornings were devoted to nursery cares and domestic chores; getting Nan off to school and Roger out in his carriage. Old Melissa came back to help take care of him, for her daughter's children were grown out of babyhood, and she longed to return to her profession. Friends came to us, since I could not often go to them, and frequently dropped in for lunch. In the afternoon I kept vigil in the nursery, writing sometimes, sewing, and having an eye to the older children as they played out-of-doors, racing over the neighbors' fences and yards. There were sixteen boys and girls on our block; some of them my music-pupils, all Nan's schoolmates, and an extremely merry crowd. They were very much at their ease in our house, which was one reason for my wanting to be there afternoons.

One's children's comrades out of school hours are of immense importance to the family life. The music scholars very often came in to practise as well, when their mothers were using the family parlors for company or for meetings. On stormy days they were very apt to have a study hour in the dining-room for the sake of sociability and a sort of prestige which they felt to be attached to this privilege, because silence was a condition of their being allowed to come. It was not uncommon for a guest to find a girl or boy performing on the piano, several more studying at the dining-room table, a group in the nursery playing dolls with Nan, and perchance a lone reader tucked into a big armchair. I invited my older callers to come upstairs to my room under those circumstances, but even then there was chance of an interruption at five, the hour when it was possible to tease a fairy story out of "Aunt Ruth," which appellation designated extra-territorial affiliations, as it were. On bright days they all played out-of-doors except those who had to do special lessons, and I could see them from my window, dashing about, counting blindfolded with forehead against the maple tree or shouting "All in!" at the end of a game.

They were not above squabbling and playing tricks on one another, and running upstairs to complain. Boys accused girls and girls boys, and I began to be tired of tattling after a time. So we decided to turn that into a game, which was called Trial by Jury. And that it was, in effect. The disputants eliminated themselves to two, and must each choose an advocate from among the rest, to put their grievance before the court; they were not supposed to tell their own story. The successful advocate was understood to be the boy or girl who could be an absolutely accurate and impartial witness, and after the taking of evidence the jury, which consisted of the rest of the group, retired to the nursery to arrange its verdict. It was astonishing how seriously the youngsters took it. There were no punishments except apologies and restitutions, although once or twice imprisonment was suggested. Nevertheless each of the quarrels was settled amicably, and I rather suspected now and then that a dispute was framed in order to bring on court action. I officiated as judge, but rarely needed to harangue the offenders, and became very fond of the bad boys, as well as of the good. The system made for truthfulness.

My own child was quite as often disciplined by her mates as any other one; in fact everybody was equally welcome under our shingled roof, and all claimed a sort of tacit family connection. They were avid for stories, especially fairy tales, and when the long spring twilights came they gathered after their supper on the front porch, coming much too early usually, and besieging us while we were eating dessert. The story lasted till eight, when parents called their children to bed; any boy or girl who did not go at once on order was barred next night from the company. There was woe when we ourselves were entertaining at dinner, and now and then a wistful child peering in at the window and having to be apologized for by the hostess. But aside from these skirmishes they all romped and climbed and shouted healthily, and made an interesting study.

One cannot be a real child-lover unless one can enjoy other people's children, and do them justice. If I had known in those days what a good training I was having for a future vocation, I should have been even more interested in those afternoon encounters. Roger, a serious baby, watched them solemnly.

When my chickens were in bed, I wrote and wrote: magazine articles, letters to newspapers, sometimes controversial; columns for the little magazine. I fear the essays were preachy; the flavor of the Bishop's study *would* get into them. My pen had been trained to the transcription of hortatory exegesis, and ran it off involuntarily. But sermons did not pay as stories did. *Munsey's Magazine* was making a hit in the late nineties, and used to print short tales which were called storiettes. I sent one, hoping to get enough money for a much-needed coat, and to my surprise received a check four times as large as I had expected, with news that the story would be published in the regular columns. Years after, when my husband was editor of *Ainslee's Magazine,* a man in one of the far southern states sent him that very story, probably thinking that enough time had passed to make the plagiarism go unsuspected.

13

Sorrowful events made the summer of 1897 very different from our untroubled winter. That which concerned the family life most deeply was the death of my husband's mother, the mainstay of her children and the solace of her invalid husband. It left a very empty place in our household, where she had been used to spend one day a week—a happy time for parents and children both. I was always strengthened by our talks as we sat sewing together, for her clear mind and her understanding of her son's mind made my own comprehension far more complete. I had thought our mutual confidence was primarily a matter of kinship, but I know now that it was a wise and self-effacing counsel that made me depend more and more on her judgment. She and her brothers and sister had been educated abroad; there was an element of cosmopolitan tolerance in their outlook and a breath of view that counterbalanced the Puritan inheritance which she shared with her generation. This broad-mindedness she owed, as we did, to the grandmother who left Calvinism for Unitarianism. Her likeness to our Grandmother Huntington was pronounced, and her face had the same strong lines which we had seen in Aunt Bethia's face and in the pictures of Elizabeth Phelps—the long upper lip and delicate nostrils, severity softened by sweetness of character.

The 1897 Christmas holiday was again a busy time for the Consumers' League. We knew we could not count on the newspapers to help this time; another way of advertising the exemplary supper-providers must be found, and I think it was the New York League which set the example of printing small flyers which we distributed by thousands to be wrapped in bundles with purchases. It was not a very hopeful method of advertising, but it was the best we could do, and we did not see how many of them were left over; they were considered a nuisance by the bundlers. However, there had been a slight improvement in the arrangements for sales-girls, and meantime our investigators had achieved more than in previous years. I had made a few speeches that winter, and found audiences a little more responsive; it was becoming fashionable to call public attention to glaring evils, as well as to reform legislation. At Girls' Friendly conferences there was a nearer approach made to an understanding of the members' backgrounds and the effect of those backgrounds in lowering standards.

The neighbors' children still annexed themselves to our menage, playing and studying and bickering. Nan asked more questions now, at the age of nine; why didn't women vote, what were women's rights, what did *noblesse oblige* mean? I heard her explaining it later to a comrade. If you had a nice grandpa or daddy, not rich of course, but lovely, you had got to be nice to everyone else, you know; you were *obliged* to have the *noblesse*; it was a French way of spelling niceness. And what if you had neither a grandpa nor a daddy, the interlocutor inquired. Well, in that case you would have to make up some niceness of your own, suggested Nan. But little children who had poor homes and not enough to eat and no bathroom couldn't be expected to make up niceness for themselves, so you had to do it by being very friendly with them, don't you see, and having to do things like that was the *oblige*. *Obleege* was what they called it. You just couldn't be stuck up, because it was only an accident that you had bathrooms anyway. By which time the argument was abandoned as raising too many issues.

A blow which amounted to a national calamity, took place in October of that year—the sudden death of Henry George. He had become more and more of a power in the affairs of Greater New York, and had been nominated by the Jeffersonian Democrats as an independent candidate for mayor, with Seth Low running on the Republican ticket, and with Van Wyck the Tammany candidate and tool. His chance of success was strong, with the backing of vigorous anti-Tammany groups. But his doctors—and one of them was my old friend Felix—had warned him that he had not strength for the campaign. The stress of active political work wore on him. The quiet, intense philosopher and prophet was fighting for the great principles to which he had dedicated his life, and could not listen to any plans for withdrawal.

In the midst of the battle he was struck by a sudden seizure, and lived only a few hours. Then the world knew that one of the greatest men of our times was gone. His body lay in state in the Grand Central Palace, and a hundred thousand people filed past it. Messages came from four great countries of Europe and from Africa, Australia, Japan, and China. His funeral was a simple, majestic service, with clergy of three protestant churches, a Rabbi, and a Catholic priest, Dr. McGlynn, who had suffered in his own church for his allegiance to George's doctrine, and had, after excommunication, been restored to it by order of Pope Leo XIII.

A long procession, led by a band playing the great funeral march of Chopin, and the *Marseillaise*, carried his body on a high bier drawn by a double line of horses to Brooklyn. It was in the evening, so that the working people might join in the "vast winding column" which followed it while crowds looked on from the sidewalk. The next day there was a quiet little ceremony, with two Episcopal ministers, in his own house at Fort Hamilton. My brother James was one of his sincerest mourners. They had been together in Europe in 1890, and were in deep sympathy; he had performed the wedding ceremony of Mr. George's son Richard, the sculptor.

The election day which followed three weeks after Mr. George's death was sorrowful for those who had enlisted under the great leader. Our own household was subdued. Nan remembers still, after forty years, how her father came in that night; she heard me call out softly from my room as he stole into the dark hall, "Who got in?" and his answer, "Oh Lord! *Van Wyck!*" The Tammany success seemed to spell not only defeat, but disgrace.

14

WEARY PATRIOTISM

From friends in England, the Muirheads in particular, I had recently heard much of the Fabians, and had felt a greater interest in that development of the socialist movement than in the party which represented it in this country. The Fabians were intellectuals of the middle class, and were not agitating for drastic revolution but for gradual education of society; the gentler title of their brotherhood was less repellent than that of the organization which, to conservatism, represented little less than a plague and a menace. Graham Wallas, Sidney and Beatrice Webb, William Morris, even John Burns and Keir Hardie and other leaders in the Labor movement, were more than mere names to us. Although the political interests of my own country had by this time superseded the flair for contemporary British history, we had followed such reports as could be gleaned from the reviews and from the speeches of visiting Englishmen.

Such men as Shaw, with unassailable positions in the literary world, were more or less intrenched against open attack, although not immune to thrusts of ridicule from conservative men of letters and of science as well; even the social scientists had trained heavy guns upon their assumptions. Shaw, however, could never be downed, however daring his aggression. Midway between the aristocracy and the proletariat, he could send his flashing shafts in all directions, and in a measure blazed the trail for the more patient arguments.

Our own middle class comprehended little of the doctrines of Marx, nor did it trouble itself to understand the Fabians. Socialism, in its theoretical sense, was not branded as actually dangerous, but rather as a delusion, a ridiculous idea that the human race could achieve equality by pooling all the money in the country and dividing it up, thereby producing a dead-level of living-standards and a drab existence for everyone, with no hope or initiative. That was the general attitude of nineteenth-century society, but some of our young intellectuals, taking comfort in the self-flattery produced by finding themselves able to enjoy the Fabian essays, confessed to belief in the new doctrine.

It was the burden of many discussions in the Social Reform Club and in various intimate groups. Our dining-room, with its quaint fireplace, was turned into a small forum on many Sunday nights, when we kept open house for supper. A few friends dropped in from week to week, and shared the family meal. Old Melissa, who had come back from a long visit at her daughter's to take care of Roger, would put the children to bed after a quiet day, and I cooked the supper, which was cleared away to make room for a circle round the fire. Let me not give the impression that those were gatherings of the *salon* order, intellectual feasts with the sparkle of wit and the stimulus of philosophical argumentation. There were seldom more than five or six people, often differing widely in mental calibre and outlook.

Now and then there would be solitary individuals who came simply for a rest and a meal, and a chance to air their views. Some of them tended to quibble in discussions and showed a fly-like persistence in coming back to the ego and its standpoint. Then there was one mild anarchist who, though not precisely disputatious, managed to infuse polemics into the conversations, especially when conservatives were about. Once he had as antagonist a distant female relative of ours who was a Christian Scientist. They began by getting into a hot and perfectly futile argument, and ended by going off together toward the lady's home, not being able to stop talking, each hoping to convert the other, while the relieved survivors settled down to confidential discourse.

Once we came back from the summer vacation on a Saturday night, and Archie disclosed on Sunday noon that at least three people had found we were coming and were figuring on supping with us that night. He recommended planning for six. I had no provisions in the house save the fall supply of potatoes and apples in the cellar, and a very few groceries; but I made a plentiful supply of French-fried potato crescents, and heaped a blue platter with baked apples, their bubbling juicy contents flavored with brown sugar. This, with tea and bread and butter, constituted the meal.

It turned out to be one of our really brilliant evenings, with Leonora O'Reilly there. She was out of the sweat-shop now with a better position, and was greatly interested in the possibilities of a Women's Trade-Union League. There were very few crafts in which women were organized, and the Union leaders took little or no interest in forming new ones. In fact, it had become clear that the girls themselves must fight for their cause if there was to be anything accomplished. Since 1885 the Unions, under Gompers, had increased as the Knights of Labor diminished. Gompers was shrewd and influential, but bent on keeping the original order and power of the crafts unions intact and excluding all the unkilled and less solid groups. There could be no actual strengthening of forces except on limited lines. The only real weapon labor possessed was the strike, and thus far strikes, even the most disastrous and determined, had failed to accomplish anything more than a public upheaval and a subsequent return to the suppression of the workers.

Leonora built her hopes on the education of the woman worker, and also on her eventual enfranchisement; but it was a long slow process, with discouraging returns from both employees and employers, and no help from the law. It was not merely the flame of the wood-fire that flushed her cheeks that night as she told us of efforts to open up a broader horizon to the girls who had worked under her, and the lack of ambition which long toiling hours had engendered in them. She made us all listen to her, and feel with her, but she little knew what a foundation she herself was helping to lay in the outer world for the solidarity of wage-earning women.

In March of that year, 1898, President McKinley took the oath of office. Cleveland's second term had been a difficult one, for him and for the country; commercial panic, financial panic, the Demo-

cratic President fighting for low tariff, the Republican party for
protection; money hard to get, gold going out of the country, a
silver standard threatened; jibes and jeers at the administration,
at the marriage of the Chief Executive to a charming young woman;
a rebellious Senate, an income-tax declared unconstitutional by
the Supreme Court, five to four. The old rhythm of capitalism
again! And boundary disputes in South America, an uprising in
Cuba; finally another election campaign and the nomination of
McKinley a gold man, against the Democratic William Jennings
Bryan silver advocate. People's domestic affairs were too absorbing
to be disturbed by the political earthquakes; cradles rocked plac-
idly while states were shaken. The new Republican President
promised tariff revenue, quiet, and a balanced budget, and Congress passed a bill, the invention of one Dingley, which was expected to bring more money into the country at the expense of
foreign traders.

But after Mr. McKinley's inauguration there was a good deal
to take his attention from this hopeful programme. The grave dis-
agreements with Spain and the revolt in Cuba had been going on
for months. Admiral Dewey was in the Philippines, and celebrated
May Day, 1898, by demolishing the Spanish fleet in Manila Harbor
without losing a single *American* life, said the triumphant reports.
Our navy was now "second to none" in glory of achievement. In
July Roosevelt and his Rough Riders made their spectacular charge
up San Juan Hill, and the North applauded. The Cuban survivors
came back in the autumn, and were paraded—a sad, listless company
—through the streets. They listened passively to the applause from
the sidewalks, and perhaps found more satisfaction in the occasional
groans of pity which reached their ears. Veterans. Old before their
time, and with just that one adventure stamped into their brains
for the years to come. Admiral Dewey came back too, and we took
the children up to a roof on Brooklyn Heights to see the victorious
ships steam up the harbor. I can remember the thrill of it, and the
reflection that we had done our duty by Nan and Roger in giving
them this great event to remember. And I think we went over

later in the day, and sat at a window on Fifth Avenue, to watch the victors themselves as they drove past in open carriages.

We reached home in a state of weary patriotism that day, and Archie had a lame shoulder from carrying his heavy young son. I doubted privately whether the remembrance of it all would contribute to the boy's future value as a citizen. I had not been able to put heart or enthusiasm into the war, and all my horror and hatred of that came back with the review of its victims. But the Rough Riders and brass-buttoned naval uniforms were received with furious acclaim; later the psychology of the conquering hero worked itself out in Theodore Roosevelt's fame and eventual political life.

There was more or less aftermath, which children could feel. Roger was not so much stirred by the patriotic fervor of his environing world, as by the bands and brass buttons. He could not yet talk, beyond a queer jargon which served to acquaint the family with his desires. But he sang, from morning till night, in his bath, his baby-carriage, and his bed, reproducing all the popular melodies and war choruses, with isolated syllables for words—usually *wa*, a contraction of *Hurrah*—but perfectly correct and recognizable in time and tune. People used to stop and demand the name of the "singing baby," and asked for *Marching through Georgia* or *My Country 'Tis of Thee,* which were delivered with entire indifference to the beholder.

Marching through Georgia . . . . I thought of the songs which had echoed through the Boston Common in the sixties, in through the open windows of Ninety-eight Boylston Street, where Father and his friends discussed the war and God and the country's statesmen, while the fourth child hid from the blare of bands, too near. The revolving wheel of history had once more arrived at the same point, through the complication and conflict of the intervening years. And in 'ninety-eight we ourselves were discussing war and God and the country's politicians—and our own child was objecting when the band came too near, shaking his head indignantly, listening again, then begging to go after it.

15

SEASON'S MUTATIONS

There came a sunny spring morning, the morning of Whitsunday, 1899, when I sat by my window at sunrise, watching the early church-goers, with their prayerbooks and their rosaries, pass to the sound of bells in the distance. A light breeze stirred the maple leaves; across the street between brick walls I could see a blossoming apple tree; a robin was calling; shafts of sunlight were lengthening across the pavement; overhead the sky was clear blue. My heart was beating with happy anticipation in tune to the chime, for another child was on its way to us, and I felt sure it would come in time to be a Sunday baby.

My family was still asleep, so I had that happy hour by myself, and five hours later our second boy, a tiny but healthy creature, arrived as the bells were ringing for service again. He was a merry little person, with an equable nerve-outfit, and even in his early babyhood made few demands on the attention of his elders. We named him John, after Archie's father, who had died a few weeks before. Roger greeted him with broad smiles, and settled himself into the big-brother attitude.

We all went early to Hadley that year, because a hot wave made Brooklyn nearly uninhabitable. It had been a hard spring, after a blow in the winter-time which depleted our courage. My husband's law partner had died suddenly after a short illness, and with his going the comfort and confidence of our home life had faded. It was impossible now for one man to keep up the rent of an expensive office, or to pay a helper, without whose services the court work could not be carried on. We had been able to look forward to a measure of security for the future during those two years, and had even put by a little toward the extra expense of my illness. But although Archie managed to finish the work in hand, there was no outlook for an extension of it during the summer.

We had been through some weeks of great anxiety, and had finally accepted the necessity of his breaking away from the practice of law, and accepting a position with the publishers of the new Encyclopedia Britannica, at a small but regular salary. I could not but realize that at last Archie had found a kind of work which was congenial to him, even though it had not the promise of what he hoped to achieve at some future day. He was very thankful for regular pay again, and found the task interesting.

As for giving up the house, which seemed inevitable, a small windfall came to us through inheritance, and would pull us through for the year to come; one worry settled. I had been lame the previous winter with a phlebitic trouble which kept me on crutches, on one floor for a few weeks, but the children could be out-of-doors all day. The family at the old house came back and forth, helped with the nursery work when old Melissa was recalled by her daughter; and my older brother and his children, five boys and a girl, the eldest now an instructor at Dartmouth, kept us much alive. Nan and the babies went over each morning to see their grandparents, with Cleve, the big dog, for guardian.

The Bishop read aloud to us, after the earlier fashion, Trollope's *Last Chronicle of Barset,* to which the older children could now listen. The baby lay on a comforter spread over the grass, and cooed to himself; Nan rowed with her cousins; Roger had abandoned his vocal exercise, and begun to put words properly together. Molly was the children's delight; Arria was busy with a new book, *Under a Colonial Rooftree,* a story of the old house and the earlier life at Forty Acres. In the midst of all this activity, I could lay aside anxieties and take in the peace of the Valley as preparation for the more strenuous winter.

Little did we think how our lives would be changed after another season's mutations. But we returned to town in full vigor, and there were many demands on our time. One of my friends in Brooklyn had gone south, and left me her box at the Metropolitan

Opera House for one evening a week, and another friend gave me her box for afternoon concerts, while she went away for a few weeks.

Walter Damrosch was then conducting a series of young people's matinees, one of the most important moves in the history of American music. I took Roger to one of those; he was three now, and more musical than ever, always wanting to be at the piano, where he touched one note at a time, prolonging it and listening to its last vibration, and then perhaps playing a chord, stretching his small fingers apart and striking the keys almost timidly, with a smile to himself. He never attempted tunes.

I was a little doubtful about giving him the excitement of hearing an orchestra, but still longed to try its effect on him, and decided to let him come with me. We sat in a proscenium box, the second tier, and the concert began with the *Pilgrims' Chorus* from *Tannhäuser*. Listening so intently that I had forgotten the small figure beside my knee, in white kilts which made him look particularly infantile, I happened to turn my head toward the audience once, and noticed that people were looking toward the box and smiling. Roger was standing there with one hand in the air, following Damrosch's baton with absolute fidelity, beat by beat, a broad grin on his countenance. He kept it up unconsciously until the very last notes of the overture, for I hated to interrupt him; then he climbed up in my lap, still smiling but saying not a word.

I must say I was rather more moved, however, by hearing him give a whoopy and quite unexpected cough before the entertainment was over, which mingled some regret with my joy at having been able to bring him with me. As a matter of fact he did develop whooping-cough, and had a long siege of it; that one concert constituted his entire musical experience for months to come.

Then came the dawning of the twentieth century. The populace welcomed it with bells and blare, from the iron throats of machines to whistles and penny horns and cat-calls. Press and prophecy proclaimed it; the thoughtful said among themselves that there was no limit to its possibilities and its obligations; they made resolutions and beginnings, and promises, many promises. The old, in dread of change, reflected on the wickedness of the world and the menace of war; the clergy preached and prayed.

But I think there was a feeling of sadness in many minds. The closing years of the nineteenth century had been filled with premonitions of change, of a parting of the ways and a loss of the secure, perhaps too confident sense of abiding comfort and safe, ornamented living to which the Victorian age seemed to have attained. At any rate, we two people did not greet the age of machinery and magnificence with very hopeful hearts. We were finding it harder than ever to make both ends meet, and to plan for the children's future advantage. The salary on which we were trying to subsist was too small for the necessary outlay; the little old house, for all its joys and its possibilities, grew more costly each year. We felt it must be given up for more modest quarters, and that by spring some sort of decision would be forced upon us.

We had talked over the situation and its possible remedy, again and again, during the year. What if we should go off quietly, without letting our friends know where to find us, and live among the people who had been so long on our hearts, wage-earners with no greater resources than ourselves and no particular ambition? And do what, we asked ourselves. We must both work, of course.

I tried to sketch out certain ways of earning, one of them being dressmaking. Visions of a bare dining-room, with table pushed back and a long mirror on the wall, were conjured up. "And let the babies crawl about among the pins and swallow them," suggested Archie. No, that was harrowing beyond words. Although it was said that children learned to avoid pins. But dressmaking seemed to be the only profession which could be carried on in the home, and my going out to work was impossible. Furthermore, we both knew the conditions of the slums all too well, and rents were pretty nearly prohibitive, even in tenements. Besides all this, the distress of our relatives would be a hopeless obstacle. Neither of us would think of living with one another's people as an alternative to life in the tenements, either. We used to break off these futile discussions in a mood for shelving all plans and passively awaiting some decision which might be made for us, rather than by us.

One day the blow descended upon our heads. We had had a particularly happy day, for the weather was bright, and the children had been able to play out-of-doors, since Roger's whooping-cough was almost gone, and so far little John had not shown any signs of contracting it. But when their father turned in at the gate I saw trouble in his face—a whiteness and weariness that boded defeat of some sort.

It was not long before the news came out; the firm for which he had been working was to move to London, closing its New York office. A blank curtain had been dropped, cutting off our view of the future, of our life, it seemed to us. This time we both sat staring ahead of us, silently and hopelessly. The one possible avenue to restoration of hope and ambition had been cut off. They wanted us to go to London, Archie said, but there was no certainty how long a position would last, even if we could afford to make the move. And there was no alternative now but for him to bend every energy toward getting a new and more profitable opportunity to continue in the publishing business, without capital, with expenses eating us up, with the children's needs increasing daily.

It was then that a thought which had been coming into my mind with persistent appeal, began to renew its claims. It had dawned upon me that if only I could make it possible for my husband to be free of all cares and goading expenses, and if he could have a year or more in which to buckle down and find his own level in the literary world, a scope for the talent with which he was plainly endowed, and which he only needed time and opportunity to develop, it would be the chance of his life; a chance he had never known before. If there were some way for me to make a home for the children and at the same time provide for the family expenses, taking all care from him, I knew well that he could work out his destiny and fulfil the promise which all his friends had recognized, but to which the four of us who were dependent on him were barriers. There was no question about that; many a time I had felt that our families must be aware of it. Not that there needed to be any sentimental recognition of the fact, but it *was* a fact.

In spite of all the preconceived, traditional views of the essence of matrimonial responsibility, all the ordinances of social life which made a wife a dependent under the law, it was an absolutely clear conviction in my mind, growing with each year of marital experience that the mother's obligation for the support of her children was as great as the father's. Her share of the work for the household might with equal propriety consist in wage-earning.

I had never said very much about this to my husband because I knew the pang it gave him, both in pride and sense of obligation. Yet he had agreed with me in theory when we were discussing the demands of our world, and so long as it did not cut into our own personal conditions we could both of us look upon it as a principle to be applied to all married people. What if we were to be put to the test after all? Were we afraid of our own convictions, or ready to sacrifice ourselves for them?

In the end we had only a few days for coming to a conclusion. I had written to my father that we were giving up our house on the first of May, pending a decision about further possibilities, and that I wished we might find something to do in New England. I believed that my husband's Harvard training had equipped him to teach in the English department of a college, although I knew that he would rather undertake creative work of some kind.

The letter reached the Bishop at Forty Acres, whither he had gone to make plans for spring planting. He met his old friend, President Seelye of Smith College, in Northampton next day; by chance —he said. They discussed common responsibilities somewhat, and then my father mentioned that it would be a joy to him if his daughter and her husband could get back to New England. "I want my grandchildren," he said, "to grow up in the spirit of their forefathers." Mr. Seelye caught his meaning. He had no opening to propose for a man at that time, but for the Bishop's daughter— was she the author of a recent article in the literary Saturday issue of the *Times*, on *Children's Reading*? He had been interested in it. Would she be willing to come to Northampton and open a house for students? They needed more off-campus houses, and he thought a very good dwelling might be found; he would be glad to help.

There was one on Round Hill, not far from the site of the old hotel, and also near the college. . . . .

I shall not tax the reader's patience by describing the steps, painfully surmounted, by which we reached an agreement to accept this offer. It was not easy to make, and yet the very fact that we loved one another deeply, and wanted the best for our two selves and for our children, kept it from being a tragedy. For each one a door of opportunity was offered; freedom with its inescapable price of isolation, sacrifice that would be keen and possibly bitter; hard work; a complete readjustment of our plan of living. Things we could not face all at once, nor even work out with the imagination which set itself to appreciate them.

We could look back upon that racking choice in later years, with thankfulness, for all its harsh demands on our devotion and discernment. Each had tried to save the other when crises threatened. Now we found out how much stronger the will becomes when two characters lay hold upon a common problem. But for my part, I could see no opening and no promise as yet. I faced the relinquishment of a life in which we had found companionship, children, hospitality, opportunity; through it we had come to a sense of oneness with all humanity, of daily living permeated with faith. And now to go back to a quiet New England town to earn support for one's children and one's self through the commercialization of everyday comfort; to sell one's household labor, and count achievement in columns of red and blue lines, in dollar-marks and dots and ciphers; was that to be the sum of achievement?

Involuntarily I recalled the fate of other women who had met defeat on that same road. Of one or another it had been said, in the familiar Victorian term, that she "had come down to taking boarders." Down. If only that word had been suggestive of possible ascent or of some bright goal! But instead, the vision itself was Browning's Childe Roland at the Dark Tower; a windowless dungeon in a hopeless landscape.

> *Gray plain all round—*
> *Nothing but plain to the horizon's bound.*
> *I might go on; naught else was left to do.*

My imagination carried the figure further. The "hoary cripple with malicious eye"; that was the gossip of observers about the "come down" of a woman who had been spendthrift of privilege and birth and education. A boarding-house for students—the most that could be hoped for. This time, though determined, I succumbed to a completely dreary mood. "And all the doubt was—should I be fit." Browning had gripped my will, however, and given me the courage of desperation.

But another person had been reminded of Childe Roland too. My husband and I were very fond of the Rector of St. Mary's, the little Brooklyn church to which we had attached ourselves at the time of our uptown move in 1893. It was very like an English church, standing in a shady close with its rectory and parish buildings in the midst of an unpromising factory district. The young priest was a warm friend. In one of the characteristically short notes that are sometimes better than the spoken word, he struck the impelling tone I needed.

Dauntless the slug-horn to your lips you have set.

So music was once more to play its part in deliverance. The beauty of the slug-horn's blast is that its reverberations remain in the immediate atmosphere, and come back to one with many an echoed note of joyful defiance.

It is curious, too, how suddenly a tragic situation may be relieved by some trivial interruption. When we waked on the morning of our departure from the "Bird House," to see a squad of wreckers, so to speak, descending upon it, and a gaping van preparing to swallow up our precious furnishings, there seemed naught but black disaster before us—the Dark Tower on wheels. It remained for the youngest member of the family to divert that mood.

As there was no one to hold him, small John was fastened into his crib by a shoulder-strap, and lay there gleefully watching the spoilsmen as they carried away bureaus and beds and chairs. His parents were rushing from room to room giving orders, and Roger was making frantic attempts to escape from a young girl guardian, when suddenly there was a call.

"The baby's gone!"

Apparently he was. A glance into the denuded room disclosed an empty crib and a silent space within four walls. It was an utter impossibility for anyone to carry him away without being seen, but the whole family stopped work and began a dazed hunt. From cellar to garret, every corner and cupboard was examined. Finally, going back in desperation to the crib, the searchers heard a chuckle. John had wriggled himself over its edge next the wall, and was lying *perdu,* suspended by his shoulder-belt, absorbed in reaching for a red ball which had fallen to the floor.

People laughed and cried simultaneously, one old mover even mopping an eye. The worst moment was over, and we crowded into the waiting hack, taking a final view of the house and the picturesque group on its porch. Annie, the tall negro girl who had been our friend and buoyant helper for two years, was standing there amid a small company of her relatives, male and female, who had come to help her close up the premises and were clasping various cast-off articles to their breasts. Their brown faces shone in the morning sunshine. Annie herself waved an energetic farewell with a large cracked Canton platter which had been her heart's desire ever since she let it drop a few weeks before. The neighbors sang out good-byes from their porches, and bade us come again soon. So, with sorrowful resignation cloaked by these saving emotions, *finis* was written under the last chapter of our Brooklyn life.

Northampton

1

NEW ENGLAND AGAIN

We had a happy summer, since Archie came up from New York, and spent weeks with us in Hadley. We did our own housework at the farm, took long drives with Charlie, the old horse of Englewood days, harnessed to the accustomed carryall, both retained at Forty Acres for ten years. We painted the blinds of the Phelps house, to relieve its brown walls with a fresh green, and the little boys watched their father as he wielded his brush.

Through July and August we let the children stay up to watch the sun go down. We taught them to listen to bird songs, and to know the wildflowers, whose names their Aunt Molly could always give. Little wild animals still crept out of their holes, and made acquaintance with us; the squirrels ran madly over the roofs, and leaped across from the pine-branches into the elms and maples. There was a woodchuck's hole in the middle of the north dooryard, and the old fellow used to come up and look about him warily when we were eating dinner. We watched him, but did not disturb him; he was surveying territory which was his own by right of occupation. When we were visiting friends in another country-house, Roger inquired politely, after being shown their horses and dogs and cows, "But where is your woodchuck?"

As for our two parental selves, we were no longer in the throes of despair at the coming separation. We had each begun to plan and to look forward to freedom and work; we could enter into one another's hopes and share ambitions. It did me good to see my husband eager for the future he had previously renounced, and was now planning to recreate.

When I moved to Northampton in the fall of 1900, he came

back, and helped me settle into my new abode. I was to take the house of which President Seelye had spoken to my father, and board four freshmen who had not been able to find rooms on the campus, reserving one room in which to put up visiting parents.

The house was attractive, situated on the lower side of Round Hill, and with a lovely view of the eastern hills from its rear windows. Mount Holyoke lay to the southeast in an altogether different setting from that of our Hadley outlook; the low range always reminded me of a sleeping lion, stretched out beyond the valley plain. To the west, between housetops, we had a view of Mount Pomeroy, a horizon which was quite new to me.

Just below us, on Elm Street, stood the house which my father's oldest brother, the Honorable Charles Huntington, had built and occupied in long residence; opposite that the two Misses Brewer, once the gayest girls of Northampton, and nieces of Judge Lyman, were living; they welcomed the child of their erstwhile associate, and had the merriest stories to tell of youthful pranks, memories of which kept them in touch with the younger generation. Miss Fanny was tall, erect, handsome, positive; Miss Hannah small, dainty, clever, vivacious. Three other members of the former circle in which my father moved, Christopher Clarke and his two maiden sisters, were original characters, picturesque personalities with old-time touches in their garb and a quaint house in the residential district that was originally populated by the first families. The Clarke sisters had a lot of old letters, bits of amusing verse, and other trophies, witnesses to a lively and select company which in their younger days had earned repute for Northampton as a centre of cultivation and wit. And music also, for their brother Christopher and his colleagues had founded a lyceum which had brought famous artists and lecturers to the town. One of our elderly friends remarked that "it was taking a whole college to raise the tone of the present generation to anything like the standards of fifty years before!"

In making my own venture, I was the recipient of blessings and curses both, to put it baldly. My family supplied the blessings, but other relatives were divided in their minds as to the propriety, or even decency, of exchanging the prestige of a lawyer's wife and what they were pleased to term "good birth", for the inglorious career of a landlady. Quite different, argued discerning Boston, from that condescension which ladies of Cambridge, for instance, had practised during many years past in accommodating a few paying guests of a student or professorial character in their own houses, dispensing cultural advantages thereby. Yes, quite, *quite* another thing.

This attitude seems incredible today, and luckily I was unaware of it at the moment. However, my cousin Fanny Quincy, whose heritage from Betsey Porter may have accounted for her large-heartedness, sent me some dessert-spoons with colonial markings, and a friend of my father added a French-enamelled outfit of bedroom and parlor furniture, with cordial benedictions. This was pleasant, but I was absorbed in calculating and planning and learning how to cope with artisans and merchants. If I thought at all about my future social status, it was to feel the satisfaction of being able to rank myself among the wage-earners and be recognized by them.

My conception of a woman's college in the year 1900 was, like other inheritances from a romantic age, somewhat ahead of reality; and the conversion of ideals into ideas was bound to be a little slow.

The campus as we had seen it in summer months was thus far only a bare and rather dusty yard, with tall elm trees and transverse paths and closed brick buildings: no hint of life during the period of our stay at Forty Acres. It had never seemed like a part of the town, and we had thought it a bore to exhibit it to strangers. It formed no actual setting for the vision which had always remained in my mind, derived from Tennyson's *Princess*—and not yet disturbed, even by acquaintance with many collegians—of gracious women in academic garb, moving about under the spreading elm branches, followed by fair young girls who gazed at them adoringly and listened to words of wisdom from their lips. In my teaching days at Utica the school had given, under Emily Griffith's direction, a most charming performance of *The Princess,* with artistic costuming and very good dramatic representation. So I looked forward with some amusement to a modernized version of the drama.

It was a great comfort to find that my four girls, of different types but with good backgrounds, were able to fit into family life as well as into a college schedule. I have always had a particularly warm affection for that quartette, and a deep respect for the up-bringing which made them truly helpful during our common no-vitiate. Through them I learned how to meet the combined de-mands of matronhood and hostess-ship.

I knew little or nothing of the regulations in the other off-campus houses, except from the good advice of a very successful matron whose disciplinary principles awed me exceedingly, and made me quite hopeless of ever imitating them. I had to content myself for the time being with making the house regimen simple and orderly so that it might not interfere with college regulations. The children were taught to fall in with this, and learned to go to sleep in the midst of noise and motion, but were more or less re-moved from it in their big room at the back of the house.

The girls, and their many friends, who ran in and out of the house much as the Brooklyn children had done, played with the little boys, taught John to walk, and amused themselves with Roger. We had discovered soon after his third birthday that Roger had taught himself to read, we never knew how. Our visitors, girls and young faculty women whom I had come to know, used to make him recite bits from Shakespeare, setting him up on a table, to hear him declaim with infantile gusto, *"Friends, Romans, Countrymen."*

It was a comfort to feel that the children could have outdoor life, sunshine and bracing air, with Forty Acres only six miles away and a chance meanwhile to grow up in a community of scholarly habit and tradition. The task of developing system and economic foresight was bright with discovery; now one could have done with sordid calculations and fears.

I was asked to join the Monday Club; the most interesting of the town associations, I discovered. I found myself, rather timidly at first, accepting kind overtures from women of the faculty who had either known my family or had followed up commendations of friends. There were at that time comparatively few men on the staff of the college, and one found these women (divested of Tennysonian robes!) very delightful company after one had overcome a certain awe which was no more than their due.

They were fine women. It seemed fitting that Eleanor Cushing, who dealt with the higher mathematical values, should have been endowed with a classic beauty of countenance, with dignity and reserve. When she came to pay her first visit she brought with her a little dark-haired vivacious lady who displayed such familiarity with the doings of the town that one did not suspect her of any connection with the college. I concluded that Hatfield house, inscribed on her visiting card, signified a small hotel of some sort. I had not yet mastered the campus geography, and did not at the moment dream that I had had the honor of a visit from the star of the English faculty, Mary Augusta Jordan. But after attending one of her classes I could appreciate the brilliancy with which, as analyst and lecturer, she held her audience spellbound.

It was always good fun to visit those classes, for she had a fashion of flinging little asides, over the girls' heads, to adult listeners, and frequently turning from the more commonplace subject of the moment to indulge in an intellectual fusillade which delighted the company. One could well understand that the talented girl would seek her training, even if it implied biting though constructive criticism. And somehow, in spite of her small stature, abrupt manner and cryptic nods or shakings of the head in place of words, she was an impressive figure on a commencement platform.

Then I enjoyed Julia Caverno of the Greek department, who out of the dry background of classical research brought human and friendly approach to an ancient civilization, and made its language fascinating. She was a delightful person to meet and greet in one's daily walk, with contagious humor in her smile, and a freedom from pettiness that might well be the outcome of dealing with the immortals.

Elizabeth Hanscom was slight and rosy-cheeked and quick-moving, but uncompromising in her principles, and deaf to all appeals of the non-studious; her Shakespeare course brought out so much in her recognition of the dramatic and poetic values in their relation to life, and so keen an exposition of the essential and eternal humanity of the great dramatist, that the girls looked upon it as almost a fitting in itself for a literary career. They knew her, too, outside of the classroom, and loved to visit her in the little house where she lived with her mother.

But among them there was hardly one greater, if the observation of an onlooker counts for anything, than Jenette Lee, who, with her husband Gerald Stanley Lee, had already gained distinction as a writer of that period. Her faculty for making her pupils' minds work was amazing. A small figure in a sober brown gown, she sat relaxed before a crowded classroom, and led them in criticism of a given book or essay with scarcely a word from her own lips; merely a pithy question now and then to draw out opinions, and not a suggestion of her own point of view. It was a course for upper-classmen, and the required work was heavy. Receiving each effort courteously with no more than a twinkle of her brown eyes, and simply calling, when they finished, for someone else's point of view, she achieved astonishing results. I loved to watch her do it, and to hear afterwards the discussions of some of the girls who came to our house, for I had the joy of knowing some especially brilliant seniors that first year.

There were a few men on the faculty, but nothing like the proportion of men there today. Professor Gardiner of the Department of Philosophy was one interesting character who was loved by townspeople and college both, for his learning and his social qualities. There were others: scientists like Professor Waterman of the chair of physics, and Professor Stoddard of the Chemistry Department. Professor Ganong, a botanist of outstanding repute, was warmly loved by his many pupils. And there was Dr. Irving Wood, the professor of biblical literature, a course which I was told had been established in obedience to a decree in the will of Sophia Smith, but was something of a departure from the Calvinist interpretations of Scripture which had been her guide in girlhood.

As a matter of fact, I myself still had enough traces of fundamentalism in my make-up, to be rather shocked at some of the modernization in the text of the Old Testament particularly. Dr. Wood was giving a course on the prophets, if I remember correctly, and the girls brought reports of the ruthlessness with which he demolished the haloes of those worthies. My image of the great Jewish leaders of thought had been derived from Michael Angelo and Raphael and the Renaissance. I pictured them in flowing robes and thrones and scrolls, with clouds about their heads, and commanding postures; had heard their utterances reverberate in the tones of Bach and Handel and Mendelssohn. What was my horror, therefore, at hearing from a flippant freshman that "Proffy" Wood had said Isaiah was a politician! As a matter of fact that word had been used only to convey the idea of statesmanship, but I was overcome with anxiety lest the foundations of Christianity were about to be shattered. Incidentally, I mentioned the fact to my sister Arria, who passed it on to Father. In her next letter she quoted him as saying, "Tell Ruth not to worry. There is no danger in truth. I wish we could have a few Isaiahs in Syracuse politics."

There was much plain speaking in the Bible department, and some idols overthrown; however, the girls were indeed getting truth, and no one could accuse Dr. Wood of attacking anyone's theology or of not knowing his subject through and through. His knowledge of the Orient and of ancient history was unassailable, and I had good reason to be grateful to him later for some invaluable help which he gave me when I was teaching a Bible class and giving a course on the journeyings of St. Paul. It made me realize how ignorant and presumptuous I had been.

But the dominating figure in that first experience in a woman's college, was President Seelye, the product, it seemed to me, of that which was finest in New England tradition. I had first seen him at one of the famous Ashfield dinners, when, among a group of distinguished colleagues with more or less rationalistic sympathies, he made the inspiration of the Scriptures the subject of an after-dinner speech. It was an eloquent and impassioned defense—a courageous one, in fact, and the audience was impressed by his courage and sincerity. To me it was like Moses reading from the tables of stone. "He might be Amos or Jeremiah," a man behind us whispered. I think it was one of the last pleas of its kind in the aftermath of Higher Criticism.

Recollecting it, I saw in the college chapel exercises, and in his comprehensive prayers, the same powerful faith. The girls gave him a devotion that was in itself a strong influence and a stabilizer of their moral outlook. His geniality was no less a force in town-and-college relations. I found him from the first a friend and sympathetic adviser, and was grateful for his backing. It semed to me that I had always lived in New England, and known its ways; it was the place of all others where I could best rear my children, and fit them for a useful life.

2

There was some private limitation of ardor in this settled existence after the activities of the last few years. I missed the discoveries, the meetings, the progressive plans, the risks of reform work. It did not take long for me to become aware that my chances for moving in an advancing world and keeping in touch with efforts for social betterment were now very slight. There was disquieting news from abroad; the United States was trying to run the Philippines for the benefit of vested interests, said rumor. I had already become an anti-imperialist. We heard accounts of American soldiers torturing Filipinos to subjugate them, and of traffic in native girls and government-owned houses of prostitution—all reports with some truth as their basis.

My resentment was stirred up by these stories, and also by the indignant denials and accusations of disloyalty to our country which were heaped upon those who believed the stories. The press transmitted both. The assassination of President McKinley revived and aggravated a fear of violence. Theodore Roosevelt, advanced from the vice-presidency and settled in the White House, was faring forth, always courageously if not too wisely, upon a sea of difficulties and embarrassments. In Northampton even organized labor was taboo, and its friends were looked upon as dangerous radicals; the Industrial Workers of the World, the I. W. W., was an organization begun in the mining camps. Its members were suspected of sinister activities, and hunted down; the privileged applauded all vengeful attacks upon them.

The Consumers' League, free from interference by law, but still accomplishing its end with difficulty, was looked upon by certain elements as an interfering body. As to votes for women, only the masculine type of female would even *want* to vote, said the enemies of that movement, in their "torpor of assurance". Why bother?

One amiable lady observed, one morning when I met her down town the morning after addressing our club on the Organized Vice proposition (which, let me say, came to a natural and speedy death of itself), "Dear Mrs. Sessions, when there are such lovely topics for discussion, like Art, and Beauty, and Travel, why not forget the unpleasant things, since we can't prevent their going on?" And one might agree with her, had not one's pesky New England conscience got after one for being a mollusk and paying no heed to the sufferings of humanity. It was an old song, perhaps better forgotten, one thought, till there came a sharp little thrust of memory, suggesting moments in one's own experience when one had learned a little about hunger and fear and pain—enough to make one keep on understanding those things.

Toward spring, I realized that the house on Round Hill could not possibly accommodate enough students to be profitable. The problem of finding a larger one, however, looked almost insurmountable till our kind neighbor, Mr. Oliver Walker, discovered a fine old mansion on the broad street which bordered the college grounds. It was for sale, and could be altered and enlarged to suit my purpose perfectly.

Standing on Elm Street, its gambrel roof shaded by huge elms, it was in a commanding position. It had an interesting history, and I shall quote from Harriet Kneeland, the distinguished chronicler whose little book on *Old Houses of Northampton* is the best authority of her time.

The first Jonathan Hunt, coming in 1661, built near the corner of Prospect and Elm Streets. A son, Captain Jonathan, whose wife was Thankful Strong, built a little later where the Burnham School now stands, and still another Lieutenant Jonathan lived in what we have always known as the Bridgman Place.

This was the house which was to be my possession and later that of Smith College. It was built about 1700, Miss Kneeland goes on to say, and that date is recorded on the stone tablet set in one of the fireplaces, and was given by will to the Lieutenant's son John in 1738.

So elegant was it then considered, with its big brass knocker and gambrel roof, that that part of the town was called New Boston until the fine elms set out by this same John Hunt in 1753 gave its present name to the street. Of the large family born under this roof-tree, Rev. John Hunt was pastor of the Old South Church in Boston. . . . . Martha Hunt, a daughter, married Judge Samuel Henshaw, and the name Madam Henshaw was associated with all that was stately and elegant and hospitable. The place, reaching from Round Hill Road to Prospect Street, was known far and wide as the Henshaw Place; and the coach and footman were the envy and delight of the town, and a spacious wine-cellar would seem to attest a lavish hospitality. Tradition says Burgoyne passed a night in this house on his retreat to Boston, sleeping in the big south chamber.

To find that the owner, Mr. Sidney Bridgman, was willing to sell his delightful old house was a great satisfaction, and the upshot of that discovery was that my mother made the purchase for me. The loan was an investment which I was able, in later years, to pay off and justify fully.

The Henshaw house was built in a familiar old pattern, with large rooms, low-studded but airy, built around a huge chimney which furnished two fireplaces on each floor, and crowned its roof, another chimney giving similar fireplaces in the rear. The big front door, with its stately knocker, opened into a tiny hall between the two first-floor drawing-rooms, and a staircase ascending crosswise, of fine woodwork with a picturesque railing. At its summit I had to make a slight change, cutting through a narrow hall beside the chimney, in order to connect the front of the house with the back hall, from which two very steep stairways, one up and one down, led to the dining-room below and the third story. The latter extended over the ell, and we put four small bedrooms there, but kept that addition in conformity with the proportions of the main building,

An architect whose age and experience made him competent for the task, planned these alterations, and also drove about the county to search for old verandahs, that we might run a porch along the east side of the house. He succeeded in finding one after a long hunt, with a row of arches at its top and a broad flooring which by rights should have sloped a little, close to the ground, as the truly antique ones did, for the sake of having the water run off it when it was washed; but this we had to sacrifice in order to keep a narrow path beside it. All that summer, while the building was going on, the townspeople used to drop in, and watch the carpenters; they were terribly afraid that my additions would spoil it, and what wonder? It was good to see their interest in it, and to be able to satisfy them that there would be no innovations tending to mar its antiquity or its comfort.

My husband came up during the summer, and his taste, too, on which I relied, was satisfied with the success of the alterations. He himself was deeply happy, for he had been made editor of *Ainslee's Magazine,* the very goal toward which he had been working during the summer, and for which he was so manifestly fitted. It was a glorious piece of news, and its effect upon him had justified to the full our decision to work out separate destinies with time and liberty. He spent the first few days with us at "109," as the house came to be called, and we established the babies in one of the long second-floor rooms. There was an ample back yard for them to play in, with some old fruit trees and a little dog-house for Nan's collie.

It can be imagined that my "undertaking," as it was termed by friends and relatives, who perhaps thought that a trifle more high-sounding than "boarding-house," looked somewhat tremendous and demanding. All sorts of help was provided; advice from authoritative sources, encouragement from college functionaries, and an equipment of good workers, among whom Mary Brown, a large-hearted and capable soul, stood out preeminent as ruler of the kitchen and disciplinarian of the children, who of course had to be trained to revere her authority. I don't know how I could ever have undertaken that first year's venture if it had not been for Mary's great popularity with the younger generation, and her good sense in meeting its wants without overrunning the regulations of the house. She was a hostess in herself, and began by serving a sumptuous meal on the evening of the girls' arrival; fourteen of them, from north, south, east, and west; fresh-faced young creatures bringing suitcases, mothers, and trunks, and settling in with all the twitter of southbound birds in a big elm tree. They sported golf-capes, most of them, of gray or black or brown with plaid linings, Scotch patterns or otherwise, also tams, which were soon discarded, however, since the college girls went bareheaded in their own district. Their hair was twisted into little knots in the nape of the neck, or, in the case of a few, turned up behind and surmounted with a bow; they wore buttoned shoes, high or low, and nobody carried powder-boxes; the natural complexion was still preserved. They answered, "Yes, Mrs. Sessions," or "No, Mrs. Sessions," quite punctiliously, when interrogated by the housemother.

The parents were all prepared to go with their daughters to the Registrar, and oversee their arrangements for lessons and were quite solicitous for their comfort, as well as for the furnishing of their rooms. Some mothers displayed a grim determination, even after the first day's experience and eye-opening, to keep on steering their progeny; others gave in. I felt for them all. I don't know how many times I promised to try to see that the children donned winter flannels, considered indispensable in those days, and remind them of their rubbers; but without assurance that I could be responsible for their taking these wise precautions. They provided their own desks and scrap-baskets, curtains and cushions, and had washstands in their rooms. The walls were immediately adorned with banners of all types and dimensions, and hanging photograph racks, or fishnets looped about here and there. Cots were covered with colored spreads and thus converted into sofas. This storm of *decor* was very exciting; an avalanche of youth, with nothing Tennysonian about it to be sure, nor yet a hint of art; but with vigor and spirit that reminded me of my own vivid adolescence. I felt myself enlisted already in the cause of the Coming Generation.

When we had our first house-meeting, I found little to announce except to stress the fact that we were all equally implicated in the matter of loyalty to the college and observance of its rules. Between us, we must systematize our common life to make it a fit setting for the winter's achievement. The girls were to make their own beds, receive clean sheets and towels at stated intervals, and have their lights out at ten o'clock; and they would find a pitcher of milk and a plate of cookies in the upper hall at half-past nine, as Mary Brown's contribution to the general welfare. And I was to consider them my helpers in the up-bringing of the children, with full freedom to discipline the boys, since I was not the lioness type of mother. The children were kept to a hard-and-fast rule that they should never enter any room on the second floor, save their own nursery, under any pretext whatever, nor accept so much as a cracker in the way of refreshment. I must gratefully bear testimony to the fact that the students carried out these regulations nobly, and abstained from exploiting the boys. The two were brought up on alternate petting and snubbing, which made for unselfconsciousness. Theories on the education of small children were not yet in the market at that moment, with the exception of Froebel's teaching. It was the day of oatmeal and raw apples, for the most part, and pre-digested foods were yet to come.

College activities were over by six o'clock, and except for occasional lectures, theatre, or a good concert, everybody had a holiday hour after supper, from seven to eight. A number of us liked reading, and there were enough Dickens-lovers to bring about a nightly gathering in the library at the close of the after-dinner dancing. I read Dickens aloud, with *Our Mutual Friend* as the first book. The attendance was entirely spontaneous, and kept up for seven years, until the number of evening committee-meetings and other engagements made it impossible to go on. The company never wanted to stop at eight o'clock, though now and then studious ones slipped away early. We read at least two books in the course of a season and I think the two favorite ones, if I can trust to the memory of our count, were *Bleak House* and *Nicholas Nickleby,* each one read four times. Sometimes friends from outside dropped in at that hour, and listened. No other author could hold our public so well.

On Saturday nights there were usually entertainments in the different houses. Nearly every campus house had its individual shows and its talented performers. At our house we entertained the usual quota of Sunday dinner-guests, and had a Sunday-night supper which at that time was a special kind of hospitality, informal and with many groups and amateur waitresses. It was a "lap tea," as they used to call those informal collations in Boston.

Athletics, however, had become an increasingly important part of the college scheme. The picture of Senda Berenson, head of that department for years, comes to the fore—a slight graceful figure fascinating to her pupils, with a faculty for putting common sense into the heads of her countless adorers, and a charmer among her colleagues and drawing-room followers. She and her sister Elizabeth, also in the gymnasium, were high-ranking alumnae of the college. The annual basketball game was an outstanding event, with energetic cheering and singing from the crowded galleries.

But so were the dances. Even then the "Junior Prom" had its garden-party and ball in May, chaperoned by the higher officials and selected housemothers. And on Washington's Birthday there was a large meeting in College Hall, with a speaker of note and a patriotic address. The girls were seated by classes, wearing white frocks with sashes of their class colors. My first household was mostly composed of 1904's who wore the royal purple, and that dignified shade is especially associated with the events of the first four years, as I recall the loyalties, the triumphs, the enthusiasms into which I found myelf entering. Somehow or other the fourteen girls, the children, Mary Brown and her helpers, the collie, the cat and I had welded ourselves into a family before the end of our second season.

If a student was asked in those days to state frankly her reasons for coming to college, she would have answered that she came for the living as well as the learning: the *Life*. I am afraid I shall have to repeat that word many times, in one connection or another. Books were not all, said they; they must have experience. Not only the country girl, whose opportunities might have been limited, but the daughters of the privileged, wanted to get away from conventionalities and leading-strings into a freer existence and a wider companionship.

If some of them tended to put social advancement ahead of

their academic pursuits, it was apparently because of a lack of balance and perspective, often attributable to home or community backgrounds. They were not like the graduates of English colleges, as I had seen them, nor like the hard-working students one met in Germany. And yet they had the power to change the face of American life, later on, as wives and mothers, voters, scientists, writers. Some day our universities would not only be turning out statesmen and stateswomen, but shaping them; at present they appeared to be spending most of their energy in protecting them.

So, in thinking over this question, and watching one personality after another, I was reminded sometimes of the time when I was sixteen, and sat looking off from the summit of Mount Warner at the distant buildings of the two colleges, one almost a century old and the other just beginning, meditating on the Fine Art of Liking People and feeling vaguely that it had something to do with the enrichment of existence outside the realm of letters. And when my college children came out of the classroom with a disappointing readiness to discard the loftier intellectual values and turn with fervor to basketball or dancing or masculine attractions, I understood. I too had much to learn, and the faculty of making rapid adjustments, inherent in youth, was a more serious challenge to the adult. Well if we can acquire that before it grows too late! More life, and fuller; that was to be mine too, and please God, I said to myself, my husband's, my children's. The Dark Tower had disappeared, and the landscape bloomed where thistles had been.

I am sure the pattern of living in the Henshaw House was partly, at least, a product of the former existence under its roof-tree. We developed customs which our visitors sometimes called New-Englandy; little ways of making the house life inclusive, not setting it off as a mere unit; and inventing simple enjoyments.

A custom started in the early days of our history was the search for a secret passage on All Saints' eve. There really was such a thing; I had discovered it in exploring the old structure of the house, and had also heard an ancient legend which told of an underground gallery, leading from our cellar to the Connecticut river. This stupendous piece of masonry loomed high in its imaginary setting of historical tradition, but was never logically explained either as an escape from Indians or from the English, although General Burgoyne became involved in it to some degree, which made the report of his having spent a night in the house doubly intriguing. No one could ever quite determine, by the way, which of the two south chambers sheltered him. However, the search for a secret staircase was enhanced by this rumor, and the search became a permanent institution.

"Mountain day" was one of the high-spots of the year's activity, and we had our own way of celebrating it. We owned, for the moment, a trolley-car, placarded PRIVATE, and driven by a skilful motorman who felt a measure of proprietorship in our party, and answered with a jocund acquiescence to its demands; the same man each season. In this chariot we sped eastward to the Pelham Hill range and its scattered villages—the most brilliant of landscapes on a clear October morning. In the course of twenty Mountain Days I remember scarcely any weather but the marvelous clearness which brings out the regal magnificence of autumn color. Just once it failed us. We started from home on a humid morning with the thermometer at seventy or over, and nobody thought to bring rubbers or heavy coats. We changed our programme and went to Montague, at the north end of Mount Toby, by trolley, to be served with dinner by the ladies of the church, and dance afterwards in a ball-room with an old-style spring floor. The day seemed auspicious, but I felt doubtful of a gray cloud which gathered over the Deerfield hills as we sped northward along the banks of the Connecticut. Just after we left Greenfield a cold wind and a heavy snow-squall met us; by the time we reached Montague the temperature had dropped almost to the freezing point, and the trolley-car's passengers tumbled shivering into the inn, glad of a blazing fire. The dinner was sumptuous, and the dance very jolly and warming; but the prospect of driving home in an open car, with no protection from icy blasts save a few thin jackets, was devastating to the spirits of the housemother. I was sure that half the party would be down with pneumonia before morning if something was not done about it.

I slipped away to interview the leading merchant of Montague with regard to providing extra clothing. Nothing in that line but men's denim overalls and gingham shirts. No flannels; but there was one resource left. I bought four large rolls of cotton batting, and returned with it to the cloak-room where our inadequate outer garments had been stored. One by one the girls were called in and padded, shaking with laughter, their shirt-waists lined, and special attention paid to knee-joints and wrists. They emerged with a wobbling and cautious gait, and an obvious difficulty in holding the wadding pat.

They would have reached Northampton intact, however, had it not been that on our arrival in Turners Falls somebody proposed that we should all get out and make a trip to the waterfall. The trolley-car was not supposed to make any stops, but they got round the motorman with fair words, and dashed off *en masse* when he screwed down the brakes. The casually-pinned battings came off as they ran, in a trail of little flakes which made the main street of the town look like the aftermath of a game of hare and hounds. But little recked the hares; they were back in ten minutes, quite unconscious of the effect their sally had produced. Nobody would confess to being chilled on the way back, but all the brooms in the house, next day, did not remove completely the traces of that excursion.

3

THE INEVITABLE

In the summer of 1904 there was one more gathering at Forty Acres; a last reunion, which made us feel its nearness to the world beyond. We had sometimes spoken of the certainty that some change must come, for the Bishop had been growing weaker all through that year; his memory was going, he had a tendency to great lassitude, and now and then a wandering consciousness followed by a bad chill.

On the eleventh of July, a perfect midsummer day when the stillness of the air was intense and almost breathless, we sat watching him breathe more and more softly, his wife close beside him. The farm life was going on as usual; under the window two young Jersey heifers were cropping the grass, a sound he loved; a cat-bird was giving its gentle cry now and then, and we heard other sounds from the old attic above; a nest of swallows in the chimney, the stirring of little squirrels among the beams.

There were reporters, from the larger papers of New York state and Massachusetts, all about. Every half hour or so they would come quietly into the house, that my husband or I might tell them of changes in my father's condition. For Archie was with us, our mainstay, as always, in sorrow, and this time he took the place of both my father's sons, for our oldest brother was ill in Hanover, and my brother James was not able to reach us until the next day.

It was an uplifting day; there was no dread or sense of tragedy. The end of a life like our father's could not be calamity; it was merely a quiet passing from this world's turmoil and uncertainty into calm for the worn body. We could envy him, and pray, *Let perpetual light shine upon him,* when the afternoon shadows lengthened under the windows of his room, reaching across the yard as the cows came back from the pasture. My mother was still sitting at his bedside, where his opening eyes had sought her for a fortnight past.

For the last time, young men came to the door. There was no more sound of breathing in the east chamber. Mother had gone back to her own room; the rest of us were going quietly about the tasks which must be accomplished before night. Archie and I were able to tell the press what it needed to know of plans for the coming days, and to send the many dispatches that notified relatives and friends.

I shall always remember the tact and gentleness of those reporters. They had to drive to Northampton—there was no telegraph line from Hadley then—but the news was flashed to the great cities at once, and we were told afterwards that it had reached Syracuse just as business-men were leaving their offices at five o'clock, and that many of them turned from the bulletin-boards in tears. One of the papers the next morning had for its headline, in great letters, THE BEST-LOVED MAN IN SYRACUSE over a notice of his death. The working-people asked to have a little button made; it was struck off by the thousand, and worn by telegraph boys, factory-hands, salesmen and women, wage-earners all over the city. I have one now, with his face on a black ground, and the words, *We mourn Bishop Huntington.*

My husband made me go back to the Phelps House early that evening, since I had lost sleep the night before, and there would be much to do next day. Telegrams were coming, boys bicycling over from the Western Union with great bundles of them; I fell into a deep sleep at once, but with the thought in my mind that I must write a long letter next morning, and send it off by early mail to my beloved brother in Hanover. He would want to know more than the dispatch we had sent could say.

I got up at half-past five, and in the misty stillness wrote ten pages, telling him how sorely we had missed him all that day, how my mother longed to see him as soon as he could come, and how much it would mean to her to have her oldest son take his father's place, and be able to lean on him. The letter was to go at half-past seven, by the mailman who passed the house.

At seven, when Archie came into the room, I gave it to him, stamped and directed. When he took it and held it a moment, I said, "Hadn't you better take it right out, so that it will be sure to get off early?" Then he said, "I can't, dear," and put his arms around me as he falteringly told me that George, too, was gone from us; he had died very suddenly of heart-failure, barely three hours after his father's going; word of that had not reached Hanover till afterward. My mother had found the message among the other telegrams brought to her.

For me, the world seemed to have crumbled. The numbness of despair, without relieving tears, descended upon me. Two fathers gone; only fellow-mourners left. The exaltation of the day before turned to darkness.

We left brave young Nan, who had the most treasured recollection of us all in the remembrance of her grandfather's last smile, to care for the little boys, after we had told them of his going. They too had a special memory. They had been taken over to say goodnight to him a week before; a bird had sung softly as they stood by his bed in the sunset light, and Roger, then eight, always remembered that Grandfather opened his eyes and smiled, saying, "Hear that? It is the robin's vesper song."

Somehow the sense and symbol of mourning could not be associated with the two people whose obsequies were to be carried out. My mother dreaded a church funeral, and so we had a simple service at the house.

My brother George's body was brought from Hanover, and his wife and children came to us, so our diminished family circle was together in the old house. James had reached us the day before; his luminous spirit, like a torch, kept our faith and hope rekindled, and even a spark of humor flickered here and there; for the two sleepers, with calm and peace written on their faces, lay in the long room side by side, the sun shining through the syringa bushes, and the doors only partly closed, so that we had moments of feeling them still among us, and included them in the family congeniality.

We liked to speak of things which would have made them smile, and to remind one another of their sayings. Some of the leading clergy of the diocese were among these guests; many more of the Central New York clergy were to come, vested, to meet the funeral train at the little Hadley cemetery. Some two hundred people from Northampton and Hadley and from other states were gathered there. I recollect the ring of strong men's voices as we said the Apostles' Creed at the house, and its affirmation of the faith for which the father and son had stood, their lives its witness. Then the little train of carriages—and we had seen to it that they were open country vehicles, not city wagons—drove slowly down the road behind the two more funereal ones. It was like a triumphal procession, for as we went, the church bells of all the neighboring villages rang. We could hear, in the afternoon stillness, not only the Hatfield bell, which all its life had been a familiar sound, but the lighter tone from the little North Hadley belfry, the solemn notes of Old Hadley's tolling, with deeper, distant echoes from Northampton.

"For all the neighbors held him half akin," wrote our kinsman, Dr. William Huntington later in *The Outlook*:

> "Scholar and prelate? Yes,
> But here, to them, long summers had he been
> Plain farmer too, no less.

> "Nay, always that; a master seedsman he;
> The furrows knew his tread;
> As ever, with a faithful hand and free,
> He sowed the children's bread."

The procession was met by a train of white-robed clergy at the head of a little lane leading to the graveyard, and the vested choir of St. John's Northampton. After the first interment we walked over to my brother's grave, on the northwest side, for the second committal service; and there, as we stood singing, we who had learned from him to find messages to our souls in bits of nature's beauty, noticed a pair of homing swallows which, flying past, dipped so low over the open grave that their wings almost brushed our faces. A white moth lighted on the casket as it was lowered.

I went over, at my mother's wish, to keep house for her during the next two months of the vacation. The children came there with me, and my brother's boys and girls visited us from time to time. There was a silence and a sadness about the old place, especially at evening. Its soul had gone, and a young life was beginning to take the place of the old; some things would never be again. But we were happy and hopeful, reading aloud together, and answering the many letters, eight hundred of which came in the first month. My brother James, who stayed on for some time with us, helped us answer these.

In August I got away for a few days, with Lucy Watson, who had been with us in all our family gatherings at the time of Father's death. We belonged to the Companionship of the Holy Cross, an association which met each year for conference at Adelynrood, an old house near Newburyport overlooking the green marshlands, with the sea beyond.

Then in September I came back refreshed to my houseful of girls. There were new ones with me every year; I took them for only their freshman and sophomore years, and they went to the campus as juniors. For our immediate family there came changes and promotion. Roger went away next autumn; his capacity had carried him beyond the age of the children in our little private school, and we felt he could advance better among boys and men. We had not realized, however, that a child who is more or less precocious and uneven in development cannot be thrust into a crowd of average youngsters, without some of the martyrdom of the misfit. He came home at Christmas time a bundle of nervous terrors, and we felt we must find a new school at once, where a moderate, sympathetic headmaster would handle those fears by quietly carrying confidence with him. I was in the mood to beg my small son's forgiveness for the mistake we had made, and felt that we could never make adequate reparation for that great blunder. But we found the best possible conditions in the Campbell school at Essex Fells, New Jersey, whose principal combined the very qualities we sought. Meantime Nan, who had been sent to boarding-school so that her equipment for college might not be too heavily permeated with experience of the *Life,* begged to spend her last year of preparation in Northampton, and was willing to bargain for that by taking a room at the house of our neighbor Mrs. Bridgman, and coming to the old house only for meals. Her town connections kept her successfully out of the college sphere, so that she could enter the class of 1909, with the proper freshman attitude and no sophisticated notions. Sixteen was too young for that, as we all realized later; but since she obtained high rating in examinations, there seemed no object in keeping her back.

The next years passed calmly and life at "109," went on without perceptible changes, though a quiet progress continued and from time to time one noted an increased academic enthusiasm. I recall the appearance of Everett Kimball on the faculty, announced by a lively ebullition of argument among his pupils, manifest at our mealtime discussions. It was his delight to raise objections, to combat established theories and even principles, and shatter cherished traditions; exactly what was needed to revive their mental alertness, and make dry bones rattle.

It seems to me as I look back that the nineteen-sevens and 'eights, and 'nines, while very "dressy" young women, wearing silk blouses and dangler-necklaces to their classes and pale-tinted fabrics to Sunday dinners, were none the less acquiring better habits of study and more interest in the real objectives of the college curriculum. They took their mid-years as desperately as ever, sitting up till all hours with wet-bandaged foreheads and drinking strong coffee, occasionally falling by the wayside, burdened with conditions.

In the winter of 1909 my mother died. To the very last she has kept her alertness, her reading of French and German, her church-going and interest in all manner of people and affairs. She was beloved by the little club of old ladies which had met in our neighborhood for years, and welcomed in younger circles as well,

since her social gifts made her congenial with people of all ages. I
had written her daily for the five years after our father's death, and
my two sisters had cared for her devotedly, Arria having given up
many civic connections in order to be more with her in the little
house they had taken after the Bishop's death, while Molly had
been always her close companion. Her passing left much to be
settled at Forty Acres, which had been exclusively her property.
None of the descendants could undertake the sole management
of the place, nor could they have borne to see it pass to strangers
after its long family history. It was finally arranged that the old
house and its surrounding land should be left in the keeping of
our brother's five sons and daughters, thus remaining a Huntington
estate, and that my children and I should live on in the Phelps
place, since this had been my Father's expectation in adding it to
his property. My sisters retained a share of the land also; my brother
added his portion to mine, to make it possible for me to start farming, with my share of livestock and tools; some of the larger machines were to be shared by our nephews and ourselves. My quota
of livestock was five cows and two calves, and with my share of the
money left to the estate, I built a small house for a manager, and
made over the old barn, adapting it to hold a larger herd; then a
married couple was settled there to take care of the place and make
it earn its way by supplying our Northampton household with
chickens and eggs and milk.

Our summers at the farm were busy times. We all worked; there
was much to do in the fields and in the haying and corn-cutting, and
I had the thrill of driving the mowing-machine now and then—an
exhilarating experience on a dewy June morning—and sometimes
the hay-rake on hotter afternoons when a bathing-suit, of the decorous pattern which we wore in those days, was the most comfortable
costume. The boys helped our farmer. John had always been devoted to the land, and we like to think that by inheritance he was
fitted for tilling the soil as his ancestors had done and thereby
earned their acres, which were never used for market speculation.
When the question of private ownership of land was discussed, I
had secretly indulged that thought, with a joy in possession which I

felt must some day be sacrified, but which made our love for Forty Acres all the stronger. Roger preferred weeding to harvesting, and spent long mornings wielding a hoe between the rows of corn. He preferred that monotonous occupation because it left his brain free for musical conception; occasionally, however, he would slip away into the woods at the call of a bird, forgetting the implement and the task for too long a time.

Some summers I did the housework as well, giving my Northampton maids a paid vacation and not always engaging a substitute. I liked to be up early with my people, slipping down into the kitchen at half-past five to start the breakfast biscuits, doing the morning chores with the stimulus of the coffee aroma. We were always glad to have guests from the circle at the old house, or to give a waffle-party for younger visitors, cooking the waffles over the fire of shingles, which were replenished by armfuls brought in from the woodshed.

It was always hard to break from that life when the time came to go back to town, just as we were having frosty moonlight nights and long sunny days, hearing the clack of the silo-filler and seeing the great loads of tasselled corn come up from the meadows. I felt the rejoicing of the farmer over fruitful acres, and loved to plan the crops for the coming year. We were running a milk-route then, and I kept a waiting-list of the prospective customers, buying a new cow when a group warranted the purchase, and adding five or six names at a time. John ran the route successfully, and I occasionally went along on the little truck, to familiarize myself with its demands.

4

DEPARTURES

By the spring of 1910 a need for expansion had developed at Northampton. The Henshaw house could not accommodate the number of students who were now applying for admission; my waiting-list was large, and we needed a substantial addition. Our friend Mr. Huxley, who justified his inheritance of the great scientist's name in being a supremely intelligent builder, and whose understanding and human insight made him the most helpful of planners, worked out a design for enlarging the old building without disturbing its proportions unduly, copying measurements and patterns of woodwork, and getting round the old chimneys and massive beams with a tact that saved new changes from being innovations. Sixteen rooms and a number of bathrooms were added at the back, and on the ground floor, beyond the dining-room, a good-sized recreation-hall with a wide fireplace at one end and a long window at the other; a broad staircase ascended at one side, and a door opened on the old verandah; the ceiling was studded with little lights which were not obtrusive in the daytime, but converted the place into a ballroom at night. It was dubbed the Hilarium, and became a gathering-place for all kinds of groups, from Sunday night suppers to Hallowe'en hunters.

The year 1910 was memorable for many reasons, especially in the college. Its long-loved President retired that year, after thirty-five years of service; and though we were still to have him in Northampton as a citizen and friend, the departure left a very sad and apprehensive atmosphere among the directors. A mourning faculty and student body, not to speak of the hundreds of alumnae, realized that there was more than personal loss to be considered.

He stood for that which was strong and abiding in the movement for the higher education of women; had conserved the best traditions and principles, fought unswervingly for the validity of the old faiths; and kept to a safe course with a scorn of experiments and superficialities. Not only had he built firm foundations, but a progressive, economical system of housing and provision for an annually increased body of students, and a combination of discipline with democracy which kept the morale of that body at a high level. But with his going, many certainties seemed now doomed to be swept away. That which was new would come in through the door that closed after him. The realization of this inevitable change was in the minds of the trustees when they met to consider the next step. When the public, which for us in Northampton represented our own corner-of-New England conservatism, learned that they had decided upon a drastic departure and were preparing to bring a gifted and liberal young man from the west to undertake the office, anxious surmise attacked the community. Looking back on my own experience as a child, I could not but feel that the change from eastern to western leadership might open up new paths for the college, and enrich its life. Yet on the opening day the students, for all their eager anticipation, were somewhat sobered. "We missed even the long prayer," some of them said. Marion Leroy Burton was a person strikingly different from his predecessor, but he came into his place without display of any sort and was welcomed by town and gown, as was his pleasant wife. They had been lovers when fellow-students at a co-educational college, which perhaps made them interesting as individuals to the students. They affiliated themselves with the Congregational church, and fitted excellently into the social life of the community as well as the campus. From my own observation I felt this an auspicious beginning. One did not at once observe many signs of change in the general attitude of the faculty or student body; the girls took kindly to their new president and fell in with his wishes as they developed.

My own children were making some departures from earlier plans. Nan was graduating from Radcliffe, not from Smith; it had seemed wise to let her have part of her college experience away from home, and spend some time in Cambridge where she lived for two years with Professor and Mrs. Emerton, and later with Mrs. Cooke, the "Aunt Mary" of my Boston days. Her aunt, Adeline Sessions, gave her as a graduation present, a trip to Europe, where she went in 1910. She was then just the same age that I was when I had been there more than twenty years before, and my youthful excitement at meeting Celia Thaxter in England was matched by a larger group which the broadened interests and contacts of our family could offer Nan. Her letters brought glowing accounts of friends whom she met through her father's previous visit there, and Romanes (then the outstanding scientist whose faith in the Christian religion had held against the doubts and denials of many of his colleagues) to whom she was introduced through his friendship with my brother James, after one of his visits there. She visited the Rookes, whose daughter had been for many years on the faculty at Smith College. At a Suffrage meeting at Queens Hall, she met the Pankhursts who had recently influenced our own ideas on suffrage. In Switzerland she studied both French and German at the house of a charming French family on Lake Thun. All these things and more served to prepare her for her next year of teaching, and the welfare work upon which she subsequently entered.

We read Nan's letters together at the little cabin which had been built for my sisters on the top of a hill between Amherst and Forty Acres. Father had given them the wood-lot, with its view of the mountains and the river valley. They were supremely happy there, studying the birds, the butterflies and ferns. Cousin Ellen had sent a little Christmas sketch of that view from the front of the house, as one looked westward across the blue, undulating horizon-wall of hills—a bit of sandy road, with a fence long since gone, and a few dull-green-and-brown sweetfern bushes beside it in the foreground. Underneath it she had painted, *"Denn so das Klarheit hatte, das da aufhöret, vielmehr wird das Klarheit haben, das da bleibet."* 2 Cor. 3.11, which is even nicer than the English translation by Moffat: "If what faded had its glory, then what lasts will be invested with far greater glory." I think that the fadelessness of those eternal hills will never be any more clear to those who come after them, than it was to Arria and Molly.

Roger entered Harvard in the fall of 1911; at fourteen he was large and strong, with the appearance of a sixteen-year-old. But he was mortally afraid of being recognized for the youngster he really was, and had a nervous terror of publicity. He and Nan, therefore, were quartered for two winters in a little apartment on Brattle Street, with an elderly maid to look after them. Roger had definitely decided on a musical career, and had written, two years before, a miniature opera scored quite correctly for an orchestra of twenty instruments. It was composed in the manner of Wagner, and contained various motives. He named it *Lancelot and Elaine*; I recollect that he had made the Guinevere motive, as he told me with all the earnestness of a romantic twelve-year-old, the most attractive one of all but with less *meaning,* because, though very beautiful, she had no soul. He was never especially willing to play his productions, always asserting that he could hear them just as well without; and they were not taken with him to Harvard; he already felt them to be childish.

Vacations, short though they were, brought my husband back to the children and me. And now and then I went to New York for visits which he made especially gay, taking me to theatres and concerts and attractive restaurants. He was amusingly adequate in the role of *galant,* looking as handsome in his evening clothes as when he had come from Harvard to escort me to the opera in years past. It was a source of deep happiness to us all to see how completely he had found his destined work at last. We went back to our tasks after these interludes with memories of moments when a chance touch had brought the old thrill, or a meeting of eyes betrayed some sudden emotion, *innig* and unexpressed, which gave us wordless assurance of fealty. In those slight mutual revelations there was a pledge renewed; a preservation of the spark which might have gone out under the pressure of an unremitting dual struggle with defeat. We reminded ourselves of that in our long intimate talks at the farm, when after the children's claims had been satisfied we found ourselves alone by the fire late at night or sat under the pines in the moonlight, discussing not only our affairs but the problems of a larger world, as we had always faced them together. We had given ourselves a holiday to go to Kent for Roger's graduation—a satisfying experience and a joy to the boy himself, for both brothers felt the lack of paternal companionship, and were thankful to have their father share in any achievement.

Our college household gained, I think, from enlargement. It had reached a better capacity, and through greater numbers touched more interests and problems, some of which looked larger to the outside world than to ourselves. One question was asked by friends whose churchmanship was unqualified; *What do you do about religion?* I always felt that it put me on the defensive, for when I was obliged to answer, "Nothing; only just try to live it," they were apt to look puzzled and pained. It was such a wonderful opportunity said they, with a household of girls, at the impressionable age, surrounded by temptations to forsake their parents' faith for the modern rationalistic outlook. Even the societies for Christian work in the colleges, it was urged, were more or less limited by a spirit of so-called breadth which must be pervasive in an evangelical body representing many creeds.

I had to acknowledge that the typical college Sunday was anything but an ideal Sabbath devoted to rest and worship; it began with late breakfasts, went on into forenoons of shampooing and manicuring and letter-writing, dressy dinners and later a vesper service which was practically a sacred concert, with a short address from some outstanding denominational preacher. It was of no use to stress the benign influence of beautiful organ-playing, nor to plead that after all many faithful young church-members slipped away to early services or visited other places of worship at the conventional hour; nor to suggest that my own regular church attendance might be an encouragement to the spirit of worship. These excuses, if such they were, did not exonerate me in the eyes of sundry splendid people who had a right to think me neglectful of my duties, but did not quite understand the deeper instinct which had kept me resolved to leave my college children's faith to the God I believed in.

Little by little, however, since religion is itself an instinct inherent in the fabric of individual life, however obscure its pattern, there developed an expression of it which is often recalled as a cherished bond of unity. On Sunday nights, a little while before "lights out" was signalled, the Hilarium was darkened, and I would play in the dark a very simple hymn, Baring-Gould's words set to Barnby's music; that often reminded me of the lessons Joseph Barnby had given us at Pontresina years before. The girls sat about on the floor or the stairs, the embers in the fireplace lighting their faces; one could kneel or not, as her impulse prompted, when we repeated the Lord's prayer at the end of the hymn. Nobody knew, I think, what her fellow-worshipers were doing. In later years we came to say a little collect as well, about going deeper into the mysteries of life and being interpreters of life to our fellows. Then came a long silence like the silences at a Quaker meeting. It was not imposed upon us, but developed quite naturally because the worshipers lingered, finding the stillness restful. I do not know that it was always used for formulated prayer, but I do know that in those moments—and they were intense moments—there came into our midst a Presence which made the room a sanctuary, and hallowed our common life. When at last we stirred, there was a surge of energy and a series of spontaneous goodnights. I never wanted to make that service a defense when accused of indifference to the religious training of my "lambs." It only showed that their souls' good was in higher hands than those of their housemother!

5

INHERENT PACIFICISM

The quiet German people who had once taken me so confidently into their family life, were going about in black garments, acquiescing silently with the aggression of a mad government, and praying to a god of war to give its army victory. The marching armies which I had seen in Germany in 1881, suggested glory and might, but not bloodshed. At that moment of comparatively peaceful Germany history, the German army had been pure pageantry, and the fear of destruction from it was not in our minds any more than the opposite fear that the Germany I had loved would be destroyed by its adversaries. But as the months went by, and America was taking on the passions and hatreds of the conflict, even urged on by the Christian church, there was nothing for me to do but pin my faith to a possibility which I could not really believe: that Wilson could hold America neutral.

I was in New York on the day when the news of the Lusitania disaster came. I think it reached America after the morning papers were printed, but the word spread with that appalling rapidity reserved for a national calamity. At once every human being seemed to know it; horror was written on the faces of hurrying businessmen and women, truckdrivers, newsboys; voices calling, vehicles speeding, bulletins changed every few moments as dispatches brought fresh details. It crossed the United States on wires and flying trains and was caught up and carried into far village districts. For days reports kept coming; mourners multiplied; the bravery of officers and passengers on the sinking ship put heart into their fellow-men at home. It would not have been possible to stem the tide of indignation, lust for revenge, pity, and challenged courage, that swept over the mass of American people. I think there were no doubts after that that we should enter the war, though a few kept up hope. It was no surprise, at all events, to a group which was standing in the hall of our house on a bright afternoon, when Roger came in with the first edition of the paper in his hand, and said in the quiet tone that always reminded me of his father, "I hate to tell you, Mother, but *war is declared.*" And I remember saying solemnly, "That is the end of Wilson."

At once the country seemed to swing into action. Sight and sound testified to that; I heard the soft clicks of innumerable needles, and saw girls knitting, knitting, as they stood and sat and lounged and traveled, and the gray scarfs, the long stockings, the hanks of yarn; the flags, the bulletins, the buzz of voices in the Red Cross rooms; the boys in khaki.

I had hatred and horror of war in my blood, and my stubborn mind held inexorably to the belief that taking of life, whether organized or involuntary, was *wrong*; that one idea possessed it, and I made no attempt to dispel the convictions thousands of voices cried, that America had done right in going into the conflict; the Church quoted the sayings of Jesus Christ to prove that point. Patriots, older and younger, not only defended but lauded our fight for the honor of our country and championship of the nations attacked. They prayed for our army and our noble allies. My heart would not respond. I was not an absolutist; I could not take the ground that work for the soldiers of the hospitals was a support of war which involved the individual in its guilt. I could not see that disagreement with the military party, however intense one's feelings, absolved one from that duty toward the suffering. My friends were loyal and loving, but I worried them; they were terribly afraid that I might make some unguarded speech which would bring me into actual danger. But there was no fear of that, for I knew that my college children must be left free to follow in the path of duty as they saw it, and as their parents and brothers saw it. We did not discuss the matter, they and I, though they knew how I felt, with the instinct which our mutual confidence engendered. And they, too, were loyal, to the very core. So I did not get the martyrdom which, from the militant standpoint, I deserved, and was willing to endure. A few townspeople avoided me, sometimes crossing the street when they saw me coming. I had a government job, which meant going about to the stores and getting records of prices or something of that sort; my little horse and runabout was sent over from the farm, and I drove from store to store; a certificate which was sent me in acknowledgment of this service to my country smote me with a sense of hypocrisy. What *had* I really done for that country, I said to myself. Not given my life for it; did I owe it that?

Roger had graduated from Harvard in 1915, and spent the next two years at the Yale Graduate School of Music. He was awarded the Steinert prize for an overture, delivered with great success and excellent comments at the Commencement concert, a number of critics coming from New York to hear it, and extra instruments hired for its performance. Meanwhile he had been asked to come to Smith college as an instructor in orchestration, and had gladly accepted the position. He was known to have taken a pacifist stand, however. President Burton was told that just before the declaration of war he had, according to report in the newspapers, signed with four other men a telegram urging President Wilson not to declare it. It was reported that Mr. Burton said he fancied the young man would appreciate the need of being careful, or something of the sort. But from that time on he was more or less under suspicion, and the accusations against me for being "pro-German," as it was put, were occasionally strengthened by attacks on my children. I learned not to be surprised when told that my son was said to be a degenerate, a drunkard, and later a draft-dodger, when he had been rejected by the draft-board because of an eyesight-deficiency for which he had worn glasses since early boyhood. Those things were simply effects of war-hysteria, and I always asked not to be told who had reported the untruths.

Smaller things were far more annoying. My bitterness was augmented by having to rise when the *Star-Spangled Banner* was sung, on all occasions, for my ears revolted at every note, as they had protested fifty years before. And when Karl Muck was dismissed by the Boston Symphony orchestra directors, and Fritz Kreisler banned in many cities from playing his violin, even musical patriots revolted, so that we could find consolation in their company.

The other children were not with me, though I found my pleasantest recreation in visiting them. Nan had finished her courses at the school for Social Work in Boston, and had been sent by the S.P.C.C., after special training at its Boston office, to Berkshire as its representative. I heard with pride from the Judge of the District Court, that she was doing especially fine court work in Pittsfield. Her younger brother John was at St. Paul's, Concord, and enjoying outdoor sports with a schoolboy's keenness. He graduated from there in 1917, handing me rather shamefacedly a silver medal which signified the highest honor which could be bestowed by the school, with the observation that it was the sort of thing mothers liked to have, and I might keep it if I wanted to. He entered Harvard the next autumn, and was given an honorary scholarship that winter by the class of 1920, then sophomores, for being an "all-round freshman." He particularly liked people, of all sorts and kinds. It was less a Fine Art with him, however, than a natural instinct, not too selective to be wide in its application.

News from abroad was bringing Russia and its distractions to the fore. The hopes aroused by the Kerensky revolution were lost when it was followed by the Kornilov rebellion and the Bolshevist uprising. Madame Breshkovsky, "the little grandmother of the Russian Revolution" as she was called, had been brought back from exile by the government and acclaimed by thousands as she drove through the streets of Moscow. The account of it had stirred the people of America, for she had visited this country in 1904, in an interim of her persecution under the Czarist regime, and had made many friends. She came to this country after our own war, under the protection I believe of returning Y. M. C. A. workers, and made a stop in Northampton, staying a night at our house, and addressing the student body in the large auditorium. But from a strong woman with a faultless physique and an inextinguishable flame of purpose, she had become an enfeebled figure, still alert in mind, yet timid. She wore the Russian headdress, a black square of soft cloth, over her white hair. It was such a great event, that visit, that a very large assembly gathered to see and hear her; for the moment we were carried out of our absorption in the nation's entanglements. Yet when she faced a thousand people in the auditorium of Smith College, all of them eager for the tale of persecution and struggle which they expected to hear from her, she was suddenly seized with an emotion which seemed to drive the subject-matter out of her head. She said a few words about the Russian crisis, with an assurance of her confidence in her own people and country and belief that some day right would triumph; then she began an impassioned description of the impression which the great college had made upon her, and told her audience of the thousands of Russian girls to whom education was at last a hope for the future, explaining what such an opportunity would mean to them, and to the life of the nation.

Later Leonora O'Reilly also came. She spent a week-end with us, gave a talk at our Northampton Monday Club, and spoke to my own girls on a Sunday evening. It was the younger generation that listened most understandingly; I did not feel that the women of my own age were sympathetic with what she told them of the American working-woman's struggle for better conditions, and need for fairer wages: to the girls she talked, as Madame Breshkovsky had done, of the opportunities given them as privileged children of an era of wealth, begging them to use their education thankfully, and wisely, in acquiring a deeper knowledge of economic and social conditions. She was deeply interested in the Woman's Trade Union movement then, and I know that she aroused the interest of her audience.

6

NEW ORDER

In the autumn of 1917 came another change at Smith College.
President Burton was called to a western university, and it was a
disappointment to his many friends to lose him from Smith. He
had contributed much to its progress. He had enlarged its curriculum; had shown discernment in grasping new truths and opportunities. But even warm adherents had been aware of a certain lack of
depth in his administration, as compared with the widening of
other dimensions. The scholarly element, the conservation of foundations built upon treasures of past accumulation, the dignity of
authoritative wisdom, seemed, although venerated, to be no longer
perpetuated in the government and life of the college. The one
man to restore these things it was felt, was William Allen Neilson
of the Harvard faculty, who was not only recognized as a man of profound learning, the recipient of degrees from the universities of
England and master of the English language, but a liberal in
thought and spirit, a gentleman and a scholar and a canny Scotsman
as well; the type of character best fitted to become the President of
a New England institution, and to assume that office with calm
and poise in the face of national upheaval and distraction. The
town itself accepted him as counsellor. Even opposing factions
listened to him when he was settled within our gates.

It was a time of questioning and criticism; changes, not only in
our universities but in the whole fabric of civilization, were coming
upon us with such swiftness that dissenting voices found few listeners. Both apathy and objection were left behind in the trend
toward new standards. The trustees were proud of their choice, and
the younger generation accepted the regime. We who felt all this

through the students and through friends on the faculty, became aware that in any move toward peace, any increase in international fellowship, President Neilson's sympathy would be warm and responsive. His counsels to young men, of whom my oldest son was one, helped them to maintain a balance of liberal thought even while feeling conscientious objections to military service.

We had an event in the family during the first winter of the American participation in the war—a military wedding. Nan was marrying Paul Andrews, the son of our friends in Syracuse, whose father, an eminent Justice of the New York Court of Appeals, had been the stripling at our early games of Prisoners' Base in Syracuse. The engagement was already a year old, and Paul was expecting to be sent to France in the spring. Roger played the march, and I an accompaniment to a violin obbligato, by a student in the music department, while an old English wedding-hymn was sung and the married pair knelt after the benediction; it was very reverent and lovely. Then, as they rose from their knees came the dramatic feature of the occasion. Roger sounded the strains of *The Star-Spangled Banner* from the large trumpet, the tones of which filled the hall. The guests were already standing and smiling—bringing the affair to a triumphant climax at which I might well have felt moved. But the spectacle of the musician, his cheeks full and tense as he solemnly pumped air into the unaccustomed instrument, brought a fit of amusement which I could hardly control. This supreme sacrifice of our pacifist predilections and agonized musical sensibilities upon the altars of Hymen and Mars was too much for pent-up emotions. I dared not look round at my husband, who was standing decorously beside me with every outward indication of sympathy; he was a perfectly consistent patriot and even his own sensitive ear endured the trumpeting. But I did give him a slight jog of the elbow—and primmed my unruly lips into an expression of respect. Our son mopped his perspiring brow as he eased his lungs, with a twinkle in his eyes that met mine. Even if the "brass" was a trifle off key, however, the *finale* had made a great impression. It is only fair to own that thereafter I found myself looking upon our national anthem with less aversion. As an instrumental solo

divorced from the explosive text which rasped one's peace-time
pride, I could bear to listen to its tones.

The year 1918 was a strenuous one from its very beginning. The
departure for France of the Smith unit, made undergraduates eager
to give their services in intensive work for the army and the
wounded. At home there were exigencies to be met which appealed to all the local charities. The Children's Aid (which a
group of friends had founded some years before) took on new
problems; now we had unmarried mothers and war-babies to care
for. Private resources were drained to meet these needs; prejudices
had to be revised in the name of patriotism. And there was always
the endless discussion and argument over patriotism itself; how
far external observances of it should be enforced, how severely
dissenters should be punished.

For me it was always a comfort to get away with Lucy Watson
to conferences of the Fellowship of Reconciliation, where Rufus
Jones and an earnest group of peace-men kept the spirit of its
gatherings at a high level. We found the Quaker meetings not only
restful but intensely devotional. The Friends' Society was carrying
on in Europe with an unobtrusive persistence which made its work
more truly a copy of Christ's own ministrations than any other
undertaking. There was no ban on its care for the wounded and
starving, of whatever nation; but the American Red Cross, taken
over by our Government, could no longer labor impartially, though
its accomplishment was superb. Everywhere, at home and abroad,
it was manned by fine leaders and organizers and devoted nurses.
I was glad, too, to get away to Boston for an occasional visit at
Denison House, with Helena Dudley and Euphemia Mackintosh.
Helena was bravely outspoken in her condemnation of war, and
sometimes alarmed her friends thereby; but she came to no harm,
and her courage heartened us all. At Wellesley Alice Brown and
Vida Scudder gave their prayers to the peace cause. Vida's vision
was strong and clear, her stand convincing. Yet not all our Com-
panions were absolutely at one in their shades of feeling about
America's entrance into the war, and the attitude of the House of
Bishops in the Episcopal Church, over which I had frequent argu-

ment with my brother, was then discouraging to many of us. At
Adelynrood there was spiritual unity if not always complete una-
nimity, and we gained from our effort to maintain it.

In the spring of that year, I traveled to Syracuse, to visit my two
sisters. We were very anxious about Arria. She had been closely
identified with the life of the city and with the great national issues
at stake. All manner of causes looked to her for support; she had
been made the first woman member of the Chamber of Commerce;
was called in council by benefactors of public charities, and buildings, even, were named for her; her work for girls had widened out
into larger circles. But now, after fifty years of intensive usefulness,
she was suffering from a nervous breakdown and great despondency.
At the end of the summer she was taken, by her own wish, to a quiet
private sanitarium near Syracuse. For my sister Molly this was a
crushing blow. It meant giving up the pleasant apartment they had
shared, and leaving the church people by whom she had been
dearly loved; an uprooting of much that was precious to her. She
came back to us at the farm each summer, but not with the old joy
and zest. The empty cabin on the hill-top, its doors and windows
nailed, remained for succeeding years a place of sad remembrance.

After the 1918 Commencement, I managed to slip away from
home for a little visit with my daughter, who, with her husband
and another couple, had taken a pleasant old house at Harvard,
near Camp Devens. Its pillared porch overlooked the camp from
a hill some two miles to the east, and it was reached by lovely
country byways. Roger was working at the Soldiers' Club at Ayer,
and had met me at the station when I arrived. I was aware, however,
of a certain reserve in his greeting. "Nan's out there in the car," he
whispered. "I think Paul's gone. I went over to camp this morning
and the Brigade headquarters were empty, the General's and all.
I haven't asked her any questions and she hasn't said a word; I
imagine she isn't supposed to let out anything for a certain number
of hours; maybe till after the transport has sailed. But I'm sure they
must have left in the night; they always do."

Nan was very bright, looking festive in her white afternoon
gown. We stopped to chat with various people on the way to her

house, and later some of the officers' wives came in for tea. All seemed in good spirits, but their eyes looked weary. After supper, as we sat watching the sunset, Nan said unemotionally,

"Mother, I can tell you now. Paul's Brigade left last night." It was a moving story, told with calm. The boys had received sudden orders to leave, and the two husbands were allowed a few hours at home for packing up and bidding farewell to their wives.

"We knew we shouldn't crack," said my daughter, "for we've been keeping ready all these last weeks."

At half past nine the men left, with an everyday goodnight; no sign given servants, or other witnesses, of an unusual parting. The two were fellow-officers on the General's staff. After that the wives had sat on the dark verandah, hour after hour, watching the distant camp lights. Excitement kept them buoyed up during the last dragging moments of their vigil. At one in the morning they could see that lights were extinguished; then there was stillness, for the tread of softly marching feet did not reach their ears. A train of empty cars had waited on a siding for days. By and by came a faint sound of grinding wheels, a few light puffs from an engine; the train pulled silently out, unheard by a sleeping community. What its destination was, the narrator did not say, but I imagined that the transport had sailed from Boston. I think mothers take lessons from their children with better grace than from their parents; at any rate mine had given me an example of fortitude, which I counted among the salutary, if somewhat racking, experiences of the war.

7

"COOK AND HOUSEWORKER"

Life at our own farm was increasingly complicated. All country communities were feeling the lack of masculine workers. A trying experience with a manager who turned out to be a draft-dodger and was retired from his job in disgrace, forced us to call upon the younger generation for help, and four boys in their teens, headed by my own younger son, took up the task with remarkable capability. They whistled and sang as they drove the cows home from pasture and tossed hay into the mangers. Seated on a three-legged stool, John trolled out college choruses in his hearty baritone, accompanied by the rhythmic tinkle of milk as it flowed into the pails. Lee, a lad who had grown up among us, carried on the milk-route and the work in our still primitive dairy; Albert and Arthur looked out for the chores; all four, on shifts, put through the digging of a drain from the barnyard to the east ditch, as practice for work in the trenches later on. They accomplished the harvesting of rowen-crops and, with help from the village carpenter, built a long tool-shed against the barn ell and painted it. Their straight young bodies and tanned skins were good to see.

I was cook and houseworker, and one of my 1922 freshmen, a niece of General McNair, came to work with us for a week or so, since many of her friends were going out as "farmerettes." She walked the six miles over from Northampton carrying her overalls in an appropriate bundle. An old man in a wagon picked her up on the North Hadley road, and upon being told where to leave her inquired,

"Be ye Mis' Sessions' hired gal?" that delighted her greatly and caused her to adopt the title. She wanted to try every species of farm labor, and trundled a wheelbarrow with buckets of "swill" for the pigs, curried the horses, or borrowed the paint-brush and mounted the ladder which stood against the shed-walls. After our lively evenings she was apt to sleep late, and remembers being called in the morning by a recital of the breakfast menu, as "Betty, *muffins!*" or; "Omelette, Betty; hurry and get down before it falls!" I see her, a slim, bright-haired creature, standing in the doorway of the barn with head erect, and hands clasped behind her back, or poised upon a load of green sword-bladed cornstalks with long hanging tassels, headed for the silo-filler, which kept up its metallic din for hours together. Overhead brooded the blue September sky, faintly misty and dreamy, and our wooded hill, bedecked with scarlet branches, made a background for the picture.

I was proud of my young son's managerial achievement, and now and then indulged a secret hope, developed from my own love of the soil, that I might one day see him squire of Phelps Farm. But no vision was bright enough to dispel a foreboding sadness; he was going on leave from Harvard to spend a term at the Yale Artillery School, his choice of a military training-place; he was keen for an acquaintance with the guns. Once more I buried resentments, thinking of the thousands of braver mothers who through all time had been called upon to sacrifice their sons, and meditated upon that curious quality of the maternal mind which can maintain a calm front at the agonizing moment of parting, but succumbs to tears over the darning of stockings or packing of kits.

It was during the war years that I became aware of a change which had come over the American girl since the beginning of the century; she, too, had taken on poise and judgment. We could see it in her assumption of collegiate responsibilities. Most mothers no longer felt it necessary to *bring* their daughters to college, or introduce them to teachers and housemothers. Undoubtedly the improvement of preparatory schools had something to do with the change; certainly the average freshman no longer needed protection. She could settle herself intelligently in new quarters, with a fairly clear idea of the aims and objects to be pursued during the four years ahead of her. One heard less about the advantages of *The*

Life; the whole of life, and its interwoven pattern was little by little opening to her contemplation; she was listening more soberly in class and lecture-room. One noted a trend toward occasional reflection, and I recollect some of the talks we had. Often when I came upon a group of debaters they would reach out a hand and draw me in with the question, "What do *you* think, Mother Sessions?" or would call to me as I passed a door and make a place for me among their sofa-pillows in a moonlit room. Youth was beginning to surmise that with the return of the army there would be problems to meet; there were already happenings to be sober about. Yet neither my college children nor I could have prophesied how tremendous a claim that return and its aftermath would make on traditions which society had hitherto taken for granted.

Calamity was close upon us at that moment, in the fall of 1918. The influenza epidemic, brought to this country on the transports from European war-centres, swept the United States, spreading from camps to populations, and attacking the college with special virulence, it seemed, when it reached Northampton. Every house, on or off campus, was quarantined. We had fourteen cases at our house in the first ten days, and some of them were obliged to wait for entrance into the emergency-infirmaries, which were set up after the city's hospital was filled. We turned one of our rooms into a ward, and took care of patients as best we might till that could be regulated. I found I could stand night-duty, and there were no nurses to be had. Most convalescents were sent home; some twenty, mostly immune, remained with us. After that our cook and assistant cook and one waitress were sent to the hospital with severe cases lasting several weeks. Minnie, a gentle elderly soul who had been like a family nurse to the girls for twelve years, carried on upstairs with one helper; in the kitchen I took over the cooking, with the help of the remaining waitress, a rosy brown-eyed German girl, vivacious and briskly capable. Rose and I worked shoulder to shoulder; wakened at five, and descended to the kitchen to bake a hundred breakfast-cakes or half a dozen big loaves of cornbread, and pack luncheons for seventeen uninfected girls who were allowed to do farm-work for the sake of life in the open. We gave them an early breakfast, and at seven, three or four dusty old cars would draw up in front of the house, ready to transport them to neighboring villages. After the cars drove away we had a quiet day, with light luncheon-duties and time to prepare a hearty night meal. Doing up table-linen, making butter-balls and cleaning silver were some of my duties beside marketing. Minnie and her assistant swept twenty rooms and made beds, while Rose set tables, washed dishes, scrubbed the kitchen and sang folksongs the while in a clear soprano which supplied rhythm for our activities. I always thought of such adventures as happy opportunities which gave one the sense of the solidarity of human endeavor, and the joy of labor among singing workers.

The girls came out triumphantly with their field-work. One group cutting and stacking it, harvested the corn-crop for an old man whose sons were in the war; all of them escaped the "flu," and returned each night tanned and toughened and ready for sound sleep. The epidemic subsided almost as quickly as it had descended upon us. Classes resumed work, and we forgot the interruption. Stirring events in Europe were filling the public mind with alternate hope and fear; the French soldiers were still shouting; *à Berlin!* Roger ran in early and late with news to which our household had no other access. One morning soon after six, we were wakened by a blare of factory whistles. Sonorous tones from our own nearby mills, an answering blast from Easthampton, echoes from Holyoke and Springfield, made a volume of sound that told of some stupendous event. I sprang to the telephone to ask what had happened, and the answer came back; *"Treaty of Peace with Austria!"* Trembling with excitement I dashed out into the halls, knocking at every door and cried, "Children, wake up! Peace is coming; this is something for you to remember all your lives long!"

"Only Austria?" they asked.

"Yes, but Germany will come next. The war is almost over!" We had already learned of the surrender of Bulgaria and Turkey. And only a week passed, in fact, before the whistles wakened us once more, and this time the church-bells followed; newsboys were shouting in the streets. "Armistice! Armistice!" The word echoed on every side. Flags were going up, the telephone-lines were crowded. Our house was alive with calling voices, hurrying footsteps, windows flung open to hear the sound from without. Some girls came to my room after breakfast, asking;

"Mother Sessions, can't we have a service? Will you say some prayers, thanksgivings, you know, and can we sing hymns in the Hilarium? We *must* do something."

I was delighted to fall in with this plan, and set them at once to looking up hymns, but prayers were harder to find; I was most unskilful at extemporaneous praying, and my Prayerbook seemed only to contain expressions of gratitude for good harvests and recoveries from illness. I thought fretfully that the church ought to have anticipated a celebration of this sort. Certainly we were not singing the praises of military conquest like the Old Testament warriors. But I was shamed into dropping self-consciousness; eloquence was not needed for spontaneous and simple thanksgiving.

Roger turned up just then, all excitement.

"Rodge, you must play something! What can you play to celebrate?"

"The Ninth Symphony, of course," he responded promptly. "There couldn't be anything better; wait and I'll run over and get it while you do the singing and praying." He did fetch it, and played it completely through, adagio and all, the girls moving about meanwhile in restless excitement. When he came to the Joy Hymn, however, they stood about the piano and beat time with hands and feet. In a corner, I was hearing the *Gewandhaus* chorus, all sound shut out except the orchestra and voices, as I had heard it thirty-six years before. My hands were over my eyes;

> *Seid umschlungen, Millionen!*
> *Diesen Kuss der ganzen Welt*
> *Brüder-über'm Sternenzelt*
> *Muss ein lieber Vater wohnen.*

The vision of that vast embrace encircling all the nations of the earth, swept one up into its glory for a brief moment. Now the company scattered, carrying felicitations across the campus. By afternoon rejoicing was in full swing. The staid old town went wild. There was a procession of cars, and every sort of vehicle from a haycart to a handcart, galloping horses, barking dogs, long strings tied to the back ends of buggies with tin cans dragging from them; streamers of bright paper, tooting of horns, shouts and songs and flag-waving; a leaderless mob up Elm Street abandoning itself after long repression, to unleashed frenzy. Later on dispatches arrived with news that this was not the real armistice, and that peace must still be arranged; but it did not discourage the populace, which had worked off its first jubilation in the preliminary stampede. On the eleventh came the authentic announcement, received with more dignity and celebrated by a great gathering in the Auditorium. I think no one who attended it and heard President Neilson's readings from the Bible could have doubted his innate spirituality. There was a deep reverence in the silence which followed. That evening the Neilsons threw open their house to town and college and a long line of sympathetic friends streamed through the rooms offering congratulations and eager handclasps. Everyone felt keenly the relief to Mrs. Neilson, after months of anxiety for her people in Germany.

But the days which followed were not joyful ones. The community was by no means content with the cessation of hostilities. For hundreds of young men, eagerly expecting call for service in France, it meant disappointment, openly acknowledged. Intense feeling set in against Wilson; the peace-machinery was held back by complaints and quibblings. The war was not over. Old shibboleths were revived and familiar scandals and stories repeated. One afternoon early in 1919 I was told that a man who said he had come from the United States Government, wanted to see me. I descended blithely, while good Minnie, rather anxious, lingered in the hall to be near me in case of need. She had heard rumors that I was liable to investigation of my suspected "activities". I found a middle-aged man of quite uninteresting appearance, and a manner which suggested salesmanship rather than military authority; was I to be approached, I wondered, for subscription to some liberty-bond scheme or other patriotic enterprise, since the gentleman was in civilian's garb? I greeted him cordially, but noticed that he seemed a trifle put about. He moistened his lips.

"You'll be a little surprised to see me, I guess," he began, "but I'm from the War Department and I want to ask a few questions. It's about your son; his name's Roger, is it? I hear he's an instructor in the college and is rooming in an apartment with a young man of the name of D——— who we understand is a German. Can you tell me anything of him and how your son happens to be associating with him?"

"He has a German name," said I, "but I believe he was born in this country. There isn't a trace of foreign birth about him. Futhermore, I understand that his father is an American citizen and fought in the Civil War." The statement about the war was a mistake, which I did not find out till years after, but it produced a marked impression.

"Well, that puts a different face on it. I had heard he was a spy."

"The best thing you can do," I suggested, "is to go to John Spencer Bassett, of the history department, in which the young man is an instructor and let him get that idea out of your head. I'll give you his address and you can see him at once."

The man reddened, and his flat face took on a more aggressive expression. "I've got to find out something else," he said. "Your son himself is on our list. It seems, to begin with, that he signed a telegram which was sent to President Wilson last year asking him not to declare war. That was a traitorous act; it was going against the Government. He hadn't ought to have done it; it made him liable."

"According to the newspapers," said I, "Professor Phelps of Yale signed that telegram also. Are you getting after him too?"

"He isn't on my list," said the visitor evasively. "But I presume they'll see him. We're going right on looking up people who are suspected of anti-war activities."

"What, now?" I exclaimed. "Why, the war is over; there isn't any war."

"Yes, but there are just as many traitors. We're getting them, right along; sending them on to Leavenworth and other places. I hold my job till the fall, anyway."

"I'm glad you're assured of steady employment," I snapped. "Now, what else?"

"Well,"—he hesitated. "I don't know whether you know about it, but they say your son belongs to a crowd that meets every Saturday night at a drinking place down street, where they have discussions of a radical sort. Are you acquainted with any of those people?"

I could hardly subdue a smile. "Certainly," I answered. "They are all older than he, and mostly faculty men. A number of them are Harvard graduates."

"Oh. They have a lot of radicals at that college."

"One may hope so. I hear a good deal about their discussions, because Roger usually stops in as he comes home on Saturday nights, and tells me about it. I'm apt to sit up late, reading. They are all interesting. Perhaps you'd like to meet some of them. There's Professor Kimball of the History department, and Professor Fay, Mr. Bassett of course, the Greek and Latin men, Mr. Lieder, Mr. Locke of the music department, Mr. Churchill—why, he is a most genial person! I don't know how many of them belong to that particular group, but you'd find them wide-awake men. You might see President Neilson, and ask him about them; why not do that?"

There was no response whatever to this proposition. My visitor switched to another point of attack.

"What are your own views, Mrs. Sessions, on the subject of the war?" I told him I was very glad he asked me that, because I had found it difficult to formulate my views. My objection to war had been an inherent personal antipathy. But it was not a thing that could be made an influence; the time had come when one must put prejudices aside and rationalize one's mental attitude. "If you want me to tell you where mine has arrived," I said, "I will say that it coincides with the point of view of the British Labor Party. That's very important, you know, and Great Britain is our foremost ally."

"What is it? A union? We haven't any use for those fellers. I. W. W.'s make a lot of trouble; they shoot 'em up out West."

I hastened to assure him that there was no alliance between the two. I brought down the Labor manifesto, of which I had a fine copy, to show him, and made him go over it with me. He actually brightened up, and seemed quite interested, especially when he heard of the men who had been imprisoned and then released, like Ramsay McDonald.

"I never knew about that party," he said. "You're a real smart woman to find out about such things. I guess it's a good thing to have an education. I never had one myself."

It seemed an appropriate time to break off this amusing interview and speed the parting guest. I offered him my copy of the British Labor Party's principles, but he declined it; it wouldn't be the thing, he said, to be carrying papers about, and it was too big to go into his pocket. I urged him to make sure of higher advice on the subject of the young instructor with the German name, and sent him on his way. As soon as he was out of sight, I called up Professor Bassett and told him of the call he might expect.

"Good," he said; "I'll settle him." Which apparently he did, in short order.

8

WOMAN SUFFRAGE

Even if the Peace settlement still moved slowly, there was one cause, and that a very big one, making forward strides. The campaign for woman suffrage had kept up all through the war; national upheaval could not hinder nor demolish it, in America or Europe. The work of women in hospitals and on battlefields had raised them to a commanding position, and more and more of them demanded the vote. After seventy-three years of agitation, the movement was gathering momentum, and had penetrated every state in the union.

Born and bred in the stronghold of suffrage, and closely associated with its promulgators, I had taken it as much for granted as my very religion. But the fight itself had not come conspicuously into my foreground until after the first ten years of the twentieth century; it was a widely-accepted principle but not a battle, despite skirmishes here and there and struggles with obdurate legislatures. Since the 1875 convention in Syracuse—and it had existed before that in connection with anti-slavery agitation—there had been a band of older women, in that city, some of them intimate associates of my mother and sister; the Mills family, the Sedgwicks, the Mays and Wilkinsons, the Mundys, the Millers of Geneva and other old New York families who upheld it. Arria had been an active campaigner; Mary Raymond Shipman Andrews had been prominent in it and had used her influence and pen; Susan B. Anthony, by that time retired from the presidency of the National Woman Suffrage Association, had visited in our house, and Anna Shaw had spent a day or two with us at Northampton.

The Nineteenth Amendment to the Constitution had been rejected by Congress in October, 1917, but had won quite a sensational victory in the following January, just as the House of Lords conceded the vote to British women. Now came the fight to get it through a reactionary Senate, and those of us who had hitherto been content to let our braver sisters lead the van swung forward into action with them. I was one of those who with shame for their passivity found themselves called to the front, as it were, and spurred into the intensive work without which victory was well nigh impossible. Both political parties had alternately opposed and furthered the Amendment; the South was to a very large extent against it. The liquor interests were fighting prohibition, for the Eighteenth Amendment, too, was at stake, and the anti-suffrage forces were thereby strengthened.

We found plenty to do in Massachusetts, and by the spring of 1919, even standing for suffrage, let alone speaking for it, became a matter of aggressive tactics. Making speeches was more amusing than difficult, but one had to conserve one's wits, for clever opponents assailed the speaker with all manner of questions and objections. Their prophecies reminded me of the days of the pompadours in Consumers' League meetings.

Dire predictions were voiced. Women would leave their babes and their kitchens for the polls—which one was led to believe would be places of daily resort—and thereby break up the sanctity of the Home. They would vote for the political interests of their husbands, to the detriment of other women's husbands. They would *not* vote for the political interests of their husbands, but for the furthering of their own ambitions. They would give themselves to office-seeking and wire-pulling; they would let themselves be bribed. The good women would neglect their voting-privileges on election-day, and the bad women would seize the ballot and vote against prohibition. The South would be laid waste by the enfranchisement of the negro woman. In fact, the working-people of both sexes would rule everything and everybody, and refuse to labor.

"Do you want," said one lady, "to have your maid have a right to go to the polls and vote against you?" And women would smoke, and probably end by wearing trousers. They would aspire to cabinet-positions, would even try for the presidency, and would speculate themselves instead of letting their men do it.

I smile to think what good officials some of those women have made since they had the un-wished-for vote. I made no prognostications myself, however; I was not prepared to promise a millennium as the result of giving the franchise to women. The one real reason for it which my stubborn mind would concede was that it was *right*; plain justice.

The students at Smith were beginning to wake up to suffrage agitation. Women on the faculty wielded a considerable amount of influence in discussions, but there were opponents of woman's suffrage among them. In town circles we made slow progress, though there were fine workers; at meetings (which were more successful if preceded by a supper) we had good chairmanship and excellent speakers from the great centres. Lucy Watson came to us for one of these; she was easy and persuasive on a platform, and I was proud of her impressive argument. When the alumnae came for their 1919 commencement, there was a large increase in adherents to the cause; it was hartening in the midst of national and international instability.

We ourselves, as individuals, learned a good deal in the course of the campaign. It became possible to analyze the different types of objectors, to get one's self in trim for an encounter with the purely belligerent, to avoid sarcasm as a cheap and ineffective weapon, and to find out the sort of person to whom one should listen patiently and answer her argument with a calm, "I see; of course." The "of course" was important, for it deluded your adversary into believing that she might be converting you, and encouraged her to go on and exhaust her powder, after which you might gently change the subject and leave it at that; for, by the time one had heard plenty of long and satisfied asseverations, one knew that words alone would have no effect. It was really a matter of salesmanship, the psychology of which was not familiar to us in those days. And all for this boasted *finasserie*, I am quite sure that I never personally won over a single *anti*.

One of the most effective speakers who came to us during that period, however, was Max Eastman. He had a pungent wit, an original set of illustrations well applied, and a human appeal that was irresistible. He urged suffrage for women on the ground of its benefit to their own characters, in added responsibility and interest. It illustrated clearly the many-sidedness of so great and slowly-advancing a movement as the enfranchisement of women or of backward nations and helpless minorities. Still far from its goal, it actually made over individual characters; and the suffrage struggle, with its inspired and intrepid leaders and its fight for a principle that transcended and conquered political opposition, may be incorporated in history as an endowment to civilization.

I went to my first parade in Boston with conflicting sensations of heroism and criticism. I had never outgrown the notion that it was childish to flaunt one's self before the public to the music of a brass band, even though as a child I had loved Church processionals and vestments. I joined the line of march on Beacon Street. I had always, since the days when my short legs took me to my music lesson at Mlle. de la Motte's, considered Beacon Hill a tiresome ascent. But when we were started, at a pace which at first seemed impossibly brisk (with the responsibility of keeping step to several discordant blaring bands) we lost all consciousness of our past prejudice, and we *floated*, the corpulent and slender side by side, on wings of sound, up to the State House. My heart pounded with fervor for a noble cause, and in my exalted frame of mind I decided that the one way of achieving the devotion of an individual to a creed, was to make him march for it.

My friend Mrs. Henry Dyke Sleeper was one of the active participants in the Woman Suffrage movement. We had worked together for the Children's Home and were at one in our sympathies with the interests of Labor and the struggle for peace. Lydia Ludden, business manager of the *Hampshire Gazette* was also a stalwart upholder of all progressive action. She, and Marion Dodd, manager of the Hampshire Bookshop, and I were taken into the Northampton Chamber of Commerce that year, its first woman-members. I have a vivid memory of the meeting we attended in a crowded hall which made us less conspicuous. We had a good deal of curiosity with regard to the gatherings of the Chamber, especially since we were not representing high finance or ambitious civic projects. Everybody was extremely polite to us, and we were much chagrined when the gentlemen proposed to relinquish their cigars as a concession to our sex. We saw that that would not do at all when women were entering public life, and protested. It was effected for that one evening, but conceded to be only a gesture of welcome. Marion Dodd had brought some chocolate cigarettes which she handed to Miss Ludden and me, and we nibbled them, smiling, as the smoke-wreaths faded. But we appreciated the compliment from the men, and looked forward to meeting them at the polls, the long process of ratifying the Amendment was now well under way.

9

NINETEEN TWENTY

The twenty years at Smith College, almost a third of my whole lifetime, had meant caring for four hundred and fifty girls; a vast number it seemed when one came to count them. And that amount of responsibility could not be carried indefinitely. I had not been really well in 1920, since my eyes had given out, and I was obliged to have a secretary for all desk work.

But in the spring I grew stronger again, and in June came Roger's marriage to a brilliant and fascinating student with whom he had been in love ever since the beginning of the war. They had been engaged for eighteen months, and Barbara had been living in a little annex to our old house, with five other girls, during her senior year. The two had studied together evenings, in our library, taken long walks, and heard concerts. Barbara played the violin very well and their mutual enjoyment of music was intense. They planned a honeymoon at the farm, where they could be alone for a week before I moved there for the summer, and decided to have their wedding the day after examinations closed, escaping from commencement ceremonies. My husband and sister and I, with John and Nan made a quick trip to New Hampshire, where Barbara's parents lived; it was a home wedding in their lovely house, and we all enjoyed meeting them and beginning a new friendship. Our young people were marrying with no more realistic idea of the implications of matrimony than their forbears had had, and we elders wondered with some anxiety whether life would destroy, or sublimate, the romance and imaginative rapture which these temperamental children were bringing to their union. They were completely absorbed in one another.

They were sure they could live on the small salary of an instructor, and they were eager to work together. They had picked out a tiny house in Hadley village. So we fathers and mothers stood by and heard them plight their troth to one another with the hope and pride and sympathy that had inspired our own parents. They went directly to the farm, but as commencement approached, Barbara's teachers were dismayed at the idea of her being absent from the graduation-ceremonies, because she had received high honors. We found it difficult to induce her to go there without breaking the news to her, but it was managed somehow by enlisting Roger's services, and in the end she was on hand to receive the *summa cum laude* which she had well earned.

We had the families all together at Phelps Farm that summer. Paul Andrews was back from France; John, a Harvard senior, was returning after a triumphant season as football manager, which had consoled him after the disappointment of parting with the Yale guns.

Our brother James, too, made us one of his unforgettable visits. He was still in the "prime of life" at sixty-six, a striking figure in his monastic garb. He walked easily, up hill and down, accompanied by the nephews and nieces. My brother George's widow was now living at Forty Acres, invalided but alive to all the interests of her five sons—a professor, a publisher, a doctor, a clergyman and a businessman—and her daughter, who was my godchild and the cousin nearest Nan's age. They had been with us much since their childhood and were like older brothers to my own two boys. All of them were eager for companionship with their uncle and it was amazing to see with what keen understanding he entered into their confidence, not only taking the objective and occupation of each personality into his thought and experience, but teaching youth to find a stimulus for its own living in the performance of the task itself. In the evenings the young men walked back and forth with him along the road between our two houses, their bursts of hearty laughter echoing, as did the chorus of katydids in the elms, from the wooded hill east of the farm, while we elders waited ungrudgingly for a chance to have him to ourselves. In the forenoons he was exclusively

Molly's property, for strolls in the woods or talks under the pines. Archie came to us at the end of the season; he had become very fond of Barbara, and delighted in the way with which she fitted into the family life. He was getting as much satisfaction as ever out of his work and his circle of friends, one of whom was O. Henry, to whom he had been useful in starting a recognition of his undoubted talent and originality. He had already told me much about the man's charm and his pungency of characterization, and the definite importance of his previously unencouraged literary achievement, which, by that time, had become successful. They had been extremely congenial, and after his death, my husband was chosen to write the introduction to the last edition of his books.

Another interest, also, had come into my husband's life. He had begun to do some writing of plays, for which he had only evening-time, but which promised real success. He was working with David Belasco over one of the plays, which they were planning to produce together. The two were excellent friends; Belasco was very enthusiastic over its possibilities, and over the subject-matter, a bit of American history not yet appropriated for drama or fiction. This was of course an absolute secret for the time being, and at first was imparted only to me, which gave it mystery and importance. The enterprise filled him with hope, the hope he had cherished for twenty years of being able to provide, after a little longer waiting, not only for the needs, but for extra indulgences which we had not been able to achieve thus far. With our children all self-supporting and no longer in need of financial help, we could make a home together again in some quiet spot, and live simply; the success of the play would put us on a footing of ease, if not actual luxury.

I remember observing one night that our best gains had come to us as surprises, and that perhaps it was as well that we could not see into the future. I was none too good at air-castle-building. Archie laughed and said, "Yes, but you love to look forward to tomorrow; you say that is the essence of happy living." "But not farther," I insisted. "One tomorrow at a time." There were yet to be many tomorrows. A friend once said to me; "Have you no villain in your book? No story is complete without a villain." I laughed and said that villains were boring to write about. But there was one, of whom I could not write; the false friend who stole, and sold, my husband's play and broke his heart; the heart that had withstood the ravages of the great blizzard thirty years before, but was not proof against mortal treachery. We try to forget the crime and remember only the happy visions that were never realized.

10

"THEY TELL ME YOU'RE GOING AWAY"

The autumn of 1920 found our old house in Northampton full and flourishing. I had never appreciated so keenly as in that post-war year, the expansion of the college. There was a difference in the student body. Girls were coming now from families where national, as well as domestic issues were a matter of concern; they longed for foreign travel and wider opportunity and were ready for the contemplation of problems which their forerunners had never faced. Self-support was looked upon as a universal objective. Even the recreational side of the campus life was taken more seriously; in athletics there was less individual rivalry and more group-competition. One heard about "worth-while" courses and new clubs. Parents, and even a few alumnae, recoiled to some extent from the scientific frankness of professors in the departments of Psychology and Sociology, and the startling revelations in the lecture-rooms of all the colleges seemed likely to be upsetting. But post-war conditions which must be taken into account, had brought sex-questions to the fore, and adolescents were strangely aware of facts from which their elders had vainly sought to protect them. Whether they realized it or not, a burden of responsibility had descended upon their youthful shoulders. Furthermore, if women were to be entrusted with the ballot, which was by the autumn of 1920 a *fait accompli* (though not yet used) they would eventually have to deal with public evils as well as with grave problems in their own circles. The president of Smith College was patient, watchful and liberal; upon that the alumnae and the world at large might count; he was not upset by criticism.

Meantime there were other changes which sooner or later were bound to affect our own household. The great increase of students had outstripped the housing-provisions on the campus and made the building of new dormitories imperative. Outside houses were numerous, some of them filled by invitation and occupied by seniors who secured chaperons and managed expenses. It was difficult to insure the keeping of rules, although heads of houses did their best to cooperate with the administration; social rivalries threatened the democracy which had been strong at Smith College since its earliest days. Most of all, however, it had become clear that so large an institution demanded further centralization and regulation, as a stronger backing for the student-government which was answering more and more effectively to the demands made upon it. The president and alumnae were convinced that there should be campus-accommodation for every student of the college, with uniform laws and privileges. The heads of private houses were already contemplating this eventuality and were beginning to make plans accordingly. I had long expected the change and heartily appreciated the need for it.

But the idea of turning our time-honored mansion into an apartment-house was hopeless. Even the resourceful builder who had solved such problems hitherto, could realize it. The great central chimney stood like an obstinate giant in the way of all plans, and could not be blue-printed out of the foreground; the low rooms and narrow halls were prohibitive; the heating-apparatus and plumbing unadaptable. A faculty-house, too, was out of the reckoning, since for the most part the older teachers were settling in apartments, and the younger ones in small groups. Yet for a valuable landmark with so many historic associations, to be pulled down and done away with, seemed a cruel sacrifice. I knew that I must give up my work before long, and take an extended rest from care, but I did not know how to bring that about. All this was the problem of so many other women that one could not talk about it nor complain, but it underlay the bright life at "109" for months, until at last I gained courage to take my anxieties to President Neilson, whose large-heartedness and kindness brought it to a settlement; the college would by the house at the terms I offered, as a "going concern," furniture and all, and set me free to drop all burdens, finding a substitute even before the end of the season, if I felt I must give up at once.

It was clear that this plan would be best. I had six weeks in which to go through garret and cellar, ridding them of the accumulations of years; at the farm, that time was used in making necessary alterations, putting in a furnace, and otherwise preparing the Phelps house for residence in cold weather. It was better to keep busy than to allow too much leeway to one's emotions, for now and then presentiments of a great lack and emptiness in my life came to me darkly. To live without the tonic of association with youth; the swift motion, the eagerness, the mirth, the welcoming faces, the flash of a gay good-morning, the knock at one's door for a good-night; how could one keep young and hopeful in spirit, failing those daily confidences and reminders? In late afternoon there would still be a soft light over Paradise Pond, groups coming up from the boat-house, crossing the street, loitering on the sidewalk, with sound of laughter and hurrying steps along the porchway; I should picture it many, many times and long to be with my children of the college; but it would be part of a vanished past. Unless, perchance—and that was always a bright thought—I might live to go back into it all as an onlooker, some day, and see, in the personalities of their daughters, what sort of mothers my girls had made; that vision restored my courage and shed a hopeful light upon the immediate prospect (which after all was not a gloomy one) with its promise of rest, and time, and freedom from care. It would be much easier to have the parting come when my girls left for their vacation, with plans ahead and home-coming a joyous anticipation. I made much of the fact that I should be only six miles away and easy to reach, and that they would always find me at the farm, whither they had often gone for a night's camping-out on the hillside or a day's picnicing in the woods. I bade them farewell when the day of spring closing came, with its usual excitement. As the baggage-men were tramping through the Hilarium and up the stairs, an open-faced, cordial young fellow stopped for a moment.

"They tell me you're going away," he said. "I'm sorry about

that, 'cause you've let us set the victrola going when we carried up the big trunks; it makes it so much easier, you know. I hope the next one will do that too." I felt a regret and a heart-warming both together; it was one of the nicest goodbyes I had.

By two o'clock the few belongings of my own which were to go with me were gathered in a lower room. There was no necessity for keeping my helpers, and I did not want to prolong the parting, for they were loyal friends, and we had worked together with satisfaction and affection; they, too, had pleasant vacation-plans. When they were gone, and I was alone in the empty house, there was time for a long letter to Archie, who was to come up to the farm for the week-end, and to my sister Molly; part of the plan was that she should spend the rest of the season with me, and we hoped very much that Arria would come back to us before another Christmas.

At five o'clock I went to meet the treasurer of the college for a final business transaction—the sale of the house. I have dim recollections of a shady office, of some pleasant gentlemen, of signing my name once or twice on dotted lines pointed out to me, of shaking hands rather formally and cordially. Then I came out into the sunny street, without the faintest idea what I should do next. I ran into my friend Mrs. Sleeper. We had met crises of various descriptions together in the course of the years, and I felt that Fate had led her to the spot.

"Well!" she said. "Have you been finishing up the business part?"

"I certainly have," said I. "I haven't a debt in the world, nor a care, nor a single thing to bother about. And I've a queer, light-headed feeling, as if my feet weren't really on the ground; am I walking straight?"

She laughed. "You can't fly just yet."

"Will you come and have supper with me somewhere, and then —we'll see what we can do."

"I know. Let's go to the moving pictures. In the college vacation, you know, they always have some play that the country people like. Tonight it's a revival of *The Old Homestead*. The place will be crowded, so we'll get there early and talk till it begins."

"Perfect. It's restful, at a picture show, like lying on the deck of a steamer; no past and no future, no regrets and no plans."

We supped at The Manse, and talked of dress-making, of city planning, of Bertrand Russell. We lingered over our coffee. At the theatre there was indeed a crowd of people, from all the neighboring villages; men, women and children. "Not an intellectual in sight," we observed to one another. We laughed with them at every joke; for all I know, wept with them in tragic scenes. After it we had a pleasant walk home, and I left my comrade at her door and let myself into my silent dwelling for the last time, and fell asleep, not in the west room which was now swept and garnished for my successor, but in an east chamber, with windows open to the sunrise.

*   *   *   *   *

ON THE STOOP AT FORTY ACRES. July 15, 1936

I have come over here to look at the sunset. The long gallery is empty, for the inhabitants are away. In the west, a sinking sun is still above the crisp horizon-line; the luminous green of the meadows stretches to a shining river, beyond it is the white spire of Hatfield's meeting-house, with its gilded vane and the long line of elm-shaded roofs. This place is still, yet now there are moving figures here and there. Two young people who have just stepped out from between the willows, with oars over their shoulders, are George and Arria; they are coming up from the boat, marching in the old hexameter-rhythm which our brothers taught us when we were children. I can see Arria's blue boating-dress, and the straw hat pushed back from her forehead. They pause a moment under a huge elm which Father called the perfect wine-cup; its branches still droop in graceful symmetry.

A lithe fourteen-year old girl with a crop of curly brown hair for all the world like that of her next-older brother, swings herself down from the gnarled branch of an apple-tree. It is Molly, and she lands in a clump of wild tiger-lilies, soft red and orange, which have always grown on that orchard-bank; they were never allowed in the garden where grander blooms were tended and favored, so they have kept aloof for a hundred years and more, and make a tall background for the slight figure. Molly, the shy, the keen, the daring critic, the amused looker-on!

Our father and mother, two white-haired people, are walking between the rows of hollyhocks, farther back. They stand now, looking upward at a flock of circling swallows in the midst of their mystic sunset-dance. Already, one by one, the swallows drop and disappear into the unused chimney over the ell. At the window sits Aunt Bethia, remote, self-abnegating; her face, with the long upper lip, the high cheek-bones and brilliant eyes, a replica of the countenance of her grandmother Betsey Phelps. Beyond, on the road, a boy and girl are walking together, thrilling as their hands touch. Cousin Ellen is waiting for them on the steps of the Phelps house. They are walking away, but the others are coming toward me now, the last of my generation, who can never be lonely when they answer so readily to the call of memory. For, as Havelock Ellis says, the meaningless turmoil of the moment falls silent before the things which come out of the past and are incorporated with the texture of one's own soul.

Overhead I hear a young man's voice, chanting; it is James, at the little window of the prophet's chamber. The text of an old evening psalm comes to me, with a long rising and a falling note as the monks of the Middle Ages intoned it; *Nisi Dominus aedificaverit do-mum: in vanum laboraverunt qui aedificant e-am.*

Moses Porter's labor was not in vain. The house has withstood fire and flood and earthquake for almost two centuries; the foundations underneath me will hold another hundred years. The Lord must have been its Master Builder. And there was another line in the psalm; *Cum dederit dilectis suis somnum.* That was what we said when my brother's eyes were closed to this mortal world a year ago.

The sun has sunk behind the hills and left a golden sky above them; one last ray touches the valiant weathercock pointing northwest. The long cool bars of cloud lose their rose-and-violet tints, but the orange lilies make little points of light against the darkening background of the orchard-bank. I feel a twilight dampness; there come the tiny flutings of the frogs. Tomorrow will be a splendid hay-day, and perhaps John will mow the alfalfa in the lower meadow.

If what faded had its glory, then what lasts will be invested with still greater glory.

Chart and Index

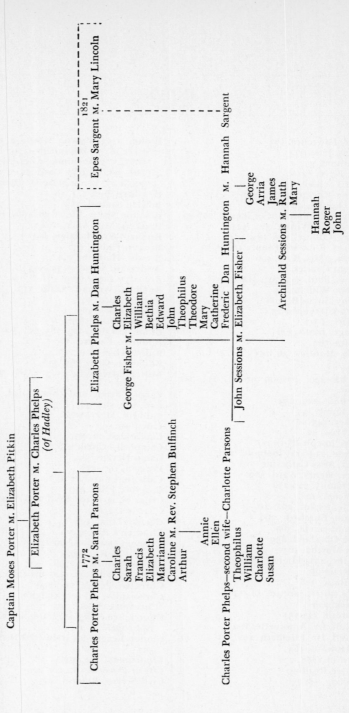

Captain Moses Porter M. Elizabeth Pitkin

Elizabeth Porter M. Charles Phelps
(of Hadley)

1772
Charles Porter Phelps M. Sarah Parsons

    Charles
    Sarah
    Francis
    Elizabeth
    Marrianne
    Caroline M. Rev. Stephen Bulfinch
    Arthur

        Annie
        Ellen

Charles Porter Phelps—second wife—Charlotte Parsons

    Theophilus
    William
    Charlotte
    Susan

Elizabeth Phelps M. Dan Huntington

    Charles
George Fisher M. Elizabeth
    William
    Bethia
    Edward
    John
    Theophilus
    Theodore
    Mary
    Catherine
    Frederic Dan Huntington M. Hannah Sargent

John Sessions M. Elizabeth Fisher

             George
             Arria
             James
Archibald Sessions M. Ruth
             Mary

                  Hannah
                  Roger
                  John

1821
Epes Sargent M. Mary Lincoln

SOME DESCENDANTS OF MOSES PORTER

INDEX

Abbott, Lawrence, 163
Addams, Jane, 314
Adelynrood, 377
Adler, Felix, 321
Agassiz's School, 11
Ainslee's Magazine, 335, 366
Alcott, Louisa, 98-99
Alexander II, Emperor of Russia, 226-227
Allen, Annie Winsor, 321, 324
Amherst College, 112, 163, 174
Ancestors, 8-10; see Family tree
Andrews, Mary R. S., 406
Andrews, Charles, 63
Andrews, Paul, 393, 395, 412
Andrews, William, 74
Anthony, Susan B., 406
Appleton, Tom, 22-23
Armistice, 400
Armitage, Jacob, 306
Athletics, 369
Atlantic Monthly, 36, 154

Bach, 229-230; passion music, 233; see
    Music
Bachschule, 229, 239
Bacon family, 57
Baedeker, 243
Balze, Miss, 22
Barnby, Joseph, 250-251
Barn, the, 113-114; footnote, 113
Beecher, Miss Catherine, 101
Beecher, Henry Ward, 309
Belfry family, 229-230
Bell, Helen, 22
Bell, Lieutenant, 202, 210
Berenson, Elizabeth, 369
Berenson, Senda, 369
Bernese Oberland, 239
Bianci, Martha, 163
Bible, the, 151; Higher Criticism of, 279;
    see Religion
Bird House, 326
Bishops, 46-48; meeting of, 148
Bismarck, 224
Blacksmith, 133-134
Blackwell, Dr. Antoinette, 100
Blackwell, Dr. Elizabeth, 192
Bliss, Howard, 163
Blizzard of 1888, 276
Books, see Reading
Boston bag, 17, 23

Boston, 1-53; Beacon Street, 3; Berkeley
    Street, 6, 7; Bostonians, 170; Boylston
    Street, 1, 2; Common, 3, 32, 237; Music
    Hall, 38; Public Gardens, 2-3, 4, 32;
    speech of, 18-19; State House in, 3, 409
Bowditch family, 1, 40
Bowles, Samuel, 157
Boylston Street, life at 98, 16ff., 101
Brackett, Miss Anna, 102
Breshkovsky, Madame, 390
Brewer, Fanny, 356
Brewer, Hannah, 356
Bridgman, Sidney, 135, 365
Brooklyn Eagle, 329
Brooklyn Woman's Club, 313
Brown, Alice, 394
Brown, Mary, 365
Bryant, Clara, 167, 170
Bulfinch, Ellen, 129, 185, 225, 300
Bulfinch, Thomas, 128
Bülow, Hans von, 245
Burgoyne, Gen., 365, 370
Burton, Marion Leroy, 382, 389, 392

Cabot, "Peter" and "Nora," 243, 244, 248
Cail, the, 304, 307
Calligan, Mary, 285
Calvinism, 9
Cambridge, 11, 357
Campbell School, 378
Camp Devens, 395
Carmen, 197, 237
Catholic Church, 252
Caverno, Julia, 359
Cedar Square, see Roxbury; Sargent
Chartists, 250
Cheney, Edna, 102
Children's Aid, 394
Chimney swallows, 120-121
Choate, Helen, 250
Choate, Rufus, 22, 298
Choir, in Windsor, 212, in Leipzig, 229
Christian, Prince, 214, 250
Christianity, 95; see Religion
"Christmas closet," 25
Church, see *Religion, Lutheran, Catholic,
    Episcopal*
Church League for Industrial Democracy,
    307
Churchman, the, 305
City of Brussels, 197, 201
Civil Service Reform, 303

Civil War, 31ff.
Clarke, Bishop, 46
Clarke, Christopher, 356
Clothes, 22, 82, 167
Cobleighs, the, 83
Coccius, Herr, 217, 221, 340
College girl, 367, 369-370, 378, 398, 408, 415
Composers, see Music
Congress of Women, 1875, 98ff.
Consumers' League, 313-320, 329-331, 336, 363
Cooke, Mary, 17, 48, 383
Corinthians 2, 3.11; 383, 421
Cornell University, 178
Courtship, 19, 180-182
Coxe, Bishop, 47
Crosby, Ernest, 321
Croly, Jennie, 101
Crown Princess, of Germany, 225-226
Curtis, Annie, 302
Cushing, Eleanor, 359

Damrosch, Walter, 184, 346
Denison House, 394
Devereux family, 57
Dewey, Admiral, 342
Dexter, Annie, 219, 239
Diamond Nell, 77-78
Dickens, Charles, see Reading
Dickinson, Austin, 163
Dickinson, Emily, 163-164
Dickinson, Lavinia, 163-164
Dickinson, Ned, 163
Dodd, Marion, 409
Dows, Jane, 182
Dreier, Mary, 300
Dresden, 234-235
Dudley, Helena, 394

Eastman, Max, 409
Education, see Huntington, Ruth
Elvey, Sir George, 203
Emerton, Prof., 383
Emmanuel Church, 1, 12, 39
Englewood, N. J., 274, 277-278, 285-286
Episcopal Church, 12, 210, 250
Equal Suffrage group, 100
Excursion days, 141ff.

Fabians, 323, 339
Fairchild, Charles, 310
Family tree, 424
Faneuil Hall, 36
Farming, 379
Faust, 235, 247, 248
Fellowship of Reconciliation, 394
Ferry, North Hadley, 142, 145
"Fine Art of Liking People," 175, 370, 390
Fine, Jean, 321
Fish, Hamilton, 280

Forty Acres, 12, 109ff., 183-189, 240, 271, 328, 344, 419
Foster, Barbara, 411
Free Trade, 157

Gage, Miss Mary, school of, 29-30
Gannett family, 1, 39-40, 64
Ganong, Prof. William, 360
Gardiner, Prof. Norman, 360
Garfield, President, 238
George, Henry, 276, 305-306, 322, 337-338
Germany, 216ff.; in 1914, 387
Germar, Fräulein von, 234
Gewandhaus, 240, 244
Girls' Friendly Magazine, 327
Girls' Friendly Society, 316
Goethe, 227; see Reading
Grammar of Assent, 184, 210
"Grant and Colfax," 66-68
Grant, Gen. Ulysses, 31
Gray, Asa, 117
Griffith, Emily, 268, 357

Hadley, see Forty Acres
Hale, Mrs. Philip, 72
Hamilton, Miss, 201
Hampshire Bookshop, 409
Hampshire Gazette, 409
Handel and Hayden Society, 38
Hanscom, Elizabeth, 359-360
Harper's Bazaar, 83
Harvard University, 8, 11, 12, 94, 102, 116, 155, 184, 384, 390
Hatfield, 113
Hatfield House, 359
Haymow, the, 146-149, 186
Hazard, Dora Sedgwick, 64
Heermans, Forbes, 85-87
Heidelberg, 249
Held, Ernst, 71-72, 105, 221
Henshaw House, 364-372, 381, 416
Herrnsdorf, Fräulein Doris, 216, 221-222, 224, 227
Herrnsdorf, Fräulein Isidora, 216
"Hilarium," 381, 385
Hill, David B., 309
Hill, Mattie, 69
Hingham, 8, 167-173
Hinrichs, Frederick, 308-311
Holy Cross, Companionship of, 377
Holy Cross, Order of, 279, 290; see Huntington, James
Hospitals, 79
House of the Good Shepherd, 79-81
Howe, Julia Ward, 33, 101, 104
Hunt, Jonathan, 364
Huntington, Arria, 11, 13, 75ff., 91, 116, 201, 211, 217, 219, 239, 345, 379, 383, 394
Huntington, the Hon. Charles, 356
Huntington, Dan, 9

Huntington, Frederic Dan, 1, 2, 6-7, 10; Rector of Emmanuel church, 12, 17-18—21, 26, 34, 39, 40-41; becomes a bishop, 46-53; in Syracuse, 65, 67, 75, 79, 88-91; at Forty Acres, 110, 114, 116, 118, 122-124; in Northampton, 135-136—138, 148-149, 150-155, 240, 253, 271, 279, 300; in *Cail*, 304—262-264, 349; death of, 373-377

Huntington, Mrs. Frederic, 11, 12, 21, 23, 26, 32, 40, 48, 119, 138, 178, 281; death of, 378

Huntington, George, 12, 94, 116-117, 161-162, 278, 345, 374-377, 420

Huntington, Mrs. George, 412

Huntington, James, 14, 26, 34, 37, 47, 61; religious ideas of, 94-95—112, 131, 132, 157, 190; becomes a monk, 241—250, 276, 279, 288, 290-292; with Knights of Labor, 303-304—338, 412

Huntington, Mary, 15, 23, 42, 50, 60-61, 82, 158, 379, 383

Huntington, Ruth, birth, 11; childhood in Boston, 1-52; in Syracuse, 53ff., 177-182; at Forty Acres, 109ff.; in Hingham, 167-173; meeting with Archibald Sessions, 183ff.; London, 206-210; study in Germany, 216ff.; teaching in Utica, 266-269; engagement of, 261
    Education, in Boston, 29-30; in Syracuse, 61ff.
    Music, study of, in Boston, 41-45; in Syracuse, 71-73; in Germany, 221ff.
    Marriage, 270. (See *Sessions*, Ruth Huntington)
    See also *Music, Reading, Religion*

Huntington, William Reed, 306, 376

Huxley, Mr., 381

Imitation of Christ, the, 188, 254

Indians, 69-70

Indian relics, at Hadley, 111-112

Influenza epidemic, 399

Irving, Henry, 209

Italy, 252-253

Jackson, Miss Mary, school of, 61, 66, 68, 88, 98

James, Henry, 103

"Jerusalem crickets," 16

Johannesgarten, 248

Jones, Rufus, 394

Jordan, Mary Augusta, 359

Kelley, Florence, 314

Kemble, Fanny, 38

Kent, 385

Kerensky Revolution, 390

Kernan, Mr., 310

Kimball, Everett, 378, 404

King, Edward, 319, 321

Kneeland, Harriet, 364

Knights of Labor, 250, 303-304

Labor, in rural New England, 122ff.

Labor conditions, 290-291, 313, 341, 363

Laighton, Oscar, 207

Leavenworth, Gen., 60

Lee, Gerald Stanley, 7, 360

Lee, Jenette, 360

Leipzig, 216ff.

Letters to Turnip, 159, 176

Leiderkranz, 73

Lincoln, Abner, 8, 170

Lincoln, Abraham, 32, 35

Literature, see Reading

Littell's Living Age, 36

Little Dorrit, 161ff.

Livermore, Mary A., 100, 103

London, 202-203, 206-210

Low, Seth, 302, 309, 337

Low, William, 302

Lowell, James Russell, 37

Lowell, Josephine Shaw, 314

Ludden, Lydia, 409

Lusitania, 387

Luther, Martin, 230, 234, 242

Lutheran Church, 233-234; see *Religion*

Lyman, Judge, 356

Mackintosh, Euphemia, 394

Manlius, 61

Manse, the, 419

Marsh, Master Builder, 125-126

Massasoit House, 109

Matty, Mr., 122-124

May, Miss Abby, 102

McKinley, President, 342

"Melissa," 284-285, 333

Mendelssohn Quintet Club, 73

Mendelson, Dr. Walter, 243, 249, 253, 276, 338

Mill, at Hadley, 127

Miller family, 51

Miller, Mrs. Gerritt, 100

Mission school, 91

Mitchell, John A., 171

Mitchell, Maria, 100

Modern Christianity: A Civilized Heathenism, 94

Monadnock, 141, 143

Monday Club, 358

Montgomery, Col., 217, 225, 227, 234, 238

Morgan, Geraldine, 256

Mosher, Dr. Eliza, 293, 295

Motte, Mlle. Gabrielle de la, 42-45

"Mountain Day," 371

Mount Warner, 144, 174-176

Muirhead, Annie, 243, 254, 323

Muirhead, James, 241, 244, 248, 323, 339

Munsey's Magazine, 335

Music, 32, 34; in Boston, 38ff.; in Syracuse, 71ff., 105, 168, 180; Sessions family's interest in, 184—202, 203; in Windsor, 209-212—221, 223, 229; in Germany, 230ff.—238, 328, 332, 346; at Smith College, 386; in the war, 389-390, 401

Nathan, Maud, 313, 319
National Gallery, 209
National Woman's Suffrage Association, 406
Neilson, William Allen, 392, 402, 415
New England, see Boston, Forty Acres, Northampton
New York, 273ff.
New York Post, 305
New York Times, 305
Nihilists, in Leipzig, 226
North American Review, 154
Northampton, 109, 110, 135-136, 355ff.
North Hadley mill, 131
"Nurse Harriet," 2, 6, 24, 33, 35, 59, 71

Otto's Grammar, 218
O Henry, 413
Opera, see Music
O'Reilly, Leonora, 287, 290, 300, 321, 341, 391
Organ playing, 74
Oxford Movement, 95, 241

Parsons, Charlotte, 128
Parsons, Theophilus, 128
Peabody, Robert, 155
Peck, Gen., 66
Phelps family, 66, 128-131; Arthur, 128; Caroline (Mrs. Stephen Bulfinch), 128; Charles, 128, 155; Elizabeth, 9, 336; Sarah, 128, 240; Theophilus, 129-130
Phelps, William Lyon, 404
Phelps, William Porter, 130-131
Phelps House, 128, 160, 297-299, 355, 379, 397-398
Piatt, Mrs., Seminary of, 261, 265-269
Piutti, Carl, 254
Planchette, 168
Poetsch family, 219, 225, 239, 256
Politics, in Syracuse, 66-68, 98, 177, 157; after 1876, 177, 268; in New York, 301-303, 308ff., 337, 341, 363
Pontresina, 250-251
Porter, Elizabeth, 8, 158
Porter, Moses, 8
Porter School, 266
Powderly, Terence V., 303
Putnam family, 24, 40

Quincy, Fanny, 357; Helen, 323

Radcliffe, 17, 382
Reading, 27ff., 89; at Forty Acres, 118-119, 141—144; in 1875, 156; at Hingham, 169, 171—177, 227, 250; at Mrs. Piatt's, 268-269—279, 280, 345; in Northampton, 368
Reform, see Politics
Reinecke, 254
Religion, 95-96, 146ff., 151-153, 187-188, 194, 201-202, 210-211; in Italy, 252-253, 360-361; at Smith College, 385-386—394
Revere family, 1
Reynolds, James, 321
Romanes, 383
Roosevelt-Barnes case, 74
Roosevelt, Theodore, 302-303, 342
Roxbury, 24, 191
Rubinstein, 245
Russell, Parson, 110
Russia, 390

St. Paul's School, 390
Sarasate, 245
Sargent, Epes, 8, 168; James, 168; Mary, 8, 24, 42, 51, 104, 169, 170-171
Schumann, Clara, 246-247
Scudder, Vida, 394, 307
Sedgwick, Charles, 64, 86
Seelye, L. Clark, 155, 349, 361-362, 381-382
Sessions, Adeline, 382
Sessions, Archibald, 183ff., 190, 195-198, 235, 242, 253, 261-265, 280, 285, 286; Young Men's Democratic Club, 302—311, 313; part in politics, 308ff.; in Social Reform Club, 321; in law, 326—344, 348, 385; play-writing, 413
Sessions, Elizabeth, 183, 336
Sessions, Hannah, 279-280, 284, 334, 337, 378, 382, 384, 390; marriage, 393—395-396
Sessions, John, 344, 351, 379, 390, 398, 412
Sessions, Roger, 327, 332, 343, 346, 378, 380, 384, 389, 393, 403; marriage of, 411
Sessions, Ruth Huntington (Mrs. Archibald), articles written, 305; attitude toward politics, 308; in Consumers' League, 313-320; in Social Reform Club, 321-325—327, 335; at Smith College, 355ff.; attitude toward war, 388, 404-411; departure from Smith College, 417. (See *Huntington*, Ruth; *Music*; *Reading*; *Religion*)
Seymour, Mr., 57, 66
Shaw, Anna, 406
Shelter, the, 77
Sherman, Thomas G., 309
Simkhovitch, Mary, 307, 321
Sleeper, Mrs. Henry Dyke, 409, 418
Smith College, 156, 175, 349, 355ff. See College girl
Smith, Oliver, 155; Sophia, 155

Socialism, 177, 250, 323-324, 339-340
Social Reform Club, 321-325
Spahr, Charles, 321, 322
Spanish American War, 342
Spiritualism, 168
Springfield Republican, 157
Standard, The, 305
Stanton, Elizabeth C., 100
Starr, Ellen, 314
Steinert prize, 389
Stoddard, Prof., 360
Stoop, the, 114-115, 141, 419
Stowe, Harriet Beecher, 120
Styles, see Clothes
Suffrage, see *Women's Suffrage*
Sumner family, 1
Sunday, at Forty Acres, 153-155
Swazey, Miss, 102
Syracuse, 46, 52, 53ff.; politics of, 98, 161, 170. (*See Huntington*, Ruth)

Tailer, Henderson, 126-127
Tammany, 301-302, 309, 338
Terry, Ellen, 209
Thaxter, Celia, 119, 207-208
Throop, Bethia, 111, 112, 178, 336
Thunderstorms, 113, 137-141
Tilden family, 1
Toynbee, Arnold, 177
Tristan und Isolde, 231

Unitarianism, 9, 27
Utica, 266-269

Valentiner, Herr Pastor, 239-240
Vanderbilt, the, 58
Van Duyn, Dr. John, 79ff., 167
Victoria, Princess, 214

Victorian Courtship, 180-182
Village store, 133

Wagner, death of, 255
Wald, Lillian, 321
Wall-flowers, 84
Walker, Dr. Mary, 99
Walker, Oliver, 364
War, 1914, 387
War Department, 402-405
Waterman, Prof., 360
Watmough, Miss, 314
Watson family, 57
Watson, Lucy, 180, 226, 250, 300, 377, 394, 408
Wedgewood pottery, 18
Wellesley College, 394
Westcott, Edward, 182
White, Andrew D., 63, 178, 224
"White List," 314-316, 329
Wilby, Miss, private school of, 13
Williams, Mornay, 321
Wilkinson family, 86
Wilson, Woodrow, 388, 402, 403
Windsor, royal chapel in, 203-204, 210-213
Women's Suffrage, 406ff., parade, 409, meeting in Northampton, 409-410
Women, Congress of, 98ff., 157, 406
Women's Trade Union League, 341
Wood, General, 63
Wood, Dr. Irving, 360-361

Yale, School of Music, 389; of Artillery, 398
Young Men's Democratic Club, 302, 308-310
Youth's Companion, 305, 327

Zakzrewska, Dr. Marie, 191ff.